My unfulfilled ambition is to write a great novel
in three parts about my adventures. I've yet to have them,
but they will be perfectly thrilling.
— Wendy Darling

All the world is made of faith, and trust, and pixie dust.
— Peter Pan

ALOHA WANDERWELL

ALOHA WANDERWELL

THE BORDER-SMASHING, RECORD-SETTING LIFE OF THE WORLD'S YOUNGEST EXPLORER

CHRISTIAN FINK-JENSEN &
RANDOLPH EUSTACE-WALDEN

GOOSE LANE

Edited by Susan Renouf.
Page design by Jaye Haworth and Julie Scriver.
Cover design by Julie Scriver.

Cover illustration: Aloha standing on the running board of her Ford Phaeton beneath the Sydney Harbour Bridge, Sydney, Australia, 1936. Photo Courtesy of Valri Baker-Lundahl. Used by permission.

Interior illustrations: all are provided courtesy of Valri Baker-Lundahl, except page 159 (top), photo by Christian Fink-Jensen; pages 159 (inset) and 362, photos by Randolph Eustace-Walden; page 323, photo copyright Bettman/CORBIS; page 324, photo courtesy of *Winnipeg Free Press*; page 332, photo courtesy Agness M. Underwood Collection, CSU Northridge Oviatt Library; and page 337 photos courtesy of Archives of the Historical Society of Long Beach. All images used by permission.

Printed in Canada.
10 9 8 7 6 5 4 3 2 1

Library and Archives Canada Cataloguing in Publication

Fink-Jensen, Christian, 1969-, author
   Aloha Wanderwell : the border-smashing, record-setting life of the world's youngest explorer / Christian Fink-Jensen and Randolph Eustace-Walden.

Includes index.
Issued in print and electronic formats.
ISBN 978-0-86492-895-5 (paperback).--ISBN 978-0-86492-935-8 (mobi).--
ISBN 978-0-86492-934-1 (epub)

1. Wanderwell, Aloha, 1906-1996. 2. Women travellers--Biography.
3. Voyages around the world. 4. Automobile travel.
I. Eustace-Walden, Randolph, 1954-, author II. Title.

G465.F53 2016   910.92   C2016-902454-7
                                       C2016-902455-5

We acknowledge the generous support of the Government of Canada, the Canada Council for the Arts, and the Government of New Brunswick.

Goose Lane Editions
500 Beaverbrook Court, Suite 330
Fredericton, New Brunswick
CANADA E3B 5X4
www.gooselane.com

For Sam and Kieran.
— CFJ

For Valri and Nile and Margaret.
— REW

PART THREE

PREFACE

THE HEART OF THE ALOHA WANDERWELL story spans twenty-seven years, from 1906 to 1933, beginning with the early years of a young girl named Idris on Vancouver Island, through her teenage debut as "Aloha" in the South of France, and across ten years of adventures on the road, travelling around the world by automobile.

Twenty-seven years is a relatively short period in a normal life; however, Aloha's life was anything but normal. Her adventures — the places she travelled, the people she met, the things she achieved and endured — would fill several volumes. The challenge in conveying her story wasn't just deciding what should go in, but making tough calls about what should be left out. That's not to say that her story was easy to tell. Many of her achievements, especially in less industrialized parts of the world, have been lost to history. And even many of her activities in Europe and North America have not been remembered or recorded over the years, so we've had to piece together many of her life's details from a bewildering variety of sources, including 254 print resources, dozens of visual archives, and the collections of family members who so generously shared what they had. Other important sources were Aloha's ghostwritten autobiography (*Call To Adventure!*, 1939), her unpublished 679-page hand-typed, double-sided reminiscences ("The Driving Passion"), her handwritten log books and diaries from the period, as well as letters, cards, notes, candid family photos, and mementoes.

Even these sources left out many crucial aspects of her life story, which is why we undertook ten years of research in archives and repositories in more than a dozen cities worldwide. Along the way, we uncovered historical documents, maps, charts, films, videotapes, microfilm, and audio recordings within university collections and museums and buried in the stacks within the Library of Congress, the Smithsonian Institution, and the National Archives at College Park, Maryland. We also filed more than sixty American Freedom of Information Act (FOIA) requests, and a half-dozen Canadian Access to Information Act (ATI) requests. As for online resources, until very recently the Internet "history" of Aloha revealed only a handful of arcane references containing mostly inaccurate information. That's not surprising, since the name, notoriety, and accomplishments of Aloha Wanderwell have long since drifted into the fog of a bygone era.

Since the 1960s, others have attempted to tell Aloha's story in various forms; Aloha herself tried to publish a second book about her travels and life experience. We know of six other biographies that also failed to gain traction due to the lack of credible sources and references. Discovering the "real" Aloha has been no easy task.

It was in comparing "official" archives with original source materials, and also against third-party accounts including newspapers, that we came to a dramatic realization: Aloha's life and times were far more sensational, thrilling, adventurous, life-threatening, death-defying, rewarding, and devastating — not to mention of greater historical significance — than even her own recollections and writings would have anyone believe.

The challenge any biographer faces is to distill the endless "facts" of someone's life into a coherent and compelling narrative. In Aloha's case, however, this task was made considerably more difficult by her dogged attempts to revise, reinterpret, or flat-out fabricate some of the events in her life. She had her own ideas about how she wanted to be remembered, the facts be damned. But facts matter, which is why we undertook such a protracted, expensive, and often frustrating research adventure. It was, truly, the only possible way to accurately reconstruct her life, tell her story, and return her legacy to its rightful place in history.

Aloha's story began over a century ago, during the social, political, and economic upheavals of the early 1900s. The events of those years set the stage: a young girl drove off on a global adventure, set world records that have yet to be broken, entertained audiences around the world, and created a life that only Hollywood could compete with.

No wonder Aloha Wanderwell became known far and wide as "the Amelia Earhart of the open road."

Randolph Eustace-Walden
Christian Fink-Jensen
October 2016

PROLOGUE

ON A STORMY AFTERNOON in December 1932 a two-masted schooner eased from the port of Long Beach, California, into a curtain of rain and fog. The boat, a ramshackle hundred-foot yacht, veered and pitched over rough seas while a small group of people gathered on her port side, holding tight to the railing and listening while a handsome man named James E. Farris shouted through the squalls, delivering a eulogy. The dead man at their feet had been carefully prepared. Dressed in his best uniform, he had been placed in a seagrass coffin and draped in an American flag. Among the mourners was a willowy blond woman, also in uniform. Beautiful though she was, her face was like granite, and intentionally so. Since childhood she had practised the art of obscuring her thoughts and feelings from others. People, she had found, were always demanding, always trying to get something from her. And today was no exception.

Hardly fifty yards away, a dozen men and one woman were clustered at the railing of another ship, watching through binoculars and camera lenses. Supposedly, they were monitoring activities, ensuring that no one tried to escape. Actually, all eyes were on the blond whose name and face were plastered across the front pages of newspapers worldwide. It was a sensational story, packed with everything that sold papers: far-flung settings, world records, beautiful girls, political intrigue, illicit sex, theft, violence, espionage, smuggling, and murder. The only problem was that no one seemed to know which, if any, of the stories were true. Some claimed the woman had driven around the world and discovered tribes in the Amazon. Others insisted that she was a Communist revolutionary or a Hollywood insider or that she'd crossed Africa, scaled mountains, survived jail and kidnapping, escaped civil wars, and worked as a spy. Such basic details as how old she was, where she came from — even her real name — were unclear. Her stage name was Aloha Wanderwell, but beyond that her true story was as murky as the weather that cloaked those two vessels.

As the icy mists turned to lashing snow, Captain Farris shouted a passage from Joseph Conrad: "May the deep sea where he sleeps now rock him gently, wash him tenderly, to the end of time!"[1] A bugler rang out "Taps" and the flag was lifted from the coffin. Then, amid sobs and a flurry of flashbulbs from the press, the plank was raised and the coffin slid overboard. A splash, a wash of bubbles, and then nothing. Just the dark sea.

The woman called Aloha Wanderwell bent forward and covered her face. Her life to this point had been a series of open roads, a steadfast journey to some other place, just over the horizon. Home as a fixed address had not existed since her childhood, 1,100 miles north on Vancouver Island and eighteen years earlier. Before she'd circled the world. Before several US government agencies had started tracking her. Before the nastiness and the extortion and the forthcoming trial. Those carefree days before another man's death had changed her life forever.

ONE

SECOND STAR TO THE RIGHT,
AND STRAIGHT ON TiLL MORNiNG.
— PETER PAN

PERSEVERE

The Arms of
Thomas Dickinson Hall
of Whatton Manor
and Broughton
in the county of Nottingham

Hand-painted facsimile of the Hall Family Arms
Crest and motto, "Persevere."

ONE

THERE'S NO PLACE LIKE HOME

O N A BRIGHT JULY MORNING IN 1912, a fifty-foot cabin cruiser named the *Inlet Queen* arrived at the settlement of Qualicum Beach on the east coast of Vancouver Island. Stepping out into the hot summer sun were Herbert Hall, his wife Margaret, and newborn infant daughter Miki. Watching from the newly painted deck was five-year-old daughter Idris.

While her parents walked carefully around the small rocks and driftwood on the lip of their new property, Idris preferred to stay on the boat, combing her doll's long blond hair. The cruiser had snug beds, a kitchen, even a living room complete with piano and gramophone. But most important of all, here they were *together*.

For as far back as Idris could remember, "home" was the place where she stayed put while her parents went off without her. At Grandpa Hedley's house in North Vancouver, Idris was scolded for being too noisy, too rambunctious, and too present, while the other Hedley grandkids were doted upon, sung to, and read to. Most of her days were spent playing alone in her bedroom while the older cousins enjoyed the run of the house. By the time she was five, Idris had firmly associated the word "home" with separation.[1] Travel, on the other hand, meant exciting times with the people she loved best. Travel brought treats and adventures and Daddy reading tales of Peter Rabbit. As far as Idris was concerned, they could keep on sailing forever.

Why leave the lovely pleasure craft when solid ground meant staying put and the end of every good thing?

❁

At the dawn of the last century, Vancouver Island was a lush rainforest paradise. Ancient fir stands stretched more than 400 feet into the air. Ravens and eagles circled the skies and kept watch over a misty, rolling landscape that plunged to a gentle sea dotted with seals and orcas. Europeans had been poking around since the 1840s, but few had actually settled. In 1900 hardly a thousand Caucasians inhabited the 5,000 square miles along the island's east coast. But for the British, the Edwardian era of colonial expansion and opportunity was in full swing by 1905, and things were beginning to change.

Rumours of a railway from Victoria in the south to Port Hardy in the north drew settlers from around the world with the lure of newly arable land, plentiful natural resources, and the promise of well-paying jobs. Territory that had been populated by Coast Salish, Esquimalt, and other Indigenous peoples for millennia was suddenly crawling with Americans, Germans, Russians, Scandinavians, Chinese, Japanese, and most of all, English. The collapse of English agriculture in Great Britain, combined with a weak stock market and rapid urbanization, had removed the gilded sheen from the English upper classes. Landowners suddenly found themselves without tenants and, consequently, without a stable source of income. Estates that had belonged to families for centuries were being liquidated, their heirs flung out to the far corners of the British Dominion to prospect for new sources of wealth. One such Englishman was nineteen-year-old Herbert Cecil Victor Hall.

Herbert, or "Bertie," was born June 26, 1887, at Tickhill, Yorkshire, and came from a well-known Nottinghamshire family that had once controlled vast properties. Herbert's grandfather, Thomas Dickinson Hall, had served as the sheriff of Nottingham and Lord of the Manor of Whatton, a sizeable village. Herbert's father had been a captain in the Boer Wars and had sent his sons to Haileybury Imperial Service College, a school once attended by Rudyard Kipling. For Herbert, however, the rigors of a service college were too constricting. Though he respected military tradition and understood the responsibilities of authority, he saw no place for such discipline in his own life. Schoolwork didn't interest him nor did the conventional attitudes of his fellow students. He had few friends, and thanks to an injury suffered while riding on the Hertford Heath in 1903, he did not compete in any sports. Herbert dreamed of a more exciting, freewheeling sort of life. By his second year at the school, Herbert was regularly running afoul of school authorities, most seriously in the spring of 1905 when Housemaster A.A. Lea caught Herbert with "smoking materials." By September, Herbert had left Haileybury and was at the Manor Farm Agricultural College at Garforth.[2]

After less than a year there, Herbert received a letter from an older brother regarding investment opportunities in Canada. Unlike England, Canada was bursting with chances to earn a fortune in farming, mining, logging, fishing, heavy industry, and especially real estate. A national railroad, the Canadian Pacific Railway (CPR), had been in existence for just twenty years, and by the early 1900s the trickles of westward immigration swelled to a flood. In 1906 Canada's population was just over six million people, and of these, nearly a million had arrived in the previous ten years.[3] It was, in other words, a nation waiting to be made.

Herbert quit the Manor Farm and set sail for Canada, where he would complete his education at the High River Agricultural School, just south of the city of Calgary. It was, at long last, his chance to set out on new adventures.

Herbert's ship docked in Montreal in the early summer of 1906. He made his way west, by train, across the prairies. The High River School of Agriculture had been founded in 1903 by fellow Englishman Oliver Henry Hanson of Cambridge. Hanson was one of many English "agricultural experts" who came to Canada to train prospective farmers. He advertised his school as a place for young English gentleman farmers. Tuition was fifty pounds per annum and the course lasted two years. According to one source, "Hanson supplemented his income by imposing fines on his trainees for infractions such as being late for breakfast, not shaving and not having their hair combed."[4] By 1909 Herbert had left Alberta[5] to settle in the town of Salmon Arm, British Columbia, a fruit and vegetable growing microclimate.

Salmon Arm was settled predominantly by English. The town boasted a country club, cricket matches, lawn bowling, and a soccer league. Herbert probably came to Salmon Arm to explore farming opportunities but instead wound up discovering an Englishwoman named Margaret Jane Hedley—tall, elegant, a few years his elder, with an exciting disregard for convention and a fondness for giant hats. She was, like much else in Herbert's life, an unusual choice.

Unlike Bertie, however, Margaret was not to the manor born. The eldest of six children, she was raised in the coal country of northeastern England. Her father, James, had worked in the collieries, and although he had risen to the position of foreman, family life was frugal and luxuries scarce. Finding a long, tiring line of would-be suitors unappealing, Margaret made a life-altering decision. Marriage would have shackled her to the duties of a coal miner's wife, the likes of which she had seen many of her female friends endure. Around 1901, at the age of twenty-two, Margaret found her own way out, taking a CPR steamship to Canada. Eventually settling in Winnipeg, she fell in love with a CPR employee named Robert Welch, who, ironically, hailed from a town barely 5 miles from Margaret's birthplace. Five years later, on October 13, 1906, Margaret gave birth to a daughter. Idris Welch was born at 77 Hallet Street in the Selkirk district of Winnipeg. According to Idris's birth certificate, her mother was Margaret *Hadley* and her father was Robert Edward *Welsh*.[6] The certificate claimed that Margaret and Robert were married, but there is no record of the marriage.[7] It was the beginning of a cascade of errors—sometimes accidental, sometimes wildly concocted—that would persist in official documents throughout Idris's life. It's unclear when the couple left Winnipeg to move west and settle in Salmon Arm, or even what finally became of Robert Welch (a piece of family correspondence between cousins suggests he fell off a ladder and broke his neck), but by 1908 Margaret Hedley was single again.[8]

Photographs taken in Salmon Arm show a scowling, three-year-old blond girl seated on a horse-drawn wagon in the company of her mother and several adventurous-looking men with prodigious moustaches, all wearing

OPPOSITE: Margaret Jane Hedley Hall, Aloha's mother. Photo taken about the time of her marriage to H.C.V. Hall, British Columbia, 1919.

INSET: Baby photograph of newborn Idris Welch (Aloha), Winnipeg, Manitoba, October 1906.

Herbert Hall in his canvas tent on the newly purchased Hall property on Qualicum Beach, Vancouver Island, British Columbia, 1914. While the plot of land was being cleared and the initial living quarters were being built, both he and Margaret stayed in the tent .

their Sunday best. These were probably a series of wedding day portraits of Herbert and Margaret's marriage that took place on October 16, 1909, in Herbert's own home with local Baptist pastor H.P. Thorpe presiding.[9]

The ink had hardly dried on their marriage licence before they packed up and moved to the west coast of British Columbia. Margaret's father had emigrated with the entire Hedley clan to the scenic slopes of North Vancouver and Margaret and Bertie decided that familiar family surroundings would benefit them all, especially a growing Idris.

North Vancouver was a thriving town of five thousand souls and had earned the nickname "the Ambitious City." Herbert became a partner in a branch office of the Manitoba Fire Assurance Co. and was soon dabbling in real estate development, building single-family dwellings.

The decision to move west proved a good one. North Vancouver's industries couldn't hire fast enough and news of the good life attracted an influx of working-class families. Before long the Ambitious City became "the City of Homes." The extended Hedley-Hall household was quite content.

However, the Halls were accustomed to being Lords of the Manor, and North Vancouver already had its established wealthy families. When rumours of a new railway line on Vancouver Island surfaced, Herbert saw his opportunity. The line from Victoria, north to Port Hardy would open vast stretches of prime real estate. New industries and settlements were bound to follow, just as they had done in Salmon Arm and North Vancouver.

With funds from the sale of their North Vancouver properties, Herbert bought heavily forested property along Vancouver Island's east coast. Idris was left behind with her cousins and grandfather in North Vancouver, while Herbert and Margaret spent much of 1911 living in a canvas tent, clearing the most scenic part of a forty-acre promontory in Qualicum Beach. By early 1912 they had built a cabin to serve as a temporary home until the family manor could be constructed.

❁

As it turned out, Qualicum Beach was the highlight of Idris's childhood. The arrival of a little sister — baptized Margaret, but nicknamed "Miki" — provided Idris with a playmate, and in future years both sisters would

(L-R): Idris Hall, baby Miki and Herbert Hall enjoying their oceanfront property at Qualicum Beach, British Columbia, 1913.

ABOVE: Young Idris standing thigh-deep in the Salish Sea at the foot of the Hall family property, Qualicum Beach, British Columbia, 1913.

RIGHT: (L-R) Miki, their nanny, and Idris at the foot of the Hall family property on Vancouver Island, Qualicum Beach, 1914.

treasure the memory of their time there: days spent exploring the forests or summers spent paddling "in the shallows (while) mum 'dipped' in her cumbersome bathing costume, sometimes even removing her stockings."[10] The sisters befriended the deer that braved human contact in exchange for crackers, apples, and on more than one occasion, their daddy's beer. On sunny summer afternoons, Margaret would pack a picnic lunch and box up the gramophone. The trio would march down to the shingle beach, where they'd twirl their skirts and croon along to the hits of the day, especially, Idris recalled, the song "Beautiful Ohio." One 78 rpm record contained ukulele music. Playing it would prompt Idris to begin a slow hula-style dance, wearing an imaginary grass skirt. Sometimes Margaret would play this record for dinner guests and ask Idris to "do your Aloha dance."[11]

It wasn't all flights of fancy and wooded kingdoms, however. Idris watched as her father applied his Haileybury and High River Agricultural School training. Forests were pulled down, timbers sawed and planed, and all that wood repurposed as buildings, fences, and signposts. Ranch land was created, the first schoolhouse erected, and a ribbon of road was laid along the coast to the huddle of shacks that served as the town centre. As his crowning achievement, Herbert worked with architects to design the Hall family manor, scheduled for completion in two years' time. While the town around them sprouted into existence, Margaret and the kids tended the family gardens and readied the stable buildings for horses.

For Margaret, a life lived close to the land and sea was happily familiar. Although she had grown up in a mining community, she had often travelled to the North Sea coast on family outings. Striving to attain the trappings of a newly minted middle class, the Hedleys managed a few niceties, and as the eldest, Margaret benefited. While schooling was limited, as it was for most young women of the time, Margaret was able to learn equestrian skills and sailing, pursuits that made Vancouver Island — so dependent on horses and sailboats — feel like home.

For Idris, too, Qualicum Beach imprinted itself on her mind: this was, finally, home. No longer just one of the cousins, she was now part of a stable family — and one that was thriving in a vast and beautiful setting. Nothing could shake Idris from this idyllic life. Or so she hoped.

In April 1913 their boat, the *Inlet Queen,* sank during a promotional trip to Nitinat on Vancouver Island's west coast. Maritime author J.A. Gibbs gives an account of what happened:

All went well till the *Inlet Queen* left dockside. Nasty winds were fanning the Strait of Juan de Fuca, and all the way to the Nitinat Coast the craft took a terrible pounding. The passengers became violently seasick. In crossing the Nitinat Bar, the craft ran hard aground and the passengers were forced to struggle ashore, sick, wet, and discouraged.

Despite the setback, including the total loss of the *Inlet Queen,* the real estate firm was persistent. They still planned a resort similar to those on the coast of southern England.[12]

Although the disaster did little to dissuade Herbert (after all, the Hall family motto was "persevere"), the assassination of Archduke Ferdinand in faraway Sarajevo was about to test the whole world's perseverance.

ABOVE: The Hall family launch, *Inlet Queen*, docked at the foot of Victoria Harbour in front of the Empress Hotel. Note the square portholes.
Victoria, British Columbia, 1915.

BELOW: The interior lounge aboard the Hall family launch, *Inlet Queen*,
Victoria, British Columbia, 1915.

✦

England's declaration of war on Germany caused skilled labour to vanish overnight. During the war's first week, the Canadian militia requested that twenty thousand men sign up for service in Europe. One hundred thousand men responded. Herbert, whose military training made him a natural candidate, would have been expected to leave at once but Margaret begged him not to go. She reminded him how much he was needed in Qualicum Beach, not just by his wife and daughters but by the many families he employed. It was an excruciating decision for Herbert and he tarried through 1914, doing his best to mothball his numerous projects until the war was over, hopefully by Christmas. As 1914 passed, however, the news coming from Europe was cataclysmic. Germany had wiped out the Russians on their Eastern Front and had progressed so far into France they'd nearly captured Paris. The world was in shock, and the failure of the Allied forces to halt Germany was widely blamed on a lack of troops.

Pressure to join the fight became a tidal wave that swept over Canada. War propaganda was everywhere. One famous poster asked women, "Is your 'best boy' wearing khaki?... If he does not think that you and your country are worth fighting for — do you think he is worthy of you?"[13] It wasn't long before businesses and entire towns were being run by wives and daughters, while the men signed up and were shipped to England

Studio photograph of Lieutenant Herbert Cecil Victor Hall, Durham Light Infantry, London, England, 1914.

for training and dispatch. For Herbert, raised in a military tradition and schooled at a college whose motto was, and continues to be, "Fear God, Honour the King," the call of duty was eventually too powerful to resist.

On May 3, 1915, Herbert, now twenty-four, signed his attestation papers for the Canadian Expeditionary Force (CEF), committing himself to serve for as long as His Majesty King George V should see fit.[14] He was commissioned as a private and placed in the 29th Battalion of the CEF, otherwise known as the Vancouver Battalion.[15] He kissed his wife and daughters goodbye and just two weeks later was in Halifax where, on May 20 — amid a throng of rowdy recruits, many of whom had never fired a rifle — he boarded the SS *Missanabie* and sailed for England. In June the men of the Vancouver Battalion were sorted and sent for training in Romney Marsh, Kent, a flat, treeless expanse that simulated the denuded landscapes of rural Belgium, where Herbert would soon be assigned.

✻

Herbert stayed with the Vancouver Battalion for less than six months before transferring to the 12th Battalion of the Durham Light Infantry (DLI), where he was tasked with overseeing the construction of new trenches and facilities and was the keeper of maps for his unit. In a few short weeks he had gone from building houses with sweet-smelling Canadian pine and cedar to piling limp sandbags in a pit and fortifying shelters with scrap timber and flattened tin cans. The British General Staff had a policy against making the trenches too liveable, based on the notion that comfort discouraged "the offensive spirit."

In Qualicum Beach, Margaret did her best to keep up appearances. She wore her biggest hats to all the church functions, kept the horses well brushed, and made sure her girls' dresses were neatly pressed. Inside, however, she was collapsing. As a child, her birth mother had died suddenly. Then, her first love had been killed in an accident.[16] The thought of losing Herbert was more than she could stand. It certainly didn't help that the teatime talk among the ladies from town was dominated by rumours from Europe: whole fields of infantry cut down in neat rows like wheat by German machine guns. Some women were astonished to hear the men were even fighting on Sundays and when it rained. According to one young woman, "Every boy I ever danced with is dead."

Worse than the news from the front, however, was the lack of it. Letters from the front to Canada took as long as four months to arrive. It often happened that a cheerful missive would arrive from a soldier weeks after his family had received the telegram informing them of his death.

As the months ticked by, Margaret began to withdraw. She no longer wrote to the family in North Vancouver, especially since her brother, James, had also gone to war. She hired a nanny to watch and tutor the girls, much to Idris's consternation. Although she didn't understand the full scope of events, she was old enough to see that her mother was unhappy, that her beloved daddy was away, and that her comfortable life was under threat.

✿

When a telegram arrived in early July 1916 saying that Herbert had been injured in France and was recuperating in England, Margaret made up her mind. The distance and the wait were simply too much. She and Miki packed their bags for England. Idris, however, would be left behind. Perhaps Margaret felt she would be safer in Canada or that she should continue her schooling or that she would be too big a handful to manage, given the situation. Whatever her reasons, Margaret made arrangements with a Victoria boarding school.[17] For Idris, it was the start of yet another separation from her family, but also perhaps the first record of an error in her birthdate. Somewhere in the whorl of moving from North Vancouver to Vancouver Island, and from Qualicum Beach to Victoria, her birth year was changed from 1906 to 1908. It's unclear whether Idris actually knew her true age — both dates crop up in documents spread across the years. This uncertainty about her birthdate would come to have serious consequences.

Herbert convalesced at the Cambridge Military Hospital in Aldershot. Miki and Margaret found Herbert in good spirits, though his right thigh had been littered with shrapnel during battle at the Somme.[18] A photograph taken during an afternoon stroll around the hospital grounds shows Herbert leaning on his cane and smiling at the camera, while Margaret, in a pinstriped dress and large flowered hat, looks down at little Miki, wandering

(L-R) Lieutenant H.C.V. Hall, Miki, and Margaret, taken during Herbert's convalescence from a wound suffered during battle, Aldershot, England, 1916.

wandering the overflow tents in her white frock. The expression on Herbert's face is, unmistakably, fatherly pride.

While Europe was torn to pieces, Idris was waging her own kind of war. Unhappy to be confined in the school dormitories, she regularly escaped (usually to attend the cinema) and was placed under house arrest for pummelling a boy who called her a sinner. Later, when Herbert's brother, Algernon, came to visit in his Ford Model T, she convinced him to teach her how to smoke. It appeared that Idris's school career would turn out rather like Herbert's. She was restless and she wanted to be with her family. So deep was her desire to get to England that, in later years, she claimed to have left Canada in January 1917, even describing life in a London cold-water flat with a collapsible Primus stove, the alarm of Zeppelin raids (one blast levelling Miki's nursery garden), the clang and shriek of trains grinding into Victoria station, the sight of fresh troops departing Charing Cross, people kissing in public, and everywhere the "acrid reek of coal smoke, steam."[19] However, ship manifests plainly reveal that Idris was in Canada until after the war's end.

✸

Once Herbert was returned to the front, an uneasy routine settled upon Margaret and Miki through the spring of 1917. One of Herbert's letters noted that the men were working non-stop, though Margaret could not have imagined how literally he meant it. The 23rd Division was part of a colossal mining operation at a place called Hill 60, near Ypres, Belgium, one of the most feared theatres on the Western Front. The project's objective was to mine the whole of the Messines Ridge, occupied by the Germans. The rise, although hardly as high as a second-storey bedroom, was one of the few vantage points in the area, and any view of opposing trench lines was invaluable. For ten months Australian, Canadian, and British troops had rooted under the ridge and along a smaller opposing escarpment called the Caterpillar, laying mines. While the DLI 12th Battalion was not directly involved in tunnelling, they were responsible for defending the trenches and conveying explosives while the digging continued.

By early June the tunnelling was complete and the explosives in place. At 1:00 a.m. on June 7, 1917, the British moved to their jumping-off positions. At 3:05, the troops were instructed to lie flat on the ground. Five minutes later, close to a million pounds of explosives were detonated inside nineteen tunnels under the German front line. The result was a man-made earthquake that instantly killed ten thousand German soldiers. It shook the bed of British prime minister David Lloyd George at 10 Downing Street and rattled pint glasses in Dublin.[20] It was the largest human-created explosion in history up to that time.

Following the blast, the left flank and most northerly unit was the 23rd Division. It was up to them to fight off what German resistance remained and secure the capture of Hill 60. On June 13, six days after the detonation of the mines, Herbert was working with two other officers on a construction detail in an area of Ypres called Battle Wood. Late in the afternoon, the 12th Battalion's forward position came under German shelling. One explosion caused a trench wall to collapse. As soon as the dust settled, the troops scrambled over the debris towards shelter. Just as the last men were clearing out, another heavy shell fell directly into the trench, badly injuring two

106012/7. (C.3.A.L.)

DEPT.
MILITIA & DEFENCE
MAY 18 1921
H.Q.
CANADA

MISTERS OFFICE
REG'D.
MAY 17 1921
REFERRED TO
DEPT. M. & D.

CERTIFICATE OF DEATH.

Certified that according to the records of this
Office Temporary Lieutenant HERBERT CECIL VICTOR HALL,
Durham Light Infantry, attached 12th (Service) Battalion,
was killed in action in France on the 13th day of June, 1917.

Percy Taylor

incorrect:
H.C.V. Hall was
killed at Ypres
Belgium

for the Secretary, War Office.

Dated at the War Office, London,
this 9th day of October, 1917.

Official British military 'Certificate of Death' for H.C.V. Hall dated October 9, 1917,
but retrieved from Canadian archives in May 1921. Aloha's own sticky note
corrects the information, stating Herbert died in Ypres, Belgium, not France.

officers and vaporizing Second Lieutenant H.C.V. Hall. Bertie was gone. Not so much as a fingernail was recoverable. He was mentioned in dispatches "for gallant and distinguished service in the Field" and posthumously awarded a service medal.

❖

Margaret was bereft. In the weeks that followed, she tried her best to look after the family's affairs, including the reading of her husband's last will and testament. Documents had arrived from the family's barrister in North Vancouver, stating that Margaret was to act as sole executrix to Herbert's estate. According to the will, Herbert's possessions in England were to be divided between his brothers, Henry and Algernon. This amounted to some dusty furniture, a few pictures, a gold watch, and a battered cigarette case. Herbert's Canadian property and possessions would pass to his "beloved and faithful wife" Margaret, with the exception of the family silver, which he bequeathed to his daughter, Margaret Verner Hall, Miki. There was no mention of Idris at all.[21]

Idris had been too young to remember her birth father, Robert Welch. When Margaret and Herbert wed, she was barely three years old. The revelation contained in Bertie's will forced Margaret to tell Idris the truth: Herbert had been her stepfather. Idris was numb with shock. Margaret told Idris to be strong. As the older sister, she needed to keep her chin in the air and a smile on her face. To set an example for her younger sister. Idris was by now ten years old, still not old enough to tell her mother to go to hell — that would come later.

The effect Herbert's death had on Idris is evident in surviving photographs. Where once there had been a smiling, gregarious child, there was now a distant, hollow-eyed, vaguely angry young girl of indeterminate age.

The hand she had held on those long beach rambles turned out to be an empty glove. No wonder she had been left behind in Canada. No wonder she felt she had nowhere to belong and, once again, had no place to call home.

Idris Hall, age fourteen, dressed as her silver screen idol Mary Pickford, 1920.

TWO

BRAINS, BEAUTY, AND BREECHES

B Y JUNE 1919, SEVEN MONTHS after the last shot, the war to end all wars finished with the signing of the Treaty of Versailles. That same month, after a lengthy train trip from Vancouver Island, Idris stood on the shuddering deck of the SS *Melita*, watching the ship's propellers churn the cold Atlantic waters. She was twelve years old, and she was travelling solo to England. It had been three years since she had last seen her family. Never small for her age, Idris now stood at almost five seven. Her face had thinned and lengthened, revealing strong cheekbones, large, deep-set eyes, and full lips. The biggest change, however, was in her attitude. Idris had always been a high-energy child and boarding school had proved an intolerable prison of starched collars and chalkboards. The only thing that had made her dull life bearable was the cinema. On the silver screen, Hollywood's stars led exciting and glamorous lives. And in 1919 no one was more glamorous, more adventurous, or more famous than Canadian actress Mary Pickford. Idris became obsessed with Pickford's persona, copying her spunky style, her bravado, and her disregard for authority.

Idris's ship departed from Montreal and sailed for eight days. Like Idris, many passengers were returning to salvage the scraps of their former lives or to claim the possessions of lost relatives. But there were other worries too. Since the war's end, a new and vicious strain of flu was sweeping the globe, killing with incredible speed. An innocent sneeze at breakfast could mean approaching death by dinner. Governments scrambled to contain the disease — the state of Arizona outlawed handshakes and France made spitting a legal offence — but to little effect.[1] On board the ship, many passengers wore masks throughout the voyage and avoided contact with others.

The ship's manifest doesn't record if anyone accompanied Idris, and there are no Halls or Hedleys listed on board. She may well have travelled alone. It is ironic that Margaret left her in Canada through the war, only to call her to England at the height of the most virulent illness the world had ever seen. According to those records, Idris was headed for Margate, Kent, to attend school, but this was never likely. As she wrote years later, "Mum had no desire to settle in England — she had become a colonial misfit among her own."[2]

Idris arrived to the bustle and sooty air of Liverpool harbour on June 25. A day later, on the southeast coast of the country, she was reunited with an emotionally distant mother and a still playful, but bigger sister. Three years of separation had been, for all of them, a transformative time.

At first, Margaret was devastated and pined for the life she'd had with Bertie. But as the weeks passed her sadness turned to fancy, even consulting an astrologer to have her charts done. She came to believe it was possible that Bertie was not actually dead but only wounded or a prisoner of war or suffering from amnesia. Such things happened all the time. Without a body or even a personal effect to prove that he'd been killed, perhaps he was out there somewhere, smoking his pipe, twisting his moustache, waiting to be found.[3] At the very least, she had to go to Belgium and see where he supposedly fell, to visit the grubby railway dugout where a small white cross marked his empty grave.

✿

Idris arrived with her mother and sister at the Belgian town of Heyst-sur-Mer, or "Heist" as the locals called it. A summer holiday town, it was as relaxed as the towels that covered its wide sandy beaches. Postcards of the era show women in ankle-length skirts and children in striped bathing costumes frolicking in the surf or reading books under tipping umbrellas. But Margaret had not chosen Heist for its sand and surf. During the war, the town had been a German command post, a few miles from the terminus of the Western Front. This made it a convenient location from which to

Idris Hall (C) and Miki Hall (R) at the window of their apartments with unknown woman, Heist, Belgium, 1922.

explore the fields where Herbert had fought.[4] Margaret leased a four-level apartment that served as an annex to the Hotel des Bains, newly repaired after heavy German shelling destroyed much of the original façade. While Miki stayed with a nanny, Idris and Margaret spent two months taking day trips across northern Belgium, looking for Herbert. Nothing could have prepared them for the shattered landscape they encountered or for the mutilated veterans they found begging in the streets and train stations. As Idris would later recall, "Mum yet hoped for some miracle among shell-shocked drifting fugitive prisoners of war trudging westward, dazed, haggard, sometimes mindless."[5]

Margaret's fantasies might seem naïve, but the general public had only the vaguest ideas of what had happened during the war.[6] The 1914 Defence of the Realm Act gave the British government sweeping powers to control citizen activities, especially regarding the communication of anything war related.[7] For the duration of the conflict, virtually no stories indicating the true number of casualties or the horrors of battle were published in any newspaper in the British Dominion. It was feared that real images would shock the public and erode support for the war. The reality — the fields of rotting, mangled corpses, the undependable supply lines, the rat- and

ABOVE: A studio photograph of Margaret "Miki" Hall, age six, London, England, 1919.

LEFT: Idris and younger sister Miki on the beach at Heist, Belgium, 1918.

disease-infested trenches, the angry hopelessness of soldiers — was carefully guarded from entering the public imagination.[8]

By summer's close, with no sign of Herbert, Margaret was again packing her daughters' things into a large cedar-lined trunk. She and Herbert had talked about a "continental education" for the girls and this was her chance to fulfill that wish.[9] The girls became boarders in the Catholic girls' school Monastère des Bénèdictiones, Religieuses Françaises, two hours south of Heist in the town of Ooigem. Idris dreaded life in yet another boarding school, but at least this time Miki would be with her. The school was a collection of boxy, ivy-clad dormitories with orange tile roofs and a long, rectangular teaching hall, lined on one side by tall arched windows. In summer, the grounds could be beautiful, offering spacious green courtyards and the security of 20-foot-high brick walls. In winter months, however, the barren trees and dead grass made the grounds feel more like a cemetery.

From Margaret's perspective, the school was ideal. A convent could offer all the opportunities of a secular boarding school, but at a much better price

Idris (C, back row) and Miki (kneeling second from L, front row) in student class photo, Monastère des Bénèdictiones, Ooigem, Belgium, 1920.

and with the possible added advantage of being strict enough to handle a tall twelve-year-old who enjoyed a good scrap and rolled her own cigarettes.

Miki, the cherubic little girl who was as retiring as her sister was outgoing, settled in quickly. Photographs show a small, slightly plump girl with dark, bobbed hair and a round face. Everyone liked Miki, and it wasn't long before she'd learned to "genuflect gracefully" and otherwise stay in the nuns' good books.[10] She learned French easily and was soon deemed ready for her First Communion. Idris's experience was somewhat less positive.

> Mine was a grudging progress, only belatedly acquired by din of Benedictine zeal. All innocent? Not I! Happily compliant? Not likely! Mother spoke of it as "a mind of her own" and did not deny me. I was promptly admonished with some acerbity, forbidden to shoot orchard apples with a slingshot, or to whistle. "Makes the Virgin Mary cry." What a pity.... Problems faced in earlier schools began.[11]

The nuns labelled Idris uncorrectable, but that did not prevent her from gaining a degree of success and popularity.[12] Idris noted the quiet rivalries that existed between the nuns and formed convenient allegiances. But there were genuine friendships too, most notably with the Mother Superior, Abbess

Marie Pia, who recognized that Idris had her own kind of spirit. At the opposite end of the spectrum was Madame Headmistress, a "gross despot" who used her girth and booming voice to tyrannize students.[13] Idris was one of the few who dared to defy "the Battle-Axe" and often suffered for it, though never with the severity visited upon the other girls. The nuns were only too aware of Idris's close relationship with the Abbess (whom Idris referred to as "Mother of Leniency") and measured their punishments. It could also be that Idris had discovered something that gave her a degree of power over her tormentors. She would later write, "In this rigid cloistered order, under vows of abstinence and chastity, only Headmistress was permitted to share her bedroom with another nun."[14]

❖

Idris turned thirteen that fall and, like Herbert, yearned for a life of adventure, not piety. Late at night, after the nuns had passed her door en route to their evening vigil, Idris lit a candle and lost herself in the contraband books she'd snuck into the convent after weekend visits with her mother: Kingston's *The Three Midshipmen*, Conrad's *Java Sea* tales, a stream of cheaply produced, serialized adventure tales for boys, and, of course, *Silver Screen* magazine.[15]

For Idris, the hair-raising adventure stories were inspirational. Before long, she was scrawling her own variations in a book she called her "fantasy journal." There were tales of stormy sea adventures, of young girls overcoming despotic nuns, of true love threatened by blackmail, and of lovers separated by natural disasters and cruel parents. Whatever

A studio photograph of Idris Hall, age thirteen, London, England, 1919.

42

the crisis, there was always a swashbuckling heroine who bore an uncanny resemblance to Idris Hall. Idris shared her stories with some of the more wayward girls of the cloister. On free afternoons, during hikes along the gentle River Lys, Idris and friends would stop in the shade of ancient oaks to perform impromptu dramas based on her scripts.

❁

At the school, both Idris and Miki contracted scabies. When Margaret heard of this, she promptly paid a visit to the headmistress, demanding that immediate measures be taken. Madame Headmistress coolly informed Margaret that, even in the presence of disease, the Benedictine Order *did not take baths.*[16] There was a total prohibition on nudity: the girls could not even view their own bodies when changing. Bathing was never immersive, but done with a damp sponge under clothing.

This was not a complication that Margaret had anticipated. "You people," she hissed, "must be the last holdouts for St. Jerome's sanctimonious advice about female nudity. I'll take cleanliness next to godliness!"[17] She paid a quick visit to the Mother Superior and then to the convent's patriarch priest, whom she plied with a five-star cognac. The next week two full-length zinc bathtubs were installed in the convent dormitories, for Miki's and Idris's exclusive use.

In the meantime, Margaret ensured her girls received proper medical attention. It was an experience Idris would never forget.

> The cure became my first experience of standing totally nude before
> a man, a young Belgian physician. In the presence of my mother his
> gloved hands rubbed my body forcefully in every area with a stinking
> sulphur compound of Peruvian balsam seed benzoate. Standing head-
> level to him, anticipating every sensation, cringing inside...I stared
> wildly at Mum.[18]

❁

Idris and Miki were permitted occasional trips to visit Margaret in Heist, where the trio spent lazy days wandering the wide beaches, collecting shells and stones, or visiting local cafés for treats of warm milk and petits fours.

For Idris, though, half the adventure was getting to Heist. She no longer looked like a child and often attracted the attention of male passengers — a development that both frightened and fascinated her. Clattering rides north were spent keeping one eye on her sister while coolly pre-empting men's attempts to engage her in conversation. It was no different at home in Heist, where she regularly endured "vulgar Continental annoyances." Even the owner of the hotel was prone to holding Idris's arm rather too intimately.[19] When Margaret noticed, she counselled her daughter to employ what she called the Frigid British Stare. "If it's an impudent look," she said, "just give your eyes the cool dismissal. If the bottom pinch is *too* marked, just kick 'em in the shins, 'arry!"[20]

Margaret will have known all about the attentions of men, even now. Margaret was a panther among tabby cats: an independent woman from the new world, accustomed to handling her own affairs and quick to dispense with civilities when bored or affronted. Her strong, tempestuous character was put on public display when, during an afternoon stroll, Idris and Margaret witnessed a peasant brutally goading a tired horse with a hayfork, blood oozing where the prongs had pierced.[21] Spewing an invective of incomprehensible *Frenglish*, Margaret charged the bewildered farmer, snatched his pitchfork, and walloped his backside with it. Amused onlookers cheered her on.

※

In early 1921 Margaret abruptly announced that she would return to Qualicum Beach to "see what could be retrieved of the family fortune."[22] She had finally accepted that her vigil in Belgium was futile; Bertie was gone. Back in British Columbia, however, Margaret had to face the fact that almost all the family's commercial land holdings had been auctioned off to pay for property taxes and her Canadian friends and the families of the men Herbert had employed could not, or would not, offer the beleaguered widow assistance. Go home to England, they told her, and forget about Qualicum Beach.[23]

Idris, meanwhile, was chafing with boredom. The world beyond the cloisteral walls was churning with excitement while she missed it all. Even in sleepy Ooigem there had been a thrilling procession of Marxists through the town centre. Fearing a revolution, shopkeepers had shuttered their windows, and churches had locked their doors. The nuns sent the girls to chapel to chant the rosary and pray for safety. Idris, however, watched from a third-storey window while passionate young men with "Gregorian voices" boomed the "Internationale" and waved banners. She had little concept of what the Communists stood for, but she understood that change was at the heart of their message — and *that* was something she could believe in.

Then, in a way she couldn't have predicted, change arrived of its own accord. During some routine snooping, the headmistress discovered and read one of Idris's fantasy journals. Its tales of violence, monastery intrigue, and wild plans for escape scandalized the sisterhood. Even Mother Superior could not quell the shock and outrage that Idris's lurid stories provoked among the nuns.

According to her later accounts, Idris was summoned to the headmistress's office where she was excoriated for, as her journal would later say, "conceiving such irrational events."[24] The diary had been her best friend and to see it so sneeringly violated was unbearable. She lunged to retrieve it, but the headmistress yanked the book from reach. Before Idris could stop herself, a fist shot out and crashed into the nun's mouth, sending her sprawling in a puddle of black and white fabric. Shrieking expletives, Idris kicked aside the sister's fallen rosary and plucked her precious journal from the floor.[25]

It is impossible to know if this account has been embellished since we have only Idris's word for it, but it is true that Margaret received a cable from the Mother Superior of the Monastère des Bénèdictiones, explaining the discovery of the journal and the necessary disclosure of its contents — after all, it contained the girl's avowed intention to run away from school. The nuns, she wrote, could no longer cope. Idris was to be expelled from the cloister. Margaret hastily leased the remaining Vancouver Island properties for logging and ranching. Together with her war widow pension, the funds would meet life's expenses with little left over for luxuries. At this point, according to her daughter, she hardly cared. She was tired of hauling her unhappiness from shore to shore. She "cabled a sailing date for the French Riviera, imploring, 'Patience 'till we meet!'"[26] For her part, Idris vowed to be "très sage."

✼

In late April 1921, the sisters, now fourteen and nine, dressed in tweed capes and took a train to Paris, where they boarded an express for the French Riviera. The train came to a stop in Nice, where Idris and Miki tumbled out onto the platform, wide-eyed at the soft air and warm sun. The girls soon spied their mother and ran into her outstretched arms.

A large black taxi delivered the reunited family to the Villa Marie-Thérèse, a rustic thick-walled villa built in the late 1600s. There were large fireplaces, deep-set windows with rippling glass, and heavy doors on every room. For the girls, though, their new home's best feature was the elaborate private garden, overflowing with citrus fruits, roses, orchids, and mimosas. It was a stage for fantasy, transformed during the summer into Peter Pan and Wendy's Neverland, and, in view of the garden's fig trees, the Garden of Eden.

> Well, there is something wrong with that story. I (had) no sooner strung large leaves fore and aft across Miki's bare betweens, than she began to scream, dashed for the pump, tearing off the apron. The back of those leaves was worse than poison ivy! The Written Word lost some of its power for us.[27]

Though Idris was content to spend the summer naked in the garden, Margaret wanted to keep the girls more productively occupied. She enrolled them both in ballet classes at the Victoria Cinema Palace under Madame La Sédova, formerly of the Imperial Ballet, and in equestrian practice with a Cossack ex-cavalry officer who had recently fled the Bolshevik bloodbath. Miki, it turned out, had a knack for horses, while Idris excelled at dancing. She was soon dreaming of a career on the stage.

At summer's close, the girls were registered in the tiny Raspini Pensionnat de Demoiselles on the Rue de France, N° 107.[28] It was another convent school, run by two "gaunt as parchment"[29] nuns. Idris steeled herself for another spell of regimented boredom, but consoled herself that at least this time she could spend weekends at home with her mother.

When school began, Idris was pleasantly surprised. In contrast to the banal uniformity of the Monastère des Bénèdictiones, students at the Raspini were ethnically diverse and culturally sophisticated. The school was also less strict than the Belgian cloister had been, with the unstated aim of "finishing" privileged girls in preparation for a successful marriage rather than a life of abstinent piety. In her journals, Idris noted a blond, olive-skinned Corsican, a "sultry" Romanian violinist who made her classmates swoon to Godard's *Berceuse de Jocelyn*, several hot-tempered Italians, and above all, an American girl of uncertain ethnicity. Like Idris, Eliza was tall, outgoing, and looked older than her years.[30] She introduced Idris to make-up, pedicures, ballroom dancing, wine, and urbane literature, especially the work of Madame de Staël. Eliza's mother was a poet and a friend of the French writer, Colette. In later life, Idris wondered if Eliza was the model for Colette's famous would-be courtesan in *Gigi*.[31]

☼

No high walls surrounded the Raspini school, and students were afforded relative freedom, but Idris enjoyed more than most. She was given her own room and was permitted to leave the school on weekends to run errands for her mother, now less than an hour south by tram. It was a liberty Idris cherished and sometimes abused. Occasionally, on early evening trips home from a matinee or shopping at the Place Masséna, Idris would pass by the local bordello. "They were corpulent, painted — wore wigs, I thought. If daytime, we smiled at them and they smiled. Raspini girls recognized them all by sight but remained strictly aloof." Margaret said she felt terribly sorry for these women, and Idris was shocked to learn that the girls there were legally and forcibly inspected for syphilis. Yet she was fascinated by them. "There was something about their mien," she wrote. "Something about the way they walked."[32]

Now fifteen, Idris was increasingly interested in fashion and conscious of the changes that time and ballet were effecting in her body. Margaret noticed the changes too, telling her that her shape "would never be better."[33] When a Côte d'Azur beauty contest was announced, Idris begged her mother to allow her to enter. The first prize was a picture contract with a well-known French company.[34] In the end, Idris didn't win, but the experience of being fawned over and admired whet her appetite.

(L-R) Mother Superior, Miki, and Idris, age fifteen, at the Raspini Pensionnat de Demoiselles, Nice, France, 1922.

✸

Idris was happier in the South of France than she had been in Belgium but still resented the drudgery of classes, homework, and school rules. Like Herbert before her, she longed for excitement and adventure. Then, in the spring of 1922, while on one of her many sorties from downtown Nice to the Villa Marie-Thérèse, she paused at the local aerodrome to watch the planes crisscross the tiny airfield and twist through the Mediterranean sky.[35] She imagined herself in the cockpit, with goggles and scarf, climbing through the air, soaring over great distances.

And while Idris watched the planes, the pilots began watching her. Soon a handsome war hero named Marc Maicon[36] strolled over and introduced himself. They chatted for a while and he offered to give Idris and her groceries a ride home — not in his Caudron G.3 airplane, but in his cherry red Peugeot sports car. She took one look at his wavy brown hair and big brown eyes and handed her groceries to Maicon.

By the time school recessed for the summer, rides home from the aerodrome were regular occurrences. With Margaret's approval, Marc began teaching Idris how to drive. Naturally, Idris was soon infatuated. "Had (mum) been aware of my immediate captivation, things would have been quite different."[37] But it wasn't just Marc that Idris was falling for. She loved the speed and mobility of driving. *This* was independence — and it didn't hurt that these wheels came complete with a dashing owner. "I was to remember how the confines of a car, its reassuring purr and motion, breeds an extraordinary sense of isolation, intimacy…privacy."[38]

Even if Margaret fancied that Idris might make herself a good catch with the war hero pilot, she likely had little sense of how rapidly things were really progressing. Idris's journal recorded how with each meeting the caresses grew more insistent, the romantic talk more serious. During one lesson, as he leaned across Idris to help her steer, he proposed they find some place to be alone. Idris declined at first but eventually "agreed to go with him to a small villa near the aerodrome."[39] They drove to an out-of-the-way house where a plump matron showed them to a small room on the upper floor. After some initial awkwardness, he manoeuvred Idris to the single bed and began unbuttoning her shirt. He praised her smooth skin, her nascent curves, and blossoming breasts. "You should be wearing a *soutien gorge*," he told her, "or those little tetons will begin to droop." As he ran his fingers over her, Idris, not exactly sure what they were doing, began to giggle uncontrollably.

Perplexed, Marc asked if it was her first time. "No, of course not," she lied. But the giggles would not stop. Fearing the moment would be lost, Marc leaned over and kissed her. Although she was still in her skirts, he lay on top of her, pressing her legs apart. His motions had the desired effect. Perhaps surprised by these new sensations, her laughter trailed away. But soon, too, did l'aviateur. His pleasant movements ceased completely.

To Idris's great shock, he seemed to be crying. He lifted his head. "Excuse-moi, cherie. J'ai…j'ai réjoui sans toi." Idris hadn't the slightest idea what he meant. *"He has rejoiced without me?"*[40]

✵

In the fall, Idris and Miki returned to the Raspini where, as usual, Miki flourished and Idris chafed. In her journal, Idris describes being "tortured by strange yearnings" and frustrated that she and her mother could not "speak the same language." Compounding matters, her friend (and co-troublemaker) Eliza had not returned to school from Paris. After the excitement of summer, school felt lonely and restrictive. Idris wanted something exciting to happen, but there was, she believed, nothing to look forward to.

Shortly after Idris's sixteenth birthday, she was in her room at the Raspini, gazing through her window at the wide and inviting Mediterranean. White masts dotted the waters, a hundred specks, each connected to some ship, moving towards some glowing adventure she was not a part of. Depressed, she flopped on her bed and began leafing through *Le Petit Niçois* newspaper until an unusual article caught her eye: a "quixotic American, racing an automobile around the world" had arrived in Nice. According to the article, the Wanderwell Expedition was making movies of its travels and would be screening them the following evening at the Victoria Palace.[41] An accompanying photograph showed the handsome expedition leader, Captain Wanderwell, wearing a kind of military uniform and leaning nonchalantly against a racy, fenderless, doorless roadster. Idris was intoxicated. The question was not *whether* she should sneak into town to see the show, but *how*.

The solution proved easy enough. "I had no conscience about cutting school — just advised La Directrice that Maman requested my absence. Then . . . I was out on the street, alone . . . at dusk."[42] She made her way to the Victoria Palace theatre and used her smile and swagger on an admiring doorman to let her in without paying.

In the crowded lobby, Idris studied photographs highlighting the expedition's adventures: American president Harding autographing the hood of the car, General Pershing shaking hands with Captain Wanderwell, a car dashing through Mississippi floods, the Prince of Wales saluting Wanderwell's crew, which included, Idris noted, two females. The captain himself looked to be in his late twenties, blond, lean but muscular, with a square jaw and smiling eyes that expressed confidence and amusement. His uniform

A staged photo op of Walter with two unidentified girls in his party, London, England, October 1922. This was just prior to travelling to the South of France and meeting sixteen-year-old Idris Hall.

consisted of gabardine jodhpurs, black Pershing boots, and a jaunty field service cap.[43] In no picture was anyone ever out of uniform.

For almost an hour, "speaking in broad Yankee twang...sparked here and there with French words," Captain Wanderwell treated his audience to the towering redwoods of California, the deserts of Mexico (including a visit with revolutionary Pancho Villa), the Florida Everglades, the engineering miracles of New York City, as well as scenes from Cuba, South Africa, South America, Scotland, and England before concluding with images of Paris filmed only days before.[44] At that time, perhaps only Burton Holmes could offer audiences such a feast of world vistas.[45]

Idris was gobsmacked. Here, in the flesh, was a man living a life more adventurous than anything she had dared dream in her journals. After the show she snuck backstage, only to find that others had the same idea. "A line of fans already waited for the privilege of shaking hands with this young daredevil." She pushed her way to the front of the queue but, "His dazzling smile overwhelmed me and I could only stammer, 'My felicitations.' 'Ah, you speak English', he said. 'Great — come along.'"[46]

In the company of other fans, she followed the captain outside. There he signed autographs and answered questions about the aims of his expedition. He was, he said, engaged in a race around the world with another car. The goal was to see as many countries as possible before the next World's Fair, scheduled to be in Chicago in three years' time.[47] The race had been nicknamed the "Million Dollar Wager" because the winner would be awarded all films, photographs, and other memorabilia from *both* teams, as well as, it was said, all rights to their use, the value of which would approach seven figures.

When he turned to sign Idris's souvenir pamphlet, Wanderwell seemed to recall why he had invited her along. He snatched a newspaper from a nearby crew member and flipped to an interior page. He pointed to an ad at the top. "Right now, I'm looking for an interpreter," he began, "and

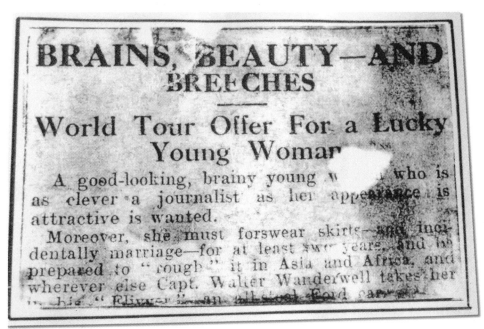

BRAINS, BEAUTY — AND BREECHES

World Tour Offer For a Lucky Young Woman

A good-looking, brainy young w   who is as clever a journalist as her appearance is attractive is wanted.

Moreover, she must forswear skirts — and incidentally marriage — for at least two years and be prepared to "rough" it in Asia and Africa, and wherever else Capt. Walter Wanderwell takes her in his "Flivver" — an all-steel Ford car.

The original newspaper clipping that started it all. From the English-language *Paris Herald*, Walter Wanderwell seeks a young woman to join the Wanderwell Expedition, December 1922.

somebody who can act or sing." Idris was momentarily stumped but then told him that she could dance, if that was any help. He smiled. She was invited to visit his hotel the next morning, the Normandie.

☼

Idris walked back to the school, transfixed by the newspaper that Captain Wanderwell had given her.

BRAINS, BEAUTY AND BREECHES
World tour offer for lucky young woman

> Captain Walter Wanderwell is seeking a lady secretary to join his world tour by auto.... A good-looking, brainy young person, who is as clever a journalist as her appearance is attractive. She must forswear skirts, and incidentally marriage, for at least two years. Be prepared to rough it in Asia and Africa, to record the adventures of the party, to learn to work before and behind a movie camera.[48]

This was everything she'd ever dreamed of. She imagined herself in the Wanderwell uniform, lecturing audiences, earning money and applause. Then, like cold water down her back, she imagined her mother. Somehow she had to make her mother see that further schooling was pointless. Somehow she had to convince her that she was ready to join an expedition that aimed to traverse, often for the first time, some of the most forbidding lands on the planet.

The first professional studio portrait of Idris as Aloha, France, 1923.

THREE

SATURDAY'S CHILD
HAS FAR TO GO

IDRIS STOOD AT THE DOORWAY of an adventurous life. It was a golden opportunity, and yet, in many ways, typical of the winds blowing through that era. In the fall of 1922, people the world over were reinventing themselves, taking risks, throwing off recent history like an old coat. Indeed, the whole of Western culture was entering an era that few could have predicted. Only a few blocks from the Raspini school, Henri Matisse was working on a series of unconventional canvases he called "Odalisques," evoking the pastel reds, pinks, blues, and oranges so abundant in Nice to give life to his subjects. In Paris, one thousand copies of a book called *Ulysses* were being printed. Across the Atlantic, in California, a man named Walter Disney was picking up the pieces of his bankrupt Laugh-O-Gram Studio and trying again. And in New York, poet Robert Frost had published a collection of plain-language poems, including one whose ending Idris might have found especially apt: "But I have promises to keep, And miles to go before I sleep..." The twenties were beginning to roar.

❋

On the morning of December 20, 1922, an early winter storm was raging through Nice, whipping palm fronds and frothing the deserted promenade. Idris arrived, soaking wet, at the lobby of the Hotel Normandie ten minutes before the 10:00 a.m. meeting time. She found a leather bench and watched as hotel guests — mostly English vacationers — peered through rain-splattered windows with expressions of undisguised annoyance. By eleven o'clock the captain had still not arrived, nor by lunchtime. It was, according to Idris, after one o'clock when a khaki-clad figure finally sauntered through the entrance door and saw her watching him. With a wince and snap of his fingers, Wanderwell apologized for forgetting their meeting. He placed a hand on her elbow and directed her to the hotel café, where he ordered two glasses of milk and began describing expedition life. Yes, there was plenty of adventure, he said: travel, film, photography, press interviews. But even more important were the letter writing, the postcard sales, and the promotional agreements — these were the tasks that bought their bread.

> We also advertise the products we use: petrol, tires, film, hotels, so forth; a barter system. The main cash income is from the sale of illustrated brochures, the history of our Expedition. Each member gets fifty percent commission of her brochure sales, ten percent of the value of ad endorsements. From earnings, the member pays "personal" expenses. I pay all transportation and accommodation expenses. Luxuries are scarce; there are hardships along with the adventure. Our uniform is breeches, boots and tunic — it's practical for climbing in and out of the car — there are no doors.[1]

At the end of his summary, he paused and said that there was one other important requirement. "Members agree to remain single for the duration. I guess only a *very* young person can readily adapt. You need daring and fortitude to stand up to the rigors of our active and very public life."[2]

He took a sip from his milk and leaned back in his chair, awaiting her response. She was, she said, not afraid of hard work and certainly had no intention of getting married any time soon. She asked for a chance to prove herself. He looked her over and, smiling, agreed.

❀

Idris cobbled together an outfit from one of Herbert's old sets of tunic and breeches and arrived at the Royal Theatre the following afternoon. She was introduced to the two other crew members. The first was an enthusiastic Italian man she referred to only as "il giornalista." The other was a gruff

One of the many souvenir postcards produced by the expedition promoting their scheme around the world — this one printed in French — circa 1923.

Texan named Helen Raeburn who'd left her boring husband to see the world. She had a facility for striking coy, demure poses and acted as an interpreter for the captain, or Cap as the crew called him. Idris dubbed her "la Divorcée."[3]

Idris's first task was to help sell postcards during the matinee's intermission.[4] The job sounded easy enough, but she soon learned otherwise. While the others earned fistfuls of cash, the girl from the cloister found it difficult to approach strangers, let alone ask them for money. In a panic, she watched Wanderwell freely converse with anyone in "truncated versions" of whatever language they preferred, able to engage and move on without ever losing his smile or composure.[5]

After the show, Idris found she had earned approximately one-tenth what the Italian journalist had managed. Still, the captain complimented her work and assured her that selling would get easier. Besides, he said, hawking postcards and brochures was only one small part of the job.

I was called to work the solid day, winding up commitments on advertising contracts, each sponsor requiring documentation of our campaign: press clippings, photos, showbills — (a) complete rundown of how well their product or agency was brought to local attention...

It was all very novel, curious to me. The effort to keep up with instructions, memorize files, containers, required considerable concentration. . . .[6]

The following day brought more of the same, except that instead of returning
to the school, Idris stayed overnight at the Normandie, sharing a room with
the "American lady member."[7] La Divorcée had signed on for the London–
Paris–Monte Carlo–Nice run and was set to leave the expedition. The two
settled into their room, chatting as they unpacked. Idris was shocked, however, when Helen changed from her uniform into a racy nightgown in plain
view, all the while disclosing extremely personal details about her life, her
family, and the dullard husband. She also volleyed questions that Idris didn't
feel prepared to answer, especially about men. Perhaps realizing how naïve
Idris was, she offered a little sisterly advice: "'All Italians are giornalistas.
The press card gives them dazzle. In fact, half the men you meet on the
make are journalists.' She changed her tone, looked at me hard and rattled
on, 'Now the Captain, he's on the square. You'll be perfectly safe with him,
so don't worry. He'll take care of you.'" Idris was plainly startled. The Texan
paused, squinting. "Kid, you're not totally innocent, are you?" Idris laughed.
"Of course not!" though she wasn't quite sure what the crazy divorcée had
meant.[8] Obviously, there was more to this expedition than driving around,
making movies, and getting famous.

But if Idris had misgivings about joining the Wanderwell Expedition,
they were soon banished. The next afternoon they drove 18 miles east to the
small town of Menton, near the Italian border. She rode in the front seat of
the car labelled Unit N° II and watched as forested hills, citrus groves, and
a shimmering turquoise sea rolled past. She chatted with the captain as he
drove, captivated by his easy laughter and his wonderful storytelling. He
described some of the towns they'd been to in France and where the best
money was to be made. It all sounded so wonderful. She told him that she
was ready to do whatever would be of most use to the expedition. Smiling,
he suggested that, perhaps rather than sell souvenirs, she could try her hand
at interpreting, especially now that the Texan was moving on. It would give
her a chance to see how she liked it up on stage. He did not have to ask twice.

The Eden Cinema was small but lavishly decorated. Idris would perform at a matinee and evening performance, both of which had sold out. She chewed her nails but was desperate to make amends for her lacklustre performance in Nice. This was her chance to shine. She thought of Mary Pickford and did her best to imitate the captain's easy nonchalance. She climbed to the stage, blushing at the audience's applause, but then, as the film began rolling, her bones went hollow, her mind blank. She forgot the names of places or misremembered film sequences; even her French deserted her. Rather than simply pass over troublesome portions, she attempted to find just the right word, all the while falling further and further behind in the narrative. Her "performance" soon dissolved into a slight, inarticulate gurgling. Afterwards, Wanderwell gave her some advice: "Speak to the last man in the last row — your voice will have the right volume and you won't be intimidated by the sea of faces at your feet."[9] It was a tip she never forgot and it had immediate effect: the evening show went much better. She spoke confidently and felt in control of her voice. The earnings were high and by the time she collapsed in her hotel room shortly after midnight, Idris had experienced her first taste of success.

As Idris found out, sleep was not one of the tour's luxuries. Shortly past dawn, Wanderwell banged on her hotel room door. He was dashing across the border to Italy to get a permit for his car before returning to Nice. He wanted her to come along and see how one could get a car across the border without paying duties. The duo drove into Italy near Garavan, where they got a French stamp on the car's "carnet de passage en douane." The carnet was a new concept in professional travel. Backed by the Royal Automobile Club, it eliminated the need to pay duty for the car at every border. If the vehicle was sold or wrecked in a foreign country, the RAC would pay the resulting duty. Carnets are still in use today, though seldom for cars.

According to her later journals, Idris was back in Nice by 11:00 a.m., thumping on the door of the Villa Marie-Thérèse. As the door opened, she thrust the newspaper at her mother. She pointed to the ad and confessed her adventures: her absence from school, the expedition, the wonderful films, the cars, this crazy chance of a lifetime to see the world, to be in films, to earn money for the family. Just today she had already been in two countries! It was everything she'd ever dreamed of and an opportunity that would never come again.[10]

Naturally, Margaret said no. Not under any circumstances. In fact, she was already familiar with the so-called Wanderwell Expedition because she'd read an article about it in the *Paris Herald* some days earlier.[11] Certainly, it sounded exciting. But how could a mother allow such a thing? Idris was barely sixteen and had not yet finished her schooling—and who knew what these world-roving vagabonds were really like. Still, she couldn't help smiling at her daughter's raving enthusiasm, especially since she too loved the thrill of packing up for points unknown. Years later, at another crossroads, Margaret wrote, "The Gypsy in me said move on. That itching foot of mine is the surest warning that the stage of being 'put' is likely to come to an end...the problem was not when to move, but where and how."[12]

Idris reminded her mother of her youthful travels. At twelve, she had travelled unaccompanied by train across Canada and by steamer across the Atlantic. With the Wanderwell Expedition, she would be in the company of other experienced travellers. After much pleading and negotiation, Idris convinced her mother to meet Captain Wanderwell. If all went well, perhaps Idris could participate in some local shows to see if she had any talent. Margaret relented. She would meet this Wanderwell fellow but made no further promises.

One of only a handful of professional studio portraits of Aloha. Note the Clara Bow–style "bee stung" lips — a popular fashion statement in the 1920s.

✦

The next morning, Walter Wanderwell arrived at the villa, his brass buttons shining and his car parked out front. Passersby regularly stopped to examine the vehicle's many badges and slogans. "You're probably wondering how I got into this enterprise," he said over tea, and proceeded to outline his version of the events of his life. His real name was Valerian Pieczynski and at fourteen, he'd run away from his native Poland, lured by the "Cabin Boy to Captain" ads he'd seen in German magazines. By sixteen, he was sailing on an English merchant vessel and at seventeen, he had rounded Cape Horn and landed in Chile. In the years that followed, he continued to crisscross the globe, visiting ports in Europe, Africa, South America, and finally North America. When war was declared, he decided to stay in the United States, setting off on foot to explore the country. He made his way doing odd jobs and speaking at clubs, where he sold brochures outlining his adventures. After a few years, he settled in Atlanta to serve with the Volunteers of America — a faith-based non-profit organization. According to him, his wartime marriage had failed but he and his wife, though legally separated, remained friends.[13] Both were interested in travel, so they hatched a plan to race each other around the world. His wife, Nell, was currently piloting her car, called Unit N° I, across the United States, Canada, and Mexico.

To support his amazing story he produced several scrapbooks bursting with documents, personal recommendations and seemingly endless press clippings. "A splendid performance," Idris would later write. "As we scanned this impressive array, I could see mum's scepticism slowly melting. How could anyone doubt the ability of this self-confident, captivating man who had already packed several lifetimes of experience into his twenty-six years?"[14]

The captain outlined the aims and structure of the expedition, and highlighted the need for someone who could work both behind and in front of the camera. "Our crews may change with the countries," he said, "or sign on for limited periods, but I do need a permanent member to feature in the picture I'm producing who will appear on stage with the film. I think your daughter has the right spirit and good health to be a success."[15] Margaret thanked the captain for his time and said she would think it over. Idris panicked. She had hoped for an instant answer and this delay wound her into knots of worry. What if Wanderwell decided not to wait, or hired someone else? Or what if Margaret simply said no? The risk of letting this opportunity melt away was too awful to think about — how could she ever return to a joyless and boring convent school after this? And so Idris began to create a Plan B.

She was leaving no matter what.

By the following week, Margaret had still not made a final decision, but she did consent to a trial run. Idris could work with the expedition during its stay in southern France. Wanderwell would provide training and Idris would see how she liked the work. For the purposes of the tour, however, the captain was obliged to become her guardian — he would cover all her expenses and guarantee a minimum commission. If she wanted to resign, he would pay her fare home. For Margaret, this final point was a deal breaker. Idris must have an exit route. To Idris's surprise, Wanderwell agreed. It was, she wrote, "the dreamed of 'open sesame.' All problems could be overcome… I knew everything would be okay."[16]

✿

On the morning of December 29, a calamitous rattle and clang announced the return of Captain Wanderwell and his car to the Villa Marie-Thérèse.

The ever-present American flag affixed to the vehicle's trunk was another example of Walter's grasp of public relations. He knew it would attract as much attention in foreign locales as the vehicle itself, but the flag also served another purpose, as Aloha stated in her journals:

> The car…drew waves and shouts. "OK Americains, bonne chance!"
>
> Suddenly I became American, caused by the prima facie question, "Where are you from?" As the Captain explained, the public's interest was in the Expedition, not the individual, hence the answer and the unavoidable assumption.[17]

The vehicle was bizarre: covered with autographs, advertising slogans, and a giant planet-shaped logo that read "Around the World with Walter Wanderwell." The body was constructed of 22-gauge sheet metal, riveted into an aerodynamic shape, including a tapered "fastback" design that

Aloha and Walter with two of their "improvised" Ford Model T automobiles, Tokyo, Japan, 1925.

Wanderwell would eventually patent. There were no doors, but it had removable floorboards (for easy access to both the transmission and hidden compartments), pressed steel wheels (wooden spoke tires were still the norm), and telescoping axles that allowed the car to travel on railway lines. All of it fastened to the chassis of a Ford Model T.

None of this mattered to Idris at the time, of course. Her attention was on her expedition uniform and how she looked. She cut a striking figure — and with the addition of her new riding boots, stood almost six feet tall.

One more adjustment was required. "Idris," a name she'd never much cared for (it was a boy's name to begin with), didn't sound exotic enough for a grand expedition, let alone public stage performances. She had promised Cap that she could dance, and since one of her favourites was her Hawaiian "Aloha dance," she adopted the name. Idris became Aloha.

She chirped a hurried *au revoir* to her mother and bewildered sister, then jumped into Unit N° II, blowing a last kiss while the captain cranked the engine and put the car into gear. As they pulled away, a sixteen-year-old Idris caught herself smiling in a window's reflection. Aloha smiled back.

❀

Aloha's first days on the road were a gentle introduction to the vagabond life. She and Cap managed a two-day engagement at the Olympia Cinema, payment for which included two rooms in the best hotel in Cannes, the

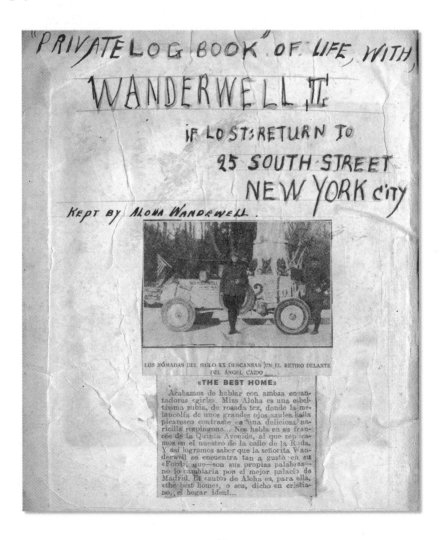

RIGHT: The original Wanderwell Expedition pamphlet featuring sixteen-year-old Aloha from late 1922. She is listed here as "Aloha Hall," not Wanderwell, and her job is listed as "Mécanicienne" (mechanic), not interpreter.

OPPOSITE: The first page of Aloha's "Private Log Book of Life with Wanderwell II" begun in Nice, France, December 1922.

Pilote
Capt. G. Armstrong

Aloha Hall
Mécanicienne

Eva White
Secrétaire

Amahuaca Norden
Interprète

Tour du Monde
Concours d'Endurance

Le Tour du Monde en automobile a été décidé en 1919 aux Etats-Unis.
Commencé à n'importe quel moment il doit se poursuivre jusqu'à la prochaine Exposition Universelle.
Le prix du concours sera décerné à la voiture qui aura parcouru le plus de kilomètres géographiques et le plus de pays.
Afin de faciliter le contrôle, chaque équipe doit produire des preuves écrites et des autographes officiels.
Les concurrents s'étant engagés à ne se faire appuyer par aucune corporation et à ne posséder aucun argent autre que celui provenant de leur travail, les écrits, annotations et films sont leurs seules ressources.

Carlton. "Round the world on 15 cents is right," she wrote in her journal. But, as she soon discovered, there was little time to enjoy the luxury. Each new venue brought a multitude of compulsory tasks. Evenings and afternoons they presented travelogues at the cinema. In between, they zipped around town, drumming up interest for the show, selling brochures, talking to journalists, and shouting endorsements for their sponsors. Ad copy was painted on the hood and tires of Unit Nº II.

Although she was now advertised as one of the expedition's key attractions, Aloha's first dance performance was, as she put it, "an absolute failure." A band had been hired, but there was no time to rehearse. "I had had no practice for two weeks...the music was too short and also a piece I had never danced to before." But the worst came when, "the elastics on my sandal broke. I slid to the floor, made a few *forte bras*, which included taking off my sandals and got up to finish the dance. I was frightfully sorry for the Capt."[18]

Aloha's self-doubt was intensified by the stir she and the captain caused in the hotel lobby. While other guests sported glamorous 1920s couture — gauzy lamé dresses, beaded cloche hats, sparkling high-heeled shoes — she trudged around in riding breeches, boots, and a tunic. She was an adventurer, yes, but she also loved being admired for her looks; the beauty contest had made that clear. Was there some way to make her Wanderwell uniform more attractive? The question punctured her self-confidence until she felt overwhelmed by teenage insecurities. The captain assured her that things would get easier, that all she needed was a bit of time and practice. But then he did something that made her previous insecurities seem irrelevant.

> I was still standing mid-room (undressing)...when there was a knock at the door.
>
> The Captain had arrived with more instructions and questions about preparedness.
>
> "I think you'll get along fine," he concluded, "in our day-to-day encounters. It's a matter of sizing up whatever is at hand, learning patience with people you're dealing with. You've got to have the right stuff."
>
> He was standing at a distance, lecturing. Then he was holding me at arm's length at the shoulders. Not suddenly, just firmly, smiling, eyes probing, trenchant, he drew himself to me and placed his lips carefully and tenderly to mine.[19]

The above quotation, from a collection of unpublished reminiscences, goes on to describe how the kiss was a "sacred consecration" that merely confirmed "he could love me." It's impossible to know exactly what happened, or if a single kiss was the sum of events, for we have only Aloha's version as a record. Whatever the case, Wanderwell — the married adventurer with a taste for young girls — had a new one at hand.[20]

✳

The last day of 1922 was the duo's last day at the Carlton and they were in no hurry to move on. They were enjoying their moments of luxury. "Why not enjoy life while it lasts?" she wrote in her journal. While she worked on her writing, crafting appreciative descriptions of the view from her window, the captain wrote letters to various world politicians regarding his proposal for an international police. His idea was to create an apolitical international body that would control armaments worldwide. It was as much an antidote to the raw memories of the First World War as anything else; certainly, it was wildly unlikely to be taken seriously by sovereign states concerned about borders and national safety in the uneasy years between the two world wars. In his vision, the international police would operate under the auspices of the newly formed League of Nations, an international body tasked with safeguarding the peace of all nations. He'd already sent the League an outline

Aloha and Walter in the first days after she joined the expedition, Cannes, France, December 1922.

of his plan. According to Aloha, the captain was consumed with his concept and spent endless hours concocting strategies to promote it.

A voracious reader of news dailies, Cap had followed the rise of Mussolini's Blackshirts and was impressed by the bloodless coup they had achieved. In tribute, he created an olive-coloured flag for his international police concept, the emblem of which included a fasces, the ancient Roman symbol consisting of a bundle of sticks bound to an axe. Although fascism would later introduce horrors beyond anything Wanderwell could have imagined, in its early days Mussolini's Italian fascist movement was widely welcomed as a bulwark against the spread of communism. For Walter, and even for much of the Western press at the time, Mussolini was a visionary and a model of decisive, effective leadership. Just as fascism's efficient, no-nonsense approach would restore a crumbling Italy, so Walter believed a powerful international police would put a damper on militarism and allow Europe's economies to focus on rebuilding a prosperous civil society.

Aloha could not have been less interested.

✵

In Toulon they played to capacity audiences at the Femina Cinema Palace. Aloha still complained of stage fright and felt her performances were hopelessly amateurish. But the compliments and sales rolled in, and the applause, whether for her ability or her looks, echoed long in her mind. Back at the hotel that evening, they piled the "dirty paper-money bills" onto the bed and counted it like thieves.

The next day, the captain suggested she try her hand at piloting Unit Nº II. Aloha climbed into the driver's seat and roared confidently forward — or so she'd hoped. In fact, her Italian sports car skills did not translate to a stripped-down, heavily modified Ford Model T. The intricate ballet of gas, clutch, throttle, choke, steering wheel, and brake was arduous, and just getting the vehicle to start was a task bordering on witchcraft. Stopped at a roadside, Cap explained that before turning the hand crank, located at the front bumper, it was vital to ensure the spark was "retarded" so the engine wouldn't kick back. Also, the crank handle had to be held loosely in case the engine *did* revolt and send the crank flying in reverse, possibly breaking a thumb or wrist. While cranking with one hand, the other had to simultaneously operate the choke via a wire poking out from beneath the radiator.

At one point, driving up a particularly steep incline, the car began sputtering. Aloha assumed they were low on gas and began pulling over to fill the tank, but Cap just laughed. He told her to turn the car around and put it in reverse. The 1917 Model T had no fuel pump and relied on gravity to feed gas to the engine. If the tank was below half, the engine could easily starve while climbing uphill. The solution was to drive backwards. Soon the pair was soaring through the French countryside, past ancient Roman markers, among vineyards and olive groves, surrounded by craggy peaks that reached 1,600 feet. Backwards.

✿

As 1923 began, Aloha settled into expedition life and asked to try as many jobs as possible.

> I found myself with multitudinous duties but it was the chance to learn, to make myself *indispensible* [italics hers], especially to familiarize myself with the gall and gallantry of the wee Iron Maiden. …N° II was such a little thing to spend one's life aboard — it amounted to that. Her motto: *omea meo me comporto* — everything I own I carry with me. Aboard this piece of scrap iron I was to build my golden memories.
>
> Maintenance rituals became pleasure. Swabbing mud away, revealing honourable travel scars, her enamelled brass emblems' peak sheen … when the Captain was well pleased, I was pleased. Tires pumped up, courtesy flags trim, astern the Stars and Stripes unfurled proudly on its staff. Shipshape, we launched each day ready for endless scrutiny of Lizzie of Serendip.[21]

One morning, just as they finished giving the car its spa, the captain turned over the empty wash bucket and sat down. He had a surprise, he said. To support his international police idea and convey their aim of world peace, they would paint the car olive drab. Aloha laughed but soon realized he wasn't kidding. Khaki is a colour of war, not peace, she said. It is an *ugly* colour. They weren't here for looks, Cap said. People needed reminding that safeguarding world peace could not be left to chance — it was a job that needed doing. Besides, he'd already bought the paint. Aloha hated the idea of driving a car the colour of rancid burlap, but it wasn't until the first few strokes on Nº II's hood that she hit on a more compelling argument: khaki would photograph poorly. Their livelihood depended on catching people's eyes with film and photographs. Ugliness would alienate their audiences. "After patient coaxing, he saw it my way, so I quickly sent him for a bucket of water before he could change his mind."[22]

As Aloha was discovering, the captain was flighty. Shortly after the paint idea, he announced they would not head for Italy or Spain. Her journal entry for January 3, 1923, barely conceals her disappointment.

> Cold sunless day, all hopes of spending a few weeks in Marseille to make a fortune were blown away as Captain announced his intention of going immediately to Geneva to see the League of Nations, present our new International flag and hand over the idea of an International Police. I wasn't quite in favour of the move, but then it wasn't really my business, so said nothing.[23]

The captain's obsession with disarmament and his idea for an international police stemmed, he said, from his wartime experiences. His father and brother had been compelled to fight for the Germans. In America, he had been treated with scorn and suspicion, largely because of his accent and weak attempts at disguising it. Worst of all, during the war the borders were closed and travel was restricted. According to Aloha, he believed that his welfare, his way of life, depended on an enduring world peace. Even after the lessons of the Great War, even with the dazzling technology of the 1920s, peace was a fragile sprout in need of protection.

Hôtel de Strasbourg, Genève

Postcard of the hotel where Walter allegedly "fell," Geneva, Switzerland, 1923.

The expedition swept into Geneva late on January 5 and began work early the next day. Cap needed to drum up interest in an international police force and the expedition needed a Spanish translator. The captain was aware of Aloha's reluctance to come to Switzerland and promised her that the next leg of the expedition would take them south again. Wanderwell had already wired ads to *La Suisse* for the translator position while in Marseille and the duo were soon deluged with multilingual young women eager for a trip to Spain. It was enough to refresh Aloha's stores of patience. A few extra days in Geneva seemed endurable after all.

But what happened next would cause Aloha to exclaim in her journal: "Most frightful day I have ever experienced. Entire world expedition collapse!"[24]

That afternoon, Cap had been "scheduled to raise a flagstaff from his window just above the parapet of the steel glass marquee" with reporters on hand. The international police flag would be unfurled with Unit Nº II parked below. The purpose of the photo-op stunt was to announce the Wanderwell Expedition's arrival in Geneva. But no reporters had shown up. According to Aloha, the captain went ahead anyway — they would take their own photos — and leaned out his window, stretching to untie the flag, but then he "slipped" on the icy windowsill. As she watched in horror, he fell and crashed through the plate glass roof of the restaurant below, stopping with a sudden yank. He hung in mid-air, saved from hitting the ground by a decorative iron spike that had buried itself his leg. "Police were arriving and there would be a long session of questions. It was really awful! Cap was in such agony, the doctor gave an injection, and took him to hospital." Following the crash, hotel witnesses claimed Wanderwell had been raving about his girls.

By afternoon, newspapers were jammed with reports of the "suddenly insane" Captain Wanderwell and his delusions of being a pasha with a harem. One particularly unflattering article, which ran in the *New York Times*, carried the headline "World Auto Tourist Suddenly Loses Mind."

Seized with suicidal mania, Captain Wanderwell leaped from a window of his hotel. He fell on top of a glass-roofed veranda, smashing through the glass, and remained hanging on the steel framework. His legs were severely cut. He was rescued from his dangerous position and subsequently taken to an asylum.[25]

Similar stories appeared internationally. Aloha later destroyed her journal entries relating to the captain's mental state, a telling act. There was something here she did not wish the world to remember.

Walter was taken to the Asile Canton d'Aliens, a care hospital for foreign nationals. It is possible that the reports of insanity originated through a combination of his incoherent ranting following the injury and the fact that in French a long-term care hospital is sometimes referred to as an *asile*, or asylum. While some newspapers wrote that Wanderwell had slipped from his window, others claimed he'd jumped or was pushed. Some insisted he'd been placed in a straightjacket and locked in a padded cell, a story, which given the nature of his injuries, seems unlikely.[26]

WORLD-RACE MISHAP

Captain Wanderwell Falls from Hotel Window

A man's motor-car race round the world in competition with his wife has been almost tragically interrupted.

Captain Walter Wanderwell, one of the two competitors, an American, while at the Marquise Hotel, Geneva, fell from the window of his room.

Fortunately his fall was broken, for, after crashing through glass, he was caught and held by some iron bars; but it was only after much difficulty that he was extricated from his perilous position with an injury to the leg.

Captain Wanderwell had just arr⋅ed at Geneva, after motoring across America, England and France.

The race thus—at any rate, temporarily—spoiled is the result of a bet between Captain Wanderwell and his wife. With him were three young women, all of whom were

MISS RAEBURN.

pledged to forswear skirts and matrimony till the race was over in two years' time.

They were all wearing breeches.

Miss Helen Raeburn (23), the secretary, startled London during her passage through by walking about in a leather jerkin, a bandolier of cartridges, breeches, a racing helmet, goggles and big gun.

Newspaper report of Walter Wanderwell's tumble from a Geneva hotel window in January 1923. (Unknown source. Found inserted in Aloha's Logbook.)

Not knowing if the captain would recover from his injuries, sixteen-year-old Aloha returned to the hotel room and collected the expedition's papers and printed materials. She placed the films and cameras in Unit Nº II's hidden compartments and arranged with the local Ford dealership to have the car stored in a locked garage. She left a forwarding address at the Asile Canton d'Aliens and, by 8:00 a.m. the following morning, had boarded a train bound for Cannes.

> I don't remember much, save arriving in Cannes at 11:30... and spent the night at the Hôtel des Voyagers. I have never felt so alone before in my life, but after a good old cry, I dropped off to sleep by the tune of a jazz band from a nearby cabaret de nuit.[27]

If nothing else, the challenges showed that Aloha could, in fact, take care of herself.

> Monday Jan. 8, 1923, Cannes-Nice,
> Simply glorious morning, but Oh! my head is in such a muddle. Instead of going straight on to Nice, I walked down to the seashore. The sea breeze and sunshine helped things greatly and when I felt sufficiently myself, I trundled back to the hotel, got my baggage and left with the "twelve" for Nice. The first person I met was the American girl who interviewed Captain when we were staying at the Royal Hotel Nice,[28] of course she was very sorry to hear the news and voiced her thoughts. Everyone stared. They always do.[29]

That afternoon Aloha was back at the Villa Marie-Thérèse. When the door swung open, Margaret hardly looked surprised. "Ah, I knew you were coming dear, I had that feeling."[30]

❀

Aloha was distraught. What would become of the captain? And what would become of *her*? She confided to her journal that it seemed cruel that just when she thought she could take on the world, the world slipped out of reach. Not one to pine, Aloha went with Miki to a dance at the Victoria Palace on her third night home. It was a gala given by *Le Petit Niçois* newspaper in aid of the city's poor. Their dancing received gushing applause, complete with baskets of flowers and a feature in the following day's paper.

It was one full week before a telegram came from Switzerland.

AM READY FOR WORK, COME AS SOON AS YOU CAN.
— CAPTAIN WANDERWELL.

Walter Wanderwell in a publicity photograph, United States, 1920s.

FOUR

IN LEAGUE WITH NATIONS

My dear Aloha!

This is certainly the best lesson I have ever received in my life. Instead of getting Publicity [*sic*] for the League of Nations, I got you in a nice "Mess." But I hope that your mother will understand and let you travel with me. I am still weak from the dreadful experience, but am getting better. That is the reason my writing is so bad. Please come as soon as possible, I certainly need you and you will be remunerated a thousand fold.

Nevermind [*sic*] about writing if you got enough money on hand to get on a train and come here. I didn't know how much you were to me until I had to be shown. You know what I said: "We are all from Missouri!"[1] Now don't worry because I don't worry either, as my conscience is clear and Jesus Christ is my guiding example in everything I do. Now Au revoir! Come soon.

Your Captain Wanderwell[2]

WALTER WAS PUTTING THE GENEVA "misadventure" behind him. Aloha's relief was channelled into several days of intense activity. She met with local press *Le Petit Niçois* and *L'Eclaireur de Nice* to announce Wanderwell's recovery, ran errands for her mother, sat for portraits in her Wanderwell uniform, and renewed her passport with her professional name so it read "Idris A. Hall Wanderwell."[3] Amidst the hubbub, however, she still managed to creep to town each day to "see a man about a dog" — twenties slang for having a drink. The captain had firm ideas about health and fitness, so if she wanted to indulge a few vices, this would be her last chance for a while.

☼

Aloha boarded the early morning express for Lyon on January 21, but the train arrived an hour late and she missed her connecting train to Geneva. She had to take a hotel room, skip supper, and make due with just a cup of black coffee at sunrise — "a thing I dislike immensely"[4] — as her funds were low. A further mix-up sent her to Chambéry, where she spent her last pennies on a ticket to Culoz and an afternoon connection to Switzerland.

It was Monday evening before she reached Geneva and the captain was not at the station to greet her, having expected her the day before. Annoyed and exhausted, Aloha was eventually met by a hotel porter who'd been placed on lookout by the captain. Hurriedly grasping her luggage, he explained that Cap had gone uptown on business after spending most of Sunday and all morning waiting for trains from Lyon. It was not the reunion Aloha had imagined. "Nor was he to be found at the hotel, so I took my old room, unpacked and tidied and presently his lordship put in an appearance."[5]

Her attitude changed once the captain arrived. Although he was now using a walking stick, just seeing him well again, full of his old vitality and raring to resume the roving routine, set her mind at ease.

Cap shared my glee being on the road again; a lot of Peter Pan in him. When excited he crowed — every inch of him radiated exaltation.... Let's race! Let's go! US here we come! So, like Wendy, I too soared.[6]

They went for a quick supper and then a walk to watch the lights of Geneva shimmer on the waters of the nearby lake.

Cap rehearsed [sic] his days in the Asile of which he remembered every instant, painful as it was (to me). I listened, answered questions till it came my turn to give an account of my two weeks' absence.[7]

✼

For a while, everything seemed normal again. Aloha worked on her usual expedition tasks: post office, journalists, pictures, printers, and correspondence. But the captain was soon back to his favourite topic. His international flag concept had, he said, been received by the League of Nations as "a good idea, and nothing more." Now he envisioned colour postcards of the olive flag design that they could sell at the shows and in the streets. It would generate publicity and give the Wanderwell Expedition a deeper sense of purpose.

Aloha sighed, "This idea of course entails a thousand jobs, and also a prolongation, I am very sorry to say, of our stay in Geneva, a town of which I have a perfect horror. Still, what would you I ask? I'm on the staff...boy I'm on the staff."[8]

Her mood improved when an afternoon visit to the post office produced a cheque for £52 — about $4,000 today and a fantastic sum in 1923 — from the Macintosh Tyre Co., in payment for the advertisement they'd placed on Unit N° II and carried for thirteen weeks. She spent the next week organizing theatre engagements, writing newspaper articles, and lobbying sponsors. Walter, meanwhile, worked on convincing officials at the League of Nations to meet with him. After endless queries, he was granted a meeting with the director of the Information Section at the League of Nations. The captain's agenda was still how an international police might control arms. For Aloha, the League was just another obstacle on her path to worldwide adventures. "They are such slow-minded people that it may be necessary to stay here for donkey's ages before they hand us a final answer."[9]

Aloha may have had no use for the League of Nations, but she was impressed by their facilities, housed in the Hotel National, a majestic five-storey, 225-room building overlooking Lake Geneva.[10] As they arrived, a young Englishman greeted the captain and Aloha. He showed them to a row of oak chairs, thickly upholstered in red velvet. Their contact, Mr. Arthur Switzer, was in a meeting that had run overtime but could meet with Mr. Wanderwell at 4:00 p.m., in an hour.

Aloha sat in one of the chairs as Cap paced. She was content to soak up the atmosphere and make notes in her journal. The building was awe-inspiring, filled with great doors, innumerable corridors, massive furnishings and intricate tapestries more suited to a palace than a warehouse for bureaucrats. What caught her eye most of all, however, had nothing to do with the building.

> The chief attraction being the *lady* secretaries. Blondes, brunettes, bobbed and otherwise, tall gaunt sticks, fat chubby dumplings, tall gracefully wispy glossy haired maidens that glide swiftly out of sight…black, bob haired Parisians, damsels floating along seeming very proud of their "contracts," and enumerous [*sic*] others.

And, much to her satisfaction, it was clear the admiration was mutual.

> I for the moment am the centre of attraction [*sic*], or at least my fair curls and riding breeches. One girl has passed at least a dozen times in the last hour (we are waiting) always with the same sheet of paper. Less fearless ones keep peeping through the curtained glass doors.

When Cap finally left for his meeting with Mr. Switzer, Aloha continued her diverting amusements.

> I'm all alone. A very nice looking English boy passes for the third time then finally returns with a couple of illustrated London newsies! Yes he is English, but for devilment I thank him in French.[11]

✤

In the days that followed Walter's meeting, Aloha booked a one-week engagement at the Royal Biograph. The negotiated rates were much lower than usual, but "I urged Cap to accept it. For one thing it would clear expenses…and secondly it gave him a chance to think of *autre choses que* the League of Nations."[12] As if colluding from afar, a letter arrived from a former Wanderwell girl, Mollie Bryan, and included some clippings from English newspapers that featured articles about the "suddenly insane" Captain Wanderwell and the calamitous end of his Round the World attempt. "What a rag!!!" screamed Aloha in her journal. The story spurred the captain to not only agree to the engagement at the Royal Biograph but also to an interview with a reporter at the *Tribune de Genève* that very afternoon. Aloha was thrilled. This was her chance to get the expedition back on track.

The Royal Biograph, with a seating capacity of four hundred, was designed as a cinema (rather than a converted theatre, which many venues were at the time), so there was no stage. To lecture, Aloha stood on a table and towered over the first rows, closer than she'd ever been to her audience. Rather than feeling intimidated, however, the strange arrangement set her alight.

The evening show was one of, if not my very best, the place was simply crowded. A few naughty young boys in the front started hooting and whistling, to see, I guess, how much I could stand. But oh! boy I love it. The more noise they make the better I like it and presently I cracked so many jokes that they cheered every time.[13]

Her assured performance did not go unnoticed. Aloha was later to write that Walter finally saw she had something special. She handled the hecklers, she knew how to improvise, but most of all she exuded confidence. She had *swagger* that he could build on. He wrote a letter to the prefect of police, requesting a permit for a .25 Decker automatic pistol. It wasn't the first time a Wanderwell girl had used a gun as part of her stage persona. One of the English articles about the captain's accident concluded with a description of Helen Raeburn, the Texan divorcée, who had earlier been part of the expedition and had "startled London during her passage through by walking about in a leather jerkin, a bandolier of cartridges, breeches, a racing helmet, goggles and big gun."[14]

Following an interview with two police inspectors (Walter and Aloha were questioned separately), a permit was granted. The next day a female journalist interviewed Aloha, asking for her life story alongside the usual inquiries about the Million Dollar Wager and the curious olive flag they flew. When they were done, the reporter told Aloha that she was "the first woman I have ever seen look so femininely elegant in such a masculine costume. I notice you are carrying a revolver accompanied by a bouquet of violets, a contrast such as I have never before seen. I congratulate you."[15]

Aloha's manner of dress would hardly raise an eyebrow today, but in 1923 her "masculine costume" was still considered cross-dressing. (Coco Chanel would not introduce fashionable pants for women until 1925 and Marlene Dietrich's signature film, *The Blue Angel*, would not appear until 1930.) A beautiful young woman cavorting in men's clothing aroused the attention of men and women alike. As for Walter, he liked the look of girls in pants, and anything that generated attention was good for sales.

☼

A telegram from the Macintosh Tyre Co. in Manchester, England, arrived on February 1, instructing Wanderwell:

CALL ON MONTEL RAMBLA CATALUNA 100 BARCELONA
—MACINTOSH

Aloha was ecstatic. The message meant escape from Geneva and signalled Macintosh's intention to continue the sponsorship agreement they had begun several months earlier. "This telegram is the best news we have received for donkey's years; it decided Cap to go to Spain after all. If it does nothing else, it will take him away from politics and all the mess of this part of Europe."[16]

☼

Unit Nº II soared through the cold, mountainous countryside. The French border came and went without difficulty (the Swiss guards were so excited by the expedition's arrival they forgot to check passports). With no theatres to book and no interviews to give, they could stay at hotels of their choosing or stroll into restaurants without a thought for appearance, covered in mud an inch thick. *This* was the carefree adventure Aloha had signed up for.

' Eventually, they responded to Macintosh.

WILL TIME ARRIVAL BARCELONA FEBRUARY SIXTEEN.
—WANDERWELL

They had eight days to cover 500 miles, a leisurely pace even in a time of dirt roads and infrequent gasoline depots. Walter said he thought Aloha would enjoy Spain, but he'd love to show her Florida, especially the bit of property he owned in Miami. He hoped to build a house there one day. "I'm game," she recounted in her diary. Encouraged, he described how he planned to get there. "We'll put the car on a sailing ship and work our way from Japan to San Francisco... Take three month[s]."[17] It all sounded wonderful.

They made it as far as Pézenas, France, before the spark plugs started giving them trouble. "From then on, every few miles Cap had to get out and get under to fix his little machine."[18] Their progress was further impeded by poor roads and the pre-Lent Carnival celebrations happening in every town.

When they finally crossed into Spain, Aloha and Cap revelled in the hot summery air and the freedom of driving along the windy roadway with their jackets stowed, shirts open at the neck, and sleeves rolled up. They made it as far as Calella, a small town of about five thousand people, 175 miles from Béziers and only 34 miles from Barcelona. They spent their first night in Spain at "what the natives respectfully call a hotel." To Aloha it looked more like a farmhouse. The portly proprietress eyed the couple with scepticism.

> The first question she demanded before giving us rooms was "Are you German?" to which Cap (gave) an emphatic "No" and whilst he was still wondering as to her motive she popped out with "Are you a married man?" "Yes" (with pride). The way in which all was said was so screamingly funny I could have shrieked with laughter but waited until the maid showed us upstairs, then we gave vent to our mirth, whilst taking off a little of the day's dust.[19]

On Friday, February 16, they made a "glorious little run down the coast of Spain" to the long-dreamed-of Barcelona. Aloha was at the wheel, electric with excitement and marvelling at the sparkling port, crowded with sailing ships and ringing with bustle. At the Hôtel d'España Aloha spoke "to the manager who immediately gave us rooms on condition that we made... 50 ft.

of film[20] of the Hôtel." Aloha was discovering that the promise of film footage could melt almost any resistance.

While Aloha charmed hotel managers, she in turn was charmed by the Spanish girls.

> Heaps of pretty señoritas, with the most beautiful black hair you ever set eyes on, not to mention snappy brown eyes and that curve of the lip! Oh! Boyo! Cap is lost in admiration.[21]

❁

Within days, the Wanderwells had convinced the Lord Mayor of Barcelona "to come out of the city hall and sign his autograph on Wanderwell II." The ceremony was filmed and sold the next day to form part of a Gaumont Graphic newsreel. Overnight, newspapers were eager to cover their story. The Spanish press coverage gave rise to several of the myths that would follow them around the world — the foremost being that Walter and Aloha were *brother and sister*.

> "Grin and bear it," said Cap. "There's nothing we can do. Explanations will only confuse them. We'll straighten things out once we get out of Spain." The Greeks had a word for it: *Ti en onomati* — What's in a name?[22]

Aloha secured a week-long showing at the Teatro Novedades, a 2,500-seat theatre. The booking was wildly optimistic since they still had no Spanish speaker to assist with the narration.

When the hour of their first performance arrived, they still had no translator and the theatre and surrounding streets were jammed. The crowds were so thick that Aloha couldn't get through and the show began almost fifteen minutes late. Finally, the stage lights came up and the manager introduced "Captain Wanderwell, his sister Miss Wanderwell and Company." As the film and orchestra started, Aloha left the stage to wait for the five-minute intermission when they could sell their cards, assuming any of the audience remained. Then, to everyone's surprise, Cap began guiding the film in a competent Spanish, accompanied by the orchestra's vividly humorous sound effects.

His few essential Spanish Catalan and Mexican terms led to humorous wordplay. His timing marvellous, his brisk fun-poking tickled the effervescent Barcelonese. He recalled his first day, ordering a stack of three buttered tortillas — correct words for Mexico, but here (he received) three layers of omelettes covered in lard. The light-hearted effort was re-warded. At intermission, souvenir folders sold like wildfire.

At the end of each performance, lights down, we drove the car, headlights flaring, on stage, a spot flooding the Catalan flag. We saluted while the full orchestra played a patriotic Catalan hymn. The 2,500 (strong) audience raised the roof! Contributions for pamphlets and requests for autographs so overwhelming — later I could hardly use a pen.[23]

It was a master course in showmanship. This was success beyond anything Aloha had imagined. They were selling as many as a thousand postcards and folders at each show, all by donation, generating so much money that Aloha had to sew her pocket buttons on with wire.[24] To brighten the mood still further, they met an English cinematographer who had been travelling around Spain for a year. George Armstrong was a tough-looking man of medium build, a strong chin, slightly protruding ears, and close-set eyes. He went by the title Lieutenant Armstrong after his rank in the British Army. When he told Wanderwell how he'd almost joined an Ernest Shackleton Expedition, the captain was sold.[25] Aloha was equally impressed, writing that the lieutenant "knows nearly all the countries round about plus their languages. Of course he loves the vagabond life and wanted to join us." Then they received word from a Spanish-speaking girl in Geneva that she could join the crew on Monday, February 26. "I must say we are living in the lap of luxury," Aloha wrote, but also added, "I wonder how long it will last."

It was a good question, and one the captain had been considering too. He understood that their success in Barcelona was a short-blooming flower and that the road ahead would be tough. He wanted Aloha to be prepared and began lecturing her on the need for discipline, exercise, a vegetarian diet, reading, cold showers, and spiritual awareness. "Simplicity ensures happiness," he told her. "Eliminate trivia, study the Buddhist line, learn a calm channel." He assured her that "reliable standards would carry [her] through when things [got] off key."[26]

At sixteen, Aloha was not so interested in the wisdom of her elders. She was fast becoming a major draw to the expedition screenings, and the captain worried that when luxury vanished and the money got scarce, she might bolt. As further insurance, he asked her to help improvise film stories on the road. Pretty pictures are fine, he said, but it's the stories that get people excited.

Suddenly, Aloha was eager to leave Barcelona and begin work on the "Adventure Film," as they came to call it. The captain was impatient too, but for different reasons. Newspapers had been awash with news of an archaeological discovery in Egypt. On February 16, 1923, the same day the Wanderwell Expedition had arrived in Barcelona, British archaeologist Howard Carter had opened a sealed wall in the Egyptian Valley of the Kings. Inside, he found a burial chamber complete with the three thousand-year-old sarcophagus of King Tutankhamen and more gold than anyone could have imagined.[27]

Egypt was not the only possibility, however. Across the water to the south, Spain was waging a war against indigenous Berber tribes in Spanish Morocco. The so-called Rif War was claiming tens of thousands of lives on both sides of the conflict, with a little-known general named Francisco Franco helping to command the Spanish Foreign Legion. Many Morocco-bound soldiers left from the port in Barcelona. "My heart ached for the weeping women dockside," Aloha would later write. "I wondered if the Rif would be as glutted with blood in '23 as Ypres was in '17. The press gave only heroic accounts."[28] News of the conflict set the captain thinking about the League of Nations again. Footage of the carnage might convince people that an international peacekeeping force was needed. When Aloha asked him if they would actually see fighting first-hand, he replied, "It's an idea. [We could] cross at Gibraltar to Ceuta.... A lot of action to film, then [we could] work our way east to Egypt," but he quickly added, "I've got to see Bilbao and A Coruña again and *you've* got to see it with me. There we'll add Portugal to the record."

So long as this man held the keys to such an adventurous life, to Aloha's shot at wealth and possibly even fame, she would be his pupil, his factotum, his whatever. Under his guidance, she believed she could face anything.

The evening of February 26 found Aloha and the captain at the Estació de França, where the expedition's new recruit had finally arrived. Aloha rode to the station on Cap's newly purchased Indian motorcycle, just in time to see him "aiding a frail sweet-faced girl into the Hôtel car. I heard her voice, speaking in English with the delicate accent that comes only from a French education." The interpreter, named Fate (possibly a variation on Faith), was a diminutive, dark-haired girl with large eyes, strong cheekbones and a small, restrained smile. "We became friends immediately and all my fears of scrapping with her vanished."[29]

The next day Aloha took Fate around Barcelona. Together they assembled a uniform and discussed expedition duties. On their last evening in Barcelona, the crew found there was not enough room for all of them plus gear in one tiny car. "All you need is your breeches," announced the captain, which he later revised to, "all you need is your bathing suits."[30]

In Tarragona, Aloha and Fate arranged for two rooms in the best hotel in town but had no luck booking theatres. Finally, Cap approached a cinema manager and offered to show one of the expedition's reels for free. The manager agreed, allowing Cap to sell cards while the girls lectured, Aloha in French and Fate translating into Spanish. Fate's first lecture was predictably awful, the crowd merciless. When the reel ended, Cap rose from his seat and made an impromptu speech using his pastiche of Cuban/ Mexican Spanish, "which produced a roof raising hullabaloo" and ensured that cards sold by the boxful.[31]

Towns were soon blending into each other. At Castellón de la Plana, about 175 miles south of Barcelona, Aloha and Fate booked the "best ciné" and enjoyed the attentions of the local boys who cried, "¡Qué Monas! Pero están armados!!" (What pretties, but they're armed!). The town itself was rudimentary, but what it lacked in modern convenience, it made up for with sumptuous food. "The table is literally covered [with hors d'oeuvres]. Then soup, fish, vegetables, meat...at least six or seven dishes. Then dessert: nuts, biscuits, pudding and fruit." The crew ate like starving prisoners, but.when it came to Spanish wine, which Aloha found delicious, the captain refused to try any, leaving their hosts perplexed. Later, he chugged a pitcher of cold water, much to the matron's alarm. She told him it was dangerous because "many deaths in Spain were caused by typhoid germs in the water." The captain simply smiled. "I have," he said, "drunk water so dirty that it might have been anything, so don't worry about me anymore."[32]

❁

At Valencia, Cap announced he was taking a "holiday" because of his leg, which had been giving him trouble. In his absence, Aloha would be in charge. "He has given me *some* money and with that I am to get to Madrid and make money to keep the crew going; it's a sort of test for me." His announcement came with little warning; he packed his bag and left the next afternoon by motorcycle for Cádiz, 480 miles west. That same afternoon Aloha lectured at the Bataclan theatre and performed her Aloha dance "with great success." By the time she returned to her hotel room that evening, though, she was exhausted, alone, and less than confident.

> I feel suddenly years older, and look it. I suppose it is the fact that so much responsibility now weighs on my young shoulders. I am all in but the bed is literally covered with litter an' evr'y thing that must be sorted so that I know just where I stand with this business and an hour later when all the baggage is packed, I crawl into my bed, just a tired, weary child.[33]

❁

Walter Wanderwell was not the man he claimed to be. Aloha knew this. For all the ink in newspapers, magazines, postcards, and brochures, not to mention the films, his name was not really Walter Wanderwell, he was not really American, he was not really divorced, and he was certainly not related to Aloha. His Million Dollar Wager was, for the most part, a publicity stunt, and the expedition was not really sponsored by Ford.[34] Walter Wanderwell's real story was much stranger and a good deal more alarming than anyone travelling with him might have guessed.

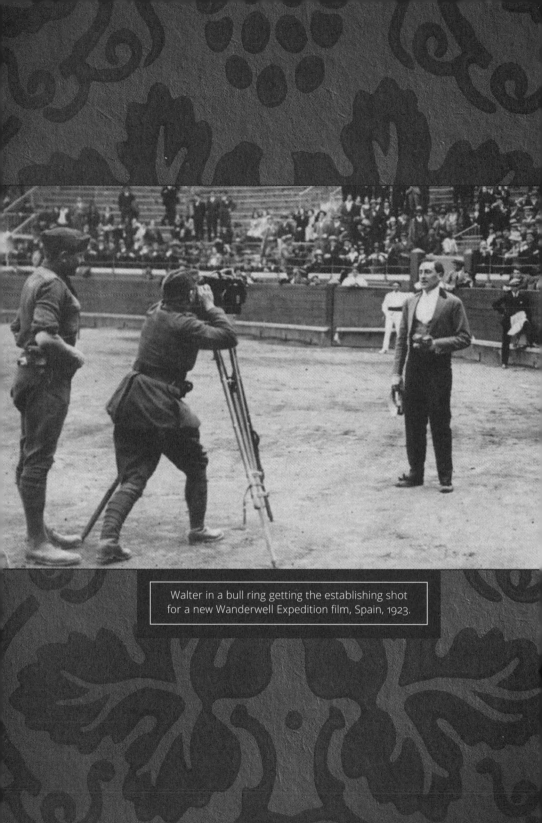

Walter in a bull ring getting the establishing shot for a new Wanderwell Expedition film, Spain, 1923.

FIVE

THE TEMPER OF
THE TIMES

BY THE TIME THE EXPEDITION arrived in Madrid, Aloha had recovered some of her nerve. She knew the routine — get to town, book hotels and theatres, start the publicity machine — and was determined to show that she could be depended upon. Things began well enough. They overcame a succession of mechanical misadventures to reach Madrid safely and, once there, were able to win free rooms at the Hotel Sud America. By March 18, however, they still had not managed a booking for it was Lent. In deeply Catholic Spain, this was a time to avoid *all* indulgences, including entertainment. Some theatres closed altogether and no one was buying postcards. Even the bullfights were suspended until Easter.[1] As the expedition waited, they became so low on cash they were "almost afraid to eat in case we are broke before leaving."[2]

Late one afternoon, a trio of reporters rang the bell on the hotel desk and asked for an interview with the expedition's female crew members.[3] Fate and Aloha conducted their visitors to the hotel's sitting room and began answering the usual questions about when the race had started, where they had been so far and where they planned to go next. Aloha described the Million Dollar Wager and the race around the world, prompting the youngest reporter to shake his head in wonder. "Only Americans make wagers like that," he said. "We Spanish never bet more than five douros [*sic*],[4] nor do we go in for such adventure…(except for) the toreadors." His shoulders sank as he explained that unless you're a bullfighter, Spanish women won't give young men a second look. Fate and Aloha exchanged glances. Aloha was on the verge of bursting with laughter when the tallest of the trio asked, "Will you come to lunch with us tomorrow, out at the Golf Club? All of you I mean." Fate and Aloha shrugged. Why not?

The next morning a grand limousine containing the three young Spaniards, plus a friend, arrived at the hotel. The group spent the afternoon eating sumptuous food, drinking delicious wine, and wandering the gardens near the clubhouse.

> We played up to our roles till we were well on our way; they were the first to break the spell, after us having hinted that few reporters in any part of the world could afford such luxuries.... They told us the story of how they had seen us so often in the streets and tried in every way to get an introduction, all in vain, till finally they decided to drop in on us as reporters.... The boy I have tasked myself to, chiefly because he speaks English so well and is tall, is the Duke Ricardo d'Estrada, the [second boy is the] "petit Moreno" Count of Granja, and the third boy a cousin.[5]

✧

Then Aloha received disturbing news. She wrote, "The situation is becoming unbearable. Mother is ill and leaves Nice for England in May. Really I don't know whether to join her or not."[6] The only bright spot was that the captain had wired, saying he would return to Madrid on April 3.

Aloha finally made a sale in Madrid, although from an unexpected source. The duke and count came calling at the hotel, asking whether Aloha would present the Wanderwell films at a family get-together that evening. They could offer her one hundred pesetas for her trouble.

> Of course I was only too delighted. 100 pesetas is not to be picked up so easily these days. Really, my poor Duke is becoming very senti-mental. Kissing my hand as an adieu is becoming a frequent occurrence these days. Oh ye American beauties that will visit Europe, beware, oh beware of the Spanish boys.[7]

After that night, Aloha's relationship with the duke turned more serious, though his family's status meant their affair had to remain discreet. Still, the idea of an anonymous Canadian girl being pursued by a Spanish duke was flattering in the extreme. "The whole situation was too incongruous for words," she would later write, "(and) I was swept away on the magic carpet of romance."[8] Aloha did not elaborate on the details of her romance, but did imply that it was thanks to the duke that the battered Unit N° II was repaired and released without charge. Their hotel fees were likewise magically resolved.

※

The captain returned from "holiday" on April 3 and was appalled. The crew was in splinters. One of the crew, Armstrong, was gone — off to deal with some family matters back in Barcelona, apparently. Fate was on the verge of a nervous breakdown, and Aloha, whom he had trusted to lead the expedition, had not booked shows, sold cards, or secured advertising.

> I am on the verge of being sent home for misconduct. I am sorry, sorry beyond words. Cap has lost all trust in me. It is all a misunderstanding and my one wish is to remain with him sufficient time to show him that every move made in the last three weeks was for his good.... This is my first break with him, it becomes unbearable.[9]

The captain announced that the expedition would leave Madrid immediately and sent a wire to Barcelona saying so, bringing Armstrong scurrying back that night. As for Aloha, there was nothing for her but to say a tearful farewell to the duke and move on. During a final visit, they exchanged photographs and he wrote her a short note: "So you will not forget this 'daddy long legs' you first knew as reporter and must not forget as a Friend." Aloha pasted the picture into her journal.

※

The expedition landed in the town of Salamanca, a quiet, hilltop town some 200 miles west of Madrid. At the outskirts of town, people began following the strange-looking, flamboyantly growling car that moved slowly over the

Walter Wanderwell was an expert at hand-lettering, and changing "signage" on the fly was sometimes a political necessity. Spain, 1923.

cobbled streets. By the time they reached the ancient Plaza Mayor at the town's centre, the car was mobbed. Everyone seemed to know who they were and where they were supposed to go.

The passing of Easter made sales easier, but the expedition's mood remained fragile.

> For the last few days there has been nothing but eruptions; Lieut is becoming awfully fed up with the whole thing. Cap loses his temper at every possible occasion and poor Fate receives the consequences. Tonight I'm sure if I had a home to go to I should go, but there is none.... Mother leaves in a few days for, I don't know where, so...[10]

It was the first time Aloha had seriously considered abandoning her adventure. The captain invited Aloha to spend the afternoon visiting the port with him. They rented a boat and admired the craggy, curving coastline. Aloha pointed out that she had now been with the expedition for six months. Cap was amazed. "Well you certainly have broken the record, no Wanderwell girl ever remained more than 3 or 4 months at the most. I congratulate you old kid!" Aloha, however, was in no mood to celebrate. "Don't be in such a hurry. I may change my mind at any moment about going all the way round.... Just the same I am quite proud of the fact."[11]

The tour trudged back to Bilbao, where Fate announced that she would not lecture. She was, she said, too well known here and did not want to disgrace herself by appearing in breeches. Exasperated, Cap let her go ahead to San Sebastián. Meanwhile, he called a meeting with Aloha and Armstrong, where he detailed his plan to build a third car. Aloha would have her own car to pilot full time.

※

By May of 1923, Spain was a dangerous place. Although Aloha had seen some of the unrest, she did not understand how serious the situation was becoming. The Spanish labour movement, known as the *Confederación Nacional del Trabajo* (CNT), had formed a military arm to fight back after years of persecution and assassinations by government and industry leaders. The general public was outraged by the catastrophic losses in North Africa, and it was widely believed that the army was corrupt and the Spanish monarchy complicit. The situation was on the verge of boiling over.

The country's gloom was reflected in the mood of the Wanderwell Expedition. Although they were making money again, Aloha was "afraid our little party is sailing towards the rocks."[12] Unhappiness reached a flash point in San Sebastián when Armstrong announced, after yet another argument with the captain, that he was quitting. Fate quickly concurred that she was "fed up wit eet all."[13]

That evening the captain asked Aloha to go for a walk with him. "We'll go for coffee, anything [you] like to do," he offered, which, in light of his prohibitions against caffeine, showed his sincerity — or his desperation. He told her he was leaving for France. Bordeaux was only 146 miles away and he would try to get a chassis and begin work on Unit Nº III. He wanted the crew to accompany him so that shows and sales might still be possible while he worked. As a gesture of peace, he even offered to let Fate and Armstrong use Unit Nº II until the new car was complete.

That evening the crew discussed the captain's plan. Fate flatly refused to return to France with "that man." Armstrong mumbled that he needed to return to Barcelona to "collect some property." And Aloha said, "While there are still pesetas to make, I prefer them to francs." Her aim, as she so often wrote, was to keep travelling. Returning to France would have felt like failure. The trio would stay in Spain and wire money to the captain. The next morning, Armstrong drove Walter to the French border where he caught a train for Bordeaux.

✿

The crew headed south to Pamplona and, once again, failed miserably. Next they bumbled into Zaragoza only to find that everything was closed following the assassination of local cardinal, Juan Soldevilla y Romero.

Although they had no engagements, Aloha instructed the crew to stay for the cardinal's funeral, a decision that prompted a shocking announcement from Armstrong that he had "long ago decided to get a car for himself... [and] that is why we're going to Barcelona."[14] Aloha could stay with them or take the car to Bordeaux. If she decided to stay, she would become a member of *their* crew and, effectively, third in command. It was a cruel humiliation but Aloha, uncertain what to do next, agreed to stay on.

Fate insisted they stay in Zaragoza for at least a week, despite not having any income. Once the funeral had passed, Aloha was anxious to move on, to make some money, but Fate would not leave until she felt sufficiently rested. By the time they finally left for Barcelona, Aloha was emphatically regretting her decision.

> In the back of the car amongst the filthy oil cans, etc., I cuddle up in one corner. I am so cold, so lonely. Out of sheer self-pity I cry. Even if Cap was a bum...he was a first class brother and pal, and I can't live like this, it's horrible.[15]

While rumbling through a dark country road (ironically, Fate had chosen to depart at night), there was an ear-splitting bang and the car came to a standstill. The crankshaft had broken and the trio were stranded on a remote stretch of high desert for almost three days without food and only some Malaga wine for hydration. By the time a rescue truck arrived, Aloha felt as though she'd been bathing in bleach: her lips and hands were cracked and bleeding, her eyes stung and she could hardly talk. The lame Unit N° II was roped to the back of the rescue vehicle and pulled slowly down the hills back towards Zaragoza. Aloha hadn't managed to move forward at all.

☼

Back in Zaragoza, a cheery letter arrived from Cap. He was in Clichy (Paris), hard at work on Unit N° III. He'd also hired two new secretaries, was selling cards and playing shows. In short, he was having a marvellous time and hoped that everything was going well in Spain.

It was Aloha's turn to be appalled. Even without car or assistance, this man was able to thrive. A man with whom he'd travelled in 1916 described Cap as "a marvellous demon — a daring, brazen, disarming and charming adventurer who could flamboyantly flash in and out of people's lives, leaving them dizzy and checking for their wallet."[16] Whatever his shortcomings, he was never at a loss for ideas, and *somehow* he always managed to succeed.

At the hotel one evening, Armstrong took Fate's hand and explained that he and Fate had fallen in love and would no longer participate in the Wanderwell Expedition. They would soon be leaving for Majorca on their honeymoon. Unit N° II would be placed in storage until they returned, and then they would drive it to Paris. Aloha could wait for them or find her own way north.[17] Aloha had had enough. She left.

The bare frame and power train of the former Ford Model T Red Cross ambulance that Walter purchased and turned into expedition Unit N° III, Paris, France, Spring 1923.

SIX

THE WORLD IS YOUR OYSTER

A LOHA ARRIVED IN PARIS WITH just one hundred francs in her pocket. She arranged to meet the captain at the Paris Ford Agency, where she was thankful they were "in the usual fishbowl crowd or I would surely have rushed up to him like a fool."[1] The agency had arranged a photo shoot to christen Wanderwell N° III — Cap's new creation and, as he spun it, the car that would represent the City of Light in the Wanderwell Around the World Endurance Contest, or WAWEC.[2] He'd built the car himself, starting with the chassis of a 1917 Red Cross ambulance to which he added a host of new components, including a gleaming dashboard, floorboards, and headlights. Most remarkable, however, was the body. Instead of the light gauge steel used for Unit N° II, he opted for aluminum. "The metal of future cars, airplanes, anything!" he crowed.[3] His enthusiasm for the automotive uses of aluminum was prophetic. Major auto manufacturers would not start using aluminum components until the late twentieth century.[4]

Aloha was impressed. "She had sleek lines, lower sides, wider comfort, leg room. It was love at first sight." Her enthusiasm doubled when the captain told her the car would be hers to pilot. "My very own Jolly-Boat. I quickly took an initial fling behind the wheel. She purred.... With muffler, her throb was smooth. [She was] built for derring-do."[5]

Adding to Aloha's excitement was the multinational crew the captain had assembled. There were two war veterans: one solidly built American named

Eddie Sommers[6] and a gangly German-Pole called Stefanowi Jarocki, former enemies who once "tossed grenades, fired at, cursed each other across the barbed wire. Now they united efforts in horizon chasing." There was also a blond Dutch girl called Lijntje van Appelterre, more widely known as Mrs. Siki, wife of a French-Senegalese boxer known as Battling Siki. Siki had recently become the world's first black light heavyweight champion, defeating Frenchman Georges Carpentier with a knockout punch.[7] Convincing a celebrity wife to join the expedition was a stroke of marketing genius.

For Aloha, though, the most interesting new member was pretty seventeen-year-old Amanda Hoertig,[8] "from South America, richly dark, handsome; she and I really hit it off together."[9] Amanda, who they'd nick-named "La Princesse," had been Wanderwell's interpreter since Bordeaux and quickly built a reputation as an *artiste de hoopla*, a free spirit with infectious energy and little regard for social norms. Even Cap, usually so serious, couldn't help admiring her expansive effervescence. "Full of the joy of living," he said, "uninhibited as a young puppy."[10]

❄

Aloha had only been in Paris a few days when Armstrong and Fate arrived, very dusty and thoroughly unmarried. Still, they were together, had delivered Unit N° II in one piece, and were now "in Paris somewhere, preparing to build their own unit."[11]

With both cars together, the captain wound up affairs in Paris and prepared to take his newly expanded show on the road.

When the captain announced the expedition was leaving for Belgium, Aloha refused to go along.

> In spite of my enthusiasm about driving N° III, I decided not to travel to Belgium again. . . . I really wanted to scoot off with La Princesse for a fling in Paris. She agreed — it was time for her sign off; Paree could be fun together. I knew Cap would disapprove. I told him that Mum wanted me home for a while. Then I wrote Mum that I was very busy (and) not to expect letters too soon, all's well, tra la la. . .[12]

Aloha with girlfriend in Paris bistro.

On the loose in Paris, Aloha and Amanda shared a room in Montparnasse, subsisting on market food and the kindness of friends. Aloha managed to do a little modelling for the French fashion designer Molyneux, and helped a showman named Chief White Elk find engagements around the city.[13] Most of Aloha's time, however, was spent with Amanda, visiting cafés[14] and markets, or arranging liaisons with various suitors.

> She was a very dear buddy to me…a bit crazy about men, especially wealthy. Sometimes we didn't see each other for days…. Seeing Paris from the rough side was much more adventurous than if lavishly chaperoned. It felt like sheer debauchery to have one's own way entirely…. For posterity La Princesse and I had pictures taken a l'Apache[15] seated at table with a bottle of vin rouge — explicitly going to hell-in-a-basket — Paris in the summer, at sixteen."[16]

When the money ran out, a change in lifestyle ensued. La Princesse moved in with one of her lovers, to whom she'd become engaged, leaving

Aloha to fend for herself. The experience was twice as expensive and half as interesting. Debauched and depleted, she was ready for the telegram that arrived from Holland. Captain wrote that the expedition was headed for Germany and he wanted her to come "at least for a few days...as my guest...can talk things over." As Aloha put it, "I wanted to dash to him but my heart said I must go home to Mother and straighten myself out."[17]

The problem was that she had no money to get to her mother, who had returned to her home in Nice. Her solution was to visit an acquaintance that Amanda had recommended. Nicknamed Old Brooklyn, La Princesse's friend ran a successful business selling surplus war tires and was known to enjoy having the neighbourhood girls stop by for "lively chit-chat and sandwiches." Aloha stopped in for lunch one afternoon and told him of her impending departure, adding that she needed five dollars. "Cheerfully he said 'Ok' and handed me out of the office...into a cubbyhole washroom. My God! I got the shock of my life! His pants ripped open, he was exposed in a flash!" According to her memoirs, Aloha rebuffed him with a loud no. "Red in the face, he flung open the door, shouting at the cashier, 'Hell, give her five bucks.' I picked up the note and walked out."[18]

Aloha arrived in Nice and stayed just long enough to wash her clothes, enjoy some home-cooked meals, and otherwise recover from the exhausting improvisations of bohemian living. When she left this time, she told her mother, she would be gone for much longer.

※

In August 1923, Aloha stepped off a train in Amsterdam and was met by the captain. His "'Old kid' greeting of a slap on the shoulder jolted any sentimental idiotic impulses." If she was disappointed by the platonic and joshing reunion, it was much worse when she arrived at the hotel and was met in the lobby by the new Dutch interpreter. "Petite, baby-faced Joannie van der Ray was very attractive in uniform."[19] Aloha gave her a crushing handshake and watched the reaction. "Her glance to Cap was for reassurance. I read a lot into that glance."[20] Cap had not mentioned the new and strikingly attractive crew member, nor that they were to be roomies.

The captain had secured visas for Germany at The Hague. Surviving passport documents set the date at October 11, 1923, expiring November 20,

1923.[21] Perhaps more than any other destination in Europe, Germany attracted Wanderwell. Although Polish, he'd spent most of his school years in Alsace-Lorraine and Solschen, near Hannover. His German was as good as his Polish and better, by far, than his English.

In 1923 conditions in Germany were appalling. The war reparations required by the Treaty of Versailles led to hyperinflation and meant the average German was so impoverished that bread became an unattainable luxury. Rumours of starvation were widespread. Still, there was hope for change. A new and moderate chancellor, Gustav Stresemann, had come to power; he aimed to strengthen German democracy, repair relations with France, and free Germany from the heavy burden of the reparations. Now, Walter thought, might be the perfect time to promote his idea of an international police.

The expedition crossed the border at the town of Malden. Here, Belgian border guards escorted them through the dangerous buffer zone to the Rhine bridge crossing at Wesel, Germany. While the crew sat in the cramped darkness, listening to rain drum on the car's canvas roof, Wanderwell entered the sentry building and spoke to the German guards. He drew attention to the "three pips" on his uniform and demanded they escort the cars to their commanding officer. To further assert his "rank," the captain instructed the junior officer to carry his briefcase.

At the designated building Cap retrieved his satchel, and ordered the guard to wait outside. We watched anxiously but could see no movement in the pale light of the upstairs windows. Several minutes passed before Cap appeared, relayed his briefcase and stepped into the car. The guard assumed this imperious officer had obtained permission to cross.[22]

Cap used the same strategy at the town of Wesel and again at the customs house where the cars were finally allowed to enter Germany.

Impressive though he undoubtedly was, Wanderwell's ability to overawe guards by the sheer force of his personality is a touch far-fetched. A better explanation for the expedition's successful entry into Germany may have lain in the contents of the briefcase he was carrying. Years earlier, in the

United States, Wanderwell had performed numerous questionable tasks for the German government that had attracted the attention of the US Bureau of Investigation. Walter's relationship with the German government may have opened doors closed to anyone else.

The expedition made a beeline for the north central part of the country, hoping that if their "ruse was discovered we could be sent to the nearest exit — Poland. We had been twenty-four hours in wet clothes, no sleep, only one hot meal. We took turns at the wheel, except van der Ray."[23]

The sights that greeted them as they rumbled north were depressing. In each town were long lines for food, bedraggled elderly, children in rags, and people subsisting on a barter system. The sights brought out old bitterness among the multinational crew; memories of the war died hard. Wanderwell stepped in.

Cap absolutely forbade making critical comments about the political situation.... [He] wanted us to learn to understand people — just as each of us had a war scar to outgrow, so also the 1914 Germans. "Individually, these are fine beings. Show them restraint and healing. Learn in a country; don't spend your brains criticizing.... These Germans are hungry for friendly gestures from the outside world. They'll whole-heartedly admire the sporting aspect, you'll see."[24]

What the captain didn't realize, however, was that Aloha was more worried about the Dutch than the Germans.

I was very keyed up about the whole situation — the Expedition's and my own. I felt sure our demure member of the voluptuous lips and come-hither eyes was just lying in wait to compound an untenable situation. On the job Cap treated us all without distinction — male, female. I simply had to outlast her.

It didn't help that Aloha's seventeenth birthday had come and gone with nary a notice.

In Hannover, shows were booked at the Dekla theatre, the city's "number one show house." Wanderwell handled the lecturing, managing to mix his

dramatic travelogues with plugs for world peace and half-serious acknow-
ledgements of local achievements. "If we get lost in the jungle, at least we'll
find Hannover's worldwide Leibniz Biscuits," he joked, shrewdly highlighting a German product that was universally *loved*. That mention alone earned
them "a hundred pounds of biscuits, hardtack, gingerbread," gifts that were
"more valuable than their weight in paper marks."[25] Audiences at the
Wanderwell shows were soon covered in crumbs as the Leibnitz company
began distributing free samples, a move that further enhanced public goodwill. Local papers offered enthusiastic write-ups, praising their courage and
willingness to travel without financial backing.

Inevitably, it wasn't long before they attracted cement-faced, green-suited
Polizei, because someone figured out that the cars had entered Germany
without paying duty. After one evening's show, Wanderwell was detained
and the rest of the crew confined to the hotel. When he returned, Wanderwell
gleefully announced that although the cars had been confiscated pending
trial, they were permitted to continue their theatre appearances.

On the day of the trial, the crew gathered at the local courthouse. The
captain entered his defence plea, describing the peaceful aims of the Around
the World Expedition and their goodwill towards the German people. The
judge was unmoved. He reiterated that the crew had "committed a grave
offense, smuggling two automobiles across the frontier" and, closing his
notebook, announced that they would be assessed a penalty "prescribed by
our prewar statutes." After much rustling of papers and mumbled discussions
with his clerks, the judge read out a fine of 35,000 marks. The captain began
to protest but was swiftly silenced.

> The judge regarded Cap. "I wish you to understand, sir, I want you
> to remember this experience. The war has left our [country] bankrupt,
> unable to adjust even our laws to inflation. You are fined according
> to prewar values. You will pay only thirty-five cents.... Young man,
> reach into your pocket and hand me in American money, the value
> of five of your souvenir brochures."[26]

Autographed photo of Aloha in front of Unit Nº IV, Europe, mid-1920s.

✿

Cookies in tow, the expedition headed east to Berlin, the capital of the Weimar Republic and possibly the most culturally kaleidoscopic city in all of Europe at that time: Dada, Bauhaus, Jungian psychology, Fritz Lang's *Metropolis*, Marlene Dietrich's *The Blue Angel*, physics (Einstein was working at the Kaiser Wilhelm Institute), Brecht and Weill's *The Threepenny Opera* — all happened in Berlin in the 1920s. This creative ferment, however, took place against a backdrop of serious political and social upheaval. Liberal, modernizing forces were colliding with right-wing militants who remained outraged at the outcome of the Great War. The result was an existential uncertainty, or what one writer so vividly called a "voluptuous panic."[27] By the time the Wanderwell Expedition arrived in late October 1923, their cars crawling like "two tiny ants" beneath the imposing Brandenburg Gate, Germans were taking full advantage of the freedoms granted by the country's new constitution.

However, both the constitution and its promised freedoms would shatter within a month of their arrival. While Aloha and Walter were preparing for performances in Berlin, on November 8 about 360 miles south in Munich, a charismatic leader and some followers stormed a political meeting and announced they had taken over the government. The unsuccessful Beer Hall Putsch, as it came to be known, resulted in more than thirty dead and injured and the imprisonment (and later trial) of its chief agitator, Adolph Hitler. The attempted coup made front-page headlines all over the world, disrupted an already fractious German economy,[28] and helped put an end to a promising coalition government. As if to underscore her emphatic disinterest in all things political, Aloha's journal entry from November 23 contains no hint of this volatile and historic event.

✿

As in Hannover, the newspapers were generous. Lavish publicity led to the expedition's biggest engagement yet: Berlin's colossal Scala variety theatre, the largest in all Europe. According to Aloha, their shows played alongside the feature attraction, Lil Dagover in *Seine Frau, die Unbekannte* (*His Wife, the Unknown*) and nearly filled the theatre's four thousand seats. As usual, the audience cheered and hissed according to their political biases, but the captain had devised a special speech to close the show.

> As the curtain descended, cheers and good-natured guffaws nearly drowned out Cap's voice. Abruptly a brilliant glare of spotlights flooded the super stage to reveal three almost dwarf khaki figures: Cap center, from either wing a young man marching toward him. Expectant silence gripped the audience.
>
> In resonant voice, Cap, "Friends permit me to introduce Private Jarocki, a better man never fought for the Fatherland...and American Private Sommers who rallied to his flag at the age of fifteen. Once enemies, today staunch friends in a common cause...PEACE and (he usually had to yell it) GOODWILL!
>
> It brought down the house![29]

Not all Germans, however, welcomed the foreign visitors. Both cars were vandalized, flags stolen, masts broke and threats made against the crew, but during such a volatile time, they could not have been greatly surprised.

When it came time to negotiate payment, Walter refused cash — trying to convert it later would have been laughable. By the end of November 1923, 1.00 US dollar bought 4.2 trillion marks, a number that, as one author put it, destroys the possibility of any rational economic calculation.[30] Instead, the expedition accepted goods in exchange for services.

❄

With their popularity soaring, Walter found a local agent and booked the largest vaudeville house in Warsaw, their next destination. The crossing into Poland in late November 1923 was filled with pomp and ceremony. According the expedition's logbook, the Polish embassy in Berlin had alerted border officials to the expedition's arrival and had arranged for the presence of a contingent of Polish cavalry. Captain Wanderwell Pieczynski and Stefanowi Jarocki, the two Poles of the expedition, saluted the troops and removed the German flags from the hood of the car, replacing them with the Polish White Eagle standard.

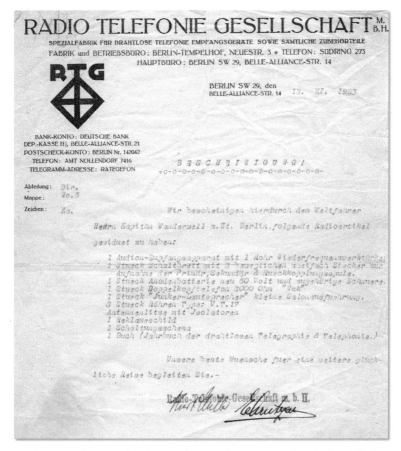

The original receipt for the "wireless" radio system Walter had installed in N° II and bartered for in Berlin, Germany, November 13, 1923.

Aloha was thrilled to be racing through new territory, although the approximate 300 miles of road east to Warsaw were rough and the weather increasingly poor, fading from sun, to freezing rain and eventually snow.

We went bounding across the plains of Poland…through endless tiny mud-spattered villages [with]…small heavily-thatched roofs… whitewashed dwellings…wooden shuttered windows. Beside each [house] a well, its quaint protruding tall arm to raise and lower the bucket.[31]

To Aloha's delight, Wanderwell had sent van der Ray to travel with Aloha in Nº III. "Cap and Sommers were in the lead, Van der Ray since being relegated to Nº III, no longer even a map reader. She was obviously unhappy."[32] Cap, on the other hand, was ecstatic. This was his first visit to Poland since his mother had died in 1917. In his absence, Poland had won its independence — the first time the Polish people were not a subjected spoil of war since 1795.

Partly frozen roads helped the expedition's speed and they arrived, splattered and smeared, at Warsaw, shortly past noon. As Aloha tells it, they were met by a long line of ancient cars that formed a parade to guide them into town. The cavalcade drove through the suburbs of Warsaw, horns and sirens blaring, throngs of people shouting and waving, until they reached the military barracks at Saska Square, where they were escorted by "crack mounted officers...sabres and all." When the caravan finally came to a halt they were "swamped by cameramen and reporters" and a band began playing *Jeszcze Polska nie zginęła* ("Poland is not lost as long as we live").[33]

It was a lavish reception, arranged by Wanderwell's two brothers, both members of the Polish military. Photographs show the captain with various dignitaries, including one taken at the headquarters of the Polish Automobile Club. Here, more than seventy immaculately dressed people crowded into one shot with the captain.

The expedition's time in Warsaw was one long celebration. They played shows at the Cirque Warsawski, literally a ringed circus in which the cars drove around a sawdust track, intentionally backfiring, and the captain told tales of his voyages around the world. One newspaper, the *Express Poranny*, described Wanderwell as a champion driver, "world famous sportsman-Polack, the modern Marco Polo."[34]

All was not sweetness and light, however. In between the celebrating and performing, Aloha and Van der Ray were warring. Aloha still struggled with her feelings for the captain and she was intensely jealous of van der Ray's obviously physical relationship with him, referring to her as "The Vamp" and "Her Ladyship." Wanderwell noticed the hostility and tried various tactics to promote harmony, initially ordering that the two always travel together, then revising to ensure they always travelled *apart*. Nothing seemed to work.

A Christmas reunion with Walter, his brothers, cousins, and old friends.
Walter is second from R, seated front row, Poland, December 1923.

Van der Ray inevitably began to acknowledge that we were spoiling for a good fight. In spite of my determination to avoid open warfare, it seemed just a matter of time before some trivia would explode my despicable temper.[35]

By December 10, the expedition was in Kraków, where they prepared the cars for the difficult passage through the snowbound Carpathian Mountains to Romania. Tires were fitted for chains and blankets were fashioned for the radiators to prevent freezing. The crew purchased winter gear, including thick sheepskin jackets. Neither Unit N° II nor N° III had windows on the sides, only a canvas that could be tied down over the roof, offering minimal protection against wind, rain, and snow.

When the tour set off again, Wanderwell was splitting his time between the two cars and his two female crew members, much to Aloha's distress. During the drive to Lwów (modern-day Lviv, Ukraine), she tried to work up the courage to express her feelings directly, but fell short.

I wished for the time when I could freely say, "This is not working, she or I must go," but he was complimenting my snow driving, the expanded smile blasting me with his pugnacious vitality. I was numbed.[36]

❀

Mid-December was an ambitious time to attempt a crossing into Romania. The expedition had only been on the road from Lwów a short time before snows became heavy. Despite the blanket covers, Nº III's radiator froze. When Nº II stopped to assist, her engine stalled and refused to start again. "Nothing in the engines moved and the cars rapidly became white mounds in the vast white landscape."[37]

Hardly six months after nearly dying of thirst and heat in a Spanish mountain range, Aloha found herself in danger of freezing to death in the foothills of the Carpathian Mountains. But luckily, a rural policeman discovered the stranded travellers and fetched military horsemen. The horses dragged the cars back to Lwów.

There was much guffawing among the riders poking fun at the poor cars, suggesting Cap hire mules to pull him around the world. Their officer kept pace beside me, joking and teasing in German. Presently he suggested Jarocki take Nº III's wheel and I ride astride with him. We trotted off through the mists of flying snow.[38]

In town, the expedition was given beds at the local barracks. Wanderwell insisted the crew turn in early as he planned to make another attempt the following day. Aloha, however, had been invited to the opera by the rescuing officer, whom she identified as Lieutenant Walek Towarczyk of the Sixth Tank Corps. Sneaking out of the barracks like a schoolgirl, she was taken to visit the officer's sister — who loaned her a gown — and then out for a thrilling evening of entertainment and drink. "What a night! Don't know which I enjoyed more — the great performance or the excruciating excitement of outwitting Cap."[39]

At the end of the evening, back in her Wanderwell uniform, Aloha was escorted to the barracks by Walek, only to find "Cap sitting against my door, fast asleep. It was so humiliating to have one's self-esteem lowered in this way." It was past four in the morning but Wanderwell was instantly awake, furious. In the tone of an outraged parent, he reviewed her offences.

> Everything from his promise to mother to protect me, to the dangers of strange army officers and the evils of cafés chantants consumed most of his argument. Then he began...all his favourites: "Every man comes into this life with a shovel, some to dig a pit ever deeper seeing less and less, others to build a mound and climb to the heights of vision." I was really getting the works!... "On this Expedition the work comes first!"
>
> I was so offended I was unable to answer.[40]

In his anger, Wanderwell overlooked the real reason for her flamboyant insubordination: Joannie van der Ray. Aloha wanted to make Walter jealous by cavorting with a *real* officer, to see if her absence would provoke *worry*. Instead she saw only anger. And to make matters worse, it was probably van der Ray who had reported her absence.

Without pausing to write a farewell note, Aloha left the barracks and made her way to the train station where she used her expedition earnings to purchase a ticket to Vienna, and onward to Nice. More than adventure or even money, Aloha wanted to be appreciated — something that Walter Wanderwell, it seemed, would never offer her. Writing of the event decades later, one can still sense the intense emotion that fuelled her decision.

> I just couldn't brave the outfit any longer. I had to get home. "Love can wait" were the words I found. Hope that trollop finds the game not worth the coin. If you're going to be a girl like that, at least one should be totally circumspect — however, gloating is one of its spices, no doubt.[41]

Wanderwell vehicle N° II parked on the back of the Sphinx, preparing camp, Giza, Egypt, 1924.

SEVEN

PILGRIM'S PROGRESS

FILM SENT TO THE DETROIT NEWS and titled "Detroit Tourist Reaches
Bucharest"[1] shows the two Wanderwell cars tearing at breakneck speed
through a crowded University Square, to the visible annoyance of one
pedestrian in a gigantic Balkan winter hat. Twelve hundred miles away
Aloha was depressed. Although back home at the Villa Marie-Thérèse, life
was not unfolding as she had envisioned. She had spent a full year on the
road, and there were no Hollywood roles, no modelling contracts, no adoring
public, and her Wanderwell Around the World dream was fizzling into
vapour. Instead of basking in the limelight as the main attraction of an
intrepid international expedition, she was sitting among the embroidered
pillows of her mother's parlour making small talk and munching on biscuits
and baked scones. She had been replaced by a buck-toothed Dutch girl.

Shortly after Christmas, Margaret invited some friends from England
to come for a visit. The Dawsins had been the Hedley's neighbours back in
England for a generation and were among the few friends to come to
Margaret's aid after Herbert's death. Like Margaret, Mrs. Dawsin had lost
her husband in the war. When Aloha had first arrived in England in 1919,
she had stayed with the Dawsins and had formed a close friendship with
Stanley, the oldest of two brothers.

Aloha and Stanley spent much of the time together, visiting cafés, riding
horses, and going for long beachside walks. After a week of mostly unchap-
eroned time, Margaret nudged her daughter, saying, "'I hope you are in love

with him as much as he is with you.'" It was a statement Aloha "was expected to consider most profoundly."[2]

She didn't.

Settling down was the furthest thing from her mind, though she did enjoy Stanley's company, and looks. "How gorgeous he was! So veddy, veddy British — tweeds and all."[3] Aloha would later blame the reluctance to marry on Stanley, but really it was *she* who demurred and sent him back to England without any commitment. Her fights with Margaret grew more frequent and Aloha concluded again that she was "really better off away from home."

> Damn my beastly temper! I had such quarrels with Mum — outbursts
> that crushed her, poor dear. Each homecoming was worse. Wasted
> her time with embroidery when all could be bought machine made;
> pridefully she enticed me to inspect her fine leather tooling, embossed
> pewter — such artiness quite démodées.[4]

By January 24, 1924, Aloha had returned to the only thing she knew how to do. She was in Marseille with Armstrong and someone she only notes as "E." Fate, apparently, had left the scene. Taking a page from the Wanderwell playbook, they printed postcards and attempted to book theatres, showing the films that Aloha had assembled in Paris. As had happened in the summertime, though, they met with very little success. "On the whole the thing is running rottenly," she wrote. "Marseille has had so many dozens of globetrotters making a mess of things, we'll have to beat it."[5] When wires began arriving from Wanderwell, Aloha decided to call it quits. She scrawled a paragraph in her journal, announcing that after "Wally's innumerable demands for my return and a long struggle with my private feelings I wired him [that] I'll meet him in Egypt."[6] Aloha returned to Nice. Stanley was waiting for her.

❀

When Aloha announced that she was heading for Egypt, Stanley offered to come along. It was an idea that, as it turned out, suited everyone. Margaret was pleased that her daughter had a reliable escort, Stanley was happy to spend more time wooing Aloha, and Aloha relished the opportunity to turn the tables on Walter and arrive at his doorstep with her splendid "fiancé" — taller, younger, richer, and more handsome than Wanderwell.

Aloha and Stanley, whom she'd taken to calling "Locey," arrived in Marseille at 5:20 a.m. on Wednesday, March 26, 1924, sleepy eyed and frozen. By nine o'clock the duo were at the offices of the Compagnie Inter Messagerie Maritime, attempting to purchase tickets to Alexandria aboard a two-funnelled, 11,375-ton steamship called, appropriately, the *Sphinx*. [7]

❀

Aloha and Locey watched at the portholes as ancient Alexandria swam into view. Even the harbour seemed exotic, with its flat roofs, its forests of masts and funnels, its Citadel of Qaitbay, its boardwalk crowded with white turbaned stevedores and camels in the bleaching sun. Here, at last, was a world made for adventure and discovery. They raced from the ship, placed their bags into storage, and headed for the post office, expecting to find a note of instruction from Captain Wanderwell. But there was nothing and no one could tell them anything.

Aloha found a bank and exchanged the twenty-eight francs she had in reserve, hardly enough to last them a few days.

> As a last recourse I decided to go to the British Consulate. Lieut. had once told me that by leaving one's passport as a guarantee, it was possible to obtain one's fare to any end of the World.... So off we went. I interviewed the Vice Consul and after a good cross-examination received the sum of two Egyptian pounds. What a relief! [8]

The best course of action, they decided, was to proceed to the expedition's next likely destination, and that evening they were on the 6:15 train south to Cairo.

The next morning, Aloha and Locey headed to Cairo's central post office to learn that Captain Wanderwell "had just been for his mail." [9] He did not leave a forwarding address, however, which meant he had not left town. By mid-afternoon they had found a cinema where Captain Wanderwell was scheduled to call at 6:00 p.m.

❁

Aloha and Wanderwell exchanged a fraternal hug, after which she introduced Locey to the captain. If Locey's presence was intended to unnerve the captain, he didn't show it. To the contrary, he seemed entirely unsurprised by everything — Aloha's presence, her partner — nor did he comment on her sudden disappearance in Europe. "At this point I was extremely surprised as he showed no signs whatever of the shock it must have been to him."

At supper that evening, Aloha and Locey were introduced to the current Wanderwell crew members. The first was Benno, a German Jew with a noticeable speech impediment who had met up with Wanderwell in Palestine. Carl Martens was a German linguist and musician, whom Aloha described as "a money maker, keen of eye and better of soul." And finally was a German girl with the unlikely name of "Fanny." Of the old crew, only Jarocki, the Polish mechanic, remained. After introductions had been made, Locey gave Aloha "a lean look to see what I thought of my new old surroundings. I laughed and reminded him that this was not the crew (I had been part of)."[10]

❁

The expedition was thriving. A letter written by the managing director of the Eastern Automobiles Supplies and Transport Company in Alexandria enthusiastically thanked the expedition for its effective "advertising propaganda" and was pleased to contribute "the sum of £30 towards your expenses whilst in the Delta. Should you decide to visit Upper Egypt a similar sum will be paid to you by our Cairo Branch."[11] Upon arrival in Cairo, not only did Wanderwell receive the promised sum and "any spare parts you want for your cars" but also a one-ton supply truck for use during his travels in Egypt.

By sunset, the expedition was motoring through Cairo's dusty outskirts, looking not for a hotel but for al fresco desert lodgings. While the sky darkened, Aloha gaped at the rolling desert, at bungalows with bursting flower gardens, and then, as they climbed a steep hill leading to a level plain, she caught her first glimpse of the pyramids at Giza. To her amazement, Walter kept driving until they came to rest "on a little flat piece of sand overlooking the Sphinx."

Euphoric, Aloha wandered out into her surroundings, leaving Locey to help the others build a camp of tents and cars less than thirty yards from Cheops, near the Eastern cemetery between the Great Pyramid and the Sphinx. Aloha removed her shoes and walked through the desert's deep stillness, in a place where every noise carried, undiminished for miles. She sat listening to some night birds calling through the empty air, until Captain Wanderwell approached and suggested they go for a walk. The two strolled out across the sands, away from camp, while "each in turn told his story." Wanderwell described the trip through Romania, Turkey, Syria, Lebanon, and Palestine, arriving, eventually, in Egypt.[12] Aloha gave a somewhat less exciting account of her activities during the three months they'd been apart. The two walked and chatted for so long that "it was getting on to morning before I finally turned in to Nº III."[13]

The next day an unexpected visitor strolled into camp: it was Lotti, a German girl who had joined the tour in Jerusalem and then left in Cairo to be with her husband. Described as a short, boisterous heavyweight, she had walked the 5 miles from Cairo to find the camp at Giza, arriving sunburnt but laughing. The men, surprised by her appearance, ran to their kits to return various items they assumed she had left behind. Meanwhile, Fanny had decided that one night of sleeping in a car in the desert was enough. She would leave with the crew's next visit to Cairo.

Wanderwell had arranged to meet a cinematographer from *Pathé News*, "but the gentleman never arrived so, like foolish kids, just when the sun was at its highest, we decided to take a walk across the desert to visit the catacombs on the far side of the Sphinx. The heat was excruciating."[14] Aloha's reference to the "catacombs" is odd since no such structures were popularly known to exist.[15]

We crossed an ancient graveyard in a flat between two huge dunes. The graves are marked by some half dozen uneven stones stuck in the sand, around which the latter has blown up forming little mounds. On we pushed, not a one daring to drop behind but when at last the party scaled the wall of stone up to the cave-like catacombs and once more found themselves in the shade, the temperature showed on our faces. We looked at each other in astonishment.[16]

Vehicles of the expedition preparing to camp for the night near Cheops and the Sphinx, Egypt, 1923.

A little later on, Aloha describes the site as "the hole in the rocks," but her notes are not detailed enough to be certain where they trekked that day. The Egyptian desert had done in twenty-four hours what months of travel through Europe had not: Aloha had firmly decided that this life, this adventuring life, was the life for her. Her notebooks overflow with observations and giddy accounts of expedition life, from the ritual of washing her face using water from an old benzene can, to becoming transfixed by the sight of two Egyptian boys walking along the crest of dune, "their flowing robes (making) a pretty silhouette."[17] Even after a night spent cramped on one of the car's horsehair benches, she was enchanted by the dawn, as the sky became stained with "pale lemons and oranges" and the sun spilled over "the cool sands, casting great shadows behind the Sphinx and Pyramids."

> There comes with this trip a complete sense of freedom which I doubt possible to be found in any other job in the world. There is absolutely nothing to worry about and the greatest of our annoyances do not reach beyond the petty troubles amongst the crew.[18]

Perhaps the only person as wowed by the desert as Aloha was Walter. There are more photographs of this spot than anywhere else he'd yet travelled, including pictures of the men climbing to the top of Cheops and a stunning photo of Unit N° III parked on the Sphinx's back.

✿

From Giza the expedition travelled to the step pyramids at Saqqara where they visited the five thousand-year-old Pyramid of Djoser, considered the earliest stone structure of its size in the world.[19] From there they continued east across the Nile on the Kasr el Nil Bridge to the oasis of Mit Rahina, which Aloha described as "the promised land," consisting of a large green valley between the Nile to the west and the desert to the east. They had come to visit "two remarkable statues," the first known as the Alabaster Sphinx of Mit Rahina (which at that time was "sitting in a pond") and the second "a most remarkable stone figure reposing on two huge blocks," almost certainly a reference to the now-famous statue of Ramses II.

The crew turned in early, expecting a dawn departure. Aloha, however, could not sleep. Mosquitoes and a variety of imaginary horrors disturbed her sleep. Then, just as the sky was beginning to lighten, an unusual noise sped her to full consciousness.

> I heard footsteps, several stealthy footsteps. They came close, there must have been five or six men. Then I heard deep gruff voices...there was nothing to do but lie perfectly still and pray that one of the boys would be awakened. The voices became louder and then died away, they were passing the camp. What ghastly suspense....I pictured a bloodthirsty attempt to capture the girls, a struggle amongst the men with the clanging of knives. Suddenly...a man stuck his head through the canvas on Lotti's side of the tent.... A general commotion...Steve[20] grabbed a revolver.[21]

A shrill exchange took place until one of the intruding men made an emphatic speech in Arabic. Lotti, the only member of the crew to understand him, responded. Whatever she said seemed to satisfy the men who turned and left the camp. The crew demanded an explanation, which Lotti could hardly choke out for laughing. "The Shiek of Mir Rahina...oh, boy, wants to know whether we would like eggs and milk for breakfast."

The Arab men, it turned out, had been sitting by the well all night long, keeping watch over the campers until 6:00 a.m. when, hungry from their all-night vigil, they began discussing breakfast and thought they would invite the visitors to join them. When the men returned, they placed food in the centre of the crew's eating area and signalled them to begin eating. As "Cap reached for the pot, the native grabbed his hand, took a mouthful for himself, grinned." Cap, "delighted by the old desert tradition," instructed Lotti to tell them that they were excellent hosts.[22]

✻

The expedition returned to Cairo on the sixth of April to gather supplies for the next leg — south towards Suez. They accepted two nights' free accommodations at the Palace Hotel and were especially grateful to "raid the bathrooms." The fuel truck was returned to Ford and passage was booked on the SS *Borulus* for April 11, travelling down the Red Sea to Aden. The crew drove due east through hot, dry air, along smooth roads like beads on a string, marvelling at mirages or spying camel skeletons until at last there came the first blue sheen of the great Red Sea, then the freighters lying at anchor, and then the square white buildings of bustling, little Port Tewfik,[23] gateway to the Suez.

✻

On May 3, 1924, Locey commandeered Aloha's journal and wrote several bizarre pages in a florid script. His entries began with a short dedication.

> As a memory to my relations with Aloha [*sic*] I am supplementing into her "log" our journey, with the Wanderwell Expedition by the SS *Borulos* [*sic*] of the Khedivial Mail Line, from Suez (Egypt) to Aden (Arabia – British).

He recounted events on their voyage, including the spectacle at Port Tewfik when two "strange looking automobiles" were hoisted onto the steamer's deck — a scene which "might be entered into the category of the, to say the least, interesting." Later he confessed his connection with "Miss Aloha Wanderwell, who, by the bye, calls me 'Locey' and claims the relationship of cousin (of the first degree) to myself, which I am in no position to either deny or to rectify." He found the Red Sea "as blue or as green as any other sea" but was excited by the promise of stops along the way in towns "with names so terrible that I could not possibly write them all here."

His writing, he claimed, was "just for the sake of wasting a little more ink," but by the close of his paragraphs, cloaked in a mock poetic voice, his purpose became clear: this was a farewell.

> You have wandered with me, Aloha, along the gentle, gay and strange French Riviera. You have sped with me across the blue Mediterranean Sea, in Oriental towns hast thou and I wandered, and under desert sun and desert stars we have sat, eaten, laughed, talked and sung. In shaded oasis, not far from the cruel sun, have we sat to think a dream, and both up and down the Red Sea have we travelled — yet you and I are just GOOD FRIENDS — oh girl, oh pal! Is that not enough?

The last line wishes Aloha success, "though it is not mine," and signs off, "Ever your sincere friend, Stanley L. Dawsin. May 3rd, 1924."

Locey's note was provoked by a serious turn of events. On arriving in Aden, the British authorities refused to accept the Laissez-Passer travel documents issued in Suez (also British). Although often used as an emergency passport, a Laissez-Passer is often only valid for one-way travel to a specified country. In this case, the documents were stamped "good for India," a certification which local officials felt was insufficient to allow Aloha and others in the crew to come ashore, even if only to change vessels. Only Walter and Jarocki were travelling on traditional passports, an event which so alarmed the authorities they threatened to reject the entire expedition, complaining about Germans, funny passports, and insufficient money. Aloha's and Locey's real passports were still with the consul in Alexandria. For three days they argued with officials, all the while living on the deck of the *Borulus*, waiting for clarification from the consul in Suez.

It was all too much for the Wanderwell crew. Aloha made a hasty entry in her journal, announcing that "the crew of Wanderwell II and III has once more broken up, as it always does and as always only I return to the one man I love, my brother Walter."[24] It's a noteworthy passage, marking the end of another crew and Aloha's first plain-spoken confession of her feelings for Walter.

> Lotti, as habituel on moving occasions got horribly drunk, Martens to spite Cap broke the lock on the back of N° III and was about to dispense with all the papers belonging to the trip when his conscience smote him and he left the job half done.... Benno with less than 15 piastres[25] to his name raged about like a madman, only Locey was silent, away on the aft deck smoking cigarets, leaving the heavens to take care of him.[26]

Of the crew, only Aloha and Jarocki would continue. For now, they travelled back to Suez, where they would scatter. Walter remained in Aden with the cars and the gear. The usual tedium of travel by sea was spiked with the shock of their sudden dissolution. The ship's captain took pity on them and gave them exclusive use of the aft deck, where they slept and filled their time with music, arguments about religion, swearing lessons (courtesy of boisterous Lotti), attempts to hypnotize each other, arguments about food, and gossip about Captain Wanderwell's recent tryst with van der Ray. According to Jarocki, van der Ray, whom they'd nicknamed "Puck," was madly in love with Wanderwell and planned to meet the cars in Bombay in May. If the news worried Aloha, she didn't let on. "Steve dislikes her (perhaps he is jealous, ha ha!) so that makes all the anecdotes lopsided but nevertheless interesting."[27]

When the ship arrived in Massawa on May 3, Aloha received a telegram. "I opened the yellow paper to read: Your passport obtained, take steamer Nippon Massawa Aden Confirm Wanderwell." Aloha was nonplussed. "Of all the things, oh! This was outrageous. Leave Steve (Jarocki) and the rest, go back to Aden. Whew!"[28]

Aloha and Lotti went ashore and made inquiries. Predictably, the Lloyd Triestino company would not issue tickets without a passport, and there was no time to receive an answer from Aden officials before the SS *Borulus* sailed. Downcast, Aloha and Lotti wandered through the hot, dusty town, stopping at a café for lunch. After discussing the situation with some curious locals, they were directed to a young Italian official who offered to help.

"After a long discussion he promised to deposit 1000 Lire with the offices as a guarantee."[29]

Aloha raced back to the *Borulus*, found Jarocki and instructed him to pack her things and give her the money that Wanderwell had entrusted them. She was, she announced, going back to Aden. "He thought I was crazy, so did the others. I went to see Locey, gave him £1 to get his passport back in Egypt. Shook a hasty goodbye with everyone, gave Steve £2 and got off the ship just before the gang plank went up, leaving on board most of my valuables which had been in Lotti's valise."

The circus that had been the Wanderwell Expedition was abruptly over and Aloha was alone.

> I was taken to my benefactor's house and duly, as expected, made love to.[30] As he didn't speak French, nor I Italian, it was a rotten position. I was scared to death but could do nothing to better the matter and was thankful when much against my will he kissed me goodnight and left the room...but it was not all over. At about 10 he returned...till as a last recourse I flew into a rage and cried. If I never prayed before, I did that night.[31]

Terrified and exhausted, the seventeen-year-old adventurer trudged up to the roof, the only place cool enough to sleep. Even in her precarious situation she recorded the sounds she heard from the rooftop, the tom-toms and hand claps that carried from some fireside, the sensation of a hundred domestic scenes settling to a close as the night became still and the village went to sleep.

The next day, Aloha was back at the shipping agency, trying to secure her passage aboard another ship, the SS *Nippon*. The agent, however, flatly refused to issue her deck passage. Instead, he placed her in first class. Aloha choked with gratitude. The prospect of good food, clean sheets, and a hot bath gave her the strength to get through one more day with her Italian benefactor. "Tomorrow," she wrote, "there will be no more of those 'emotional meetings.'"[32]

Aloha standing atop one of the Wanderwell vehicles as it's hoisted off the deck of a ship, Osaka, Japan, 1927.

EIGHT

THE LAST CHANCE TO BE FIRST

IN THE WAKE OF THE ORDEAL of Massawa, Aloha's days aboard the *Nippon* would have been languid and luxurious, providing everything her half-starved ordeal aboard the *Borulus* did not: a clean bed, delicious food, English tea, and laundry service. The Italian staff was gallant and flattering, and treated Aloha with a "polite impetuosity" that kept her giggling. But really it was the porcelain that made her swoon.

> My first request was for a bath, the passage was cleared as a steward escorted me to a spotless bagno. I found no peephole in the door, so submerged in the huge tub, the brackish water piercing like needles attacked every prickly-heat clogged pore the body over. Ah, what relief![1]

When the *Nippon* arrived at Aden's sun-soaked port two days later, Aloha was on deck, peering through binoculars to spot Captain Wanderwell. He eventually arrived, courtesy of a police launch, and was third up the gangway. Rather than the emotional greeting she'd imagined, Walter simply strolled towards her, grinning, and handed her a khaki skirt. Aloha looked at him and then her mouth fell open:

"You don't mean to say . . ."

"That was just about it, half the trouble at least — you girls running around in shorts.... The Resident asked me to beg the young lady to wear a skirt."[2]

So much trouble all because one man did not approve of women in shorts. Shaking her head, Aloha wondered if the Resident "was aware of our doorless cars!" Still, she was glad to be safely ashore in Aden, being treated "as though I owned the world" with solicitous treatment from officials who "took my new Italian passport[3] [issued in Massawa] and returned it stamped."[4]

❀

While awaiting transportation to the subcontinent, their time in Aden passed quietly. Whether because of the oppressive heat or the knowledge that they would be moving on in two days, neither one felt inclined to any great exertions. "We live like Royalty, loung[ing] around. ... When hunger pushes we go back into the native village and secure a couple of pounds of dates, some bread and fresh milk and return to our luxurious apartment."[5] And yet Aloha was not exactly satisfied. Walter spent the balance of most days leafing through ancient and derelict editions of the *Saturday Evening Post*, while Aloha listened to "oriental love songs" on the gramophone. "There is nothing to do. When away, I long to be with him and when I get back we bore one another."[6]

Aloha passed the time filling her journal with elaborate descriptions of her surroundings, from the natives' mud and wattle houses, to the myriad cafés where locals read Egyptian newspapers and shouted politics. She saved her kindest words for the beaches and Arab dhows of the waterfront, where she and Walter went swimming after sunset, despite warnings of sharks.

By now, Aloha had made up her mind to drive around the globe, a decision that, in 1924, was like deciding to grow feathers — bizarre and probably impossible. She was increasingly confident of her abilities. If she could handle Poland and Paris and Aden and Massawa, she could handle anything — including Joannie van der Ray. So, on May 11, Aloha and Walter left their hotel paradise and drove to Steamer Point, where they met the *City of Hankow*, climbed a rope onto the ship's deck, and met the waiting captain and crew. Aloha noted that some of the officers were "unmistakably astonished to see a girl there and it [occurred] to me that Walter had not mentioned my sex when procuring the deck passage tickets and arranging with the Captain about the cars. Ha! Ha!"[7] She soon demonstrated her mettle. While Walter set up his camera, Aloha arranged for the cars to be hoisted onto the ship. With ropes secured around each axle, she leapt on to the hood of Unit N° II and, grasping one of the ropes, gave a thumbs up to the crane operator. "Then what a rush … up into the air with the flivvers while Walter made stills from an upper deck."[8] It was a stunt they would reprise in several countries.

❀

The whirring eye of Prong's Reef Lighthouse signalled their arrival at Bombay's Alexandra Docks. It was Saturday, May 24, and the cars were packed and ready for unloading. As the boat drew into port, Wanderwell checked and rechecked that their paperwork was in order. Bombay was the gateway to the rest of Asia and the lynchpin of the Around the World adventure. Aloha was still travelling on a temporary passport, and Walter worried that some overzealous clerk might bar her from landing. Aloha's permits were stamped without fuss, but they lingered over Wanderwell's assorted documents until the junior official, panicked by unconventional papers, decided that someone further up the chain of command was required. "You, you must wait until Monday," the clerk insisted.[9] No relevant government official would resume work before then.

The cars and equipment could not land, but Aloha and Walter were permitted to go ashore on Sunday to collect their forwarded mail, arrange for advertising, and most crucially, book theatres. Four shows were booked for the coming week at the Madan Theatre, one of a large chain of movie houses established by Jamshedji Framji Madan, a pioneer of the Indian film industry. By the mid-1920s, the Madan organization owned 172 theatres and controlled half of the country's box office.[10] Their local dominance virtually guaranteed that the Wanderwell shows would be adequately promoted.

On Monday, Unit N° II was unloaded at sunrise. Dangling from the crane rope and amid a whorl of curious seabirds, it was placed on the pier in expectation of Walter's impending release. By mid-morning, however, no passport officials had arrived, so he sent Aloha into town to "wake them

Pages from one of Aloha's passports, this one issued in Bombay, India, and assigned to "Miss Idris A. Hall, alias Wanderwell," May 28, 1924.

up." Aloha was nervous about driving without a navigator, but directions were the least of her troubles. Before even leaving the wharf she had swerved to avoid incautious workers, dodged around wandering buffaloes and nearly collided with a "bullock cart (which) dawdled plum in front of me." The city streets were exponentially worse, filled with ambling pedestrians, bicycles, darting children, and road-hogging carts. It didn't help that something was wrong with the steering.

> Nº II has so much compression[11] it is simply terrible to steer. In fact, I have to get right out of my seat in order to make a corner. And the heat!!! If some of those fake "Round the World" cars back in the USA had ever nearly done half of what they profess, they would not, I am certain, speak so lightly of their "3rd trip around the globe."

In the stress and confusion, she forgot to drive on the left-hand side of the road, which resulted in her clipping a gharry horse.[12] The driver was understandably outraged and before long "some 150 natives had gathered

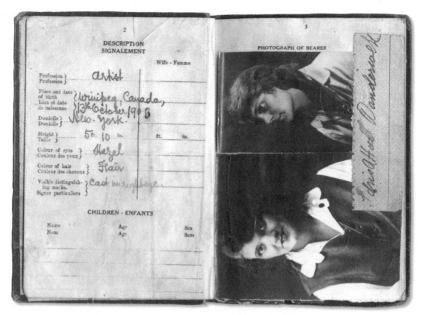

Same passport as previous page. Note that her birthdate has been "adjusted" from 1906 to 1908.

and...I could not get away!" Her luck held, however, when "a large gentleman hopped out of a car, caught the driver by the neck and hurled him across the street. That cleared the way and I proceeded."[13]

Her errand took all afternoon. The customs house was deserted, so she attempted to gain the assistance of the American consul who happened to be napping.[14] Once awakened, he informed Aloha that he would need to look into things before any action could be taken. This obliged Aloha to drive back to the customs house, where this time, officials were present and she finally discovered the real nature of the problem: they were deciding how to charge extra duties and deposits. "After some two hours of talking I persuaded [them] to allow the cars in free."[15]

Bombay flung open its arms to the expedition: the cars were pampered at the Ford garage, rooms were donated by the posh Majestic Hotel, and when they visited a film lab to develop the Egypt and Aden footage, Aloha was greeted by the "large gentleman" who had come to her rescue after the gharry incident. Mr. G.W. Allan turned out to be the Agfa Film representative for India, an organization with whom Wanderwell had already established an advertising contract in Berlin. Allan's firm provided 3,600 feet of 35 mm negative film and wrote a letter of introduction to the Agfa representatives in Hollywood.[16] Within two days, the expedition had acquired bookings, accommodations, repairs, and film supplies. Only fuel was needed to carry them forward, and even this was granted by the Asiatic Petroleum Company: 100 gallons of Shell petrol in return for "displaying an advertisement of this petrol on your entire run between Bombay and Calcutta."[17] Their success was assisted by lavish newspaper coverage and headlines such as "Young Lady to Cross India by Motorcar." "We were discovered by Bombay! The hotel gave a dance in our honour. I acquired on loan a suitable frock [*sic*], shoes.... We were swamped with invitations to be seen or be shown."[18]

By June it was clear that Joannie van der Ray was not coming. Aloha later admitted in her journal that she had intercepted a letter from van der Ray for Wanderwell in Bombay but didn't deliver it to him, leaving it at the post office marked Return to Sender.

Walter made attempts to hire local talent without success. It was time to leave Bombay, but he worried that the route ahead would prove too difficult without extra hands. Aloha felt differently. A larger crew, she pointed out, cost more and would add weight to the cars. Then there was the headache of training new members and the possibility that they would quit. Most importantly, Aloha wanted to drive N° III *on her own*. It was good for publicity and it was a chance for her to accomplish something important: Aloha could become the first female to drive solo across India — no mean feat. Walter, nervous and still annoyed about van der Ray, finally agreed. They would leave on Monday.

Everybody looked dolefully at our prospect of crossing in June, the hottest month of the year, the time of fever and the peak of the monsoon. People were full of advice about drinking water and cholera and women raised their hands in horror to think of me driving a car alone and heavy tropical rains and winds.... It certainly didn't look a very cheerful prospect and I looked forward to it with dread and fear, every day the heat was getting worse and worse.[19]

The plan was to travel an ancient highway called the Grand Trunk Road. Kipling called it "the road of Hindustan,"[20] and with portions dating back 3,500 years, the road had played an important role in the political, cultural, and spiritual development of India. For all its grand history though, in 1924 vast stretches of the Grand Trunk Road were little more than dirt tracks meandering from village to village and clogged with horses, ox-carts, and barefoot pedestrians. Bridges, if they existed, were not designed to support the weight of cars, and while there were numerous caravansaries,[21] they offered food and shelter but little else.

Their route would take them over 1,200 miles, not including detours for floods, fires, or bandits and would be run in two "laps." The first from Bombay through Dhule, Indore, Guna, Jhansi, Agra to Kanpur; the second would commence in Allahabad and take them through Benares, Gaya, Asansol, and Calcutta.

They began on Tuesday, June 4, 1924, with Aloha in the lead. Their progress was slow, barely 15 miles in an hour but even this fell by half as night set. Aloha hunched over her steering wheel and squinted through her car's feeble light, swerving to avoid the bullock carts that had been parked for the night in the middle of the road. The intention had been to make Nashik, but they were not even through the treacherous Kasara Ghat, a steep pass through the Western Ghats mountain range. Eventually, Aloha simply gave up and pulled up under a clump of pipal trees, suggesting they make camp. They were already low on water and had no rations with them save for some dried beans — a terrible oversight. Walter declared he would sleep outside on some flat rocks. "I told him if he didn't mind the snakes and the beetles, he could do so."[22] They spent the night together in N⁰ III.

The next morning Aloha unzipped one of the car's canvas walls and poked her head out. The sky was swimming with a weak orange light but already the road was busy with caravans, travelling as far as possible before the sun became fierce. Walter and Aloha knew they should do the same. Some of the country's most treacherous roads lay ahead and they wanted to tackle them before the daytime traffic became heavy.

At the Kasara Ghat, Aloha looked out over a vast and undulating rocky terrain. A loss of control could easily send the car over a cliff. She took the lead and tested the car through the first tight turns. To her surprise, she found that the area's steep drops and hairpin bends "presented no difficulty in the daylight." Her confidence surged. "I knew he must have been on pins and needles for fear I burn the brakes out as it was my first real hill, but N° III's lightness allowed her to sail down on her own compression."[23]

Aloha's driving skills blossomed. For her, the real challenge was not India's vague roadways, wandering cattle, gambolling children, or suicidal chickens, but the stewing heat. By noon, temperatures shot to over 95°F and, as in Egypt, Aloha withered. She wore her pith helmet at all times and had affixed a wimple to the hat's rear brim to shade her neck. She had no idea that the Western Ghats are one of the more *temperate* regions of India. The real heat was still to come.

By June 8 — the same day that George Mallory and Andrew Irvine were last seen "going strong for the top"[24] of Mount Everest — they'd made it as far as the Kadwa River, only to find there was no bridge. Walter, as usual, was unfazed. He approached some local farmers and, using hand gestures to explain their situation, proposed a solution.[25] He returned with several men and a team of oxen. He told Aloha to stack the blankets and luggage on the roof while the oxen were hitched to the front of her car. With everything ready, she got back into the car to steer. Walter, meanwhile, filmed. At his signal the oxen were urged forward. The ropes tightened and the car rolled into the brisk current, water cresting up against the wheels in a gurgling whoosh of whirlpools. Soon the tires were submerged and water swirled into the footwells, soaking Aloha's boots. The car jittered and seemed to slide sideways and for a brief moment Aloha wondered if she would be swept away. But after some shouts from the ox drivers, she emerged soaked but unscathed on the opposite bank.

N° II was next. Since she was already soaked, Aloha took the wheel again while Walter filmed from a slightly different angle. Once again the car nosed into the rushing river, filling the footwells. Halfway across, however, the oxen stopped. The car's heavier weight had caused it to sink into the riverbed and the oxen were unable to pull it free. With rising alarm, Aloha and Walter told the ox drivers to leave their animals and lift the car. The drivers did not understand. Walter left his camera and raced into the water. He crouched until only his head was visible and grabbed a front tire.

"Get out and lift!" he shouted.

Aloha leapt over the door and grabbed the opposite tire. This the drivers understood. Two men immediately did likewise, hoisting the vehicle while the oxen resumed pulling it forward. Back on dry land, water gushed out from the car, "shoes, topi and fruit all afloat."[26]

※

In the days ahead, water continued to be a major concern. At every village they replenished their supplies from native wells. "Peasants gladly hauled buckets of the green scum water [and] we added drops of iodine. A theory was, when there were frogs in the well, the water was OK."[27] Aloha drove with a gasoline can of water beside her, a few large leaves pressed overtop to prevent splashing. At regular intervals she pulled off her hat, filled it with water and then slapped it back on.

On one particularly hot day they spent ten hours on the road. Aloha was worn out by the heat and reeling from a searing headache. Her only thought was to find a Dak Bungalow — a government-run roadhouse. A writer for the *New York Times* described these bungalows as "not by any means sumptuously furnished,"[28] while Rudyard Kipling described them as "objectionable places to put up in...generally very old, always dirty, [and] the khansamah [keeper] is as ancient as the bungalow."[29] But to Aloha they were salvation. Arriving through the gate, she tumbled out of her car, mumbled "Mehrbani se. Chai," to the khansamah and ordered buckets of water. "I submerged in a zinc tub, shorts and all, then dragged my sopping body to a thong cot."[30]

※

After the rocky heights of the Western Ghats, the road descended to an open, fertile plateau. Aloha found it monotonous and each day longed to arrive in some village, to see people or interesting attractions, to find food and water or at least to stretch her legs and take a photograph. "We placed a vague trust in the next village.... We sought for it with our eyes, hastened towards it as though the sight of it were to cease the strain, the heat, the loneliness and the great dazzling light which seemed to be mastering us, driving us on and on."[31]

Aloha with her pet monkey, Kim.

At Gwalior they rested for a few days. Agra was next, and they wanted to be ready to film the main attraction: the Taj Mahal. They stayed as guests of a family in service to the maharajah of Gwalior, also known as the maharajah of Scindia, a line of royalty stretching from 1726. Aloha was impressed by the luxurious family home whose exterior was cooled by "coconut matting screens drenched with intermittent sloshing of water by garden wallahs." They gave a private showing of their films to the maharajah's household and, in return, were treated to a spectacle of elephants being dressed in ceremonial costume. Later on, Aloha was "asked to accept a young elephant as a gift. Be grand to tow the cars." Not knowing how to politely decline, Aloha was eventually rescued by a British resident who brokered a compromise: Aloha would instead accept a small monkey to accompany her. The monkey was a Bonnet Macaque, cute, mischievous. "Christened Kim, he would ride beside me and be on stage.... He loved to be cuddled, observed everything, hated mangy pariah dogs, bared his teeth at low caste men — he was great company for me."[32]

The push to Agra was hampered by violent dust storms, with one twister fierce enough to stall Nº III and tear the skin on Aloha's face. When Cap pulled up to check on her, "He looked at me as he might stare at a pet pony with a broken leg. He, coated ochre, his sunburned eyes ringed red. My mouth and hair, full of grit — so horrible we burst out laughing."[33]

Arriving in Agra, Aloha found the city hot, dirty, and poor. She was annoyed by the endless caste taboos, with their myriad rules governing every possible human action. Still, by the evening of their first day they could not resist heading east to visit India's most famous monument. As they passed through the gateway to the gardens, they were awed by the Taj Mahal's shimmering glow in the orange light of evening. According to Aloha, there were guards and "one lone native" but otherwise they had the monument to themselves. "I was spellbound by the beauty of the sepulchre," she wrote. "[A] monument to the love with which woman touched a man — the magic with which God touched an artist."[34]

They returned early the next morning, cameras in tow, selecting angles, planning for shadows cast by the sun, and once the camera arm was cranking, signalling to passersby that they should keep on walking and please ignore the camera. By the time they completed the day's filming, they were giddy with excitement. Walter, no doubt, was busy imagining what audiences back in the United States would say. Certainly there were dozens of showmen claiming to have travelled the world, but how many of them could *prove* it? With the exception of Burton Holmes, and Martin and Osa Johnson, no one else was constructing the same kind of ongoing, world-roving travelogue — and thanks to Agfa, the Wanderwell Expedition had all the film they could possibly need. "Through the heat of mid-afternoon I checked the exposed footage, wrapped cans in felt and stored them in the car for developing at Calcutta."[35]

✴

By mid-June the Wanderwell Expedition was nearly two-thirds of the way along their route to Calcutta and had arrived at the legendary city of Benares. Nestled on the banks of the Ganges River, Benares is the oldest city in India and one of the oldest continuously inhabited cities in the world.[36] In *Following the Equator* Mark Twain remarked on the city's age: "Benares is older than history, older than tradition, older even than legend, and looks twice as old as all of them put together."[37] He also noted that "the city is as unsanitary as it is sacred, and smells like the rind of the dorian."[38] When the Wanderwells arrived, they found Benares in the midst of an outbreak of bubonic plague.[39] At the university where they were to lecture, Aloha saw "a gutter rat the size of a cat" scurrying along. A sign tacked up at the entrance read, "Closed due to plague."[40]

Aloha loved Benares and was mesmerized by the city's confluence of religious traditions. According to Hindu lore, the city was created as the centre of the world by Shiva himself. More recently, Gautama Buddha gave his first sermon at nearby Sarnath in 528 BCE.[41] Jains, Muslims, and even Christians have had a historic presence in the city. The variety of religious expression combined with the city's astonishing age made Benares the most intriguing, and the most non-Westernized place they'd yet encountered. The pyramids at Giza were mystical, but they were monuments to the ancient dead. Benares was thronging with life.

> We stopped in the utter congestion of the banks of the sacred Ganges; miles of temples dedicated to the worship of its waters ... aware of the narrow creeds of our upbringing. As a youngster I began to perceive discrepancies, then gleaned from Cap's theories [about how] to observe not one true religion but many sources adopting and adapting from each other's prophets.... [I] no longer saw pagans or heathens, but obviously a Supreme Creator.[42]

※

By the third week of June, Aloha and Walter had left Benares and were moving through a parched landscape in the province of Bihar. Despite the heat, they had been lucky with the weather — the monsoon had not yet arrived. Hardly 80 miles from Benares, however, their luck ran out.

> The monsoon hit, flogging the parched soil with a vengeance, smacking the aluminum bonnet [and turning to] steam. The rain's advancing sheets blanked out the landscape.... Water splashed in. I got Kim [Aloha's monkey] into his nesting box and locked the unreachable clasp. I began shivering. My soaked goggles fogged, mud splashed up my shorts and slush oozed down my neck — Lord, the bitter cold![43]

Aloha and Walter drove as fast as possible, anxious to outrun the storm but the Sone River, when they reached it, was glutted with tumbling water and impossible to cross. They were stranded. With rain hammering down, they discussed their options: return to Benares, look for a village, or attempt to cross the railway bridge that spanned the river. Walter spotted some buildings at the distant edge of a field. He ran off to investigate and returned an hour later. "Fabulous news," he said.[44] The buildings were the home of a Scottish railway engineer and he'd invited them to wait out the storm inside.

A grateful Aloha and Walter were served a hot lunch and tea laced with Scotch. The railway engineer's wife was thrilled to have company and spoke almost non-stop. It was here they learned that a team of American flyers were due to land in Calcutta in a few days' time. Called the Douglas World Cruisers, the airmen were engaged in a race to become the first men to fly around the world. The engineer's wife found it curious that the Wanderwell Expedition should be attempting essentially the same feat by car. Wouldn't it be marvellous, she thought, if the two expeditions could meet? Walter's mind began whirling.

Despite their plans to visit Gaya and Asansol, Walter now proposed that they push straight through to Calcutta. Aloha agreed. When the rains lessened, the engineer organized a crew of workers to place lengths of wood across the railway bridge, moving and removing each plank as the cars progressed. After hours of effort, the cars crossed and, after a last check of their map and a thank you to their hosts, Aloha and Walter headed for Calcutta.

They flew through storms and wild temperature variations, charging across muddy plains and up rocky hills, pushing their stamina to the limit during "forty-eight hours of driving. No sleep, no dry rags."

The feat took a toll on Aloha. "I ached with wracking shivers, my fingers were seized to the wood steering."[45] The roads were often flooded and the intensity of the rain made it difficult to see. Aloha wrapped herself in a tarp and pressed on until they reached Bengal, where the rains and windy landscape gave way to soft sunlight slipping through dense jungle greenery. It was like waking into paradise. Kim squealed and chattered at the sounds of the jungle and Aloha spotted large monkeys swinging through the trees and racing alongside the cars.

Late on the second day, Cap signalled Aloha to pull over. He hobbled to her car and said he thought they could reach Calcutta by nightfall, another 60 miles or so, that is, if she could continue. "The shakes were so severe I couldn't open my mouth. With teeth clenched I shook my head up-down. . . .

It had to end." Over the next few hours the scenery continued to change. "The jungle became the old Trunk Road...villages. We drove belly-to-the-ground, sheets of water spewing out from wheels, drenching pedestrians."[46] They arrived in Calcutta just after dark on June 25, 1924, having covered more than 1,200 miles, a third of that on monsoon-battered roads. It was gruelling but they were in time to meet the American flyers. Amazingly, neither Aloha nor Walter gave themselves the luxury of realizing a world record had been set. A thoroughly exhausted seventeen-year-old Aloha Wanderwell had just become the first woman to drive solo across India.

✧

Local and international newspapers ran headlines such as "The Yanks are Coming!" In the London *Times*' "Telegrams in Brief," only the Wanderwell Expedition received mention, describing how "Captain and Miss Aloha Wanderwell...who are doing a world tour in a Ford motor-car, arrived in Calcutta from Allahabad yesterday. So far they have passed through 39 countries."[47]

The next afternoon, the pontoon aircraft of the Douglas World Cruisers settled on the Hooghly River, where they were collected by mechanics from the USS *Sicard*, an American naval destroyer that had shadowed the pilots' progress from Hong Kong to Rangoon, Burma, and onward to Calcutta. Mechanics removed the pontoons, installed landing gear, and brought the planes to a grassy area at the centre of town, where they were parked alongside the two Wanderwell cars.

A blitz of flashbulbs erupted as the two expeditions met for the first time. Walter cranked the camera while Aloha met the pilots.

They joined us on the sprawling, grassy Maidan Parade Grounds among acres and acres of people, press, cameras. A tall, young hero in cocked topi and grease-sodden overalls greeted officialdom. When I stepped up, the sight of a girl in khaki switched his haggard expression to a real grin.

"Guess you fellows are seeing something of the world down here all right. We don't see much up there," said Captain Lowell Smith, Commander of the Expedition, pilot of the DWC Chicago.[48]

Aloha meets the Douglas World Cruisers in Calcutta, India, 1924.
(L-R) Lowell Smith, Erik Nelson, Aloha, (unknown), and Leigh Wade.

Footage shows Aloha holding court with American pilots Lowell Smith, Erik Nelson, and Leigh Wade. Unit Nº III is parked beside one of the planes while Aloha leans back against the car with her elbows. This pose was typical when she appeared with men shorter than her. Other photographs show Nº III surrounded by naval servicemen and holding the American flag aloft, or what appear to be Captains Smith and Nelson dressed in tennis whites and topis,[49] leaning against Nº II and regarding a radiant Aloha.[50] The expression on the Americans' faces is a mixture of amusement, fascination, and lust.

The films and photographs are remarkable, not only for the events they capture but also for what they say about the fortitude and composure of a seventeen-year-old girl who had slept less than eight of the last sixty hours and still had reserves to parade for the cameras, offer humorous quips to the press, and entrance a band of intrepid pilots.

Aloha and members of the US Navy and the press with the
Douglas World Cruisers, Calcutta, India, 1924.

Decades later, an elderly Aloha would be interviewed for a documentary film about the Douglas World Cruisers. She recalled shaking hands with the dashing Captain Lowell Smith, who winced. "Careful," he said. "I fell off the fuselage yesterday and broke some ribs."[51] He had also contracted dysentery in Thailand, a secret he would keep until the Douglas World Cruisers landed in Seattle on September 28, by which time Aloha would be almost 1,300 miles away in the middle of a civil war.

TWO

WOULD YOU LIKE AN ADVENTURE NOW,
OR WOULD YOU LIKE TO HAVE YOUR TEA FIRST?

—PETER PAN

Advertising from the German distributor of Walk-Over-Shoe Company,
an expedition sponsor, circa 1925.

NINE

DO SVIDANIYA, TOVARISCH

BY JULY 1924, ALOHA AND WALTER had sailed south through the Bay of Bengal and into the Andaman Sea. They stopped on the island of Penang, just off the west coast of the Malay Peninsula and spent days sightseeing and sampling the island's stinky pickled eggs, papaya, and purple mangosteens. Aloha was enthralled: "I should love to live in Penang."[1] There wasn't much time to dally, however. If they were to get to America that year, they would have to make it to Japan before winter set in.

The sting of leaving Penang was soothed by the trip south along the peninsula and their arrival at the rarefied luxury of Singapore's Raffles Hotel, a colonial, fin de siècle exercise in exoticism and indulgence. Named after the founder of Singapore, the hotel was palatial, with high white columned walls, coffered ceilings, an opulent ballroom, and the most famous long bar in all Asia — where, legend has it, the last wild tiger in Singapore was shot (hiding under a table) and the Singapore sling cocktail was invented.

Walter told Aloha to enjoy Singapore's luxuries. China was next and he'd been warned that trying to cross China by car was absurd. What roads there were outside the cities and towns were virtually impassable. To quell his worries, Walter redoubled his promotional efforts. Within days, the Wanderwell cars were tattooed with company logos including Asiatic Oil, Ford, Agfa (again), and even the Bake Rite Bakery and Walk-Over-Shoe Company.[2]

Mail was waiting at Singapore's central post office, including a letter from Unit N° I. Walter's wife Nell was *still* in the United States and informed Walter that she planned to stay in the US as long as it took to earn the money required to pay for the "endurance countries." Aloha and Walter were appalled. A more anodyne letter came from Jarocki, who had made his way back to England. He was staying at the Seaman's Institute in London but said that he would soon be setting out again and could perhaps join them in Asia, "ocean is large — rendezvous is possible."[3]

While Walter looked after advertising arrangements, Aloha approached the local theatre tycoon, "Singapore" Joe Fisher. Like Madan in India, Fisher enjoyed a virtual monopoly of theatres in Singapore and could offer the Wanderwell Expedition excellent terms and promotion. He was intrigued by Aloha's brimming self-confidence, not to mention her tight pants, while she, in turn, was impressed by the Englishman's breezy, devil-may-care attitude and his occasionally ribald sense of humour. One evening he suggested Walter find himself a "Dutch nurse for the sultry Singapore nights." Eventually, he explained that a "Dutch nurse" is the local euphemism for "a bolster to separate one's legs for a cooler sleep."[4]

✿

After their Singapore run, the tour continued to Hong Kong and then on to Shanghai, where they docked at the mouth of the Yangtze River. While cargo was unloaded, Aloha and Walter sped to the central post office. There, a short clerk with oiled black hair and a starched white shirt stood shaking his head, chanting no, no, no, no. "There *had* been (mail), it seemed, but where the letters had gone to no one seemed to know." Aloha began to panic. Somehow, being beyond the reach of letters from home left her feeling deeply homesick. "All my grown-up self-sufficiency seemed to disappear."[5]

Back at the harbour, the cars had been cleared, but officials would not allow the rifles and ammunition — once again because the paperwork from Singapore had not been completed on the updated version of the appropriate form. Aloha was furious. "Embassies and consulates seem to want to move heaven and earth so that they may find a certain tint of paper on which to write a certain type of note; and then, maybe, the ink does not match." But just when things looked most dire, a visit to the British consulate turned things around. The consul was "a big, friendly man" accustomed to dealing with Chinese officialdom. "He calmed us down and, glory of glories, our mail was at the consular offices. Then he called his wife and she made a tea party for me and the newspaper men came in."[6] As had happened elsewhere, enthusiastic press coverage, combined with impressive corporate sponsorship, worked its transforming magic: obstinate bureaucrats became gracious hosts and the Wanderwell Expedition was permitted to enter China, guns and all.

Despite the success, Aloha was depressed. Interminable bureaucracy and the tedium of secretarial work and promotional negotiations made her wonder what she was doing. Why had she come to China and why was everything so backwards, so primitive, so foreign?

A little culture shock was inevitable, perhaps, but it was unfortunate that it should happen in Shanghai, because the city was *exactly* the kind of vital, careening city that Aloha had pined for in Nice and Geneva — "an exotic stew of Jewish opium traders, Chinese compradors and Viennese dancing girls."[7] When Aldous Huxley arrived on the scene shortly after Aloha, he was similarly wowed by the city's intense character. "In no city, West and East, have I ever had such an impression of dense, rank, richly clotted life."[8]

But Aloha could not enjoy it. Of the city she noted only the "noisy, narrow streets, over-crowded with smiling Chinese, slinking along single file." Even the glamorous aspects of expedition life had, for the moment, lost their attraction. She lamented the "endless society dances that keep the younger generation out of bed until the hour of dawn and at which there are *always* a scarcity of girls."[9]

※

They arrived in Tientsin (now Tianjin) in August, nearly one month after leaving India. Like Shanghai, Tientsin contained European "concessions" or trading areas administered by various European powers. Each concession contained its own prison, school, barracks, and hospital. Traders living in their concession were subject to their own national laws and made the city a kind of administrative Epcot Center. Tientsin's buildings were a blend of Chinese, British, French, Austrian, German, Belgian, Japanese, and Russian, but like any trade centre, the city's primary feature was its customs agents.

We resorted to a routine device — a statement from someone of status, viz. "To Whom it May Concern: On this date Captain Wanderwell called on me. He states that…(whatever the impasse)…is essential to his progress toward…." This pompous declaration [is] followed by status signature and STAMP. British consuls are excellent at this open sesame — spoken of as bumf…. In our jargon, we referred to these letters as "This is to certify what has been certified is certified."[10]

Aloha's mood recovered and she spent three days lecturing while Walter restocked supplies from various corporate sponsors: film, gasoline, and "longer tow lines." She was beginning to look forward to a triumphant arrival in America.

On their second day, Walter burst into her hotel room and announced that he had "just seen a real humdinger! Going down the main stem — she came spinning past in a rickshaw. *You should've seen those silk gams* stretched out behind that coolie. I want you to meet her — wanna see if you like her. Think she'd be great stuff. She's Latvian, speaks Mandarin, and Russian!" Aloha closed the book in which she'd been writing and began to laugh. "Cap was of that dashing breed; his enthusiasm genuine, dazzled by his own capacity for zest: a good audience, an open road, fine music, a new theory; encountering an unusual female." She agreed to meet the humdinger and quite agreed with Walter. "With or without the reclining rickshaw, the silk clad legs were perfection."[11] They made arrangements to meet the girl in Peiping (now Beijing), where she would officially join the tour under the name "Olga Tomska."

The local car sales agency sponsoring them insisted that the Wanderwell Expedition make use of their own guide, a husky, square-jawed fellow named Jurov who had, the previous season, made his own trip via motorcycle over "what was jokingly called 'the Way to Peiping.'"[12] He was to accompany them through rural China, leaving the expedition just short of Peiping.

So they set out with Jurov, a Russian national who turned out to be "the best piece of advice given us in China," and not just because he spoke several Chinese dialects.[13] The road north was a series of connected mud pits, so to escape the boggy landscape, Jurov directed the cars to drive atop ancient irrigation dykes where the ground was dry, though even here the going was slow. Chinese peasants believed that an auspicious burial site would bring prosperity to succeeding generations, and a raised area was considered especially propitious so the dykes were laden with cemeteries. "At places we had difficulty in passing, for some of the coffins lay open to the weather, and the skeleton was to be seen inside."[14]

The cars became stuck regularly on the muddy slopes and Jurov would hail labourers from nearby paddies to assist. It was Aloha's first close interaction with the rural Chinese and she found them "to a man handsome in their friendly expression." The experience marked a widening of her worldview and a softening of her sympathies. Once, she fetched a box of chocolates from her car and offered them to the labourers, many of them children. No one stepped forward. Jurov attempted to explain what the chocolate was, but still no one would accept. Aloha grasped one mud-smeared boy by the ear and shoved a chocolate between his teeth. "Momentary terror struck, then glee." Instantly, the others held out their hands.

Aloha enjoyed people she encountered, but she was shocked by what she called "the horror of their emaciation," recounting "signs of indescribable suffering, patient endurance," before deciding that the Chinese land could yield "but mere existence."[15]

❁

The expedition finally arrived at the gates of Peiping. Aloha recalled making a bet with Walter in Paris that she would be the first to pass through the city gates.[16] When their entrance was blocked by soldiers whose faces bore a "half asleep expression," they relied again on old tricks. Aloha smiled and offered pamphlets (to no effect) while Walter leapt from his car and strode imperiously towards the soldiers, saluting and pointing forward, shouting the name Wu Peifu, the general of the Zhili clique who, in 1924, controlled the city and its surrounding territory. When the soldiers parted, Aloha hit the gas and rolled through. The stunt caused just enough confusion for Walter to jump back into N° II and follow her though. Aloha had won the bet.

The largest city in China, Peiping did not exactly live up to its nickname, "Paris of the East." Poor sanitation meant frequent epidemics, including the plague, smallpox, and scarlet fever. The biggest killer, however, was pneumonia, made worse by the Gobi Desert dust storms that sliced through the city several times a year. One American soldier stationed there recalled that being caught in these storms meant that "every breath you took was like inhaling shards of glass."[17]

Despite the dust and dangers, however, Aloha wrote glowingly about the city.

> Peiping was swarming with humanity: rickshaw coolies; men and women and children; caravans of Mongolians with camels coming in from the Gobi desert; and everywhere soldiers — mercenaries, we were told. Yet this center of China got me by the heart strings. I do not know why, more than do many others who, once they live in China, do not wish to leave...maybe to the Occidental it is the pull of centuries piled one on top of the other which constitutes the fascination.[18]

Aloha was an instant celebrity, snatching headlines and winning invitations from the local elite, thanks in part to the city's embrace of motor racing. The Wanderwell Expedition was part of what had become a tradition of endurance races from Paris to Peiping (and vice versa) that began with a challenge issued by the French newspaper *Le Matin* in January 1907. The route was first successfully driven by an Italian team, finishing in August 1907, and by 1924 numerous cars had completed the drive between the two capitals — through the Gobi Desert and across Siberia to Moscow, then through Europe to Paris. As yet, none had come overland from India, and certainly not with a seventeen-year-old girl behind the wheel.

Aloha gave lectures in schools and theatres around the city and soon befriended two daughters of the former Chinese ambassador to Belgium. The girls loved to speak French, and Aloha was thrilled to have female guides through the city. Walter, meanwhile, was busy planning the trip through newly Soviet Russia. Mukden (now known as Shenyang), in the northern province of Manchuria, was the last station where they might secure a visa, but there was war in the area and success was far from certain. The problem was solved when an embassy clerk mentioned that a high-ranking member of the Russian foreign office, Lev Karakhan, was in Peiping, and they succeeded in getting their visas there.

As promised, Olga Tomska arrived on the scene and was fitted with a Wanderwell uniform. A white Russian, she was once the wife of a tsarist officer, and after her husband's death she was sent to a concentration camp with hundreds of other widows. "Olga's infant son died... (and she told me) that she had bought indulgences with her body from a Commandant who had visited the starving creatures in the camp, and so had managed an escape to China."[19]

At the close of an afternoon lecture, Aloha was surprised by the arrival of a former Wanderwell crew member. Not Jarocki, as they had expected, but Benno, the lisping German who had been scouting the world for a potential Jewish homeland. Dishevelled and awkward as ever, his face was, nonetheless, "bright with *Glaube dem Leben*." Photographs show him with Walter, Aloha, and the cars in front of the imperial palace. His presence also explains why there are suddenly more photographs showing Walter and Aloha. As Aloha put it, "He'll carry the camera gear instead of me!"[20]

With two new assistants, they motored north to where the monotonous dusty plains erupted into dramatic vistas of steep mountain slopes and deep green forest. Then came a valley bisected by a massive, sand-coloured structure, more like a raised single-track road than a wall, which snaked over the body of land like the spine of some sleeping giant. At Kalgan (now known as Zhangjiakou), they drove the cars onto the Great Wall of China. Spectacular film footage shows Aloha behind the wheel of N° III, crawling slowly up a steep portion, ascending towards the camera. In the bottom of the frame we can see Walter's long shadow, furiously cranking the camera arm.

❈

Peiping's English-language daily, the *North China Star*, ran a retrospective of the Wanderwell visit and wished them Godspeed to Russia. One column over, a dispatch from Shanhaiguan (where the expedition was headed) reported infantry attacks and the arrival of Italian-trained Chinese aviators. Foreigners were fleeing. The region's warlord, Chang Tso-lin (Zhang Zuolin), had recently declared Manchuria independent and, in co-operation with Japan, asserted control over the area. Just as the Wanderwell Expedition was about to set out, Chang launched an attack on northern China in what turned out to be the start of the Second Zhili-Fengtian War. "American and

British gunboats were steaming into Tientsin to evacuate nationals, and in Peiping the exodus toward Nanking was foreshadowed. On our last afternoon in Peiping, I went to a temple and paid homage to a marble god of war. I thought I ought to."[21]

Although Aloha had not yet seen war, she had no romantic ideas about it. Armed conflict had snatched her stepfather. She had seen the fields of endless white crosses. She had dropped coins into the hats of mangled veterans begging in the train stations of Europe. And if she held hope that Chinese war might be less vicious, she would have been corrected by the "supposedly illegal" postcards given to her in Peiping depicting the methods of justice applied in the north: a decapitation by cutlass, captured mid-swing, blood shooting from the neck;[22] a "flatbed wagon (with) fifteen or more bodies flopped crosswise...the arms still lashed to the frame from which they must have hung. All tortured, horrendously mutilated, dripping."[23] The images came from towns along their intended route. While Aloha "hoped the pictures were very out of date," the grim news was enough to make Benno reconsider. He would, he decided, find his own way across the Pacific. Olga, though, would not be deterred. She was determined to get to Shenyang, no matter the dangers. Aloha made it clear from the outset that *she* was the senior member on the expedition. "We exchanged a firm hand-shake contracting our alliance.... What becomes yours is yours...what is mine is *mine*."[24] Undoubtedly, Aloha was referring to Walter.

✿

A memorandum from the Asiatic Petroleum Company suggests that the Wanderwell Expedition did not proceed north by car but, instead, covered the more than 400 miles along the Mukden railroad by train.

Dear Captain Wanderwell,
   I hear your train does not leave before 11 a.m. so I am sending you a letter addressed to our Chinese agent at Mukden, who will deliver your requirements free. In case you go by road from Mukden you can obtain supplies at [several names given] from our Chinese agents. Just ask for the "Ya His Ya Ho You Kungsze."[25]

The letter seems to contradict Aloha's claim that she drove the distance, though it is possible that the note, dated September 20, 1924, was referring only to the *supplies* the expedition was shipping ahead, as they had done throughout India. Still, it was a dangerous journey. Within three days, the area north of Peiping was ruled by Chang Tso-lin. His forces, known as the Fengtien Army, were engaged in pitched battles with the Zhili soldiers of Peiping warlord General Wu Peifu.[26] There were high casualties on both sides and especially to the local civilians. After reaching the local train depot, the expedition needed to cross a no-man's land into the state of Manchuria proper. Aloha and Walter were soon taking photographs gruesome enough to rival the postcards purchased in Peiping. "Bodies lay sprawled on the ground in advanced stages of putrefaction and the stench nauseated us." One photograph shows a peasant woman face down at the edge of a field. Her hat and basket rest neatly beside her. When Aloha asked Walter what he thought might have killed "the bodies which (lay) apparently unmutilated," he responded laconically, "'Gas . . . or small arms fire' . . . but Cap did not want to talk of what he had seen."[27]

In Shenyang, their cars were halted by Fengtien soldiers. "The men were quite polite but they rode in the car with us and directed our progress." Unsure whether they were being escorted or arrested, they drove to a sprawling European-style house, where they were presented to an imposing Englishman. "He wore khaki shorts, a neat white shirt, and a pale blue sleeveless pull-over sweater. The right sleeve of his shirt hung limp and empty at his side." Their host introduced himself as Sutton and told them he was "sort of running the show." The introduction was hardly necessary since everyone already knew who he was.

I stared at General Sutton open-mouthed, frankly full of curiosity. This was the famed — or notorious — General Sutton, depending on how one cared to consider those things . . . . Stories about him were fabulous; he was accused of inciting the Chinese Civil War, some said he was Chang Tso Lin's right-hand man, and others said he controlled an arsenal in Mukden. I knew him as a most charming and generous host.[28]

English born in 1884, Sutton was an engineer who built railways in Argentina and in Mexico prior to the First World War. He lost his right arm at the Battle of Gallipoli (and came to be nicknamed "One-Arm" Sutton). An inventor, adventurer, and relentless fortune seeker, Sutton had obtained rights to the manufacture of the Stokes mortar in North America and the Far East. After initially offering his services to Wu Peifu, Sutton struck a deal with Chang Tso-lin to produce 600 mortars and 60,000 projectiles for the staggering sum of US $125,000 (now equivalent to roughly US $1.7 million). Before long, he was in charge of the Mukden Stokes Mortar and Ammunition Factory, producing 200,000 rounds of ammunition per day, along with rifles, machine guns, hand grenades, and various customized versions of the Stokes mortar, including a gun that threw an eight-pound shell and could easily be disassembled for transport.[29] Though undoubtedly a dangerous man (with a reputation for moodiness and eccentricity), Aloha was thrilled to be under his protection. "General Sutton relieved our anxiety, and I had infinite faith in this ex-officer of the British Army. Sutton put them up in his rambling house and asked them to show their films at the Mukden Foreign Club.

Inevitably, Walter spoke to Sutton about his idea for an international police. He had hardly mouthed the words "League of Nations" before Sutton guffawed. Walter pressed on, asking Sutton what he thought of an "all nations fire department to extinguish wars *before* the conflagration."[30] Sutton's response was characteristically circumspect. On the one hand he applauded Wanderwell's enthusiastic efforts to "put us sons of bitches out of work." On the other hand, he offered the expedition custom-made pistol belts and a tour of the arsenal and proving ground. Film and photographs show Aloha and Olga in leather helmets, loading Stokes mortars and then covering their ears against the noise. Sutton was a good host but "somewhere was the warning: Don't overdo your stay and don't brag about the arsenal."[31]

The expedition spent nearly a month in Shenyang, securing a treasure trove of film and lolling among the luxuries offered by the well-paid general. Sutton himself would stay in China long enough to see his benefactor defeat Wu Peifu and conquer almost all of China, thanks largely to an enormous arsenal of Sutton-enhanced Stokes mortars. By mid-September martial law had been declared in Shanghai, and cars (private and foreign) were being requisitioned to the war effort.[32] In the north, the expedition not only enjoyed the protection of a warlord's chief of staff but also were guaranteed safe passage and the continued use of their car.

※

By the time they were moving again it was late October and temperatures were plummeting. Aloha's monkey, Kim, was miserable and mangy looking. He often tried to crawl inside Aloha's Polish jacket for warmth but spent most of the 300-mile journey north shivering in the little sweater Aloha had knitted for him.

They arrived in Harbin near dark. A light snow was falling and the rail yards seemed deserted. Olga and Walter set out to find accommodations while Aloha waited with the cars, still loaded on the train gondola. Since Aloha spoke neither Russian nor Chinese, it only made sense that Olga should be the one to accompany Walter into town. But Aloha was far from happy. "Besides being cold, hungry, I was seething because HE has taken HER off to town 'to make arrangements.'"[33] With echoes of van der Ray, it's clear Aloha did not trust Walter and Olga to return without first testing the bedsprings.

As the expedition readied itself for the final 300-mile push to Vladivostok in Russia, Olga announced that she would be staying behind. Aloha provides two versions of Olga's departure. In the first, she boarded a train back to Mukden, presumably to pursue whatever mission had brought her north from Shanghai. In the second, Olga was offered a job by a member of the European colony and would stay in Harbin. Both accounts agree, however, that Aloha was sad to see her go, describing her as charming, engaging, and "a wonderful sidekick." Her suspicions about Olga and Walter were either forgotten or forgiven.

The expedition headed southeast towards Vladivostok. They stayed close to the local railway line, the Chinese Eastern Railway. Walter had received assurances from "the railway's General Manager, Mr. Ostroumoff, that the weekly freight to the border was guarded by an armoured car and would stop at our signal for help."[34] The line was also regularly patrolled and this, together with the goodwill of local military forces (secured through "patronage" payments to Chang Tso-lin's forces), made the trip through the rugged landscape of eastern Manchuria less dangerous than it might have been. Aloha was glad to be behind the wheel again, although she found the landscape dreary and the bugs relentless. She was also lonely without Olga and depressed by the area's intense poverty.

> Once we boarded a ferry and small boys punted us to the further side. We ate eggs, the muddy water stank, and chunks of thin ice floated in it.... Cap broke the shell of an egg and a boiled chicken popped to view. Cap was awfully sick, but the hunger-ridden eyes of our ferry lads begged for the boiled dreadfulness, so we bestowed largesse of all the eggs we had left.[35]

At Grodekovo, the Russian border guards were stiff and formal, though Aloha smiled to notice that their black uniform shirts were trimmed with pink. Walter's Russian was rudimentary and rusty and soon he and Aloha were reduced to flamboyant arm gestures, punctuated by shouts of "Tovarisch!" (comrade). For good measure they threw in some enthusiastic nodding and a generous helping of, "Ok, ok!" It was enough. Guards directed them to a timber cabin that served as the customs house. "We had no trouble; I took out the Soviet courtesy flags we carried[36] and put them up beside the Stars and Stripes which looked incongruous. This no doubt this was a breach of diplomatic etiquette, for our country did not then recognize the Soviet government."[37]

If Soviet Russia had welcomed the Wanderwell Expedition, the weather did not. "Cap bought me a pair of fur mittens to wear over my woollen gloves" but "there was an almost continuous sleet that cut my face and burned like fire."[38] The upside to these trials, however, were the stops in the fire-warmed inns along the way, where grandmothers delivered fresh loaves of black bread, soup, eggs, and sour cream. Food had never tasted so good.

Aloha is made an honorary colonel in the Nihinsky Regiment of the Soviet Army, Vladivostok, USSR, 1924.

Vladivostok was only 100 miles from the border at Grodekovo but it took Walter and Aloha two days of slow progress over rolling, barren landscape before they glimpsed the coastal town. There wasn't much to see. Founded in 1880, Vladivostok's real growth had only happened since 1903, when the Trans-Siberian Railway was completed. Streets were largely empty, save for a few wandering naval officers. Without an interpreter or guide, Aloha and Walter managed to find their pre-arranged lodgings at the improbably named Hotel Versailles.[39]

David Abramovich Zimmerman was the pre-revolutionary director of Vladivostok's harbour facilities and had owned stakes in numerous regional enterprises, from ships to salt to gold to grain. "The Bolsheviks had so far spared his life because no other port expert was available." Over supper at their dilapidated lodgings, the Zimmermans pressed Aloha and Walter for news. "Chère Mademoiselle, believe me, we are overjoyed to have you among us. Tell us of beloved Paris...Nice."[40]

Aloha relished the luxuries the Zimmermans were able to offer, and Walter was grateful for their insights into Vladivostok's geography and politics, learning where to go, where *not* to go, and even arranging for a French-trained hairdresser to cut Aloha's hair. As helpful as the Zimmermans were, however, associating with them was not without its dangers. Walter and Aloha soon became aware that street police had begun watching them. Walter responded by paying a visit to the local police commissar and handing out souvenirs to officers they met.

One afternoon when Aloha was in her room at the hotel and Walter was out attending to business, a "soldier entered, saluted and began shouting—assuming, as usual, that shouting would make his message understood." He handed her a letter stamped with a hammer and sickle and indicated that she should follow him, making a steering motion with his arms. Once in No III, he directed her in a familiar direction. "Good Lord! We were heading for the execution grounds!" When they arrived Aloha saw an entire regiment lined up, together with a brass band. The soldier motioned for her to get out of the car. "My knees were weak as a short dark officer stepped from the line." He addressed her in Russian, then switched to German, which Aloha could at least understand. The officer announced that while the Third Nihinsky Regiment could not yet organize an official reception for such important visitors, they wished to "accolade you for being the first Demoiselle to pilot a motorcar to Siberia. We wish to present to you the title Honorary Oberst (colonel)... [My] knees were ready to collapse. I glimpsed No II racing up." Cap leapt from the car and set up the camera and tripod. What followed were long scenes of Russian soldiers marching past the camera, occasionally pulling crooked faces, followed by the brass band, several "very small boys and two dogs." The scene would become a staple in the Wanderwell film shows for years, amazing "prejudiced global audiences with the whimsy display."[41]

Aloha's precious gold Russian cuff, presented to her in Vladivostok, USSR, in 1924. In 2001 the bracelet was valued by PBS's *Antiques Roadshow* as being worth at least $20,000.

✸

October 13, 1924, was Aloha's eighteenth birthday. She spent a quiet morning in her hotel room, writing in her diary, and worrying that despite her many experiences she was growing old before she had accomplished anything remarkable.

That night, the Zimmermans threw a farewell dinner for the Wanderwells and did their best to cheer up Aloha. They extended their sympathies on the occasion of her birthday, "not for the accomplishment, 'but because you are so young and so *far* from home, child.'" After dinner, Mrs. Zimmerman announced that they had a little memento for Aloha on the occasion of her visit and her birthday. "From a basement cache of their once handsome heirloom collection, they brought a priceless slave bracelet wrought generations ago of gold from their Arctic trading. Mine to wear forever." Aloha was dumbfounded and attempted to refuse, but Mrs. Zimmerman insisted, saying, "We exist only at their (the Bolsheviks [*sic*]) pleasure."[42] If discovered, such extravagances would surely have been confiscated and she preferred that the bracelet should find a new life in the distant world that she herself would probably never see. The imposing clasp-style bracelet was over two inches wide, cast of solid eighteen karat gold with various Asian motifs, including birds, flowers, and bamboo. It became a staple of Aloha's professional attire.

☼

Aloha described her last glimpse of Vladivostok as "the sad panorama of a ghost city wrapped in its winding sheet of driving snow."[43] Bureaucratic nonsense had almost left them stranded in Russia but some last-minute forgeries had gotten them safely on board the Holland China Company cargo ship. After a stormy two-day crossing to Tsuruga Bay, they were made to wait by white-gloved Japanese officials who interrogated them, suspicious especially of their time in Siberia. They would not be allowed to land and would be required to wait on board while official permission was sought.

Japan in 1924 was suspicious of its neighbours. The current emperor, Yoshihito, was mentally ill. As a result, his son, the future emperor Hirohito, was made Prince Regent in November 1921, ushering in an era of rapid militarization. In this atmosphere of uncertainty, foreign visitors were greeted with intense scepticism. After three days of waiting, permission arrived.

Free at last, Aloha and Walter found travelling in Japan was easier than in China or Siberia, with fine weather and a wider availability of gasoline. They also enjoyed a string of happy coincidences that made their stay easier. During a fuel stop on the second day, they were astonished to meet a "man in a brown kimono, taller than usual Japanese" offering his hand, Western style. "Have you folks really come all the way from the States as your sign says?" he asked. "I was born in Nevada."[44] He explained that his elderly father had been repatriated following the Asian Exclusion Act, so he followed along. He invited them to his home for refreshments, their first experience of a genuine Japanese home and a tea ceremony.

Their luck held in Kobe, where their barely functioning cars were overhauled by the Sale & Frazar Company, importers for several makes of American automobiles. The representative, whom Aloha called variously G.F. Drummond or MacDonald, was eager to impress them, though it's unlikely they knew why. Following the Tokyo earthquake of 1923 that had wiped out the city's tram lines, the city had placed a massive order for one thousand Ford truck chassis. As Ford's sole importer, Sale & Frazar was eager to make sure their client was happy, and as far as they were concerned the Wanderwell Expedition were emissaries of Ford himself. Walter and Aloha stayed at Drummond's elaborate home, where Aloha's first indulgence, as always, was to take a bath. "Ecstatically I hummed, 'Nothing could be finer than to be in Carolina....'" The next morning Aloha discovered she had committed a cultural blunder. In Japan people did not immerse themselves but stood on a bamboo grate and poured the water over their heads with a ladle. By jumping in and then draining the tub after her bath, Aloha had "deprived the household of their nightly tub soak — the compliment of 'first water' had been paid *me*."[45]

In Osaka they were booked for a week of engagements at a theatre on the Dōtonbori, Osaka's famous avenue of theatres. The manager, a tall man in gold-rimmed spectacles, observed that the daily commute could be tiring — hotels were far away and the streets narrow and congested. Why not sleep on the theatre's rooftop? When Walter and Aloha went to take a look, they found that "atop the fifth floor of the theatre...was a magical landscape." There was a bedroom with sliding glass doors, which "revealed a perfect miniature pond rimmed by mountains, bonsai pine and maple forest."[46] There was even a cascading brook. Dōtonbori was a former pleasure district, which could explain such accommodations, but it made for a memorable stay.

For Aloha, who had arrived in Japan once again exhausted and depressed, the country was more than she'd hoped for. She found the culture familiar enough to be comfortable and foreign enough to remain exotic. The people were friendly and refreshingly polite, but most importantly they were enthusiastic about the expedition — Walter could not print their souvenir pamphlets and postcards fast enough.

The enthusiastic mood was shared by distant sponsoring companies.

The agent for the Berlin Anilin & Company called, enthusiastic over their office reports from Shanghai, ready with 3000 [feet of] negative and 3000 positive, which meant we could print North China and Siberia immediately (and) have footage to shoot Japan and Hawaii.[47]

By the time they reached Kyoto, newspapers were flooded with stories about the American adventurers, including a near-death experience. While crossing a wooden bridge at the city's outskirts, something went badly awry. An article in the Japan *Times and Mail* described how "Miss Wanderwell's car skidded through a railing and hung within inches of plunging her to her death."[48] Photographs show that the article was not exaggerating, though they also reveal an interesting detail not mentioned by Aloha or the newspapers: it was *Nº II* that hung at the precipice. Either Aloha and Walter had traded cars or it was *Walter* who drove his car through the bridge railing — and if that's the case, it sheds light on what was considered "good PR optics" and whose reputation most needed protecting. Walter could not risk appearing inept. Events in Geneva and elsewhere (as Aloha would soon discover) had already done enough damage to his image.

No shows were scheduled for Kyoto. Instead they visited temples and took footage, much as they'd done in Benares. "Our cameras were out filming the people at art centres, exquisite parks, palaces. I had longed to see the Goddess of Mercy Temple, one thousand and one hand-carved gilded statues, and to know their admirers." Both Aloha and Walter were increasingly attracted to the quiet beauty of the Buddhist religious expression they'd seen throughout Asia. At the Higashi Honganji Temple Aloha stood alongside other worshippers, each waiting to pull a hemp cord that tolled an enormous bell. "I touched softly too, thrilled to its deep vibration."[49] For Aloha, this was what travel was all about: sharing meaningful experiences with people of other cultures.

Expedition Unit Nº II loses traction and almost goes off a rickety bridge near Kyoto, Japan, 1924.

While in Kyoto Walter and Aloha heard that the Prince Regent Hirohito was about to pass by their restaurant. Walter decided to film the prince's passage from a porch overlooking the hotel entrance. "A black limousine pulled to the steps, (an) equerry stepped out holding the door for H.I.H. Regent Emperor Hirohito [*sic*]. Cap cranking, the Regent mounted the landing. Cap and I saluted. In natural reflex, His Imperial Highness IN-CLINED HIS HOMBURG TO US and with a vague smile, vanished."[50] They soon discovered that it was considered *lèse-majesté* to view royalty from an elevated position, punishable by imprisonment or worse. However, because the Prince Regent had positively acknowledged their presence with a tip of his hat, it was as good as a Royal Warrant.[51]

On arriving in Tokyo they were engulfed by flashbulbs and the shouted questions of journalists. A single tip of the hat, it turned out, had sparked

Aloha and Walter in Japan, 1924.

national attention. Suddenly, everyone wanted to know the Wanderwell story. In most cities, they tried to reserve their epic tales until endorsements had been signed, but "there was no way to escape [or] to save it for the hotel boost." A letter from Henry Ford's right-hand man, E.G. Liebold, was waiting for them at the Tokyo post office, telling them that Mr. Ford would be pleased to accept "the first Ford car which had encircled the world," adding that "I assume that you will wish to present the same to him for exhibition in the Museum, *without any restrictions or conditions*."[52] Walter was thrilled. This would ensure them a permanent place in American history and increase the credibility of the entire Wanderwell enterprise.

After so much attention, sponsorship was easy. They stayed at Tokyo's Imperial Hotel (designed by Frank Lloyd Wright), where they were treated to a publicity dinner. Later, Aloha strolled into the Nippon Theatre, then one of Tokyo's foremost venues. Standing in the manager's office, "He and I looked out below on the crowded car. I said jubilantly, 'We can give you five days, Mr. Ohta, two performances each. The fee is $1,000 US."[53] Mr. Ohta accepted immediately. It was the highest fee they had ever charged, twenty times the rate Walter had negotiated in Osaka.

✤

By mid-November the cars had been loaded onto the *Taiyo Maru*, a luxurious steamer belonging to the Nippon Yusen Kaisha (NYK) line. A few days before their departure, Aloha nipped by the American consulate in order to secure a visa for the United States but was shocked by the outcome. "It never occurred to me that I could be refused a visa by Great Britain's closest ally.... The wind was knocked out of my sails, only momentarily." She later claimed to have solved the problem by simply approaching another official whose "morning coffee *had* agreed with him."[54] The paper record shows a rather different solution. Aloha came to the United States on Walter's visa, listed not as his employee or even his sister but, for the first time, as his wife. It was a risky deception.

Walter and Aloha with her pet monkey, Kim, in Agra, India, June 1924.

TEN

MAHALO ALOHA

THE HARBOUR AT HONOLULU was austere. Instead of palm trees and quaint thatched huts, there were military warehouses encircled by wide stretches of gravel and tarmac, a few scrubby bushes and clouds of mosquitoes. It was their last stop before California and, already glittering in her imagination, *Hollywood*. It was November 25, 1924,[1] and Hawaii was the first English-speaking place Aloha had been to since leaving England in 1919. America in the 1920s was like nothing Aloha had ever experienced. Honolulu locals frequented strange restaurants where "you drive up, sit in your car and are served — called a 'Drive-In.'"[2] They also ate oddball foods, like ice cream "floats" or minced beef in a bun or mild sausage in a roll, served by waiters called "soda-jerks" in restaurants called "greasy spoons." Most surprising though was that groceries sold only *tinned* pineapple. To find fresh, one had to travel to the plantations where the watchman might surreptitiously sneak a few unprocessed fruits.

If Aloha found Hawaii strange, the Hawaiians found Aloha equally bizarre. Disbelieving crowds asked about her name — they had never heard "the lovely word used in such a manner." Newspapers were equally incredulous, refusing to believe their stories of adventure until they produced their scrapbook of newspaper clippings and photographs. A barrage of press coverage ensued with every major paper running lavish, and in many cases multiple, positive stories — they were particularly amused that Hawaii should be included in an around-the-world *automobile* race. Their success boded well for their arrival on the mainland.

Still, shortly before sailing on to the United States, the possibility of trouble arrived in the form of a misdirected letter. According to Aloha's memoirs, the missive arrived for Walter at the Honolulu post office, except that it was actually addressed to a third party and had been sent with a Wanderwell Expedition return address. Naturally, with Walter and Aloha front-page news, the letter was forwarded to them. The letter was from Nell.

Had a letter from Walter the other day and he said he was going to Shanghai from India and expects to be there in a month or two. He also says he will be back in the States soon and I sure don't like that. I would much rather have the ocean between us...

Something happened in Houston, Texas...I met a wonderful man, Oh! How I fell and it's not over yet, I never knew I could fall so, so much in love.[3]

Aloha notes that she gave the letter to Walter, and that he was "a little sad about her wager attitude." Whether the letter actually existed, or whether it was yet another of Aloha's "massaging" of the facts is impossible to say, but her comments may have provided a convenient explanation for coming events.

❀

Aloha and Walter boarded the SS *Shinyo Maru* on December 30, 1924, and spent the six-day crossing planning their adventures on the US mainland. It was clear now that no World's Fair would occur in time to declare a winner in the Million Dollar Wager, and it was far from certain that Unit N° I would surrender its assets, including footage Walter had sent to Nell to assist with *her* film lectures. They decided to tour California before heading to Detroit, where they would declare the race ended and donate N° II to Henry Ford's museum. With luck, there would be lots of pictures in papers, some clamouring crowds, and many packed theatres. Or perhaps Hollywood would make them famous first.

Aloha Wanderwell arrived in California on January 5, 1925. As usual, Walter had alerted the local press well in advance. And indeed, despite the slow, dull fog that oozed over the harbour, reporters were on the boat before it had even docked, arriving by tug and then fanning out to find stories of interest. When the third reporter asked Aloha to spell her name, she realized that these were beat reporters — none had heard of the expedition and it was only after seeing their publicity material that one fellow pulled out his notepad. Aloha recounted the expedition's adventures, or tried to. She hardly knew where to start — perhaps the trip through Egypt, or the war in China, maybe their success in Tokyo? She said that travel had opened her eyes to the world's fabulous diversity, that she'd experienced so many wonderful cultures along the way: Slavic, Bedouin, Malayan, Indian, Chinese. But here she was cut off. The reporter wanted *just the facts, ma'am*.

> "How many times was the car repaired? How many miles have you covered? How much would it have cost if someone financed the trip from the start?" Momentarily, my enthusiasm was dashed and my high hopes shattered. I tried to explain that money could not purchase the experiences we had had. The young man was not interested in that; he didn't care a hoot where we had been nor what we had seen.[4]

Aloha and Walter trudged down the gangplank, through the gloomy fog, and into the customs office where an official held out his hand for passports and papers.

> Cap proudly produced the yellow clearance papers issued at the start of the round the world enterprise. I hated to give them up, for those pieces of paper had gone through many an international vicissitude. Often they had been dried out after a plunge through a river; they were mislaid once in India, and we thought they were lost.[5]

The clerk, however, was "unsentimental about its frayed edges, blurred purple ink and speared it down on a pin file." He asked if they had anything to declare. Aloha's mention of Kim, the monkey, produced the first glimmer of interest from the clerk. She opened her sheepskin jacket to show Kim clinging inside. "Hmm. Now some pets, no, but monkeys don't carry disease. Thirty-five cents please."[6]

✿

Aloha sat in their room at the Whitcomb Hotel, sipping coffee and searching the San Francisco newspapers. For half an hour she found nothing. Then, in the "Ships and Shipping" section of the Tuesday evening *Oakland Tribune*, page 29, she spotted a two-column inch notice entitled "World Travelers Ending Up Journey." The blurb mentioned "Captain Walter Wanderwell and his sister, Aloha Wanderwell, are planning today the last lap of a 36,000-mile journey during which they covered 39 countries." After explaining that the couple were heading for Detroit, the article concluded by noting that "'Wandy,' a pet monkey picked up by the travelers in India, attracted nearly as much attention as the hardy adventurers." Aloha looked over the page, noting the arrangement of stories. Their story appeared near the bottom of the page, after more urgent notices such as "Norwegian Ship Loads Fruit for Scandinavia" and "Lumber Carriers Are Busy Loading."

Finally, bigger stories did appear, including a piece in the *Los Angeles Times* announcing the arrival of Captain Wanderwell.

Traveler Faces Charges
    Globe-Trotter Held in Bay City for Investigation as White Slavery Suspect, Long in Police Eye.[7]

Walter and Aloha had been arrested by the San Francisco police after a tip from Agent Ralph Colvin at the Department of Justice. According to the *Los Angeles Times* story, Walter was charged with white slavery under the infamous Mann Act, legislation originally designed to prevent forced prostitution but used in this case because the authorities believed Aloha to be a minor. He was also charged with impersonation of a government officer. The newspaper article further stated that Walter was "the subject of a voluminous file in Federal offices, extending back to 1917" that investigated Wanderwell's false name and uniform, his "German" ethnicity, his purported international travels, and most alarmingly, his habit of travelling in the company of "young girls." Wanderwell's spidery character was decided by the paper's claim that "Federal officers in San Diego, Los Angeles, Spokane, Seattle, Albuquerque and El Paso, it is understood, have questioned girls who were traveling in Wanderwell's company, but no formal charge has ever been made against him."

Bail was set at $200, which Wanderwell paid, sparing Aloha a night in prison but doing little to calm her. She was understandably shocked and afraid: she was more than 6,000 miles from Nice and in the company of a man the papers were calling a possible spy, a fraud, and a pervert. Yet, she was also in love with this man, this adventurer who had shown her the world and taught her how to survive in it.

Walter was outraged and asked Aloha to stick with him. Yes, there were things she did not yet know, but the newspapers were not to be believed and he could explain everything. He hired the legal firm Ernest, Crewe to defend them against any charges (in fact, none had been laid) and to sue the newspapers for defamation. Aloha, nonetheless, was teetering.

Bureau of Investigation file photo of "hiker" Walter Wanderwell after arraignment as a possible spy and incarceration in the infamous Fulton County Tower jail, Atlanta, Georgia, 1917.

ELEVEN

ALIAS WALTER WANDERWELL

WALTER WAS NOT the man Aloha — nor anyone else — thought he was. In April 1917, during the Great War, he had been arrested by the local Atlanta constabulary and handed over to the federal Department of Justice, who kept him detained under suspicion of being "an agent of a foreign power" — a spy. Walter was grilled by federal agents convinced they had caught him in the act of collecting crucial intelligence and transmitting it back to Germany. Walter denied spying. The attorney general for the state of Georgia, acting under the direct auspices of the president of the United States, took over the interrogation.

The interviews he conducted are illuminating and are some of the few documents that show Walter without Aloha's colouring lens. They shed some light upon Walter's "activities," both real and suspected, but are still perplexing. Some even predate his first marriage to Nell and the beginning of the Wanderwell Expedition in 1919.

✲

Hooper Alexander, the US district attorney for Northern Georgia, could hardly keep up with the directives flooding in from superiors. War with Germany looked likely, and its possibility was churning up the biggest panic since the Civil War. Citizens were ready to surrender their rights and liberties in order to safeguard the country's political and social order — indeed, they were demanding it. Political trials swelled,[1] and anyone with

Bureau of Investigation file photo of "hiker" Hugo Coutandin, Walter's companion, after arraignment as a possible spy and incarceration in the infamous Fulton County Tower jail, Atlanta, Georgia, 1917.

a funny-sounding accent might be reported to authorities as a potential spy. County jails and state penitentiaries overflowed with "hyphenated Americans": German-Americans, Irish-Americans, Russian-Americans, as well as many foreign nationals. The vast majority of those arrested were in the United States legally. Many had been in the country for more than twenty years. They owned homes, ran businesses, and were active in their communities.

Two men who claimed to be on a "walking trip" across the country had been arrested in Atlanta. Their names were Hugo Coutandin and Walter Wanderwell. At least one of them, Wanderwell, had been arrested several times before,[2] and he was wanted elsewhere in the US to face civil charges relating to the Mann Act. It was this charge — defined as transporting a female across state lines for immoral purposes — that ultimately gave Alexander the legal right to hold Wanderwell indefinitely. And Alexander *was* keen to hold on to Wanderwell. Aside from maps and photographs of strategic coastal facilities in Florida, Georgia, and the Carolinas, authorities also found among the hikers' effects a "portable" two-way radio (telegraph) and two cameras. Unlike many recent detainees, preliminary information gained through the questioning of these two prisoners, and witnesses to their debatable activities, gave sufficient cause to suspect that they actually were engaged in some form of espionage.

On March 27, Alexander received instructions from US Attorney General Thomas W. Gregory advising that it would be "desirable to hold all parties if possible, using any local legislation, the Mann Act, or any statute which may be applicable."[3] Gregory's Espionage Act had just failed passage in the Senate and he was in no mood to see more potential agitators slip from his grasp. President Woodrow Wilson was equally annoyed, proclaiming, "There are citizens of the United States...born under other flags but welcomed by our generous naturalization laws to the full freedom and opportunity of America, who have poured the poison of disloyalty into the very arteries of our national life...[T]he hand of our power should close over them at once."[4] Less than a month later a presidential order arrived:

April 21, 1917

United States Attorney, Atlanta Georgia,

By order of the President of the United States, acting under proc-lamation and regulations as to alien enemies, issued April sixth, nineteen seventeen, you are ordered to arrest and detain, through the United States Marshal, at the usual place of confinement in your District, the following German alien enemies, on the ground that their presence in your District at large is to the danger of the public peace and safety of the United States: Walter Pieczynski and Hugo Coutandin.

Such persons shall be held until further order of the President.

— Gregory[5]

❖

Alexander, a tall man whose goatee, deep-set eyes, and prominent brow gave him an imposing look, spent his day in a small interrogation room of the Fulton County Tower, an antebellum structure used as the Atlanta city jail. Walter Wanderwell sat in front of him. As promised in the morning paper, the storms and tornadoes of recent days had given way to warm, sunny weather and made it necessary to place a small oscillating fan on the room's desk. The buzz-hum of the fan and the clacking of a secretary's stenotype machine filled the pauses as the fifty-nine-year-old attorney questioned his twenty-two-year-old subject in detail.

Q. Well, now, let's talk with very great frankness to one another.

A. Thank you.

Q. You know why you are held?

A. Yes.

Q. You are a German?

A. Yes.

Q. And you understand very well that you are suspected —

A. *(Interrupting)* Of being a spy.

Q. Something of that sort; that you are not in this country innocently but co-operating in some way with the German Government and against the interests of this country....

A. Yes.[6]

Walter Wanderwell, or Valerian Johannes Pieczynski, was born in Thorne, Germany, on December 5, 1895. For most of its history, Thorne had been at the heart of the Polish kingdom but had come under German control in 1793, when the city was annexed by the kingdom of Prussia as a hedge against expanding Russian influence. Wanderwell's family was often transferred from one town to another, dragged along by his father who was a veterinary surgeon in the kaiser's army.

Q. In what regiment?

A. He was transferred from one regiment to another. Altogether in the German Army twenty-nine years.

Wanderwell told of growing up in Alsace-Lorraine and Posen and Schlösschen, though he could not provide exact dates. He had attended school, mostly in Posen, until he was "going on 17" and had been a member of the Wandervögel — a German pathfinder organization similar to the Boy Scouts, though placing more emphasis on harmony with nature than survival skills. Before the Great War and in the postwar years before the rise of the Nazis, thousands of young people in hiking shorts and colourful costumes could be seen hiking around the German countryside with banners flying, guitars and rucksacks slung on their backs, in search of a better way of life — exactly what Wanderwell was claiming to do when he was arrested

ABOVE: A very young Valerian Johannes Pieczynski (a.k.a. Walter Wanderwell) with one of his elder brothers, Posen, Poland, circa 1890s.

RIGHT: A studio portrait of thirteen-year-old Valerian, Posen, Poland, 1900.

in Atlanta in March 1917. Early photographs of Wandervögel members show them wearing uniforms that bear a striking resemblance to Wanderwell's own uniform — and it was clear that the name "Wandervögel" was the inspiration for his own pseudonym.

But Alexander was not interested in arcane German youth movements. He wanted to know why, at sixteen, Wanderwell had tried to enter the German army in 1911, especially since he professed to have no sympathy for the German people. Wanderwell responded with plainspoken enthusiasm.

I was made crazy by stories of Navy life. I was very adventurous...I desired to see other countries, to see the world; that is why I (eventually) became a sailor. They (the Navy) did not accept me because I was nearsighted.

After asking Wanderwell to repeat that he was turned down by the German army, Alexander made a sudden change of tack.

Q. Have you ever been to Cardiff?
A. Yes, Cardiff, South Wales.
Q. When?
A. I don't know the year, but I was there on a Norwegian sailing ship. I will give you an account of my story, one after another. They didn't accept me in the German Navy, and I was so desirous to go to sea that, when they did not take me in the Navy, I went on one of those merchant vessels, where they give the boys training.

The exchange marked the first time that Wanderwell and Alexander vied to steer the course of the conversation, as well as the first time that Alexander demonstrated he already knew quite a bit about Wanderwell's history.

Q. Did you go on the Norwegian ship "Cambus Kanetta"?[7]
A. Yes, an old English ship, and that ship was registered under the Norwegian flag. I signed on as ship's boy.

Wanderwell described his first voyage from England, down through the South Atlantic and around Cape Horn to Antofagasta, Chile. He claimed to be in Chile on April 14, 1912, when news came that the *Titanic* had sunk. He would have been 16½ years old. He told Alexander that he sailed on the "Cambus Kanetta" for eleven months, including *three months* in Balboa, Spain, loading and unloading the ship. Given that Balboa is a hamlet of about twenty houses in

A publicity photo of a young Walter Wanderwell found amongst US military intelligence files, circa 1915.

the hills of northwest Spain, it seems Wanderwell was actually referring to the northern port city of Bilbao. It's unknown if this error is Wanderwell's or Alexander's. Obfuscation was a habit that Walter maintained throughout the interview (and indeed through his life): long-winded explanations, bloated with superfluous detail that managed to omit essential dates and facts.

Alexander asked about Wanderwell's four brothers, whether they were in the German army, whether his father was still alive. He asked for more details about Wanderwell's sailing career. Wanderwell said he'd worked on routes around the globe, including trips along Africa's Gold Coast to Lagos and the Niger River, where he travelled inland to deliver goods to the British colonies. Often there were unexpected layovers, such as two months in the Canary Islands waiting for a new ship propeller, when Wanderwell was able to do some "sightseeing" and learn a bit of the language.

While sailing to the Spanish port of Huelva, a telegram informed the crew that Austria had declared war on Serbia.

Q. When you left Huelva where did you touch next?
A. Baltimore, Maryland, United States.
Q. Do you know the date?
A. I was on the ship until ready to leave the harbour. It was twenty-five days across the Atlantic. In Baltimore, Maryland — we didn't know anything of the war; the ship didn't have any wireless outfit. When we reached the shores of Maryland the American pilot came aboard with the news that there was war declared between Austria, Germany and England, France and all the nations, and we didn't believe it — thought it was a joke.

Wanderwell said he'd demanded to be paid off in Baltimore and only got his money after threatening legal action. He never did provide the date of his arrival but instead made a statement that clearly surprised his questioner.

A. We went to the German Consul in Baltimore and reported ourselves there, and did not know what to do.
Q. Reported for what?

A. Reported for service.

Q. Military duty?

A. Yes. That is our duty, to report to the German Consul, but the main reason was to get our money from the ship.

As Wanderwell told it, because he had never served in the German army and did not have a passport, he was excused from enlisting. Alexander seemed unconvinced.

Q. You landed there about the 18th of August [1915]?

A. Something about that time.

In Baltimore, Wanderwell signed on to a ship called the *Sark*, Norwegian again, and sailed to Alexandria, Egypt. According to Wanderwell, he got the job because he could speak "Norwegian and Russian and Polish, and especially Polish." En route to Egypt, while passing through the Strait of Gibraltar, the ship was confronted by a British torpedo boat.

The commander hollered, "Where are you bound for? Any Germans or Austrians on board?" We were sitting on deck, on the hatch, so scared they would take us to a concentration camp, we didn't know what they were going to do. I put everything I had, German news-papers and everything, overboard on the other side — put things in the ventilators.... Nobody wanted to be German then.

It turned out that none of the Germans aboard had served in the army and all were under military age, so the commander made them promise that they would not leave the ship until it returned to Baltimore.

Q. Then you went on to Alexandria?

A. Yes.

Q. Did you get off the ship in Alexandria?

A. Yes, on permission of the Captain.... We went there in the Red Light District to have a look....

Q. Didn't you promise the British Commander of the torpedo boat you would not land?

A. We promised not to leave the ship before we reached the United States.... The British authorities came aboard and asked us practically the same questions, and gave us a special pass for every man to go ashore.

Alexander seemed appalled at the nerve of the sailors to disembark in Alexandria but decided not to pursue it.

Q. Where did you go from Alexandria?

A. We had to pass many submarines, French, and from Alexandria we went clean back to the Straits of Gibraltar again.

Q. Sure?

A. Yes.

Q. Didn't you stop at Algiers?

A. Algiers?

Q. Yes.

A. I was in Algiers with the "Germanic."

For once Wanderwell seemed surprised by Alexander, although he quickly grasped the question's origins.

Q. Did you ever tell anybody you were in Algiers?

A. Yes; later on I met this hiker. I never intended to make any globe-trotter of myself, but the newspapers asked me, and I told them I had been in Africa. I made these stories — didn't make them, but generally the newspapers made more than there was to it. I have never been in Algiers after the war.

Pouncing on Wanderwell's sudden discomfort, Alexander asked other questions concerning tall tales, harmless or otherwise.

Q. Did you ever tell anybody that when you were in Egypt and Algiers you got through by having false papers?

A. No.

Q. Never told anybody that?

A. Told Enden I signed on as a Russian.[8]

Q. You really didn't have any passports?

A. No. A sailor did not need a passport at that time. At the beginning of the war the situation was not so strict. If I had wanted to spy I could have done so.

Alexander was understandably sceptical and asked Wanderwell to name the master of the *Sark*, which he did. Then he asked if Wanderwell had visited the German consul in Buenos Aires. He had. Then he asked again:

Q. Were you ever in Chile?

A. Yes, but that was before the war.

Alexander knew that German agents had been operating in Chile at precisely that time, and the United States' response led, ultimately, to the establishment of the Federal Bureau of Investigation. Wanderwell denied having been in Chile during the war.

Q. Did you ever go by land from Chile to Buenos Aires?

A. No.

Q. Ever tell anybody you did?

A. I have told all kinds of stories when I was making lectures and talks.

Q. You were just "stuffing them?"

A. I have told them much of my adventures. Another boy traveled across on land on foot. He told me much about his trip from Valparaiso to Buenos Aires. I intended to make that trip with him.

Q. What was that boy's name?

A. I don't know....

Q. Do you know the date when you were in Buenos Aires?

A. No.

Knowing it would be possible to check the story against shipping records, Alexander focused on establishing Wanderwell's arrival in America.

Q. Did you quit the "Sark" in New York?

A. Yes.

Q. Do you know the date?

A. No.

Q. February two years ago?

A. Yes, that is when it was. I have it on my papers....

Q. Did you report to any Consul at New York?

A. No, not after that time; I had so much interest for America.

This, again, was a potentially volatile line of questioning. In 1915 German officials in New York — including the head of the office of Germany's War Intelligence Centre — had been caught producing forged passports that allowed Germans to leave the United States for Europe. Then, in July 1915, the German commercial attaché in New York, Heinrich Albert, forgot his briefcase while stepping off a train. By the time he turned to retrieve it, a US Secret Service agent was sprinting down the 50th Street Station platform with the briefcase tucked under his arm. Inside were receipts for funds transferred to German-American and Irish-American organizations aimed at influencing American public opinion. There was also evidence that Albert had funded a munitions plant in Bridgeport, Connecticut.[9] The discoveries had outraged the president and solidified American public opinion that Germany was working against the welfare of the United States. Author Chad Millman wrote about the mood at that time:

The California Board of Education banned the teaching of German in public schools because it was a language that disseminated "ideals of autocracy, brutality and hatred." Local libraries threw out German books, and the Metropolitan Opera stopped performing German works. Restaurants renamed sauerkraut "liberty cabbage" and hamburgers "liberty sandwiches." A Minnesota minister was tarred and feathered after he was heard praying with a dying woman in German.[10]

Wanderwell's mere presence in New York during those months was enough to cast him in a suspicious light.

During the spring of 1915, Wanderwell worked on ships sailing along the

Eastern Seaboard of the US, the Gulf of Mexico states, the Caribbean, and Cuba. Then in July 1915 he applied for US citizenship at New York.

Q. When you applied for citizenship you took an oath?
A. Yes.
Q. You said you would give up the German Emperor?
A. Yes.
Q. Said you would have nothing else to do with him?
A. Yes.
Q. Would not obey him?
A. No.
Q. Did you mean that?
A. Yes.
Q. You were going to become an American citizen?
A. Yes.

After more than an hour of questioning, Alexander was approaching the crux of his case against Wanderwell. Although he claimed to have nothing more to do with German authorities, Alexander could demonstrate that Wanderwell had, in fact, visited numerous German officials. In Chicago, Wanderwell had met with the consul on several occasions and was known to have discussed leaving the United States.

Q. Never made any effort to go to Vladivostok?
A. No. An attaché of the German Consul tried to help me, and wrote a letter to show to the German authorities.

Alexander's interest in Vladivostok was more than passing. In 1915 German agents connected with German consular offices in San Francisco, Chicago, and New York had been placing bombs onto ships loaded with munitions. The ships sailed from Tacoma, Washington, to Vladivostok. That Wanderwell was linked to Vladivostok at that time must have seemed curious.

By March 1916 Wanderwell had given up sailing. His right foot had been broken in an accident at New York Harbor and in order to relieve the stiffness brought on by three months in hospital, he began hiking. He set out from New York along the newly completed Lincoln Highway, the nation's first transcontinental road for automobiles. From New York he walked 90 miles to Philadelphia, then struck out west towards Chicago, selling postcards and lecturing at German clubs along the way. In Chicago, Wanderwell tried to see the German consul but met, instead, Carl Ludwig Duisberg, an attaché. Duisberg was not willing to give Wanderwell any money, which was sometimes the custom, but he did hand him a letter of recommendation to the German consul in San Francisco, Baron E.H. von Schack.

Q. Didn't you tell Ludwig you had made all kinds of efforts to get back to Germany?

A. Yes.

Q. Was that the truth?

A. No.

Q. What did you tell him about going to Vladivostok?

A. That was an effort to get that letter, that recommendation. He told me I could get an opportunity to go from San Francisco to Vladivostok, but I did not want to go there. I never had an intention to go there.

Carl Ludwig Duisberg Jr. was well known to the US government and had been watched for some time. His father was the head of Bayer AG and would eventually found IG Farben.

Letters of recommendation in hand, as well as some private mail for the German officials' friends on the west coast, Wanderwell struck west for Salt Lake City, where he arrived in the fall of 1916.

Q. Did you meet a man in Salt Lake City by the name of Lutzig?

A. Yes, that is the man that took us along in the automobile to San Francisco.

Q. Who was he?

A. He was traveling in an automobile from New Orleans. He comes from Berlin. His wife is German too....

Q. I don't think I ought to ask you anything about anything you did
about that woman. That might put you in the hole, and you had
better not testify against yourself.

A. I don't know if I have done anything wrong, but I would like to
tell the truth.

This, presumably, is a reference to one of Wanderwell's Mann Act mis-
demeanours, and prosecution of those charges would keep him off the streets
for a while. But if Wanderwell really *were* engaged in espionage, it would be
foolish to focus on hanky-panky while ignoring his espionage efforts. There
was something fishy about Wanderwell's activities in San Francisco.
Alexander asked Wanderwell if he had visited Baron von Schack, but he
denied it, claiming the consul was sick.

Q. Do you know where Von Schack is now?

A. No.

Q. Did you know he had been prosecuted out there?

A. No.

Q. Did you know he is in prison?

A. No.

In February 1916 von Schack and two other German consular officials
were indicted for plotting a military expedition against Canada from within
the United States. But they also had planned the bombing of ships bound
for Vladivostok and took part in an elaborate, multinational plot known as
the Hindu–German Conspiracy, which aimed to foment a pan-Indian
rebellion against the British Raj during the First World War (and thereby
draw forces from Europe). The plot was part of countless conspiracies taking
place at the time, including the Black Tom explosion in 1916 — the most
destructive terrorist act on American soil prior to 9/11.[11]

Shortly past midnight on July 30, 1916, German agents snuck into a
section of the New Jersey harbour called Black Tom and set fire to a row of
railway cars carrying ammunition that was parked next to a barge packed
with munitions bound for the war in Europe. Within half an hour, bullets
inside the cars exploded, making it impossible for firefighters to approach

the flames. Soon the barge itself was alight, and at 2:08 a.m., the munitions detonated, smashing a temporary crater in the harbour waters before raining down in a deadly storm of water, wood, and blazing shrapnel. The explosion flattened large swaths of Jersey City and was heard as far away as Maryland. Windows shattered throughout Manhattan, water mains burst in Times Square, and the torch on the Statue of Liberty was pulverized. When a second explosion occurred at 2:40, firemen working on fireboats dropped to their stomachs to dodge the flying bullets and aimed their hoses blindly over the sides of their boat.[12]

One of the German agents eventually convicted of the bombing was Polish-German Lothar Witzke, a.k.a. Pablo Waberski. It's possible that Alexander had Witzke in mind while questioning Wanderwell — especially since Witzke had been interned in Valparaiso, Chile, but had somehow managed to escape around the time Wanderwell was also in Chile. The real bombshell, however, was that Wanderwell's name appeared in Witzke's notebook.

By the fall of 1916 Wanderwell was heading east again, through Arizona and New Mexico in the company of two Germans — a small man named Fritz Gluckler and another whom Wanderwell did not name. At each town they would "hunt up the German heads" to arrange speaking engagements, sell postcards, and take photographs. In El Paso, Texas, they crossed the border to Mexico, where they were arrested under suspicion of being *American* soldiers. The German consul intervened and they were released. American soldiers had been slipping across the Mexican border looking for Pancho Villa, who had sacked the town of Columbus, New Mexico, earlier in the year. A German arms purchaser by the name of Felix A. Sommerfeld was suspected of having helped to provoke the attack — on the assumption that if the United States started a war with Mexico, it would stay out of the war in Europe. Alexander likely did not know that Felix Sommerfeld, like Lothar Witzke and Walter Wanderwell, came from Posen, Poland.

After several visits to Juárez, Wanderwell stayed at an American military camp near El Paso. At San Antonio, Walter's travelling companion, Gluckler, was arrested and interrogated but released the following day. The experience terrified Gluckler, although Wanderwell insisted that legal troubles were just part of the adventure, another interesting story they could add to their lectures. While his companions denounced the xenophobic Americans, Wanderwell insisted that there was nothing to fear and, as if to underscore it, tried to see the governor of Texas at Austin. He succeeded. Governor James "Pa" Ferguson signed Wanderwell's book and said he had also travelled through the southwestern United States as a young man, drifting from place to place and learning what the country was really about. It helped him decide what he wanted to do in life.

Since leaving California, Wanderwell claimed to have earned over a thousand dollars hiking around, a staggering amount in 1916. He had robust bank accounts in Miami, New York, Chicago, and England. But, according to Aloha's later memoir, the war also played a role in the group's success. German communities welcomed them as minor heroes: the brave German adventurers who struck out to see the world despite its troubles. Throughout the United States, Germans felt conflicted about the war, wanting on the one hand to support their new home but also feeling that Britain, France, and Russia had been unfairly aligning against Germany for years. The press's depiction of bloodthirsty Germans bayoneting babies for sport sent many tempers boiling over. Inevitably, some Germans were radicalized.

Wanderwell's travelling companions grew increasingly nervous until Gluckler decided it was too dangerous to continue hiking, believing they would surely be arrested as spies.

Q. Why did he say they would arrest you as German spies?
A. We were arrested along the road, held, searched.
Q. Where?
A. In other places.
Q. What other places?
A. In El Paso. He was, for instance, held in El Paso.

In fact, Wanderwell had been arrested in at least four US cities, a detail he was careful to omit, not realizing, perhaps, that Alexander already knew. At Christmas 1916 Wanderwell reached West Palm Beach, where he befriended a German named Hugo Coutandin. Before long, the two men were hiking and lecturing together, promoting the idea that they were racing around the world on a bet. Wanderwell, perhaps to deflect American suspicions, began introducing Coutandin as a Frenchman.

Q. You say he is French?

A. French descent. His forefathers were French; like I am a Pole.

Wanderwell and Coutandin visited countless German organizations in towns throughout central and north Florida. In Gainesville they were made honorary members of the Boy Scouts of America and were keen to play up the association as much as possible, "on account of these difficulties." Then, in St. Augustine they stopped to take some photographs.

Q. What pictures did you take there?

A. Nothing but snapshots; nothing that could have looked suspicious.

Q. What pictures did you take in Saint Augustine?

A. All kinds.

Q. Was there a wireless station in Saint Augustine?

A. Oh yes, that is right. That is the only point in the whole thing where they could get me for a German spy. We came to Saint Augustine and I had my camera along and took pictures of the old Fort, and tried to take pictures of the "Fountain of Youth." There was a light-house there and...I went up to (it), and the man told me we could take pictures.... I said, "Can we take a picture of the wireless station?" He said, "They might think you are German spies." I said, "I am English." But that picture was spoiled, and I never got anything out of that picture.

Wanderwell's story couldn't have done much for his case, especially since he suddenly claimed that Fritz Gluckler, who had supposedly left the tour in West Palm Beach, was with them when they took photographs of the wireless station. What Alexander did not say was that he possessed the testimony of Mrs. C.F. Fowler of Waterloo, Iowa, who claimed to have met Wanderwell at a wireless station in Jupiter, Florida, (236 miles south of St. Augustine) at 2:00 a.m. When she asked him what he was doing there she told her he needed a match. Alexander also knew that among Coutandin's belongings was a portable two-way radio, a strange (and heavy) item for a backpacker to carry.

Q. And you think you are not a German spy?

A. I think I am not. I know you are mainly holding me because you think I am a German spy. That is why I want to tell you anything you want to know. I am not a German spy, and not afraid to stand up for it. I am only afraid because they might accuse me of breaking a law I do not know anything about...

Q. Didn't you go to the West Coast to go to Vladivostok?

A. No; I said that to sympathize with the Germans. I am for the German people and say the German system is all right, but I say militarism is a thing of the past. I am only for one thing. I think there will come a time when the nations will come together to have a Peace League. The President of this country started that, and I think they will come to that agreement.

Wanderwell returned to his cell at the Fulton County Prison and Alexander took the stairs back to his office, where he sat at his desk for a long time, organizing his thoughts. Through his window he could see the dome of the Georgia State Capitol building blazing in the late afternoon sun. The US Attorney General was awaiting a report outlining Alexander's impressions of Wanderwell and Coutandin. It was a curious case to be sure, especially since the folks in Washington weren't telling all *they* knew about Wanderwell. In the grand scheme, the charges against Wanderwell were fairly minor: some letters couriered, a Mann Act violation, and some snapshots of wireless stations in Florida. And yet Alexander had received no less than ten wires directly from the US attorney general, several from the assistant attorney general, who in turn was working on information provided by Bruce Bielaski, chief of the Bureau of Investigation of the Department of Justice. One wire about Wanderwell seemed to have come from President Wilson himself. For some unstated reason, Washington wanted Wanderwell and Coutandin.

Alexander interviewed Hugo Coutandin two days later and prepared his reports for Washington, taking into account the country's likely entry into the war in Europe. His letter to the US attorney general, dated April 12, 1917, (six days after the US entered the First World War) observed:

In the main both of them tell a fairly consistent story. As I stated, however... there are some conflicts between them, many of them apparently not of a serious character, and yet difficult to reconcile.... Wanderwell has admitted to me that many of the stories which he has told in different places are untrue, though he has offered very plausible explanations in regard to the same...

As I stated in my telegram and in my previous letter, I have not been able to ascertain enough about any of these parties to lay any serious foundation for a charge against them, and on the whole I am rather disposed to believe that their motives are innocent. The Special Agent of the Bureau of Investigation, however, who has collaborated with me more or less in this work seems to be very much of the opinion that these men are all seeking information for the benefit of the German government, and I cannot feel that it is entirely safe just now to turn them loose.

The best opinion I can form in the matter is that it would be better to take them out of the hands of the civil authorities and detain them for the present in a military prison of some sort and until such time as the War Department may feel it safe to discharge them.[13]

Wanderwell and Coutandin were removed to a military camp at Fort McPherson and by September 1917 both had been placed on supervised parole, though officials were careful to keep them apart (Coutandin successfully lobbied for "house arrest" with relatives in Chicago). Wanderwell remained on parole, working with engineers at the Battle Hill Sanitarium just outside Atlanta, until his parole was cancelled on April 13, 1919. By August 1919 Wanderwell had married Nell Miller and was preparing to drive around the world on a bet. In the grandest of ironies, the car that Walter and Nell began their adventure in had been hand-fashioned by German POWs incarcerated next door to Walter's prison. The send-off in Atlanta was attended by hundreds, including Governor Hugh M. Dorsey of the State of Georgia.[14]

CAPT. and MRS.
WALTER WANDERWELL
PRESENT THEIR

1921-1925 Expedition

Around the World By Auto

AT THE

PHILHARMONIC AUDITORIUM

GEORGE L. SMITH, Manager

LOS ANGELES

First Automobile Journey around the world completely recorded in moving pictures—depicting in detail the adventures and unique scenes encountered in the crossing of 39 countries in 3 years. Ten reels of daring motor adventures lectured upon in person by Capt. and Mrs. Walter Wanderwell. The cars will be on exhibition at the Auditorium. Including General Pershing giving farewell to Wanderwells in 1921 at Washington. On a tramp steamer across the Atlantic—Bull Fighting in Spain—across Central Europe—Warsaw to the Pyramids or bust. Across Arabian desert—A meeting with Ex-Crown Prince. First cars across Arabia. Meeting of American Around-the-World Fliers at Calcutta, the half-way point. Through Chinese Floods and Wars. Mrs. Wanderwell, the first lady to drive a car across Asia, is honored by Red Army in Vladivostock.

FIRST SHOWING IN AMERICA

Limited Engagement

STARTING MONDAY EVENING

APRIL 27

Matinees Daily Thereafter

PRICES: Mat. 25c, 50c; Eve. 25c, 50c, 75c

A special edition Wanderwell Expedition pamphlet promoting the showing of *Around the World by Auto*, 1925.

TWELVE

A GATHERING STORM

AFTER WALTER'S ARREST in San Francisco and his admission that he needed to "come clean" about his past, it would have been understandable if Aloha had decided to quit. But after all they'd been through, and this close to Hollywood, it would take more than an arrest on "trumped up" allegations to send her scurrying back to mother. And when she heard how Walter had been harassed during his earlier travels through the US because of his "arrogant wanderlust" and his suspiciously sharp S's, she felt only sympathy. "My heart ached to see my vulnerable hero attacked — rotten shame."[1]

As promised, Walter hired lawyers to sue the newspapers for defamation and lost earnings — his reputation in San Francisco had been destroyed on the basis of unproven accusations. And, indeed, the San Francisco police soon admitted they had no evidence of any crime and were forced to release Aloha and Walter without charge.[2]

Incredibly, the bad publicity did not stop Walter from winning sponsorships — and some grand ones, too, including the Ruckstell Sales and Manufacturing Company who installed their new Model T gearshift free of charge, adding a fourth ratio and a promise of dramatic fuel savings. It was another technological leap for the Wanderwell cars, placing them at the forefront of automotive design.

※

In the early 1920s, Los Angeles was still a Wild West town. It had only just adopted its city charter and many were working to rid the town of pervasive corruption, especially at city hall and in the police force. The results were mixed at best. In one instance, Mayor George Cryer had Police Chief Louis D. Oaks "arrested in his official car while drunk and in the company of a half-clothed woman — with little effect."[3]

And yet, Los Angeles was thriving with a growth rate unmatched anywhere else in the country. No longer in San Francisco's shadow, Los Angeles had recently opened its own branch of the University of California, attracting students and academics and producing a more sophisticated business culture. Oil had been discovered in 1892, and by 1923 wells in the greater Los Angeles area were supplying one-quarter of the world's petroleum.

It was here that Aloha and Walter intended to make their mark. They checked into the Ambassador Hotel on Wilshire Boulevard, paying for a room until they could arrange free accommodation. It was not their usual strategy, but Walter was content to stay out of the public eye for a few days. He visited the offices of the Agfa Film company, which promptly provided him with more film stock and facilities to make a print of the Wanderwell travels thus far. After the difficulties encountered in San Francisco, he was determined to make sure Los Angeles was a success — not by battling a hostile press but by winning the public over. To do that, they had to make sure their films were *spectacular*. It was arranged that Aloha would cut film at Consolidated Film Industries in Hollywood, the same facilities used by some of the major studios. Here Aloha could learn about film editing from some of the best in the world.

※

Now that Aloha was finally in the city she had dreamed of for so long, she rolled up her sleeves and worked hard, outlining their feature-length film, completing her secretarial duties, selling pamphlets, and lecturing at small theatres and social clubs across the city. On March 4, 1925, Walter appeared at the Carlton Theatre on South Western Avenue, while Aloha gave a separate lecture at a private club in Pasadena. While packing up after her lecture, Aloha was approached by a heavy-set man who flashed a badge and announced that she was, yet again, under arrest. Walter had been arrested an hour earlier. According to a brief note in the next day's *Los Angeles Times*, the globetrotting captain Wanderwell and his "asserted sister" had added "another experience to their great adventure when United States Deputy Marshal Finn arrested them on a charge of wearing parts of a soldier's uniform."[4]

According to Aloha, they posted $400 to avoid spending the night in jail and returned for trial the next day. In fact, they spent several nights in prison, "having failed to keep out by providing $2500 bond each."[5] Walter and Aloha languished in their cells until March 8, when they were called to court by Judge Georgia Bullock — the state's first female judge. Judge Bullock, a big-boned, no-nonsense woman who had formerly presided over a women's only court, read out the charge against them: unauthorized use of an American Liberty Belt, regulation army issue.

Looking over her papers, the judge asked if they were guilty or not guilty. Walter responded that they were *not* guilty and that the belts were *not* US Army issue. "These are Chinese belts presented to us by Chang Tso-lin's forces at Mukden. They're modelled after the design by British Sir Samuel James Browne in 1901. The American Liberty Belt is different; it is worn over the right shoulder. Our belt is worn over the left and is for the purpose of supporting a pistol not a sword." And there he was cut off by the judge who asked, "Are you or are you not wearing a leather strap over your shoulder?"[6]

Indeed they were, as Aloha later wrote, just like "practically every elevator operator, doorman and motorcycle policeman in the country. We were proud of our souvenirs of (the Chinese) War."[7] The judge's gavel fell and they were each fined $200 or sixty days — an astronomical court fine in 1925. The *Los Angeles Times* reported that Judge Bullock warned them "not to wear Sam Browne belts or any other portion of the Army insignia in the future."[8]

On the walk back to their hotel, Walter and Aloha stopped again at the post office where a letter from the legal office in San Francisco was waiting for them. The lawyers regretted to inform Walter that they would, after all, be unable to pursue his case as discussed. No reasons were given, but Aloha assumed that somewhere palms had been greased. Walter, as ever, refused to dwell on setbacks and encouraged Aloha to work that much harder on preparing the films. Those reels would pay their way across the country, clear to Detroit where, with luck, they could meet with Mr. Ford himself.

☼

Aloha began her crash course in the highly complex art of film editing. She felt at home "working among numerous cutters — all women — the professionals who decided what to cut out, which scenes to patch together, what actions matched how the story evolves. 'Does she kiss him before or after the party?'"9 Aloha worked with an assistant, surrounded by six cloth-lined bins, rolling film from left to right and back again, checking both scenes and splices. When six sequences were cut, they were retrieved from the bins and assembled by the assistant, according to Aloha's instructions. She experimented with a number of techniques learned from her fellow cutters. If the footage for important scenes was too short she would print them twice, sometimes printing it backwards to create the illusion of new settings.

☼

Throughout Aloha's story, the details contained in the public record, whether through newspaper reports or legal documents, are often at odds with her own recounting of them. Sometimes, however, while the events themselves do coincide, their explanation is profoundly different. In Aloha's version of events, Walter suddenly decided to buy a yacht that was kept on the east coast. It was a surprising development, but he would not be gone long and in the meantime she had plenty to keep herself busy: bookings at Loew's West Coast Theatres, work at the film lab, and a scheduled installation of N° III's first self-starter.

Their last public presentation before Walter left was an engagement scheduled at the posh Huntington Hotel in Pasadena, renowned getaway for Hollywood stars.

From the rear platform, Cap saluted. Somehow I sensed he was mine; by right of qualification, perseverance, rightness.... That moment, standing below him, his good and bad points flashed like single frames: baffling, elusive, an opportunist as long as his conscience was clear with his Maker. He was often a very aggravating man but every single new thing to be seen or heard interested him. He was what he claimed to be, a traveller. Legally, he publicized his career: Wander well.[10]

Aloha kissed Walter as he boarded a train for Florida. Her notes state that, as she watched the train make it's slowly chugging way east, she felt everything was finally going to be okay. The notes also mention, in passing, that Walter needed to visit the Dade County Circuit Court where his wife, Nell, was suing for divorce.

Before leaving, Walter had introduced Aloha to Hollywood's most famous stunt flyer, Art Goebel, a tall charmer who "turned out to be as captivating in person as he had always been flirting down at me from the silent screen."[11] Like Wanderwell, Art was an incurable adventurer, though fonder of simple vices (drinking, smoking) and less prone to arrest. He introduced Aloha to some of Hollywood's biggest stars, including the British actor turned stunt flyer Reginald Denny, his friend John Barrymore, the up-and-coming child star Douglas Fairbanks Jr., and actress Joan Crawford.[12]

It wasn't long before Art and Aloha were spending their evenings together, attending movies (although Aloha would later claim there was "no necking"), drama classes, and numerous impromptu Hollywood parties where she met some of Hollywood's biggest names. Towards the end of March, Aloha was scheduled to deliver her first black tie performance for the Wedgewood Club at the Huntington Hotel in Pasadena, where she would lecture to some of the most powerful and successful people in southern California. She was undaunted. She had edited a longer program specifically for the performance and was determined to wow them. "They saw me on Europe's ravaged battlefields, in India, Siberia; greeted by Emperor Hirohito; locally by Jack Warner;[13] the acclaimed [director] Ernst Lubitsch, popular [actor] Monty Blue. Warmly applauded, I then answered questions until almost midnight."[14]

Following the show, the chairman of the Wedgewood Club told Aloha that some men wanted to see her. She was escorted to the lounge where two men in trench coats and felt hats were waiting. "What ho! The dicks! They were subdued apparently after being admonished by the Huntington hosts."[15] The officers questioned Aloha and told her that officers of the juvenile court would be in contact with her shortly.

The next day, March 28, Aloha sat on the steps of the Los Angeles central post office, reading a stack of mail, including her first note from Walter in Florida. He wrote that the divorce hearing had been scheduled for the twenty-fourth and that, although saddened by Nell's attitude, he was confident her request would be granted. He and Nell had tried to divorce some years earlier but had been rejected when they told the court that following their divorce they intended to go into business together. The judge had roared that his courtroom was not a farce and dismissed the case. This latest attempt arose from stories that had appeared in the *Honolulu Star* describing Aloha as Walter's wife. A friend had mailed copies to Nell, thus providing preliminary legal grounds for divorce.

Aloha had hardly finished the letter when she was approached by a woman "wearing a shoulder strap bag." The woman asked if she was Miss Wanderwell, and how old she was. Aloha answered that she was, as they say in France, in her seventeenth year. Nodding, the woman informed Aloha that she was, once again, under arrest.

Aloha was placed in a cell and refused bond "on grounds that I was a minor. On my previous nab my age had not affected bail or fine!"[16] The next day she was transferred to a juvenile detention facility and interrogated by officials who asked her age (she now claimed to be eighteen), her educational background, how she came to the United States, and what she was doing in Los Angeles.

> The baiter (I felt sure she was determined to feed her curiosity) looked me straight in the eye (and asked), "Are you a virgin?'"
>
> Ha! This time I had the right answer, "Certainly!"
>
> I was turned over to a nurse, my clothes taken away, handed a grey prison frock. In dazed amazement I submitted to an impudent interrogation about my health habits; head to toe examination.[17]

Following her physical, Aloha was sent back to pen number sixteen where she was occasionally joined by other girls. Their stories of prostitution, child abandonment, and even rape by their fathers shocked Aloha into silence. She was relieved when she was alone and could let her mind wander.

I noticed several important things. (I was) lucky to have a cell with sun shining through the window. A gently waving branch outside that cast shadows on the wall — very Japanese. With sunlight and movement I could live a while.

"A while" turned out to be six days, during which time she learned to hate the phrase "juvenile correction," describing it as a "sanctified mythology" that could only further warp those needing help the most. On the morning of her hearing, she was brought before the judge who gave her an academic quiz to assess her educational level. The judge looked at Aloha over her glasses and asked if she had anything to tell the court. Aloha stiffened her back and declared that she had nothing to confess. With a sigh, the judge nodded to the bailiff.

The door opened admitting a dozen people...and Cap! Cap in his uniform, his great big smile! My prayers were answered — everything would be alright.

The judge: "We are interested in your welfare in the United States. We consider you are without a guardian and you must have one."

I protested, Cap was my guardian, appointed by my mother.

"What kind of mother would allow you to go off with that globe-trotting man?"[18]

It was a fair question. Aloha, however, did not take kindly to the slight on Walter's character. Her temper began to flare, which seemed to amuse the court. Drawling, the judge said she doubted her mother was fully aware of Walter Wanderwell's character. "You know, she seems more concerned with the move from Nice and sending Miki to an Italian art school than with your safety." Aloha's mouth fell open. The judge had been reading her mail. "Bitingly, I said, 'If you read my mother *carefully*, you would learn she's a gentlewoman and that she has perfect confidence in the Captain to take care of me!'"[19]

The judge pursed her lips. She asked Aloha if she was in love with the captain and whether she intended to marry him. Aloha was shocked. What kind of court was this? She and Walter were business partners, she hissed, that's it. She had no plans to marry anyone. But whatever defiant self-composure Aloha might have affected was wiped out by the judge's curt response. "You are pregnant."

✺

Stripping away Aloha's justifications, there remains the practical reason that Walter had to return to Florida to appear before a judge to secure his divorce from Nell Wanderwell. After so many arrests, he needed to legitimize his relationship with Aloha. He understood that if he left California with her he would be arrested and charged under the Mann Act. In a series of letters to Bureau of Investigation Director J. Edgar Hoover, Special Agent Ralph Colvin had explained that there could be no prosecution of Wanderwell relating to his travel to California with Aloha since he had not technically crossed state lines. As he put it "Hawaii isn't a state, so the law doesn't count."[20]

Walter was not about to let himself be arrested again and risk destroying the expedition. So, over the course of three weeks he travelled to Florida, secured his divorce, paid the taxes owing on his property in Miami's Spring Garden district, bought some acreage along the Tamiami Trail together with four lots on the Key West Highway near Coral Gables, returned to Los Angeles, commissioned the construction of another car (to be called, stirringly, Unit N° IV), and attended Aloha's hearing in juvenile court.

✺

In all probability, Aloha knew she was pregnant. The court announcement would have been no surprise. Considering that Walter had been arrested or detained under the Mann Act a few times already, and news reports of his appetite for young girls followed him wherever the expedition went, it was essential that Walter and Aloha be free to marry. A child out of wedlock, in any Western society in the 1920s, would have meant, at the very least, ostracism — anathema to the cause of a very public, money-making enterprise.

Nothing short of the end of the Wanderwell Expedition — Walter's entire career and Aloha's dreams of success — was on the line.

✿

Aloha was released from juvenile correction and placed into the care of Natalie Ringstrom — Mrs. R, as she was less formally known — the landlady from whom she'd been renting an apartment prior to her arrest. According to the judge, Aloha was barred from leaving Hollywood for six months, presumably until after her birthday in October when she would be, as far as the court could determine, eighteen years of age.

Despite their increasingly serious troubles, Walter worked with maniacal intensity. Within a week of Aloha's release from jail, he had booked the Los Angeles Philharmonic, the city's largest playhouse. "Each side put up $2000 cash for advertising to plaster the city with twenty-four sheet billboards — a marvellous gamble. They furnished the house and orchestra — we, the show. Profits split equally. A thirty-piece orchestra for mood music and sound effects. We would open in two weeks."[21]

The prospect of her big chance coming now, so soon, erased any chance of sleep. Aloha remembered lying awake for hours every night, thrilled to be playing the largest venue in Los Angeles, but also despairing that six months of house arrest would prevent her from capitalizing on her success. No late-night parties, no overnight trips to more distant venues, no ability to be the grown-up she really was. Six months would be the longest she'd stayed in any one place since 1922.

Walter saw that Aloha's enthusiasm was waning. He took her to a late lunch at the Musso and Frank Grill on Hollywood Boulevard, "an unheard of cash extravagance — staggering from Cap." While she enjoyed filet mignon a la Frank with candied potatoes and a cup of Ridgways black tea, he spoke animatedly about his plans for the future, his words a torrent: how the new Unit N° IV car was to be hers, how they'd cross the country together with a stupendous victory celebration in Detroit. And after their arrival they'd continue their travels, making films and promoting the idea of travel as education.

In India, only a few months earlier, Aloha and Walter had received a letter from Nell when she was still wandering through North America. She

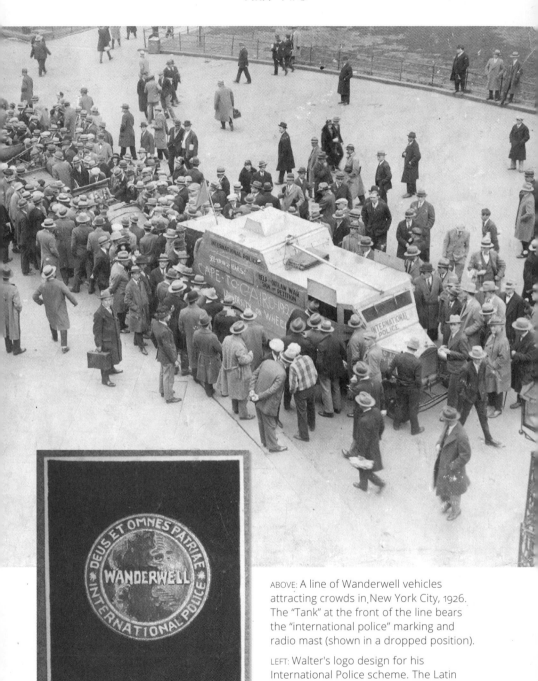

ABOVE: A line of Wanderwell vehicles attracting crowds in New York City, 1926. The "Tank" at the front of the line bears the "international police" marking and radio mast (shown in a dropped position).

LEFT: Walter's logo design for his International Police scheme. The Latin phrase means "God and country." 1920s.

had voiced concern about the many copycat Wanderwell Expeditions she had encountered in her travels. Walter didn't share Nell's concern then, but now that he and Aloha were back in America and could see cheap competition attempting to cash in, he knew something would have to be done. Aloha wrote at the time:

> Last mail before departure brought word from Unit N° I re: its "North American" competitors. There was a growing number of round the world imitators selling souvenirs on the strength of *our* overseas publicity. Some cars were almost replicas. Formats suggested various wagers: handicapped veterans, college boys working their way, Europeans seeing America First.
>
> Cap chuckled, "There'll be so many we'll have to organize a club."[22]

His solution, like so much else of Walter's promotional savvy, was simple, yet brilliant. The WAWEC logo, which until now had stood for "Wanderwell Around the World Endurance Contest," would be repurposed to mean "Work Around the World Educational Club." People would join the club and, for a fee, be trained on how to create a self-sustaining life on the road. He was safeguarding the future of the expedition, while offering Aloha the chance to continue travelling indefinitely.

And, finally, he proposed marriage.

Aloha visits new friends in Hollywood: (L-R) Aloha, child actress, Mary Pickford, Douglas Fairbanks. The newly christened "Miss Los Angeles" (Unit N° IV) is in the background, Hollywood, California, 1927.

THIRTEEN

AGAINST ALL ODDS

A LOHA WAS, FIRST AND FOREMOST, a performer. Her memoirs, like the lectures and interviews she gave, were crafted to present her experience of the world as she would have liked it and as she felt it would be most entertaining and agreeable to others. Aloha was an early "queen of spin."

By writing that Walter wanted her but that he also needed passion, Aloha acknowledges that Walter was sleeping around. Certainly, there could not have been any public display of romantic affection between them (especially since they were supposedly brother and sister), but in light of the sexual references contained in Aloha's surviving handwritten journals, as well as her jealousies of Joannie, Olga, and others, and the voluminous anecdotes of Walter's sexual appetites, it's unfathomable that they maintained a platonic chastity for the duration of their international travels.

Documents obtained through the US FOIA show that from the moment the Wanderwell Expedition arrived at San Francisco, field offices of the Bureau of Investigation in Jacksonville, Detroit, Kansas City, Salt Lake City, Seattle, Chicago, Oklahoma City, Denver, El Paso, Omaha, Phoenix, Butte, San Francisco, and Los Angeles had been co-operating to determine if Walter could be successfully charged under the Mann Act. One letter, from the Los Angeles Bureau of Investigation, was addressed to the Department of Justice in Washington, DC, on April 3, 1925, and states, "Wanderwell has just returned from Florida where he went to arrange the final matters in connection with the divorce from his wife, and that he intends to marry victim (Aloha) as soon as legal technicalities can be removed."[1]

Walter's proposal to Aloha almost certainly did not occur *after* his return from Florida, but *before* it.

※ .

On the sunny afternoon of Tuesday, April 7, Walter and Aloha drove to Riverside, California, where they were married at the home of Justice of the Peace H.D. Briggs. "The elated Justice of the Peace and his prim wife warmly congratulated, spontaneously bussed [kissed] and showered good wishes. She gave me a precious bouquet from her own garden: white fragrant tuberoses to carry away to dinner."[2] Aloha and Walter were free of the federal booby trap. Legally married, they could travel together without fear of arrest for immoral behaviour or for being the wrong age.

※

In Aloha's later reminiscences, her marriage merited hardly a page. Considerably more space was devoted to the United Artists film studio, where Aloha finally met her idols Mary Pickford and Douglas Fairbanks. In 1925 Pickford was the biggest female film star in the world and, as co-founder of United Artists, was the single most powerful woman in Hollywood. Even her eighteen-acre studio lot was the stuff of legend. Located on the corner of Santa Monica Boulevard and Formosa Avenue in Hollywood, the facility wowed visitors with its sets and stages, including a castle façade, a ranch house, New York tenements, and a pirate ship.

Surviving photographs show Aloha standing with Pickford and Fairbanks in front of the new Unit N° IV. Aloha is wearing her standard Wanderwell uniform (minus the shoulder strap) while Mary is dressed in a tightly checked dress with a sombrero, a bandana around her neck, and what appears to be a sheriff's star pinned to her chest — one of the costumes for her film *Little Annie Rooney*, which would be released in October 1925.

For Aloha, meeting her childhood heroine was a mesmerizing experience, and one that helped her own self-esteem — especially since the invitation had come unsolicited. Her name was known to Hollywood's elite, and that could only help her on the road to success.

Aloha with Douglas Fairbanks at United Artists studio, Hollywood, 1925.

Aloha would later marvel that Mary Pickford hardly reached her shoulder, even with her hat on. In the photographs the two women look roughly the same age, perhaps in their early twenties. In fact, Pickford was thirty-three, while Aloha was still just eighteen.

Pickford's husband, Douglas Fairbanks Sr., was fascinated by the Wanderwell project; he was itching to get off the studio lot and actually *see* the world. However, he had little time for far-off adventures. In addition to co-founding United Artists with Pickford, Charlie Chaplin, and D.W. Griffith, he also co-founded the Academy of Motion Picture Arts and Sciences. As its first president, he introduced the idea of presenting awards for achievements of distinctive merit in film — the Academy Awards. If Pickford was America's sweetheart, Fairbanks was the undisputed king of Hollywood. Aloha describes him as capering around like a goofy adolescent with a surfeit of energy. Walter filmed the couple and Aloha christening Unit Nº IV "Miss Los Angeles," after which "with a flourish, swashbuckler Fairbanks, arm raised, wafted Nº IV on its goodwill travels, for the camera."[3]

By 1931 Fairbanks was filming travelogues of his own in locations scattered around the globe, eventually releasing a film called *Around the World In 80 Minutes with Douglas Fairbanks*, an echo of the slogan painted on the side of every Wanderwell car: Around the World with Walter Wanderwell. Fairbanks visited numerous places, including Hawaii, Japan, Hong Kong, China, the Philippines, Cambodia, Thailand, and India. He also went on fishing holidays to Vancouver Island, where he visited the Hall family property near Qualicum Beach. Aloha's daughter would later recall summer days spent swimming with Fairbanks. According to Jeffrey Vance, Fairbanks's biographer, it was the travel bug that led Pickford and Fairbanks to divorce — at least indirectly.[4] Away for long periods, he eventually fell into the arms of Lady Sylvia Ashley, a betrayal Pickford could not forgive, although she claimed that it was the mental anguish of continued separation that prompted the divorce.

❀

The Wanderwell show played April 27 to May 1, packing crowds into the Philharmonic Auditorium's three thousand seats. It was the largest house since Madrid and Berlin, and the first with a thirty-piece orchestra. But Aloha was not intimidated. She had "eighteen years of impudence ready to tell how it was done.... Our epic looked great on the huge screen. (My) voice carried well, over the fine orchestra. Friends swarmed about with congratulations. It was one for the book — a hit run on our hands."[5]

The *Los Angeles Times* review was less effusive, describing the photography as "rather poor" and declaring, "One could wish that at least one glimpse of the Old World scenes had appeared without the two small Wanderwell cars being firmly planted in the fore part of the picture, and the Wanderwell party crossing and re-crossing in front of the lens obscuring the cathedrals, rivers, towers and lovely old landmarks with almost irritating frequency." The same article did, however, admit that "the scenes, the people[,] the views in general are of a sort not seen before. The passages of a Spanish bullfight at Madrid are the most remarkable of their kind ever filmed. At times the cameraman must have been within a few feet of the bull, in constant danger, while taking views of the matadors, the preadors [sic] and the enraged animal. The Wanderwell pictures without a doubt are splendid in their unusual glimpses of native life, native sports and famous landmarks."[6]

❀

April 1925 had been a busy month. Aloha had met several of her movie idols, was arrested (twice), married her employer, played the largest venue on the west coast of North America, and had gotten pregnant. She was not, however, ready to slow down. Their run at the Philharmonic Auditorium had been a success, but it had hardly catapulted Aloha to worldwide fame. The best course of action, then, was action. Walter and Aloha prepared to head east towards Detroit, confident they could now cross state lines without fear of arrest. A new crew was hired, including a nurse and travelling secretary named Dolly Reynolds and a fellow named Eric Owen — both of whom would play important roles in the coming months and years. Owen was a tall, slender man with light brown hair and large blue eyes, and he had recently finished his studies in criminology at UC Berkeley. He was quiet by nature but not afraid to negotiate with sponsors or authorities. Owen was put in charge of securing bookings, advertising, and sponsorship contracts, thus allowing Aloha to concentrate on lectures and interviews, and Walter to develop his ideas for the international police and WAWEC.

Dolly Reynolds was English and had worked in Los Angeles as a nurse and nanny before signing on to the expedition. Small, buxom, and brunette, she liked to laugh and, like Aloha, was known to enjoy the occasional tipple. According to Aloha, Dolly had come to the United States via Canada's Salvation Army immigrant service. Like Owen, she took over some of the expedition's chores, tending to correspondence, helping to keep the crew's communal gear in order, cooking where needed, and most importantly, tending to Aloha's needs as her pregnancy progressed.

The newly expanded crew struck out north for Bakersfield in early May, and it was with wistfulness that Aloha left Los Angeles. She would later make special mention of actors Mary Pickford and Douglas Fairbanks Sr., the writer-producer Chuck Roberts, Art Goebel (and his mother), Gloria Swanson, and the superstar evangelist Aimee Semple McPherson (yet another Canadian).

※

The road was as ragged and rough as anything they'd encountered in China or India. Aloha took the wheel of Unit N° III over the Sierra Nevada mountains and through Donner Pass, which in 1913 had become part of the Lincoln Highway. The pass's elevation made it notoriously dangerous, and the extreme altitude (over 7,000 feet) was hard on Aloha. It took several days of tooth-chipping travel over barely existing roads to make Reno. The cars had

begun breaking down, including the brand new Miss Los Angeles (Unit N°
IV) that had bearing trouble.

After Reno, the roads were little better and the expedition lost the trail
several times, once so completely that they had to make camp amid the
rocks. Aloha was excused from pitching the canvas and sat on a boulder,
sipping water from a canteen, watching the sun set and marvelling at a landscape teeming with wildlife. "There were rabbits everywhere — thousands!"[7]

In larger towns, the expedition stopped to sell pamphlets and postcards
and to book theatres. Sales were especially good in Austin, Eureka, and Ely,
where audiences were thrilled to see scenes of far-off lands. Somewhere
along the way, the expedition added two new crew members: a "buxom"
young woman called Steine and a man named Murphy.[8]

With the Nevada border behind them, they motored east along the jagged
road to Salt Lake City. The road was monotonous in this part of the country,
and as had happened in India, they looked forward to each new town with
an almost licentious fervour. But sometimes the road made its own fun. Not
long after entering Utah, some truckers had warned them that crews were
tearing up the road through the Great Salt Lake Desert, rendering it
impassable for long stretches. Their best bet was to take a wide detour north.
It would add ten days to their trip, but at least they would get through.
Naturally, Walter and Aloha ignored them. Late one afternoon, hot winds
swept up storm clouds from the east. There were ferocious claps of thunder
and lightning, but even before the rain had begun pinging the hot metal
cars, the expedition discovered what the truckers had meant. "Under our
own steam, pushing, towing each other, we, up to our knees in goo, reached
the point of lunacy where humour and curses *sotto voce* got together."[9]
Despite the cars' high clearance and lack of fenders, they were repeatedly
stuck in the soft muck, forcing them to jettison all excess weight. Each
woman drove one car while the men travelled by foot, carrying as much
gear as they could lift. After some hours of this, and just as the rain picked
up speed, they were cheered by the sight of grey tents and smoke in the
distance. The cars were abandoned where they sat.

They spent the night in the workers' camp, the women in a makeshift
storage shed while the men bivouacked under a tarp, listening to the sighs

and snorts of nearby horses. At dawn they gathered for a real camp breakfast: oatmeal, slab bacon, chops, potatoes, pie, and endless mugs of coffee. By 7:00 a.m. the burly highway workers, charmed by Steine and Aloha, had hauled the cars from the muck and towed them a mile east to where the road had already been completed. With bellies full and a blue sky promising a fair travelling day, the expedition members climbed back into their cars. In vehicles with the same horsepower as today's ride-on mowers, they had made it through the most difficult stretch of their journey across the United States.

※

At Salt Lake City the expedition added three new crew members (only one, Ayouf Gabriel, was recorded by his full name, the others listed simply as Lewis and Wagner, all male) and commissioned the construction of yet another car, Unit N° V, dubbed Miss Salt Lake City. Between lectures, Walter spent hours perfecting his plans for the Work Around the World Educational Club, which he now saw as the lynchpin of his travelling empire.

In 1925 it seemed everyone had been bitten by the travel bug. There were hundreds, perhaps thousands, of travellers attempting wild globe-girdling feats. Some travelled the world with only their guitar, others rode bicycles (including tandem ones) or milk trucks. One couple from South Africa attempted to circle the globe pushing wheelbarrows.[10] To Walter, these people didn't represent competition but rather evidence of an unmet demand: people wanted to see and to *experience* the world, and the Wanderwell Expedition, through WAWEC, could provide a means and strategy to do it. It would be, he said, a university on wheels. It would also provide an ongoing revenue stream for Aloha and for him. To Walter, WAWEC was a franchise.

※

The expedition crossed into Wyoming, making good time despite frequent stops to address mechanical troubles. Aloha was soon in love with the state's spacious skies and amber waves of grain. It helped too, that Wyoming welcomed the expedition with open arms and a sincere curiosity — the kind of welcome they had hoped for in California. When they stopped in small towns, like Green River, they easily filled the local theatre.

We would give one show; two reels: Portugal-Spain, Paris and French battle fields. Word spread quickly. Basques, Portuguese sheepmen and wranglers, war veterans, women with children — [a] lovely audience entranced to the point of proverbial pin-drop, followed by wild whoops when the lights went up. Then ten-gallon hats in hand, [they] crowded near afterwards, shy and polite, asking about my accent. Ha! Thought I had lost it.[11]

Before arriving in Denver, they had struck a promotional agreement with the rather plain-sounding Brown Palace Hotel and were shocked to discover how luxurious it was. "Its granite façades towered ten stories. With hearty greetings by co-owner Charles Boettcher, we were led into an astounding foyer encircled by balconied galleries at every floor, skyward to the glass dome."[12]

The highlight of their trip to Denver, however, was the visit to the post office, where Aloha found a stack of letters waiting, including one from Margaret who — despite announcements to the contrary — was still in Nice. Overflowing with good wishes, she asked for details about the Miami River properties. Did they include a house? Had they purchased a yacht? There were no questions about the pregnancy. Questions of house and home would have been top of Margaret's mind. Money from the sale of the Qualicum properties was fast running out, and unless new funds miraculously appeared, she really would have to leave Nice.

※

In Kansas City the expedition was pushed from the headlines by the recent victory of William Jennings Bryan in the so-called Scopes monkey trial. Aloha took little trouble to hide her opinions. "Still believing that Creation was a fait accompli in seven days, Adam and Eve were set on this planet at maturity, [Jennings] just won his case in Tennessee.... The whole country has been aroused."[13] And they were soon to experience this narrow-mindedness first-hand when a representative of the Kansas Motion Picture Censor Board demanded changes to several sequences of the Wanderwell films: "ten in the bullfight at Bilbao, two of shy little Bedouin boys with healthy naked bodies. She [the film censor] was not amused by a similar sequence where a veiled Bombay girl carrying her baby brother stood in front of the lens, plainly exhibited was his stiff little penis bound in jewellery."[14]

Much to Aloha's amazement, her husband kept his cool and even apologized to the censor before explaining that these scenes depicted old cultures who "have learned tolerance" and that he was unable to edit his films "just for Kansas." The remaining engagements were cancelled, the canisters sealed, and the crew relocated, ten minutes across the river to Kansas City, Missouri, where they promptly booked several more shows. While Aloha lectured—and now dealt with morning sickness and diarrhoea—Walter and the crew assembled yet another car, this time buying parts through newspaper advertisements. In keeping with tradition, Unit N° VI was christened Miss Kansas City.

Aloha, well into her second trimester, was at the wheel of N° III when she recognized a change in the geography and heaved a sigh. At the mud flats near Chesterfield, Missouri, the roads disintegrated into one long trough of mud. One after another, cars slid into ditches or spun sideways and had to be righted by manpower. "So hellish one could cry. Every step into the mud and out fished up more weight...you couldn't lift a leg, arms were gumbo to the elbows." Tempers flared, especially when Mac accidentally toppled Lewis into the mud. Outraged, Lewis was about to throw a punch at Mac when Steine pushed her way past them, "missing the blow but opportunely toppling the pair. We all took a breather to laugh in our agonies."[15]

But the crew's perseverance was rewarded in St. Louis, where crowds clamoured to see the cars, watch the films, and buy souvenirs. "Money money everywhere." It was as refreshing as a glass of cold water. With responsive crowds and Detroit looming just ahead, "the excitement, for us, built up hourly. We could see we were in for a good bit of popular hero worship—the thing of the day! Reaching Detroit would be such a thrill!"[16] Once again, Aloha had driven her dreams on to the next town. Except this time, that town was called Motor City.

Aloha holding newborn Valri at their compound in Miami, Florida, January 1925.

FOURTEEN

A SPECIAL DELIVERY

A LOHA ARRIVED IN DETROIT in August 1925 and found a bustling industrial city, swirling with jazz and dancing on the promise of its bright future. Immigrants from around the world had flocked to fill jobs on assembly lines and management offices. It was the town where cars were not only made but also driven — there were as many automobiles as families.[1] It was, in other words, the ideal city in which to wind up the Million Dollar Wager.

When the expedition's cars rolled through town, they were accompanied by the sirens of a police escort and a storm of tickertape thrown by cheering well-wishers. Theatres and businesses clamoured for the expedition's attention, offering free lodging, extended bookings, and product samples. And then there were the newspapers. San Francisco's dailies had turned up their noses at the little troupe, but Detroit's papers celebrated the achievements of the Motor City cars that had conquered the world.

There was much fun with newspaper rivalries — especially knock out competition between *The News* and *Free Press*.

To the *Free Press* we gave first exclusive on foreign stills in return for their Sunday rotogravure.

The *Detroit News* sent their limousine to pick us up for our first ever radio broadcast. We were ceremoniously ushered to a private office with an elaborate microphone disk suspended on the desk; were humbly requested by the editor not to mention the car's maker — "That would constitute advertising; you'll understand that, won't you?" Indeed we did![2]

Naturally, as soon as the interview started Aloha entirely forgot *not* to use the "F" word, but her enthusiastic recounting of their intrepid international adventures quickly assuaged any annoyance. The Ford company was understandably thrilled.

> The chief was delighted. On the way out, however, he let another "cat out of the bag."
> "Well, we sure scooped the Free Press!"
> To our disgust we had unwittingly fouled up our promise of first exclusive to the arch rival.[3]

The error did not seem to spoil their coverage in the Free Press, though the subtitle was a touch mocking: "Wife Is Sister Too!" followed by an explanation that Walter had been "adopted" by Aloha's mother. Ersatz headlines aside, it was the best coverage the expedition had received in America. Large photographs in the August 16 issue of the *Detroit Times* show Walter and Aloha gazing at each other with proud smiles, while behind them large crowds gather around the flag-draped Unit Nº II. The headline reads, "Wandering Wanderwells Are Home."

❀

Amid the hubbub, several crew members quit while new ones were hired. A few who had failed to meet Walter's high performance expectations were sent home. But even this hardly mattered. The Wanderwell Expedition had, for the moment, captured Detroit's imagination, and Aloha and Walter were booked from sun-up until sundown, giving interviews or "bicycling" theatre engagements — showing at two venues simultaneously.

> Running the shop at my end pretty well, I basked in publicity's glare… hounded for autographs through the lobby, stairs, outside to the (police) escort; rushed at theatres, mobbed in department stores by not always appreciative strangers — many gawkers. I gave up receiving reporters in the lobby… got on my high horse, too high hat to receive, except by special appointment, there were so many curiosity seekers — many bunkum artists. Adulation went to my head.[4]

The times were good all around. The country was in the mood to celebrate its achievements. American business was booming, Babe Ruth was batting, the Goodyear Blimp was flying, and in South Dakota a Danish-American sculptor wanted to carve the likeness of famous American presidents into Mount Rushmore. Soon after Detroit, Aloha began billing herself as the World's Most Widely Travelled Girl. She became *the* face of the Wanderwell Expedition, the main voice and authority quoted in newspapers. Walter supported Aloha's growing renown, but he also reminded her that this was the *expedition's* success and all of it a stepping stone to something greater.

❄

A tentative meeting with Henry Ford was arranged through Ford's chief assistant Ernest Liebold. Walter and Liebold had exchanged a number of letters over the years, including the recent acceptance of Unit Nº II as a gift to the Ford museum. Now Walter wanted to meet the man, to outline his idea for an international police. Aloha wondered if he would ask for Ford's endorsement, but Walter said, "I'm not going to ask him *anything*. I'm going to listen to him."[5]

While Walter waited to meet Ford, the crew continued to work the town, selling pamphlets in the streets, collecting signatures for a new international police petition, and signing on new WAWEC members. To forestall the possibility of more police interference, Walter secured a letter of welcome written on the letterhead of Police Commissioner F.H. Croul and signed by the deputy superintendent:

This is to certify that Cars WAWEC 2, 3, 4 and 9 are in Detroit.

We are glad to extend them the courtesy of the city after their absence of four years.

Trusting the officers will cooperate with them while in the city, and wishing them success, I am,

Very truly yours,
James Sprott.[6]

"The Chief of Police assigned two motorcycle escorts, 8 am and 6 pm. They picked us up at The Book [Hotel], enabling Cap...to skip through traffic on business errands. Yours truly or our ad canvassers shared the second escort." Before long, there were twenty full-time crew members and two new vehicles, including a massive armoured vehicle built on a truck chassis and referred to as "the Tank." The days were so full and the hours so long that Aloha and Walter hardly saw each other, except to sleep or go over the next day's itineraries. And then, Aloha began to falter.

On the morning of Walter's meeting with Henry Ford, Dolly Reynolds found Aloha bent over the hotel toilet, "throwing up water, bran flakes and fruit." She was sent to bed, where Dolly fed her spoonfuls of peppermint syrup. After a short nap, Aloha was up and dressed again, determined to accompany Walter. By noon, however, she realized she was not well enough to make the trip and, rather than risk evacuating on Mr. Ford's desk, decided to stay at the hotel after all. "We dashed down to the chauffeur and he was off. Standing alone at the lobby curb I had a momentary vision; some day [sic] I should have a Lincoln."[7]

Walter's meeting, originally scheduled to last fifteen minutes, lasted more than an hour — a fact that Aloha trumpeted proudly. "Cap's exuberance usually bowls people over, so evidently, the great industrialist. When Cap's allotted time was up, the Yes-man came to alert but Mr. Ford waved the annoyance away."[8] The two men discussed the trip around the world, Aloha's record-setting stretches, and the presence of Ford dealerships around the globe. Mr. Ford told Walter, "You know more of our agents than any man on earth. You know firsthand more what they think of us than anybody in the Ford Company."[9] Ford was particularly interested in the photos of Units N° II and III on the Vladivostok parade grounds. He had stakes in the burgeoning Russian automotive industry but knew that sales there would be impeded so long as drivable roads were scarce. Walter suggested that modified car designs might go a long way towards speeding the process. Ford was keen to know exactly how the Wanderwell cars had been modified: "gravity feed, deep foot pits, solid disk wheels, built-in trunk, with a hatch entrance on chains [that could serve] as a bench. Ruckstell gears, grip grooved Tilt-Lock steering wheel,"[10] and Walter's soon-to-be-patented Speed Slope body design.

For his part, Walter was deeply impressed by Ford, even if the meeting did not achieve all he had hoped. On immigration documents filed in San Francisco, Walter had claimed that the aim of their trip across the United States was to reach Detroit, where they would join the Ford Motor Company staff. That dream never materialized, nor did his wish for Ford's public endorsement of the international police. Instead, Ford stressed that businesses should remain steadfastly apolitical. "He told me I should keep free, put the work in the hands of energetic young mixed nationalities, keep free of big politicians, big financiers. Then he went on to tell me [that] sponsoring our work is out of the question 'unless you want to be hogtied to company schedules and overseers.' I said, 'No, sir!!'"[11]

When the interview ended, Walter was more determined than ever to grow his organizations, to make their achievements and ideals known to the leaders of industry and politicians around the world. As Aloha put it, "The visit had been a shining day for Cap. Any day of his life he would have traded a 'World's Fair' for this.... It was journey's end; the ORACLE, sage of industry had endorsed our way of life. Nothing finer than to give us his benign blessing and our total independence."[12]

✻

The World's Most Widely Travelled Girl had persevered through deserts, mud, heat, storms, and war. Pregnancy was, however, a different kind of challenge. After three weeks in Detroit she was too ill to give lectures, conduct interviews, or sell postcards, much less drive anywhere.

> The doctor told Cap I had colitis and prescribed sending me away to a sunny climate until my time, saying, "I can't do anything more for her." That sounded desperate to me and [I thought] I'd better get my chin up.
>
> Later Cap announced, "You're going to Miami on Thursday by train with Reynolds, you can rest in comfort there until after the baby arrives. Sorry I can't go with you but I'll be there as soon as the outfit is actually organized on tour."[13]

With Dolly in tow, Aloha boarded an "express" to Miami and spent the next forty hours and thirty-seven stops sitting in a train car, pining for a steering wheel. But by the time the smoky hills of Tennessee gave way to the flat green of Georgia and the little palm trees started just south of Homerville and the first twinkles of blue caught her eye at St. Augustine, she could barely contain the impulse to get out and explore. Even the air had changed, now warm and soft, and yet not at all like the South of France. This was another new world and she was ready to throw herself into the arms of adventure. Getting off at the wrong station, they found themselves in a bad part of town at the wrong time of day. There were no hotels so they were forced to spend the night in what Aloha called a "hot-pillow sporting house" (courtesy of a compassionate madam). Aloha refused to be discouraged. She was soon hiking, swimming, sailing, and touring the Miami area, including Coral Gables and the riverfront property that Walter had purchased six years earlier.

Aloha was proud of her regained vitality, especially *because* she was pregnant. Like many women of the time, Aloha made use of stomach-smoothing corsets to conceal her state.[14] By 1925 the medical profession had begun warning women of the dangers of "maternity corsets," but they were still widely sold and routinely used. A 1922 ad for Ferris Maternity Corsets asked women, "Will yours be a 'good' baby?" and explained how selecting the correct corset was vital to ensuring the birth of a happy, healthy, chubby, and gurgling baby.[15] In one respect, the devices were clearly effective: in no photograph does Aloha appear obviously pregnant.

✿

It would be two months before Walter joined her, arriving in late November, one month before the baby was due. He had spent his time, he said, organizing and training a WAWEC unit to work the Eastern Seaboard. As usual, his arrival heralded a flurry of intense activity. Within a week he had purchased a newly constructed houseboat that Aloha set about decorating and preparing for the baby's arrival.

By December 16 Aloha was too shy to be seen in public but still went for walks after sunset. To her horror, she had begun losing bladder control and was afraid to drink anything in the late hours of the day. Then, on 19

December, Aloha had pain throughout her body and became incoherent. By one account, she had slipped on the deck of a boat days earlier, possibly causing complications.[16] She was rushed to the Jackson Memorial Hospital where doctors feared she might be haemorrhaging.

Walter and Aloha's first child was born shortly past 9:00 a.m. on December 20.

Aloha was not well enough to return home until the fifteenth of January, when she managed to walk "unaided down the river path, feet slithering in shoes...weighing 95 pounds, Mum's new frock flapping from my bony shoulders." Signs strung across the tent buildings read "Welcome Home Little Wanderer." At the age of nineteen, after more than three years on the road, Aloha had finally arrived at a place she could call home. More than 3,000 miles from Qualicum Beach, she had reinvented the world her mother had known only a few years earlier: homesteading near the water with a boat, a young husband, and a new baby girl.

They named her Valri, after Walter's true given name, Valerian, meaning valiant and brave. It seemed to fit. Less comprehensible was their choice of middle name: Nell. Even in light of a continued friendship or of gratefulness for a divorce granted, it's hard to understand how Aloha could have permitted her first-born to bear the name of her husband's former wife. But she did. Many decades later, the authors asked Valri about her middle name. She simply shrugged and shook her head. "I have absolutely no idea."[17]

Aloha and Walter settled into a sleep and feeding schedule with young Valri, and the baby thrived. Aloha cherished those first days at home.

> That lovely lazy tropical family existence with books and recuper-
> ations and Cap and Valri all to myself—a fascinating chapter of "Life
> with Baby." Walking, nursing, boating, proudly watching our daughter
> develop, arguing [with] Reynolds about her care, fresh air, sunshine,
> swimming.[18]

It was a short-lived idyll, for the road beckoned. Just three weeks later young Valri would be left with Reynolds while Walter and Aloha put together a new expedition.

Aboard the SS *Itororo* bound from Havana, Cuba, to Quebec City. Aloha (L) next to the ship's captain, while Walter sits atop their car, Atlantic Ocean, 1926.

FIFTEEN

TWO IF BY SEA

W ALTER AND ALOHA CHOSE CUBA as their next destination. Since
the late 1700s Cuba had been a sugar-producing concern with modest
sidelines in tobacco, coffee, slaving, and piracy. Vast plantations circled the
island, but almost all were owned by American creditors whose grip on the
Cuban economy was backed by the US military. The average Cuban made
little, owned little, and in the eyes of foreign investors, mattered little. As one
Cuban historian observed, "The bank that underwrites the cutting of the
cane is foreign, the cutting of the cane is foreign, the consumers' market is
foreign, the administrative staff set up in Cuba, the machinery that is installed,
the capital that is invested, the very land of Cuba is held by foreign ownership."[1]

But the collapse of sugar prices in 1920, followed by the failure of many
of the nation's banks, underscored for Cubans the dangers of relying on a
single crop and stoked their resentment of foreign owners.

From the Cuban perspective, it was obvious that the ways of the past
could not carry them forward. If Cuba was to prosper, it needed an economy
that could ride out the bumps. Two key industries became the focus: cigar
making and tourism. Despite being overrun with mills and plantations,
Cuba retained its pristine white beaches, its swaying palms, and its soft air
scented with ginger lily, guava, and cigar smoke. There was also the unique
Afro-Cuban culture, whose music and artistic style were ready to be
celebrated by a decade in the mood for a party. Before long, Cuba was
drawing tourists from across the United States: men and women who, back
home, were respectable bank managers, civil servants, and school teachers,
were, with increasing frequency, tumbling off packed steamships with

expressions like children on Christmas morning. Only 224 miles from Miami, Florida, yet free of prohibition and social inhibitions, they thronged to Havana's bars and clubs, ready to sample the strong rum, the colourful dances, and the delicious anonymity of a foreign paradise. By the mid-1920s, Cuba had earned the nickname "Pleasure Island."[2]

Cuba's tourist boom was not lost on Walter Wanderwell. With so many people interested in visiting the country, WAWEC, he thought, would be an easy sell; and given Cuba's suffering at the hand of foreign powers, he believed that the idea of an international police would appeal to Cubans. Most importantly, though, Walter saw Cuba as testing ground for how he and Aloha might proceed with the next phase of their lives. The couple who began as slapdash travellers out to set records and raise eyebrows now found themselves married with a child to raise. Cuba was their chance to see how the Wanderwell travelling spectacle would sell without the allure of bets and races.

An ad was placed in the *Miami Daily News*:

> Work-Way Trip to Cuba. Expenses Paid.
> Apply Schooner Ainsley Morning Only.[3]

Two hundred people applied for a position with WAWEC, and seven were selected. Among the new crew was a man named H.A. Larralde, whom Aloha described as an "affable linguist with heired [*sic*] manners."[4] The names of the other new crew members were not recorded — indeed, the further Aloha progressed in her career, the less she recorded the names of her supporting crew, with some notable exceptions. In addition to the seven fresh faces, there were several returning members of expedition, including Eric Owen, who was appointed second in command. Following a week of preparations, they set sail for Havana aboard their chartered schooner.

❈

The *Ainsley* was a three-masted schooner built in Liverpool, Nova Scotia, in 1911. The ship registry listed the boat as *Ainslie* while the name splashed across its stern was *Ainsley*.[5] Also, although owned by a consortium of Canadians, it had Cuban registry and was based out of Havana.

The crossing to Havana was stormy and the *Ainsley* was forced to wait within sight of the crenelated walls of Morro Castle, the city's famous sixteenth-century fortress. When a tugboat finally chugged aport, the crew happily paid a fifty-dollar towing fee and supplied the tug operators with international police brochures. They were suitably impressed and docked the ship at Cuba's official guest wharf. The surprise arrival of an "official" vessel sent the Havana newspaper presses whirling. "Mystery vessel in harbour may be ammunition runner for Mexico," claimed one headline.[6]

Cuban customs officials were concerned. After a day of embargo, the crew was cleared to land. Aloha enjoyed the novelty of not needing to look for accommodations in town — the ship remained their headquarters — and immediately set about haranguing the masses with postcards and international police petition ledgers.

The Cuban people were welcoming and seemed to support the idea of an international police, but as Walter had predicted, it was Cuban business that was most enthusiastic about the expedition, making gifts and inquiring about sponsorship agreements. "Bacardi delivered two cases of rum with an invitation to their premises — likewise the Havana Cigar combine. The list was long. Many improbable gifts found their way quietly to the Salvation Army."[7] Cuba's warm reception translated into financial success, though some people felt the expedition was earning money the wrong way.

They spent two months touring Cuba before returning to Florida on May 11 aboard the SS *Cuba* and landing at Tampa. The *Ainsley* was left in Cuba and records show that a Captain E. Wilkie took the wheel until the vessel was sold to new owners on the island.[8]

However, there was some suspicion that the *Ainsley* and perhaps the Wanderwells were using the Cuba venture as a cover for rum-running. Prohibition was in full swing in America. On June 8, 1926, Felix S.S. Johnson, the American consul in Kingston, Ontario, Canada, wrote to the US secretary of state describing his interview with one Reverend Burgess. According to the reverend, his stepson, Hugh Leonard Douse, had served on the schooner *Ainsley* while under charter by the Wanderwell International Police Expedition and had written letters describing his experiences. "From what the Reverend Burgess gathers from his step-son's letters, cargoes of liquor are taken on board for the purpose of replenishing the vessels that are known as the rum row of New York City." The consul wrote that he was "fully convinced that the schooner is being used for other than legitimate purposes," and believed that, "If the Government would go carefully into this expedition they will find that it is a fake concern in order to hide what is really taking place."[9] The consul concluded by requesting that an investigation into the Wanderwell International Police Expedition be conducted.

US authorities had been monitoring the *Ainsley* for a long time, as early as May 1924, when Walter and Aloha were still in India. According to another letter addressed to the US Secretary of State from the American consul in Nassau, Bahamas, the *Ainsley* was known to have transferred some twelve thousand cases of liquor and large quantities of cocaine.[10] Such a cargo would fetch in excess of a million dollars (in 1926 dollars!) — a sum more than sufficient to retire for life.[11] Despite the ship's reputation, however, there was little that American authorities could do; the ship had foreign registry, and there were simply too many ships in operation and too much coastline to patrol.

One other curiosity surrounds the consul's report on Wanderwell and the *Ainsley*: his informant was a Reverend named Burgess. The registered captain of the ship was *also* named Burgess and the ship's majority shareholder was a Nova Scotian named Roland H. Burgess. Coincidence or deflection?

❈

By the end of May, Aloha was in Jacksonville, Florida, preparing for a visit to Canada. The trip was an easy way to add another country to the Wanderwell list and, of course, to add some weight to the coffers. Walter was still wedded to his international police ideal and wanted to introduce the idea to another country. Among the cars was Unit N° XI ("the Tank"), which had become the mobile headquarters of WAWEC, its side emblazoned with calls to "Outlaw War" and "Sign the Petition for International Police." Photographs show hundreds of people crowding the vehicle or standing in a line fifty people deep to scrawl their names on petition forms. In Florida, police officials seemed uniformly unenthused when a parade of battered cars bearing WAWEC licence plates rolled into their town in the company of an armoured vehicle and, usually, numerous young women in military uniform.

To sidestep those challenges, Walter booked passage for his crew and cars aboard a ramshackle, lumber-hauling Paraguayan steamer called the *Itororo*. Knowing they would be gone awhile, Walter and Aloha had spent a week in late May visiting little Valri in Miami. Now six months old, she was beginning to pull herself to standing and had the florid cheeks and wet chin of a teething child. Aloha was eager to resume her life on the road and to make a triumphant return to Canada but also hated to leave her daughter behind again.

The Wanderwell Expedition left Jacksonville on June 1, 1926, and chugged north aboard the *Itororo*. On June 17 they reached Quebec City, where the *Itororo* was boarded by Canadian officials who demanded the ship's captain explain the presence of what looked like a tank and an anti-aircraft gun. Walter intervened, explaining that he was responsible for the cars and gun. According to Aloha, intense questioning followed, during which Walter reassured officials that they posed no threat to Canada.

"Why do you carry guns? Your mission is peace propaganda?"

Cap, "People are attracted by guns and think of war. We want to distinguish our peace effort from pussyfoot pacifists. We represent youth demanding laws not war; advocating a new active force to complete the power of the League of Nations of which your Senator Dandurand is President of the Council. We advocate the actual establishment of a mobile International Police Force as differentiated from articles ten to sixteen of League Covenant. We're here to canvass Canadian opinion."[12]

Ultimately, officials shrugged their shoulders. This was an expedition of lunatics to be sure, but harmless lunatics. They could see no reason to prevent their landing in Canada but they ordered the expedition to register with police in every town they stayed.[13]

❉

In Ottawa, Aloha stayed behind while Walter paid a visit to Parliament Hill to inquire about arranging an interview with Senator Raoul Dandurand. The senator's secretary, who seemed confused by the Wanderwell uniform,

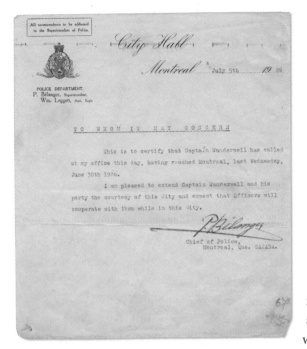

An official PR letter from Montreal's chief of police extending good wishes and the co-operation of the city's police force to the expedition during its stay, Montreal, July 1926.

suggested that Walter leave some literature behind. He handed her several international police pamphlets and explained that they would be in town for a few days collecting signatures regarding the need for arms control. The secretary scanned the pamphlets and asked Walter to wait a moment. Five minutes later he was ushered into the senator's office.

> He recalled the details vividly: Large mahogany desk, (and a) small Frenchman with white beard, furiously scribbling. Dandurand rose and came forward with the literature. They clasped hands. The Senator apologized for his hurry but explained that the House was currently in session and he was about to make a speech concerning his recent visit with the Crown Prince of Sweden. Before Walter could launch into an explanation of his International Police idea, the Senator declared that arms control was a matter "close to his heart" but that politicians had already taken the issue as far as they could. The next step, he said, was for the people to raise their voices. He encouraged Walter and Aloha to redouble their efforts, to make people see that there were better tools than guns to secure international peace. But this was not something a politician could single-handedly impose. "Yes, it is up to youth...youth must fire the engine."[14]

Walter left Dandurand's office, as he had Henry Ford's, empty-handed but not discouraged. One day his idea for an international police force would become a reality — how, exactly, was not clear but he was certain that publicity was his greatest weapon.

✿

The expedition crossed back into the United States just a month after they had arrived, but Canada had made a lasting impression on Walter. He rewrote the expedition's pamphlets to include an account of his visit to Senator Dandurand, quoting the "Genial Old Fighter" as saying, "If you want to do any good Wanderwell, go to England, go to the United States, those are the principal countries opposed to it. [It's] up to the people, up to the people."[15] The same pamphlet urged people to join WAWEC and proposed a platform of articles for the establishment of an international police, including bold type emphasizing that WAWEC was not advocating a Superstate "but an Intergovernmental Fire Department in the Service of Mankind."[16]

An article that ran in the *Christian Science Monitor* in August carried much the same message and was a snapshot of Walter's ideals. It also demonstrates his grasp of how new technologies could be used to influence opinion around the world. "The motion picture is the ideal means of solving the difficulties encountered through language barriers. I cannot speak Chinese but my pictures are my contact. I can find a theatre and a screen in the smallest town in China. I can get an interpreter at the corner and go ahead, certain that my audience will not only be interested but will be able to discern, through the pictures, what our motive is." The article's close describes how a new caravan will be organized in New York to "traverse the Southern Hemisphere."[17]

The southern hemisphere was an amorphous idea: perhaps the South Pacific, or South America, or Africa. To Walter, it made little difference, so long as they were adding new countries to the record, filming new vistas, and recruiting new members to the WAWEC and the international police (IP) causes. For Aloha, however, exhausted and missing her little girl, the idea of vanishing for another year or two or three was more than she could stand. In response, she resorted to one of her oldest tricks.

An article in the *Hartford Courant* on September 3, 1926, announced

"Husband Reports Woman World Tourist Missing." According to the article, Aloha had vanished the previous evening in Springfield while en route to the town of Adams, Massachusetts. She and Walter were parking their cars when they became separated. He later informed police that he "feared she had met with foul play because she had with her at the time $600."[18]

Aloha would later claim there had been a quick note to the captain: "Dear: Gone to Florida to see Valri. Love."[19] According to her reminiscences, she boarded a train south to Newark from where she hitchhiked the remaining 1,367 miles to Miami. There may have been another reason for her sudden need to vanish. She was pregnant again.

By mid-September, Aloha was back with little Valri at the Wanderwells' Miami property at 214 N.W. North River Drive, Spring Gardens. Nestled beside the Miami River, the isolated property was heavily treed with oaks and palms. It was a home that Aloha was happy to come back to: peaceful and beautiful and, she could still hardly believe, *hers*.

When the WAWEC units reached New York, Walter left Eric Owen in charge and sped to Florida where he and Aloha took time to try and sort out their differences, recharge their batteries, and see their wary daughter. "She had eyed us a little coolly after the first 'Hello, stranger' smile . . . [but soon] decided Cap's knee might be a jolly place for a ride . . . . Enrapt hours sped."[20]

On September 15, Aloha noted that the weather had become "suffocatingly muggy." Reynolds and Valri took refuge at the nearby Seybold mansion. The owners were away "but their staff, housekeeper, skipper, enjoyed company and gladly shared their fan-cooled quarters."[21] By evening the heat had lessened and Reynolds and Valri returned to the houseboat for the night.

The following morning one of the Seybold staff suggested the Wanderwells double up on their moorings. There had been no official warning, but the old-timers down at the pier said that something was on its way. The temperature drop, sudden winds, and an ominous increase in ocean chop suggested it could be a heavy storm. Walter had a deep respect for the opinions of old sailors, so he and Aloha set about tightening and reinforcing the lines anchoring their houseboat to some pilings and "a pair of ancient oaks of immense dimension rooted beyond the banks . . . . We cleared the decks, battened windows, filled thermoses in case the power went off."[22]

They also tightened the lines on the five canvas tents they had installed on the property as rental holiday homes. The income they generated was more than enough to support Reynolds and Valri while Walter and Aloha were away.[23]

By late Thursday rainsqualls were pummelling the area. The canvas tents billowed and snapped loudly, but held. The houseboat bobbed in drunken circles but also held fast. By morning the winds had eased although heavy rains continued, swelling the river until it began flooding the property, pooling among the oak roots and threatening the raised floors of the canvas tents. Friday brought more rain, creating new streams along the property and further glutting the river. Its normally placid and shimmering surface was frothed and carried a whirling parade of debris from upstream. "Dinghies, life belts and hatches from boathouses spun by," but Walter and Aloha were not unnerved. They were inland and the many trees along the canal acted as a windbreak. "The houseboat was sturdily constructed, a strong cypress pontoon, it rode well. If necessary we'd ride it right up onto the property." Shortly past lunchtime a small sailboat swept past them, "its foremast crushing against the Fifth Street Bridge (while) the hull clung to the south abutment."

Walter fetched his oilskin jacket and wrapped his daughter in it. It was possible that the brunt of the storm had not yet arrived and there was no sense leaving Valri in harm's way. The Seybold mansion was on higher ground and was made of brick and concrete — a much safer place to wait until the rain and flooding subsided. Aloha and Walter trudged through the soggy ground, carrying Valri back to the mansion where Reynolds and the Seybold staff had gathered in the kitchen to fill oil lamps and stockpile matches and candles. The icebox was out of ice but they had bread and crackers and a block of cheese in reserve. A metal tub had been set outside to collect rainwater. When Walter set off for the houseboat again, Aloha experienced a perplexing flicker of fear. "I was torn between being with the baby and (going) to help Cap."[24]

In the late afternoon the rain tapered to a drizzle, though the river continued to rise. Walter had managed to winch the houseboat up onto the property, away from the stream of wreckage now rushing on the river's surge. Towards evening, Aloha came wading through the property. If a storm did come, Aloha wanted to help Walter protect their little patch of paradise.

With blankets and oil lamps at the ready they settled in for a long night. Through the waving canopy of treetops, Aloha could see the sunset and was unsettled by its gangrenous green hue. Then, almost as soon as the sun had gone, the rain and wind returned. Walter shook his head, "'Babe, we have to go' is all he said.... When we stepped off the pontoon we were up to our armpits in humid water." The river had burst its banks completely. Safely back at the mansion, they rocked Valri and sipped the last of their hot chocolate as they waited for the heavy rain to pour itself out. It had been bucketing for two days, so perhaps this was the storm's final hurrah.

It was not.

At 3:00 a.m. the wind exploded in an apocalyptic hurricane. Air roared through the trees and snaked through the seam of every door and window, creating a choir of ear-splitting howls, punctuated by the explosive bangs of snapping trees and the sound of debris slamming against the house. The noise was so intense it sent tears of pain streaming down their faces. "At the height of the destruction I wondered about [our] chance of survival. Could *this* be the end of the universe?... If we were going to go, it was better to go together."[25]

By 6:30 a.m. the storm had eased. The house was still standing and the sky was lightening. Aloha wanted to go outside and check on the houseboat, but Walter warned her to stay put. There was every chance that they were now in the eye of the hurricane and that the rear wall would soon be upon them. Unfortunately, several hundred of Miami's citizens did not share Walter's experience with tropical storms. Most of the hurricane's deaths occurred when people left their sheltering spots, believing the tempest past, only to be mowed down when it returned thirty-five minutes later.[26] Walter and Aloha ventured to the upper floor to see if there was much damage. What they saw left them speechless. Everywhere they looked were scenes of destruction: "Roofs on Fifth Street taken off like kites, empty autos rammed into walls, at moments debris of all dimensions filled the air. Cinderblock buildings [had] disintegrated like mounds of kicked sugar cubes."[27]

When the storm returned barely a half-hour later, the winds were even more powerful, recorded at over 150 miles per hour. The storm's tidal surge swelled inland waterways by twelve feet, swamping vast areas. According to Red Cross figures, more than 350 people were killed in the Miami area, while as many as 60,000 were left homeless. Adjusted for wealth normalization, the Great Miami Hurricane of 1926 is considered the costliest hurricane in US history, estimated to have caused $165 billion in damage.[28] Large portions of Miami were wiped out, the damage ruined an already tottering Florida economy, and sent the state into depression three years before the stock market crash. By noon of September 19, the skies had finally cleared. Walter and Aloha donned their rain boots and put on all the clothes they could find — not to keep warm or dry, but to guard against the snakes that floated through the waters. They wanted to know what had become of their home. Perhaps by some miracle the plucky houseboat had made it through the cyclone. The trip was slow and they were cautious to stay clear of strong currents or deep water. The heat brought out the smell of decay and created a low-lying fog that made breathing difficult. "Pushing flotsam aside, we advanced among total desolation. The oaks lay in deathblow, exposed branches cluttered with planks... rags and canvas. (Then we saw) our home, lifted and turned upside down, the weight of the huge cypress pontoon had come down on the houseboat, crushing it like a matchbox."[29]

Aloha stood in shock amidst the derelict wreckage of their little paradise: shattered furniture, torn strands of clothing, the torso of a doll. Nothing remained of the canvas tents. They spent the morning hunting for items that might be retrieved but found almost nothing. Aloha's childhood journals, photographs of Herbert and Margaret and Miki, and most of her mementoes from their trip around the world had been lost. "Irredeemably submerged, my small exquisite objects... Priceless because they were artistic, or rare in handiwork, tint, native: clay madonna, Brussels lace, the jade Kwan Yin, Rubaiyat, a Haiku..." Gone too were Valri's baby things, her "handmade Lafayette, christening robe, treasures from Mum."[30]

Sixty years later, when Aloha was asked about her experience of the Miami Hurricane, she lost her usual reserve and began sobbing. "We almost lost Valri," was all she could say.

The special edition Wanderwell Expedition pamphlet promoting the showing of *Around the World by Auto*, at the Philharmonic Auditorium, Los Angeles, California, April 27, 1925.

SIXTEEN

MOTHER'S NATURE

O N OCTOBER 13, 1926, Aloha spent her twentieth birthday searching through broken trees, along riverbanks, and in the mud for bits of what had so briefly been her home. After ten days the river waters had still not subsided, and she had recovered almost nothing. Yet they had escaped with their lives and little Valri.

By the end of October they were 1,240 miles north of their destroyed land, back with the WAWEC units and looking for new ways to promote the international police initiative and make some money. Aloha received a letter from her mother who announced that she and Miki had finally given up the house in Nice and were leaving for South Africa. Miki would attend school and Margaret would visit her sister in Johannesburg. Walter and Aloha hatched a new plan: travel to South Africa and drive the length of the continent, from Cape Town in the south to Cairo in the north. Aloha had recently read a newspaper article about the Court Treatt Expedition that had driven the length of Africa, from Cape to Cairo, along sections of a newly completed motorway called the Great North Road.

> We held the council of units. It was too large a group to remain self-supporting on an African venture — so small a population, such a vast continent. The unit pilots agreed to disburse and carry on WAWEC endeavours throughout south US for the winter then north and west to Canada. My dear old buddy number three was donated to Mac and crew. We were left with Nº II, Nº IV and the Tank.[1]

In addition to Walter, Aloha, and Valri, their group would include Eric Owen and a man called F.G. Miller, whom Aloha later called "Smythe." Miller was "a short, lithe young English cockney, who answered our advertisement in New York for an interpreter, and who demonstrated he could speak half a dozen African native dialects fluently."[2]

The only outstanding detail was Margaret — would she consent to watching over Valri and caring for the new baby while Aloha and Walter crossed the continent? Margaret's cabled reply confirmed that she would watch over the children "devotionally," and bore the added news that Miki wanted to join the tour across Africa. Aloha was thrilled.

Papers and passes were hastily arranged, "British Consulate's visa 'Good for Union of South Africa, Southern Rhodesia, Northern Rhodesia,' all the seigniorial territories — and Egypt."[3] Then, on October 27, the WAWEC units held a last send-off rally in front of New York City Hall. Press photographs show the line of cars engulfed in a sea of fedoras and trench coats. On the side of the Tank is scrawled "Cape to Cairo — See you in 2 Years! — Goodbye New York!"

❖

On October 30, 1926, the Wanderwells boarded the passenger/cargo ship SS *Eastern Glade* bound for Cape Town. Aloha was three months pregnant. The ship stopped at Norfolk, Virginia, to take on coal before the ocean crossing, and "five alien seamen jumped ship." The boat was delayed while authorities investigated and levied fines against the company. "The skipper signed on two German sailors; Cap, Owen and Miller replaced the other deserters. Their able-bodied seaman's pay $30 at Cape Town."[4] The ship's skipper, Captain Thompson, was not pleased to have a woman and child aboard but was grateful that three of his passengers were experienced sailors. The arrangement meant the Wanderwell crew could make use of staff rooms and eat at the captain's table.

Rough weather soon confined Aloha and Valri to their cabin while Cap, Owen, and Miller worked through vicious wind and rain, bracing themselves against colossal waves that swept over the decks and threatened to wash the cars into the sea.[5] Alone in a dim cabin, it wasn't long before Aloha felt the walls closing in. "Stacked neatly in every corner (was) precious equipment (that) barely left room to manoeuver." Day after day was spent "trying to diaper, feed, live in such (a) tiny space with wet clammy cloth hanging everywhere."[6]

By November 12, the two new Germans had fallen gravely ill, with intense stomach pains and high fever. There was no doctor on board and the closest ship with a medical staff was 200 miles west, which, when contacted by wireless, turned out to be a French vessel. Aloha was recruited to communicate the sick men's symptoms to the French doctors: "fast pulse, blotches on abdomen, high fever, bleeding into bowel... uremic poisoning. We had none of the recommended medications, only morphine.... It's got to be typhoid!"[7] The sick sailors were quarantined, and Owen volunteered to care for the German pair. A short article published in *Time* magazine on November 29, 1926, described the outcome.

> In mid-Atlantic, aboard the USS. *Eastern Glade* [sic], bound out from Norfolk, Va., to Cape Town, S. Afr., the captain sweated to recall what simple medical skill he had stored up. Two of his crew were dying and he had no ship's doctor. Nor could his wireless, fumbling about, reach a ship with a doctor. It did, however, make contact with the USS. *West Calumb* going north from Buenos Aires to Boston. Doctorless too, the *West Calumb*'s captain sent his wireless calls fingering until he made contact with the French cruiser *Jeanne d'Arc....* The sick seamen survived. The story was told when the *West Calumb* reached Boston last week.[8]

✵

On December 2, 1926, after thirty-three days at sea, Aloha looked over the ship's railing towards the shimmer of white buildings in Cape Town's harbour. The city looked like a fairy-tale kingdom, nestled between translucent aquamarine waters and the imposing, square-shouldered Table Mountain. The warm, fragrant air, the luxurious greenery and happy, waving palms reminded her more of Hawaii or Penang than anything contained in those tales of "darkest Africa" she'd read in childhood.

At Table Bay, the troubles began. The carnet prepared for the cars and equipment in New York (and guaranteed by the RAC) was rejected by local customs officials. Permission would need to be granted by government higher-ups, who were in Pretoria, 1,100 miles away. It meant a delay of several days. The expedition used the time to find their land legs and drum up some publicity — a task they achieved, though perhaps not as they'd intended. Overnight, the press began running amusing stories about the greenhorns who thought they could drive the length of Africa by car. When Aloha outlined their plan to arrange for food and fuel stations at train junctions along the Great North Road, she was met with howls of laughter. The Great North Road, they informed her, *had not yet been built.* It was, "madness to think of driving away out there," Aloha was told, "*impossible* without complete native safari." With a shaking of heads, the locals said it would be "better that you just film a fringe of our jungle, [and then] *go back to America* with your story of Darkest Africa."[9]

It was the kind of mocking disbelief that Aloha had heard before, and she didn't care to argue with reporters. Instead, she and Walter booked a nationwide chain of theatres and contracted with Shell Oil, Agfa Film, a motorcycle manufacturer, and a chain of jewellery stores. When the cars and equipment had been cleared, the Wanderwell crew took to Cape Town's streets with their stories of adventure and their petition for an international police. It had an effect. Slowly, newspapers moderated their tone and people began to wonder: could this little band of adventurers in scrap metal cars *really* do it, after all?

❁

At the Cape Town rail yards, Aloha spied a lovely, familiar face. As she drew near, a happy but worn-looking Miki cried, "Une douche, une douche, my kingdom for a shower!" Aloha smiled and swallowed the knot in her throat. Miki "had lost none of her whimsy and vim thank heavens." The two embraced and began nattering in French, Aloha noting the changes in her sister: Miki, not quite sixteen, was much taller than before, her face older, her manner more confident. Once the words began flowing, the old camaraderie sprang to life, and it seemed they'd hardly been apart. Aloha introduced her sister to Valri, who was instantly at ease in her aunt's arms. It was the beginning of a loving kinship that would last a lifetime.

They had hardly said hello, however, before it was time to go again. Aloha and Valri left for Johannesburg to spend Christmas resting and visiting with Margaret and a Hedley aunt. Aloha had been nervous about how her mother would receive her. So much had changed since they had last seen each other in Nice. But she needn't have worried. Margaret was ready to open a new chapter in her own turbulent life; she was thrilled to have a granddaughter and seemed to have accepted her daughter's bizarre occupation and marriage.

✴

Aloha returned to Cape Town on December 26 to find Miki kitted in Wanderwell uniform and trained in IP dogma. They took on eleven new members, bringing the expedition total to sixteen. They set out east along the Indian Ocean towards Port Elizabeth, their first major stop. From there, they would make their way to Johannesburg. Among the new crew members were pretty Ann Dashwood as secretary, Afrikaner Marius de Villiers as relief driver, and "young, husky, seventeen-year-old *platteland* Boer Klaas Theron"[10] as guide, translator, and grunt. Aloha rode with de Villiers while Owen drove the Tank with the remaining crew and the captain and Miki rode on the Indian motorcycle.

Not since India had Aloha encountered such a desiccated and thirsty landscape; driving goggles were essential to keep out the dust and glare. Just past the rugged Huisrivier Pass near the town of Oudtschoorn, famous for its ostriches, the motorcycle lost traction and spun from the road. Aloha pulled up where "Miki and Cap, coated in dust, were wiping bloody wounds. . . . We washed out Miki's elbows and doctored with iodine. Cap's knees were painfully ripped."

It was not an illustrious beginning. South Africa brought them soaring heat in the day, countered by chilly temperatures at night. After every few miles they would be obliged to stop, to unlatch and then re-latch sheep gates whose signs read "Maak to die Heck — and use Cooper's dip." There was also a species of thorn bush called the *wag-'n-bietjie*, or "wait a minute" whose persistent barbs managed to worm their way into unfortunate places. Worst of all were the bed bugs that seemed to have colonized every mattress in the whole of South Africa.

✿

Arriving in Johannesburg, expedition members worked the streets drumming up support for the IP concept and selling showings of the adventure films.

By month's end, everyone was in need of a rest, especially Aloha, who was now too pregnant to continue working. While the expedition drove, Aloha travelled by train with Margaret and Valri to a seaside cottage in Durban.

On Friday, April 29, Walter drove Aloha to the Rose Garden Maternity Centre, where she gave birth to their second child. "Young Nile made his debut minus fanfare. Clenching hands, together Cap and I had welcomed our healthy Number One Son, poetically named by Miki."[11]

✿

After just ten days Aloha felt ready to resume her expedition duties. Just as bags were being packed, however, she and Walter were notified by local authorities that "South Africa prohibited foreign parents to leave their children with guardians." This was a serious problem. There was no way the children could accompany them, nor could Walter or Aloha stay behind. It was Margaret who proposed a solution: she would give up the Durban cottage and take the children to Australia where she also had family.

It was decided that the Tank and one of the crew would travel with Margaret and the kids to Adelaide in South Australia. Margaret would become the leader of the Australian chapter of WAWEC and would help to fund the children's care through pamphlet sales.

With Margaret's departure, the expedition shrank to just six members — Aloha, Walter, Miki, Miller, Owen, and Theron.

✿

And by the third week of June 1927, they were finally underway. Aloha was elated to be heading for new adventures, but also sad to be leaving her children so soon. "I am destined to make drastic choices," she wrote. "He must needs go whom the (wanderlust) devil drives...."[12]

Sloshy with dozens of fuel cans, they drove along barely discernible wagon trails in a turmeric-coloured landscape, each member wondering about the road ahead. After four hours they reached a stand of trees, beneath which was "a gaggle of black girls giggling" wearing ornate dresses and an East Indian man sitting on a stool, a Singer sewing machine churning between his knees. The tailor, a wiry man in Coke bottle glasses, explained that the mountain ahead was a platinum mine and that the girls were the wives of husbands who worked there. They spent their husband's wages attempting to create the most elegant costume possible. Aloha was wowed by their beauty, describing their "tight short sleeves fitted to a bodice consisting of a broad frill down to the nipples where firm, plump breasts gyrated alluringly with tantalizing exposures."[13] Around their ankles the girls wore dozens of yellow wooden anklets that "made a dull, melodious thunk, thunk" as they walked.[14] Aloha and Walter scrambled to take pictures, but their cameras attracted the attention of the curious, giggling girls whose interest impeded the picture taking. In the end it was Miki who managed a photograph of Aloha trying to take a photograph.

They asked the trader for directions to the Rhodesian border, some 250 miles north. It was a difficult trail, he told them, full of lions and snakes, with no food or supply stops. Lucky for them, however, his store was just ahead. Chuckling, Walter agreed to visit the shop, a predictably ramshackle affair with a hand-painted sign, tin roof, and smoke-stained windows. Aloha stepped through the doorway and was astonished. Shelves were packed to match the stock of any American general store: "canned pilchards, Crosse & Blackwell steak and kidney pie, New Zealand tinned butter, Huntley Palmer [sic] biscuits, Argentine bully-beef."[15] The shrewd tailor understood that Europeans travelling through the harsh Transvaal landscapes would welcome, and pay for, a taste of home. The expedition stocked up.

❁

A week later they reached the town of Louis Trichardt, named for one of the many Afrikaner *Voortrekkers*, or pioneers, and a place Aloha would describe as a "Boer wagon supply town" and "the end of the line."[16] It was the last major settlement before they would cross into the British Crown Colony of Southern Rhodesia, now Zimbabwe. They restocked supplies, made repairs, and surveyed the locals on the best way forward to Cairo. After wiping tears of laughter from their eyes, residents recited the usual catalogue of the hardships they could expect ahead: dense forests, animals, unfriendly tribes, and worst of all, the Limpopo River, although most seemed to agree there were not too many crocodiles about.

The expedition covered the next 60 miles, arriving at the village of Messina and catching their first glimpse of the languid grey-green waters of the Limpopo River. Across a rickety wooden bridge they could see the round, whitewashed walls of the government outpost. As their cars crossed the bridge, "two very black Askaris in military shorts, red fezzes, came to *order arms*." They cast a wary eye on the cars' rifle scabbards and watched closely as the troupe entered the boma.

The official inside was typically English, solidly built with a ruddy complexion and robust moustache. Walter presented the crew's passports and visas. "We also wish to deposit duty for our two cars," he said, commenting that he hoped Africa would soon honour the Royal Auto Club's carnet system.[17] The official was all business until the arrival of refreshments lent a more relaxed air to the proceedings. "Your wife was a member of the Russian Army. For how long? When?" Walter laughed and explained that the title was simply honorary, intended to commemorate her achievement as the first woman to drive through China to Vladivostok. She did not actually serve in any capacity. The official said nothing but continued to make notes while examining the various visas, which included every territory to be crossed northward.[18] To fill the sudden quiet Walter mentioned that he was eager to see the town of Bulawayo and asked how the roads were heading north. The official responded that the roads were "fairly well defined" and then, after asking the attendant for more tea, stood up from his desk and handed over the passports and visas. Fixing Walter with a dispassionate look, he said flatly, "I'm sorry though, you cannot enter Rhodesia."

In the shocked silence that followed he explained that officials in the capital had received word about the expedition and its itinerary. "It was decided that [your] mode of travel would be inappropriate to this Crown Colony."[19] Walter was momentarily at a loss. He set his teacup down onto its saucer and, clearing his throat, asked how they might proceed *around* Rhodesia. "You cannot," was the answer. The official explained that the Kalahari Desert lay to the west and densely forested Portuguese East Africa to the east. Neither area was navigable by car. Then, as if to close the book on the subject, he said he would "accept your word, Sir, that you will not cross our frontier at some other point. Southern Rhodesia is closed to you."[20]

Aloha felt her dreams had been dropped and smashed. She thought of the advertising arrangements, the movies to film, the records to set. She recalled the storm on the boat and the countless fees paid for visas and permits. Without another word the expedition climbed back into their cars, and headed back towards South Africa. Walter stopped his car in the open veldt within site of the Rhodesian boma and instructed the crew to set-up camp. Owen vented some of his frustration by shooting two rock rabbits which he and Miki, in defiance of Walter's vegetarianism, cooked with rice into a gruel they dubbed "Messina stew."

By morning Walter had formulated a plan: they would send a telegram to the capital, promising to head for "Tanganyika [now Tanzania] by the most feasible trail." They would "halt solely for repairs, food, sleep; sans theatres, I.P. or filming." By removing all possible objections to their presence, perhaps officials would reconsider and allow them to proceed. In the meantime they had four or five days to tighten bolts, repack supplies, and mend trouser seats. "How handy those convent training years became."[21]

It was a nervous few days.

Aloha amongst African natives, Africa, 1928.

SEVENTEEN

THE BEST
LAID PLANS

AFTER FOUR DAYS, A TELEGRAMMED response arrived. Rhodesia sent its compliments and best wishes but regretted that its decision could not be revoked. And so, just before sun-up the following day, they turned reluctantly back to Louis Trichardt.

While Aloha studied maps, Walter and Theron talked to locals for advice on how to proceed north, around Rhodesia, and met with the usual response: impossible! But by now the crew was impervious to warnings. Aloha managed to work out a possible route north, through Portuguese East Africa and Nyasaland, into Tanganyika, Kenya, then past Lake Turkana to Anglo-Egyptian Sudan, or through Abyssinia to Sudan, from which it would be a straight route north to Cairo. It was an exciting prospect, since the route had never been tried and would, therefore, not simply be a repeat of the Court Treatt or Delingette Expeditions. But getting through Portuguese East Africa by car was the challenge. According to some, the only possible route was to reach the Sabi River, follow its easterly flow to the coast and then head north. Reaching the Sabi by motorcar was, they were told, impossible.

Theron learned of a Briton named Chapman living in the border town of Pafuri. Chapman was an agent for the Witwatersrand Native Labour Association, an organization founded by the Witwatersrand Gold Mining Company in South Africa to recruit "migrant" workers (tribal peoples) for the mines.[1] If anyone could tell them about the terrain through Portuguese East Africa, it would be Chapman.

If they were to do this, they needed to travel light. Kits were to be turned out for Miki to sort through. Members were allowed to select their best clothes. Everything else would be mailed to Nairobi.

An advertising agreement was struck with the Maritz Trading Co. for fuel at half price — the empty cans could be used for trading along the way. Aloha and Miki looked for portable and durable supplies that would provide carbohydrates, minerals, and protein, settling on a "50 lb. sack of mielie-meal, 30 lbs. dried peas, [and] 20 lbs. muscatels."[2] A few small luxuries were allowed, including one can of cocoa, four tins of milk, and four pounds of sugar. Aloha and Miki were permitted to bring small mirrors and full make-up kits. The remaining cargo space held tools, spare parts, cooking utensils, knives, machetes, guns, ammunition, and a few items that could be used for trade: rock salt, safety pins, and silver *tikkies*, or coins.

Quite suddenly, the Wanderwell Expedition had become a serious exploring concern. East of Pafuri, there were no permanent roads of any kind, not even donkey trails. But the more the locals insisted the trek was impossible, the more interesting and adventurous it seemed. "Attack, attack!" Aloha wrote. "We were filled with joy at the prospect of assault on the global map."[3] A happy omen arrived just as they were preparing to leave: a stack of mail from home, including fan letters, requests to join the expedition, and a surprise note from Art Goebel inviting Aloha to accompany him in an air race from California to Hawaii. The race was being sponsored by James D. Dole, the Hawaii pineapple tycoon, who offered a stunning US$25,000 prize. As always, the temptation of elsewhere, of another even more glamorous adventure drew Aloha, but the event was to happen in August, barely a month away. The Court Treatt Expedition had required sixteen months to cross Africa.

❖

On July 2 the expedition reached the settlement of Pafuri at the northern tip of what is today the Kruger National Park, just across the border into Mozambique. Almost as soon as they spied a flagstaff flying the Union Jack, they saw a man striding along the path towards them in the company of two Great Danes. "We knew immediately it must be Chapman, the King of Pafuri."[4] His first words on reaching them were, "By Jove! What on earth are you doing *here*?" To which the crew chorused, "Trying to get through to the Sabi."[5] Chapman, a tall man with short hair, chiselled features and an athletic build, offered a bone-jarring handshake to everyone and directed them towards his outpost. The "compound was a neat, extensive — quasi official outpost of Empire.... His boys called him M'Noti, 'he who whistles' and assisted him with grinning alacrity."[6]

He invited the expedition to stay while he made inquiries about the terrain past the Portuguese boundary of Chicualacuala. His assistants showed the crew members to comfortable cabins, where they washed up and prepared some of their scrapbooks for a dinnertime presentation. Chapman was wowed by their adventures, but as the evening closed he admitted his misgivings about the road ahead. "I understand your objective to produce a film record of the first girl to drive across Africa, but... I must warn you there is only a foot trail even to Chicualacuala.... Beyond that, to the Sabi, only seasonal foot pads." He, too, advised them to turn back.[7]

Aloha would later record her reply: "It's impossible to quit now! Driving where no White woman had ventured it before *is the whole purpose of this documentary*. Besides, we're always on the verge of disaster — it's endemic."[8] They would not turn back.

The next day, Chapman sent a tall, lithe boy to Chicualacuala, 30 miles away, a note tied to his spear. It took three days but the runner returned with good news. The Portuguese official would welcome the Wanderwell Expedition and offer what assistance he could. The runner also gave advice regarding the best route to Chicualacuala, which kraals were friendly, and where to best cross the Limpopo River. Chapman marked the route on maps, while Walter took down phonetic spellings of key phrases in many of the regional dialects: "Shangaan, Bantu, Ki-Swahili [and] pidgin Arabic." When the time came to leave, Chapman signed their log with the words *Vincit Qui Patitur*, Latin for "Who endures, wins" or perhaps even more accurately, "Who *suffers*, wins." It was an apt benediction.

Chapman sent along several of his staff and oxen to help the cars across the Limpopo River. Once across, in order to reach the break in the jungle that would lead them to dry land and a footpath to Chicualacuala, they needed to *push* the cars several miles along the marshy riverbank, through brown paste, often using machetes to free vine tangled axles.[9] It took fourteen slow hours to reach the *dambo*, or open plain, that Chapman's runner had described. Exhausted, they set camp beneath a solitary baobab tree and prepared a supper of reconstituted peas.

✿

Once on the plain, the rocky and uneven ground levelled out until they found themselves travelling 10 or even 20 miles an hour over a fine dirt road. Soon they spied a village in the distance, and hardly a minute after that they were parked in front of a long orange-roofed building where a flagpole flew "the red and green bunting" of the Portuguese flag. They were greeted by a short man in an oversized pith helmet. With a boisterous smile he introduced himself as Mongoni, chief of the post office of Chicualacuala, "Colonial Deputy of Power [*sic*], arbiter of Justice and Collector of Head Tax."[10] Aloha was instantly amused, describing the man as "an animated mummy in white pyjama ducks." Walter commented on the marvellous road. They were the first to actually drive it, Mongoni said. One day he hoped to have auto races. As it was, the portion they drove constituted the entire extent of the road. Their continued progress north, he regretted, would be considerably more challenging.

They were invited to spend the night at his rondavel; sleeping quarters had already been prepared for them, including a bathtub for the ladies. He said it had been years since he'd had visitors and he was eager to hear all about their adventures. Aloha followed an unsmiling servant to her room. Unlike their welcoming host, the staff and locals eyed them with transparent suspicion. Aloha assumed they were simply unaccustomed to guests. Later, however, she learned that in the local tongue "Mongoni" meant "he who cheats the natives."

When they had settled in, afternoon tea was served on a verandah covered by an elaborate bamboo awning. The crew relaxed in wooden lounge chairs, munching biscuits and enjoying the tranquil air. Mongoni, it turned out, enthusiastically supported their adventure since it would prove the feasibility of a highway north. He suggested they dispatch another runner, this time to Massangena to discover which kraals were most friendly and whether there were water supplies along the way. Walter was reluctant to spend a week waiting but they had already burned through half their fuel, so finding the safest, most direct route was crucial.

While waiting for the runner's return, the crew explored the threadbare village of Chicualacuala. In the compound beyond Mongoni's offices Aloha and Miki glimpsed several small faces peeking at them around corners and at the edges of windows before disappearing with muffled giggles. "We calculated Mongoni kept five Native wives. We gave up on children — nimble as marmosets — there must have been thirty — all supposed to be hidden."[11] One reel of surviving footage shows Aloha sitting in a boma's doorway, holding a wide-eyed infant. She's smiling broadly, chatting with the tot's mother.

When the runner returned from Massangena, his dark forehead glistening in the sun, he explained that all the usual water sources had vanished due to drought. Even the rivers had dried and the only water was in proximity to the kraals — but those were suffering an outbreak of elephantiasis. Mongoni smiled and clapped his hands. Excellent news, he said. It would be easy to cross the waterways and sick natives were less likely to be hostile. "The highway zealot was still enthusiastic about tossing us to the lions! He assured us *in extremis* we could send back a note with the bi-monthly government runner, our desire for extra *gasolina* which he would dispatch!" Walter decided it was a chance worth taking. "Let a fool be made serviceable according to his folly," he said, quoting Joseph Conrad.[12]

At dawn the next morning, the crew gathered around the packed cars and thanked Mongoni for his generous aid. He, in turn, gave them a few final gifts: a tin of coffee, cigarettes for Owen and Miller, a gallon of elephant grease, and a quart of garlic-infused olive oil to flavour the crew's peas and mealie-meal rations. Then with a last handshake, "He-Who-Cheats-the-Natives fervently wished us 'Good-God travels.'"[13]

❀

The terrain was less rocky than the South African veldt had been, but there were countless thickets that needed clearing. And the sharp stumps of withered trees caused several tire punctures. On the third day they were stopped by the soft sands of a dry riverbed that Aloha called the "Te Kuai."

This made agonies of labour. We were forced to portage the cases of gasoline, and all provisions and equipment across the three-quarter-mile expanse. The sun blazed as we put our shoulders to the cars and pushed and hauled them over, one at a time. On the far bank we used our spades to shovel out a trail so the cars could be pushed up the steep incline. That crossing took us seven hours.[14]

❄

It was a week before a small collection of buildings came into view. This would be the second kraal that Mongoni's runner had indicated. They approached the circle of thatch rondavels in low gear, looking for locals, but none appeared. Twenty yards from the settlement, the cars stopped. Everyone sat listening for movement, for signs of life but the only sound was a slow leak coming from one of the tires.

"Let's walk into the village," Walter whispered. "If anyone *is* there, they might feel less threatened if a woman approaches." Aloha swallowed hard and nodded.

They walked slowly towards the settlement, calling hello in various languages but received no response. Here, as everywhere else, the drought had withered the leaves of all but the largest trees and a tan-coloured dust coated everything. Aloha noticed that there were many footprints on the ground yet no sound of movement. Outside the huts were grain storage boxes, wooden tools and empty calabashes, but no animals or scat. However, when Walter peered into a doorway he saw that ashes were still smoldering. Grabbing Aloha's wrist, he whispered they should head back to the cars. The engines had probably scared them off. After a short conference, the crew decided it would be best to make camp at a nearby stand of trees and hope that the villagers would eventually return. It was essential to find water, and they were unlikely to find any without help. Walter asked Theron to shout his best Shangaan greeting. "The Boer had a way with Shangaan words, better than any of us," but there was no response.[15]

Each member set about their routine tasks. Owen swung a tire iron and began mending flats. Aloha set about converting the cars for sleeping. Walter prepared the cameras (just in case) and assisted Miller and Theron in gathering thorn bush for building animal barricades and a hearth for Miki's cooking. A short while later, Miki was setting down a bag of provisions when she looked up and saw a man approaching. She called to the others and they all stopped to watch as "a tall, erect old Headman, naked except for [an] ebony head circlet and breech-apron, emerged at a distance." Walter nodded towards Aloha. She hopped down from where she'd been working and offered her broadest smile. "To our salute he spiked his murderous assegai in the ground, extended both hands in dignified welcome to *Maxaila*." Theron came forward offering a length of biltong, or cured meat, that he had been taught was an appropriate offering. The man lifted a calabash from where it hung at his side and allowed the gift to be placed inside. The exchange complete, the man turned and summoned members of his village. Slowly, from behind hills and trees, a few men and several women began to materialize. Of the approaching women, "some had babies at least two years old strapped to [their] back... [They] bent forward for the babes to see. A young daredevil reached for the radiator and shrieked with pain. The women scattered like gazelles."[16] The shock did not last long, however. Soon they were exploring without fear, even feeling Aloha's soft arms and blond hair, by now almost entirely bleached by the intense sun. "Discovering the rear-view mirror they gleefully bobbed up and down grimacing." A little later, Miki and Aloha showed the local women their make-up kits, to rave reviews. Our "precious lipstick, reserved against close-ups and our return to civilization, passed from mouth to mouth on an acreage of Native lips.... We only had to show these women once what it was for."[17]

The villagers invited the expedition to set up camp in the middle of the shamba, beneath the shade of the only tree inside the five-foot lion stockade of thorn bush.[18] The crew was invited to join the clan in some *masi*, or goat's milk. With Theron's assistance, Aloha was able to communicate that they required water. "Water, how far? Lo mati...kule?" she asked. It turned out to be nearly an hour away and several women were sent with Owen and Miller to the watering hole.

The next morning Aloha was dumping grey water at some bushes just beyond the kraal when she noticed scratches and a dark stain on the ground. Looking ahead she saw the bloody carcass of a small deer and it was revealed that a lion had been circling the previous night. Miki gasped at the news— she had been up during the night to pee. Had they not been camped inside the kraal that evening, the carcass might have been hers!

Walter negotiated with the headman for a guide to the next kraal, several days' journey away. Even with a guide, the parched land made it difficult to discern the runner's path they were trying to follow. Around noon they came to a large, dry lake bed — "pancaked hard as quarried concrete" — and saw that the opposite shore was covered in dense forest. The only way through was a wide track that had been torn by elephants. "Oh Lord! I prayed it also be the Runner's pad."[19] The guide, whom Aloha called J'tatana, indicated they should move forward, but warned them to watch out for elephants. A surprised herd would attack en masse. They crossed the lake bed with their guns in their hands only to discover something almost as awful as rampaging elephants: the bank that led to the path was long and steep. For a few moments no one said anything, though everyone knew what it meant. Because uphill travel used exponentially more fuel, Walter had ordered that the cars be pushed up every incline.

✵

Hardly a week from Maxaila, the expedition was running low on water and the crew members low on patience. Getting to the next kraal — or better still, finding a water hole — was all anyone thought about. To Aloha, the landscape seemed like some alien planet, complete with ant hills twelve feet tall and a "phantom forest, trees mere shells, the core eaten out by termites."[20] The remnant trees were paper-thin and could be toppled with a light push. All around were signs of elephant destruction — trampled earth, uprooted trees. But elephants were also a good omen: where there were elephants, there would be water.

Before long, time no longer mattered, only distance. And water. One day, they saw several buildings grouped at the edge of a green forest. The kraal was not marked on their map but a settlement, any settlement, meant there was water nearby. The cars stopped at a respectable distance, and as they had done last time, Walter and Aloha approached with an offering of biltong. J'tatana accompanied them, although clearly nervous. No one came to meet them, so they peeked inside the first rondavel to look for signs of life. They were momentarily blinded by darkness inside but slowly began to make out shapes: a broken calabash, some bones, and the dark blot of what must once have been a fire pit. The residents of this settlement were long gone.

Disappointed, the expedition unloaded and camped at the kraal. The forest would provide them some protection against animals, as well as firewood to scare off predators. They decided not to cook their meal but instead chewed lengths of biltong. They "masticated s-l-o-w-l-y four muscatels each. Tea, a quarter cup per. All urine was saved in a calabash for radiators."

Aloha and Miki slept together in one car while the men flipped a coin to see who slept in the car and who would dig a hip hole and bed on the ground. No one slept particularly well and at some early hour the Shangaan guide began screaming. Seconds later the sound of trumpeting elephants ripped the night. Everyone sprang to their feet but the old guide was already off. "Racing with flaming faggot, the Black set fire to a tinder hut. The thatch exploded, shooting fiery fronds aloft."

Almost as soon as the conflagration had begun, the crew had to run again. A river of angry snakes carpeted the ground, escaping the burning hut. "We leapt into the machines. Out of the darkness the elephants lunged up the embankment. The earth shook, the herd thundered past within feet." The blazing hut had done just enough to divert the stampeding elephants. "The old mine-boy had saved our lives."[21]

❀

It was late August 1927 and the Wanderwell Expedition was somewhere in Portuguese East Africa, attempting to follow a footpath to a kraal called Matz'Ambu that no one, including their guide, had ever been to or whose location was known for certain. They were thirsty, hungry, exhausted, and ragged. But worst of all, their containers now rattled with the last drops of water. By their calculations they were only a day or two from Matz'Ambu, but at a split in the trail they made a wrong guess and were forced to backtrack. Finally, late in the day they came to a desiccated lake with moist earth at its centre. Aloha ran to a puddle of muck and slurped up some of the slime, promptly vomiting. Walter mustered his voice and instructed the crew to grab whatever tools they could find and start digging. "Let water

A strip of 35mm motion picture film from the expedition's African adventures, Portuguese East Africa, 1928.

seep in, that'll clear it," he said. No one needed telling twice. "With our dementia, we dug like demons. Water oozed in, dark, barnyard-stenchy but combined with iodine drops, we all got some down."

The water, raunchy though it was, revived them. They settled in with light spirits and happily chewed their dried peas, muscatels, and biltong while preparing for a blessed night's sleep. Shortly after sunset, just as the first watch fire was being lit, the crew looked at one another in wonder. Off in the distance they could hear one of the most encouraging sounds imaginable: frogs.

❀

For the moment, the water issues were sorted; the looming catastrophe now was fuel. They had only what was left in the tanks. Motor oil had run out and the engines were being lubricated with a combination of Mongoni's olive oil and elephant grease purchased from the villagers. It was decided that Walter would walk the estimated 20 miles remaining to Massangena while the crew followed slowly behind. Walter would send back a runner with fuel.

Early the next morning, Walter set off across the rolling terrain, a backpack over his shoulder and a walking stick in his hand. He shouted his final instructions while walking backwards, "Don't try to ride. Save the cars." In the blazing heat of the day he expected them to push the cars across the now rolling terrain towards Massangena. At the crest of one hill they saw a long, smooth plateau spread out before them and the temptation became too great. Following Owen's lead, Aloha started her engine and began the effortless ride down. "I increased throttle, rolling smoothly at an unbelievable eight, ten mph...Miki, Miller, Theron...clambered aboard in silent relief." All they could think of was the wide flowing waters of the Sabi River less than 20 miles ahead.

Their reveries were cut short when the car lurched suddenly to the left. There was a bang followed by an awful scraping sound as the car came to a sudden halt and a cloud of dust folded over them.

> We watched the left-rear [tire] roll away spinning pitifully from the cracked buried axle.... No words. With rocks, we righted poor "Miss Los Angeles 1925." I couldn't help seeing Douglas Fairbanks posing smashingly as he christened her a continent ago.[22]

In an instant, the entire African project seemed to hang in the balance. If they could not repair the axle, the expedition would need to be abandoned, or the crew would need to be pared down. They had to get to Massangena by any means possible and repair what they could.

Miller volunteered to stay behind with Nº IV while the rest of the crew struck out for Massangena. All film and cameras were transferred to Nº II and Miller was left with water, a little food, a rifle, and the remaining cigarettes.

✸

It took just two hours to reach the buildings where they found Walter, sitting on a chair, looking washed, combed, and rested. He smiled and said they were staying as guests of the regional administrator. He also said that Owen had not arrived with Nº II.

The sisters followed Walter to the main building, on whose step was the "corpulent... Senhor Commandante, known to the locals as Wafa-Wafa." For the Commandante the appearance of cars and travellers was momentous. It heralded the end of isolation. Aloha and Miki "sank gratefully into wicker chairs on his broad veranda" and surveyed the Sabi River snaking into the distance below them. "Servants brought glasses of crystal clear water. How exquisite it looked!"[23] And although Aloha wanted nothing more than to change clothes and crash into bed, she listened while Wafa-Wafa (whose name meant "the little man indisposed to exertion") regaled them with long and detailed accounts of his numerous adventures during his fourteen years as *Administrador* of the Massangena *Subposto*.

❀

The next day Theron and a guide set out to walk the 93 miles to Umtali, now Mutare, in Rhodesia, where Theron would try to find a hunter named van Staaden. His biannual delivery of the outpost's supplies was expected within the next ten days. With luck, Theron could find a new axle and hitch a ride back to Massangena on van Staaden's donkey span.

Owen, alarmingly, had still not arrived and Miller was also still stranded with Nº IV, even farther afield. They decided to send runners to reprovision Miller, who would be running out of the food and water they had left with him.

Aloha and Miki explored their surroundings while they waited, a kaleidoscope of exotic plants, colourful birds, and animals. As far as Aloha was concerned, they could remain in Massangena forever. "Obsessively we grasped every moment — ecstasy so rich must be fleeting."

Finally, amidst a cloud of blue smoke and deafening backfires, Owen and his guide roared up the hill leading to the settlement. They had pushed the car across the rugged terrain, but were, as Owen put it "determined to bring Her *Verdompte* Tin Highness in under her own power." The car was a disaster, her cylinders unsteady, "ferociously emitting steam and smoke" as well as "the nauseating stench of sizzling elephant fat and...burned bearings." But at least it had arrived.[24]

The next morning, the settlement was roused by the barking of dogs as Miller's ragged figure wandered into a clearing. "He was exhausted, whimpering. His shirt stiff with sweat, face unshaven blistered; voice too hoarse to understand. The last runner had somehow missed him. He couldn't give a coherent account of his wanderings."

Though glad to see Miller safe, Aloha and Walter worried over the car. "Even [our] tires could become sandals before we might organize a rescue." They had no choice but to wait for Theron to return with a new axle and hope that, somehow, the car might be restored.

Towards the end of the week, Wafa-Wafa invited the crew to accompany him to a ridge at the edge of the settlement. Pointing into the distance he said that Mr. van Staaden was on his way and invited them to listen. Aloha strained her ears against the quiet countryside. Beneath the buzzing of insects and the chirps of birds she could just detect the rumble of a wagon, perhaps a shouting voice or the crack of a *sjambok*. The longer they listened, the more distinct the sounds became. When Walter suggested they cross over the river to meet them, Wafa-Wafa laughed. The donkey span was, he said, a good two, and probably three days away.

❖

His estimate was exactly right. On the morning of the third day, Van Staaden arrived with Theron, an assistant called Marius Joubert, and representatives from a dozen villages that had sent ivory tusks for sale.[25] And the expedition's axle.

The "Tank" in Johannesburg. (L-R) Margaret, Walter, and Aloha. Aloha is supposedly seven months pregnant in this photo, South Africa, 1926.

EIGHTEEN

THE INTERRUPTED JOURNEY

JUST AS THE EXPEDITION PREPARED to leave Massangena, Walter decided that Aloha should accompany van Staaden to Umtali, Rhodesia, ostensibly to buy more supplies, but in all likelihood because she was already showing signs of the illness that would soon overtake her.

Aloha and van Staaden set out at dawn for the two-day trek and by the time their caravan had reached Umtali, Aloha had passed out with fatigue. She awoke to see a real town with broad shaded streets and a hotel.

> I was so tired, only half conscious, the manager personally escorted me to a garden bedroom, sent tea and a newspaper. I couldn't believe my eyes: "American Flies Pacific — Art Goebel reaches Hawaii. Wins Dole Race. $25,000. San Francisco to Honolulu 2089 miles in 26 hours in the single engine Travelair, 'Woolaroc'... Seven pilots are missing ...search on... Goebel participating."[1]

In second place was Martin Jensen flying his Breese-Wilde monoplane named, of all things, Aloha. There were, however, no other winners. Of the eleven competing planes, two made it to Hawaii, two disappeared, and the rest crashed.[2] Ten people died in the attempt to be the first fixed-wing aircraft to fly from the North American mainland to the islands of Hawaii.

Aloha, meanwhile, was falling seriously ill. What had started as fatigue passed into quaking chills followed by a severe fever. When she next regained consciousness she was in hospital, blinded by the most intensely painful headache she had ever experienced. She had malaria, and by the time she had reached Umtali, she had probably been infected for several weeks or longer.

During a feverish episode Aloha asked the doctors about Walter and the crew — how were they doing, did they know she was sick, were they okay? She was told, "The Captain died of blackwater fever in Macèquece." In the fit of anguish that followed Aloha, had another vision, "I could see him riding a mammoth steam locomotive, waving to me, laughing, shouting, 'I'm coming. See, I'm coming to you!'"[3]

In fact, the captain was alive, as was everyone else, although most of them had also been flattened by malaria, especially Miki.

After a week, Aloha began to regain her strength. "Calm, returning to life, I had strong thoughts: the road, wind, campfire. I wanted to live!"[4] Owen, the only crew member *not* felled by malaria, stopped by for a visit and, after reassuring Aloha that everyone was fine and that the expedition would resume when she was ready, delivered the news that both Theron and Miller were quitting.

> Gone out of our lives — just like that.
>
> It is sad to lose a crew, that bond. You work, strive together months on end. Fire and flame in early enthusiasm, eventually just what we basically strive to infuse, a stronger pull…for more freedom, selection of career, expansion of companionship. Over the years I have missed them all.[5]

✻

It was late September before the expedition resumed. The original plan was to follow the Sabi River east, but given that they were now more than 150 miles north of Massengena, they decided instead to head north around Lake Malawi's western shore into Tanganyika. Crossing into the former German territory was like passing into a wholly different continent. Well-defined wagon trails made navigation easy, and there was "stacked fuel at trading posts fifty or so miles apart." At the town of Kilosa they were able to replenish their supplies of food and fuel before looping through the hilly countryside to the town Aloha called Dodomo, where they hired a Scotsman called McRae.

After Dodomo, it took weeks to round Mount Kilimanjaro, driving through a surprisingly frigid terrain, staying with Maasai where possible and losing the trail almost every day. After so many miles of rough terrain, marauding animals, blistering skies, bedbugs, joint-snapping labour, and lack of fuel, water, sleep, and the countless unforeseen calamities — any of which might have maimed or killed them — they should have been closer to their goal. But they were not even halfway.

Trying to make up time, the expedition turned northeast towards the Uganda Railway line, which they could follow to Nairobi. Near the rail lines, the ground was almost always better and the cars could make use of railway bridges for water crossings. They made excellent time, travelling nearly 65 miles northeast before stopping for the night near a water tower, where an Indian watchman and his wife insisted they overnight in one of their storehouses. There were lions, they said, *Tsavo* lions, more dangerous than any in Africa. During construction of the railway just two lions had eaten 135 men.

The Wanderwell crew was numb to danger by this point. Owen declared he would like to hunt one of the famous man-eaters, and sometime during the night he *did* hear a noise at the nearby watering hole. He fired into the darkness and then, torch in hand, crept out to see if he'd managed to kill something. "It was his first and only leopard."

Later on, they told the story to some colonials who gaped with incredulity. "How do you Americans manage to keep alive in this country? You seem to get away with everything one is supposed *not* to do. There were probably ten lions about that isolated water last night when your Mr. Owen lugged in his kill."[6]

But if expedition members now felt they could ignore local advice, they were about to be corrected. Time and again locals had warned that the trail ahead would be too much for their cars, and they were soon to discover that the "road" consisted of steep grades with slab rock ridges, each 12–15 inches high — too tall for the cars' undercarriage clearance. They had to drive the front tires up the natural curb and then use jacks to raise the back of the car and rush it forward by hand. Inch by inch and foot by foot, they nudged the grudging cars up the brittle hillside, often jacking both the front and back tires over a rocky lip, or hauling shale for makeshift ramps high enough to free some length of undercarriage suspended on rock. "After three hours the ratchet of only one jack held. If it toppled, its foundations crashed [and] we leapt."[7] Aloha later reminisced that she spent the balance of the day wishing for an airplane.

❀

The Wanderwell Expedition drove down Nairobi's wide, sunny streets. They had come through — tattered, dusty, and tired, but alive and with the cars in one piece. Along the town's main thoroughfare Aloha marvelled at the abrupt confusion of architectural styles: imposing stone façade structures nestled beside tin-roofed government offices, which sat alongside dilapidated bazaar shacks. The most welcome sight of all, however, were the white columns framing the entrance to the Norfolk Hotel, "prideful emblem of British Colonial civilization, synonymous with good taste, dressing for dinner, the pukkah Sahib and the Mem."[8]

The Norfolk Hotel was easily the most famous business in Nairobi. In 1907 it had hosted Winston Churchill. And in 1909 it had welcomed Theodore Roosevelt.[9] By 1927 the hotel had lost some of its former glory, but its famous verandah — *the* place for afternoon drinks — was a fine spot to host eager reporters.

Theatre bookings and advertising contracts came easily (the Kenya Tyre Company painted its slogan on the sides of both cars: "Fit Dunlop and be Satisfied") and the press were robustly obliging.[10]

Mail was waiting for them at the central post office. Among the usual fan mail and updates from other Wanderwell units was a letter from Margaret in Australia mentioning the loss of the Tank to a fire and the arrest of two former expedition members who had stolen piles of pamphlets and sold them on their own. Aloha also received a letter from Helen Roberts detailing the sad outcome of the Dole Air Race, a contest which Aloha would describe as "the horror I missed."[11]

❀

The rush and whirr of publicity and performance wound down on the evening of October 13, 1927. Unknown to Aloha, Miki and Walter had planned a birthday celebration in the posh restaurant of the Norfolk Hotel.

It was precisely the kind of high-class indulgence that tickled Aloha's fancy, including "linens embellished by delicate green fern fronds…[and] roses gracefully arranged by the *khidmatgar* under Miki's supervision." It was also a rarity for Walter to spend so much money. This was, after all, the man who refused to spend money in cafés, sipping water while others drank tea or ate cake. On this evening, however, Aloha's taste for extravagance was indulged. Miki had arranged for a dessert of apple pie and whipped cream while, to everyone's astonishment, the captain ordered champagne and made a heartfelt toast, "To the mother of my children on her 21st anniversary and her triumphant drive to the source of the Nile. Cheers!"

> It was always a revelation to me that others were so unaware of Cap's sentimental side. True, his attention-getting voice, his condescending but bumptious stance, never allowed members to be really close. He took outrageous risks sometimes resulting in a jail night whenever police had cause to demand "Who gave you the right?" His insouciance was often taken for gall — it vexed authorities. But to me, my husband was a friend, a stanchion, marvellous raconteur. I read him by his eyes — how else to know a man? We both loved the challenging life — always the clever twist.[12]

The Wanderwell Expedition was running out of time. The heavy rains were approaching, after which travel by car would be virtually impossible. As Beryl Markham put it, the roads north of Nairobi had, "after a mild rain, an adhesive quality equal to that of the most prized black treacle."[13] Everyone wanted to press on, and yet it seemed absurd to *not* visit Lake Victoria — the famous source of the Nile. The decision, perhaps a birthday gift, was left to Aloha. Would it be north to Abyssinia or northwest into Uganda?

After a week of driving, they reached a guesthouse just outside the town of Jinja on Lake Victoria's northern shore. The next morning they crept through the darkness to watch the sun rise over the modest Ripon Falls, then believed to be the source of the Nile. In a moment of comic understatement, Walter shook Aloha's hand in congratulation. Even years later she seemed unsure how to convey her feelings at that moment. "We had reached the Nile. Dazzlement… The roar, colossal volume pouring through nature's spillway… The earth trembled. We stood at its source at last. For me tears would have been too little."[14]

✿

From Kampala, the expedition motored north towards Sudan and Abyssinia, over a smooth landscape to the town of Mongalla in southern Sudan. "We assured ourselves Cairo was within sight. We drank in the luxuriant beauty of a smiling Africa, and counted only fifteen hundred more miles of swamp and desert land between us and the oriental city where I had joined the expedition more than four years before."[15] They had planned to stock up on supplies and ask about for the best way towards Egypt. The district commissioner, however, could bring them only bad news. Just that morning he had received a telegrammed warning that unusually fierce rains were bearing down from the north, and more troublingly, there were reports of a large Dinka uprising in British-Egyptian Sudan. Colonials and European tourists, it was said, had already been killed. For the first time in Aloha's memory, the captain took the advice seriously and, even more surprisingly, told the crew to pack up immediately — they were done. They would leave for the coast in the morning.

Walter sent cables to Mombasa, looking for steamship passage to Europe. The messages were sent with replies directed to Nairobi. Another cable was sent to the post office in Nairobi, asking them to hold on to mail instead of forwarding it to Alexandria. It was a confusing mess, but no way around it. All they could do was drive and hope.

In Nairobi word came that their proposal to one of the steamship companies, the German East Africa Line, had been accepted. They would sail on December 17. They also received a stack of letters from the US and Australia. Dolly Reynolds, still acting as secretary at the Miami headquarters, said that N° III and crew had not been heard of since Panama. "Their escort car's pilot had committed suicide at Mexico City over a love affair."[16] Margaret sent more details about the loss of the Tank but, ever persevering, told how she had mounted a campaign in Sydney, soliciting advertisers and securing the donation of a new Ford chassis. Members of the expedition then "copied the WAWEC lines in sheet metal." There was even a mention of the kids who were happy and healthy at a "loving nanny home." Valri's and Nile's childhoods were fast becoming a carbon copy of Aloha's own.

The expedition dashed to Mombasa to meet their ship — a 620-mile, tortuous two-week race through bogs and driving rain, innumerable breakdowns, hunger, illness, and difficulties finding fuel. Rolling to a stop in Mombasa on December 17, and hardly daring to turn off their engines, they parked the cars near the gate, pulled tarpaulins over both vehicles, crawled inside, and were asleep within minutes. They had spent the last seven days driving non-stop.

Their ship, it turned out, was twenty-four hours late — a fabulous ocean of time. They booked into a hotel where Aloha and Miki washed their hair, bought a pot of French face cream and some Pivear's scented powder, while the men shaved, bathed, and had their uniforms pressed. Sitting on the hotel balcony, sipping tea and rereading the Nairobi mail, Aloha reflected that "to be exciting, life must be shot with coincidence."[17]

❂

In her later typewritten reminiscences, Aloha describes their discussion of what they should do next. Their attempt to cross Africa had failed, and a new plan needed to be made. South America was raised as an idea.

> Yes, the New World to be conquered. The present passion, to spend. Not suddenly, just firmly, smiling, his eyes probing, he drew himself to me.[18]

That final sentence echoes her description of their first kiss, all those years ago in Nice — suggesting, perhaps, that something in their relationship had come full circle. Her exact meaning is opaque, but she *did* intend to suggest something. The very last sentence in Aloha's typewritten account of her travels is a quote from Cicero: "certain signs came before certain events."[19]

THREE

ALL ARE KEEPiNG A SHARP LOOK-OUT iN FRONT,
BUT NONE SUSPECT THAT THE DANGER MAY
BE CREEPiNG UP FROM BEHiND.

— J.M. BARRiE, *PETER PAN*

On board the SS *Adolph Woermann* returning from Africa, en route to Marseille, France, and Genoa, Italy. (L-R) Miki, Aloha, and Walter pose with their two vehicles, Mediterranean Sea, December 1927.

NINETEEN

WITH CAR
AND CAMERA

ALTHOUGH IT'S UNLIKELY ANYONE IN the expedition had heard, on February 21, 1927, a Swiss aviator named Walter Mittelholzer touched down in Cape Town after leaving his home in Zurich. Travelling via Alexandria, he became the first person to fly the length of Africa from north to south. It was a glorious achievement, not least because the journey took a mere seventy-seven days, but also because it demonstrated that even a solo pilot could cross vast and forbidding expanses with relative ease. In other words, even if the Wanderwell Expedition *had* succeeded in driving Cape to Cairo, it's likely their achievement would have been lost in an airplane's shadow.

Even Mittelholzer's achievement was largely forgotten after Charles Lindbergh landed in Paris on May 21 that same year, thus completing the first solo air crossing of the Atlantic and collecting the $25,000 Orteig Prize—the same sum Art Goebel had won in the Dole Air Race. Curiously, the first contestant for the Orteig Prize was French flyer René Fonck, pal of Aloha's aviator boyfriend in Nice. Fonck's plane had crashed on takeoff, though he survived.

But it wasn't just planes that were overshadowing the Wanderwells' achievements. While the expedition was off documenting the wilds of Africa, escaping stampedes of elephants, and eating pots of maggot-infested mealie-meal, people in New York flocked to see a film that had premiered on

October 6. Called *The Jazz Singer*, the film had caused a sensation thanks to the new technical innovation of synchronized sound. And earlier in the year, director Fritz Lang had released a German film called *Metropolis*, a futuristic view of technology and society that wowed audiences with special effects and terrified them with its dystopian vision. It was the most expensive and sophisticated film yet made and raised the bar for all that followed — including the Wanderwell films. Henry Ford, meanwhile, was furthering his own idea of progress, embodied by the introduction of a car called the Model A. People were quick to welcome its appearance — a car that came in any of seven body styles and four colours, *except* black — and helped the Ford Company of Dearborn, Michigan, accumulate 400,000 sales orders from dealerships across America in two weeks.[1] As for the Model T — the basis for the Wanderwell cars — the last was produced on May 26, 1927, after a run of 15,000,000 units.

✿

Newspaper accounts of the expedition's route to Europe are contradictory A surviving photograph showing cars and crew posed in a town square eases the confusion, for down in the frame's left corner is advertising on one of Unit N° IV's wheels. Magnified, the text reads: "Wanderwell Expedition – Mombasa by Marseilles – s/s Adolph Woermann – Woermannlinie A.G. – Deutsche Ost Afrika." Ship records for the *Adolph Woermann* show the route taken was Mombasa, Suez, Port Said, Genoa, Marseille.

On board, Aloha was relieved to be drifting back into a world of white sheets and bone china teacups. She was troubled, however, by the failure of their well-publicized aim — to traverse Africa and reach Cairo. Had their year in the wilds of Africa risking life and limb been for nothing? She needed to make a major film out of their adventures to compensate, and the storyline was far from clear. In any case, editing a feature-length film at a professional lab would cost a fortune, and a fortune was not readily at hand. So, it was back to Europe and back to work. This was no easy life.

The expedition landed at Marseille sometime in January 1928 and quickly moved on to Italy, where they remained for seven months, playing theatres, selling souvenirs, and stockpiling cash.

Aloha Wanderwell graces the cover of one of the thousands of souvenir pamphlets expedition members circulated and sold worldwide, circa 1929.

✿

In what can only be described as an epic omission from any of Aloha's writings, the most momentous of events resulted in not even a single note of mention. In driving to Italy from Marseille, Aloha Wanderwell had driven around the world. She had departed Nice just over five years before at the age of sixteen. She had succeeded, despite hardships unimaginable even today, to circle the globe in a car. This accomplishment cannot be understated. In the early twenty-first century, with vehicles and aftermarket modifications specifically designed for the purpose, plus satellite phones, GPS, and wireless Internet — not to mention actual roads — this achievement would still be front-page news.

A year later, German auto enthusiast Clärenore Stinnes would complete her round-the-world trek, covering more overland distance than Aloha, but Aloha tackled routes that no one else had yet dared, and she had done it by the time she was twenty-two.

✿

The expedition reached Berlin in November 1928 to find the country again steeped in political turmoil. Just as they arrived, the chief of police, Karl Zörgiebel, banned all public demonstrations in an attempt to calm dissent and steady the teetering republic. Berliners, exhausted by so many years of uncertainty, merely shrugged at the Wanderwell's African adventures. The mood was captured by one weary show-goer, a certain Joseph Goebbels whose diary entry for October 21 tersely reviewed the show he'd seen the previous evening: "In desperation I went to the movies and heard about the American Wanderwell's world trip. Why does this economic opportunist pretend to be interested in pacifism?"[2]

Still, despite unpolished reels and surly theatregoers, the expedition made good money in Europe — enough for Aloha to get started on a proper edit of the African footage. There was a Christmas in Ostrów, a snug Polish village about 80 miles west of Posen (the town where Walter went to school), after which Aloha tucked the raw African footage under her arm and made for Paris. Editing would require several months, so it seemed a perfect time to reunite with her mom, Miki, and the kids. A wire was sent, asking them all to meet her in France.

✿

There are no surviving records of Aloha's reunion with her children, but the volume of photographs suggests she was charmed by the children she hardly knew. The children seemed to like Aloha, but they *adored* their laughing, playful aunt Miki.

Aloha found lodgings at Joinville-le-Pont, a district in southeastern Paris, less than 5 miles from the Pathé film lab on Rue Villiot. The apartment, located at 26 Avenue du Président Wilson, was a narrow but charming two-storey building with a terracotta roof and shuttered windows. There was a gated courtyard where the children could play while Miki watched over them. A pastry shop up the road provided breakfast each morning as Aloha left for work. Since her last visit to a professional lab, splicing equipment had improved, and there was a menagerie of new devices she'd never seen. Some filmmakers were experimenting with sound and colour, even hand-colouring individual frames so that a black-and-white film might suddenly have yellow and orange flames at a campfire. Developing chemicals had also been improved, allowing contrasts to be more finely controlled, resulting in deeper blacks and sharper whites that could add drama to a scene.

Despite feeling like a house painter at the Louvre, Aloha managed to assemble a coherent (if not entirely accurate) visual account of the Wander-well Expedition, beginning with Aloha's arrival on the scene. The film carried audiences from Paris of 1923 through Europe to North Africa (the pyramids), India (Benares), Singapore, China (the Great Wall and war scenes), Siberia (an honorary colonel), Japan (Hirohito), the US (Hollywood, Wyoming, the devastation of Miami), Cuba, Canada, South Africa through Mozambique to Uganda and Kenya, before arriving back in Europe. Short interstitial cartoons depicted the little cars winding a dotted line across the atlas in the style of the time. Running almost an hour, the film was christened *With Car and Camera Around the World* and was by far the most comprehensive and artful account of their travels to date. Its completion dramatically enhanced their credibility and, for the moment at least, set them apart from the glut of adventuring show folk. Even among masters of the travelogue, such as Burton Holmes, none boasted so many countries visited, depicted such offbeat locales, or demonstrated how it could be accomplished with just a car and a camera. The films documented dozens of disparate cultures and environments at a time when technological advances and political transgressions were about to alter them forever.

With a newly polished film to drum up publicity, the crew swelled to twelve members, including two young Germans — Frederick Müller and Hans Wolfart — who would accompany the expedition across the Atlantic. There were also now two female Belgian recruits, Olga van Dreissche and Justine Tibesar — the latter a cherubic-faced brunette with a quick tongue, able to silence any of the male crew members. She had an affinity for long silk scarves and liked to throw them around her neck with a flourish like Isadora Duncan, before sauntering into a car or away from a boring conversation. Aloha liked Justine but kept a wary eye out as well: Walter was no less impressed.

On the strength of reviews in Paris, Aloha was able to secure a week-long engagement at London's Shaftesbury Avenue Pavilion. The theatre, also known as the London Pavilion, was the city's largest playhouse, seating over a thousand people.[3]

Aloha was anxious to show off her film to the most important city in the world. Unfortunately, while the London *Times* was thrilled by the stories of adventure and found that "Miss Wanderwell [*sic*], the heroine of these adventures, has personality, and one cannot but admire her courage and that of Captain Walter Wanderwell," they also found that "the expedition has been handicapped by a lack of professional knowledge in the use of the camera and by being forced to develop negatives under very trying conditions."[4] To sophisticated audiences of the late 1920s, death-defying adventures and never-before-seen vistas were no longer enough. They wanted a dramatic soundtrack, fight scenes, regular explosions, and a love interest or two. They wanted Hollywood's talkies.

Despite the reviews, Walter was quick to use the strength of the Shaftesbury booking to contact steamship companies: the crew would present their films and lectures on board the ship in exchange for free passage.

Walter's pursuit of sponsorship may not have been limited to steamships. A biography of Colonel Percy Fawcett (an English explorer who mysteriously vanished in Brazil's Mato Grosso region in 1925) recounts a story told by Fawcett's widow, Nina. For years after her husband's disappearance, Nina was hounded by opportunists offering to search for her husband in exchange for money — including one memorable German adventurer. "She wrote bitterly that the man had 'more than one passport, at least three aliases, and a sheaf of Press cuttings was found on him.'"[5] While there's no way of knowing whether this was Walter, it is certain that the story of Fawcett's disappearance had reached his ear. It was a tale too interesting not to follow, and Walter and Aloha were already making plans to do just that.

On October 18 Margaret and Miki set sail for Montreal from Liverpool aboard the White Star Line's SS *Doric*. Their final destination would be Qualicum Beach and the possibility of a veteran's land grant for Miki courtesy of her father. Walter, meanwhile, had managed to secure passage for his family and four other crew members with the French Compagnie Générale Transatlantique who granted them passage on the SS *Île de France*, an ocean liner decorated in the art deco style and considered the most beautiful ship then afloat. They would board at Le Havre — first class for Walter and Aloha, but, for some reason, steerage for the crew and their children.

Then, on October 25 before they left port, troubling news arrived from the United States. An enormous sell-off of stocks had taken place in New York the day before. Newspapers proclaimed, "Greatest Crash in Wall Street's History," and described the frenzy of panicked selling that had punctured the bloated market and caused prices to tumble "like an avalanche." In the days that followed, prices continued to fall, despite the spending heroics of major investment firms and prominent businessmen, including the Rockefeller family. By week's end the market had lost over $30 billion and

Aloha posing with the freshly cleaned Nº IV aboard the *Île de France*,
en route to New York City, Atlantic Ocean, November 1929.

there were whispers of imminent bank collapses. The Wanderwells had most of the expedition's money held in US accounts.

❖

Aloha and Walter were among the first on the *Île de France*, supervising as the cars were swung aboard by slow donkey cranes. The sky was grey and a light mist was falling, but the air was unusually still and magnified every sound: the talking voices, the slow rumble of the ship's engine, the clatter of chains against the ship's hull. When at last everyone was on board and busy finding their cabin or the restaurant or the ship's railing, there came a sensation of movement, gentle at first, but then stronger as the engines rumbled and the buildings and cars and people of Europe slipped gradually behind them.

It was November 1, 1929, and as the sun set and passengers enjoyed their last glimpse of Europe (and their last legal sips of champagne), no one knew for certain what they would find when they docked in New York.

Photo op in front of the Ford Motor Building, Manhattan, New York City, 1930. Aloha (R) looks at expedition member and close friend Olga van Dreissche (L, at the front of vehicle)

TWENTY

THE FORK
IN THE ROAD

B Y 1929 THE DAYS OF barnstorming were drawing to a close. Flying could still earn one a good living, but success required skill, ingenuity, and sometimes, a willingness to skirt legal restraints. One such pilot was Edward DeLarm, a status Indian who flew routes from Florida to California and Mexico. Born at Pryor Creek reserve, Oklahoma, on October 12, 1888, DeLarm was the son of a French-Canadian father and an Arapaho mother.[1] He first worked as an auto mechanic and race driver until a high-speed accident left him hanging from the branches of an elm tree. The experience soured him on professional driving but did little to diminish his thirst for thrills. He took up flying and in 1919 earned the eighty-fifth licence issued by the Aero Club of America. His licence was signed by Orville Wright, a fact that so impressed DeLarm that he legally adopted Orville as his middle name and carried his original licence in his billfold for the rest of his life.

Like Walter Wanderwell, DeLarm hated smoking, enjoyed chasing women (though he professed to being unusually slow since he only ever caught two), and loved crossing borders — especially if he earned money in the process. By 1929 DeLarm was living and working in Los Angeles, flying gold, alcohol, weapons and people for well-to-do clients, including newspaper-publishing magnate William Randolph Hearst. DeLarm's life history bore great similarity to Walter's and Aloha's, and he would soon have an enormous impact on their lives.

✿

Aloha and company arrived to sunny skies and fair temperatures in New York on November 7, 1929, three years after they'd left for Cape Town. While the ship began unloading at New York's Chelsea Piers, American authorities offered Walter their traditional welcome and detained him for questioning. He and the cars were eventually permitted entry, although he needed to supply his New York address. As an extra precaution, Walter immediately filed a Declaration of Intention for US citizenship — the fourth declaration he had made since 1917.

With immigration cleared and the cars finally unloaded, Aloha and Walter drove the crew and children to their hotel. Aloha was amazed by changes in the city. It was still recognizably New York — the forty-four-year-old Statue of Liberty held her torch over New York Harbor, the sixteen-year-old Grand Central Terminal was bustling — but there were dozens of new buildings, including a monstrous project under construction on Fifth Avenue. Most noticeable of all, though, were the cars. By 1929 there were more than sixty makes of automobile being manufactured in the United States, and all of them were on display in New York. Next to these cars, with their glossy, rounded shapes, chrome spokes, and thundering motors, the Wanderwell cars seemed merely grubby.

The wealth apparent on New York streets was impressive but misleading. Since the stock market crash, a mood of uncertainty had swept America. Bank stocks had recovered substantially from their initial lows but were slipping again. Walter was rattled. For the moment, the Wanderwells' savings were secure, but from now on he would carry several hundred dollars in cash at all times.

Within three days, articles appeared in newspapers across the country announcing that Miss Aloha Wanderwell was nearing the end of her seven-year world tour and was en route to Detroit, where she would donate her car to Henry Ford's museum.[2] An article in the *Oakland Tribune* — the same paper that had mocked Walter and Aloha on their arrival in San Francisco — announced, "Miss Aloha Wanderwell, born Gilvis Hall, is nearing the end of her rainbow and the pot of gold. But to reach it she has had to travel five [*sic*] times around the world, visiting 43 countries on four continents during

British Board of Censors "show card" would be placed at the beginning of all of the expedition's films, showing they were "appropriate" for family viewing.

a journey lasting eight years."[3] The *New York Times* confirmed that a globe-circling car would be donated to Ford and marvelled at its many trials and adventures, including Africa where it had been kept running on "crushed bananas for grease and elephant fat for oil."[4] The Wanderwells stayed on in New York to play theatres and sell pamphlets, although leaving might have been the better option.

On December 17, in its section entitled "Screen Notes and New Films," the *New York Times* announced the debut of the travel film *With Car and Camera Around the World* produced by twenty-three-year-old Aloha Wanderwell at the Fifth Avenue Playhouse. That announcement was followed two days later by what must have been a shocking assessment.

With Car and Camera Around the World walks through half a dozen reels of this film [*sic*]. The travel part of the expedition may have been Miss Wanderwell's mileage in pacing from one side of the screen to the other. True, there are views of the Taj Mahal, African huts and

A portion of the Wanderwell compound with tents and outbuildings
along the Miami River, Miami, Florida, 1928.

Venetian canals, but they all seem to be obstructed by this well-traveled girl...At the conclusion of this photoplay one feels that Miss Wanderwell is an essential part of any landscape, here or abroad.[5]

The reviewer went on to suggest that the story may not be true, complaining, for example, that the safari "fantastically jumps from two to five cars, one of which is armored. Then this last disappears and a motorcycle magically takes its place." The reviewer concluded by dismissing the film as "exactly what a majority of tourists would take with a motion picture camera."

Aloha claimed not to care what newspapers said, but the ferocity of the *Times* review must have stung.

❈

After all the talk of heading for Detroit, Aloha and Walter had realized that winter was not the time to donate Unit Nº II to Ford's museum. In the summer they could organize outdoor events and sell souvenir pamphlets. But drawing crowds in the snow would be next to impossible. A better idea was to head south for the winter.

By mid-January, Aloha and crew were back at WAWEC's Miami headquarters. The property bore little resemblance to its pre-hurricane self, but it still felt like home. Two small buildings had been erected and the area cleared of trees. While the kids gambolled around the property, the Wanderwells planned another trip to Cuba. Money was tight and they could not afford bureaucratic delays, so they decided to send just one person ahead to prepare the way. Days later, quiet Olga boarded a flight to Cuba with the newly formed Pan American Airways, and by February 17 articles appeared in Havana's *El Pais-Excelsior* announcing the arrival of the "Precursors of the International Police."[6] By the time Aloha arrived, shows were booked and tickets were selling briskly.

✼

The fifteenth census of the United States took place in 1930. The enumerator for Miami's 36th precinct, Mr. A.M. Ziegler, was extraordinarily fortunate to find the Wanderwells at home on April 7 and must have wondered at the scene he found. Unit N° II was in the midst of being repainted and repacked, and a motley assortment of tarps, canvas bags, automotive tools, printing supplies, and fuel canisters were spread across the grounds. Three olive drab tents had been pitched alongside the houses, including a military-style mess where C.W. Nicholson worked in his Wanderwell uniform supplemented by a frilled cooking apron. Valri, a deadpan four-year-old with long, blond, curly hair patrolled the property dressed in her own version of the Wanderwell uniform, complete with mini aviator goggles. And then there was little Nile, who preferred to lounge naked and spent most of his time on the porch swing or watching boats on the water.

When Mr. Ziegler had identified who actually owned and resided at the property, he listed Walter as head of the household, the value of his buildings as $4,500, and his profession as lecturer for a travelling film company. Aloha's profession was the same. Two children were recorded, ages 3 ½ and 4 ½, while 47-year-old C.W. Nicholson was listed as both "servant" and "secretary for traveling film company." The Seybold property, where Aloha and family had sought refuge during the Miami hurricane, was valued at $20,000 — the second most expensive property in the district.[7]

By the time the census taker arrived, Justine Tibesar and the members of WAWEC Unit N° III were already well on their way to San Antonio, Texas. And shortly after the census taker's visit, Aloha was behind the wheel of

Unit N⁰ II, piloting the Tin Lizzie on her final voyage, not to Detroit, but to Chicago.

Since Africa, Aloha had continued her correspondence with Art Goebel. His most recent letter said that he'd entered the cross-country air derby at this year's National Air Races, to be held from August 23 to September 1 in Chicago. In 1928 Goebel had entered the same event, flying from New York to Los Angeles. That year, none of the eleven starters had finished, although Art had flown further than anyone else, getting as far as Prescott, Arizona, in his Lockheed Vega.[8] This time he would be sure to finish, and hopefully win. After the races, he planned to stay in Chicago for a spell, giving flying lessons as part of a publicity event. Perhaps Aloha would like to learn to fly? She didn't need to be asked twice.

By July the expedition had left Florida and was in Detroit, suffering through sweltering temperatures and a city government in meltdown. The worldwide economic downturn had hit Detroit especially hard, but the newly elected and corrupt mayor Charles Bowles had filed his nails while the city was overrun by speakeasies, gambling dens, and mafia murders. Activists, however, had organized a recall vote, and by the time Aloha and company arrived, the city was about to go to the polls.

This new mood of hope may have contributed to the warm reception the Wanderwells received in the Motor City. Although there were no ticker tape parades this time, newspapers and radio stations ran flattering stories about the expedition's accomplishments and played up the promotional angle that Walter had painted on the side of Unit N⁰ II: "Only a Ford Could Have Done It!" One *Detroit Free Press* photo shows an elated Walter standing behind the car and extending the US flag, as in days of old. Inside, Nile and Valri are peeking over the side of the car. The caption describes how the car had been given an "Honor Place" in the Ford museum after being presented to Henry Ford.

After dozens of countries, thousands of miles, and countless close calls, the car that had carried Aloha around the world had roared its last. Aloha would often think about her "Princess of Serendip," with its horsehair seats,

Walter behind the battered Unit N° II as it was presented to Henry Ford at the Ford headquarters, Dearborn, Michigan, 1930. Valri and Nile are inside the car.

gun scabbards, and auto club tattoos. It was her first home on wheels and she would later wonder what had become of it.

To replace Unit II, Walter had negotiated a reduced price on a Model A chassis and, thanks to Olga, had received a "Phaeton body for the Ford Chassis for an expedition to be made to South America, gratis" from the Briggs Manufacturing Company.[9] The completed car closely resembled the stately 1930 Deluxe Phaeton, except that the trunk was rebuilt to Walter's patented Speed Slope design, allowing it to fold out and serve as a workbench or table. Decades later, a vintage car magazine would describe how the unique trunk "stored cine cameras, film, spare petrol, tent, sleeping bags, etc. Hardly any spares were carried... However, one special gadget was included: a very light-weight windlass and winch which, with a length of fine cable, three steel pegs and chains, helped to extract the car from many an impassable condition encountered on hills, gullies, mud and streams."[10] Their new supercar was again called Unit N° II.

☼

Over 1,800 miles away, aviator Eddie DeLarm and his mechanic Reid Smith were arrested in Chile and charged with conspiring to overthrow the government.[11] Chile's resource-based economy had been devastated by the fallout from the 1929 crash, and the authoritarian government of Carlos Ibáñez del Campo was deeply unpopular. DeLarm had been in South America working for Ford as a test pilot and courier, flying his trusty Ford Trimotor plane throughout Brazil and the central continent, but he had recently signed on with the New York, Rio & Buenos Aires Air Lines. According to the *New York Times*, "they worked for the NYRBA until Sept. 13, when the airline officially ceased to function and was absorbed by the Pan-American." Ten days later, DeLarm and Reid flew with five other men to Concepción, Chile, where they were greeted, almost on landing, by a retinue of carefully aimed rifles. Someone had been tipped off.

☼

With the Detroit festivities over and a new vehicle to break in, Walter drove Miki, who had arrived to share in the celebration, back to Qualicum Beach with Valri and Nile.' Aloha went on to the Curtis-Reynolds airport in Chicago. She had a photographer's pass to the National Air Races and, after the recent news coverage, everyone knew who she was.

She spent most of the week watching a sky cluttered with buzzing aircraft: there were autogiro demonstrations, navy aircraft flying in formation, several stunt flyers (including an amazing display of daredevil flying by Commander Richard Atcherley whose biplane flew close over the ground, dragging wingtips, spinning fully sideways, even appearing to fly backwards), and a war demonstration in which aerial gunners actually shot down a manned blimp. The blimp pilot parachuted to safety shortly before his deflated craft plummeted to Earth in an explosion of smoke and flame. There was a real crash, however, that killed Lieutenant P. DeShazo and two spectators. Once the conflagration had burned itself out, the air races continued while officials with metal poles poked through the wreckage, turning over what looked like twisted lengths of tinfoil to search for human remains. None were found.

Like Aloha, famed aviatrix Elinor Smith, "The Flying Flapper," was at the airshow awaiting Goebel's arrival — and she, too, had reserved a place in her heart for the dashing aviator. In her autobiography, Smith comments, "Because he had been first aviator to conquer the Pacific, Art Goebel's fame rivalled Lindbergh's."[12] She describes Goebel's arrival:

> The crowds were keyed up by the announcement that Art Goebel should be landing any minute. He was competing for first place in the nonstop race from Los Angeles to Chicago. So far Wiley Post was the winner, with Lee Schoenhair in second place....
>
> At 5:31 p.m. Art roared across the finish line, nosing out Schoenhair for second place by racking up an elapsed time of nine hours and twenty-one minutes, just twelve minutes behind Wiley, who was now the official winner. Interestingly, every ship in this race was a Lockheed, so the individual scores...were directly attributable to piloting skill.[13]

Two weeks after the air race, Aloha began her flying lessons, writing Miki that "the flying is going great, eight hours dual control now and learning to land the ship, that's the hardest part of all. We have several small shows (thank heavens) the end of the week so will have to thin out the lessons."[14] Olga was also in Chicago and may have been taking lessons too, though it seems that she had already learned to fly in Europe.

On November 16, 1930, the *New York Times* carried an article describing how an American aviator named "Orville DeLarm" had used a hacksaw blade to file the hinges off his cell door in a Chilean prison. Once free, DeLarm had "walked all night, avoiding highways until he had gained the comparative safety of the open country where he bought a horse," the start of a treacherous 500-mile journey to Argentina, through sleet, snow, and across rugged mountain terrain, often going hungry and eventually wearing out four horses.[15] The article concluded by saying that his mechanic, still in

Valri, age four, and Nile, age three, at the Wanderwell compound, 1930.

prison, had not known the real reason for their trip to Chile and that DeLarm was planning to return to the United States soon. That part, at least, was not entirely true.

❋

Aloha spent the remaining months of 1930 preparing for the trip to South America. Now twenty-four, she would, at long last, be able to incorporate aircraft into her films and travelogues. She had been disqualified from earning her pilot's licence because of a defect in her left eye, but the ban extended only to US airspace, leaving her free to fly in South America. Officially, however, Olga was the expedition pilot.

December found Aloha and her "girl world travelers" headlining the Newcomb Theatre in New Orleans, Louisiana, while Walter placed ads in the *Times-Picayune* newspaper, seeking "four persons to share part expenses motoring with me around the world. Covering South America, Australia,

Asia and Europe in special Car...$100 month required."[16] The hundred-dollar stipulation meant that no one from the economically depressed South could afford to join the expedition, and when they finally departed on January 20, 1931, aboard the Mississippi Shipping Company's SS *Afel*, ship manifests would list only Aloha, Walter, and Olga.[17]

Shortly before their departure, Walter had contacted the Brazilian government requesting permission to enter the wild Mato Grosso region — the same area where English explorer Percy Fawcett had disappeared six years earlier. A response to his request arrived from a Brazilian colonel named Rondon. The government was interested in Walter's proposal and looked forward to meeting with him to negotiate the details of the expedition, including aircraft and support crew. It was a promising start.

Aboard the SS *Lorraine Cross*, Aloha and Olga van Dreissche (wearing helmet) prepare for docking at Rio de Janeiro, Brazil, 1930.

TWENTY-ONE

TO THE ENDS
OF THE EARTH

IN 1931 THE CITY OF Rio de Janeiro was about to unveil a new statue atop nearby Corcovado Mountain. Workers on the scaffolding could look down over the fast growing city onto Copacabana and its legendary sandy beach, and across lovely Guanabara Bay dotted with ships and surrounded by a jumble of mountains shaped like cresting waves, pyramids, and sugar loaves. The view was equally impressive at sea level. Even before the SS *Lorraine Cross* had docked, Walter was rushing to load his cameras and capture the moment: Aloha and Olga standing on deck with proud expressions, the new Unit Nº II beside them, Sugarloaf Mountain sliding past.

As the unloading process began, it was obvious that the press had been well prepared — but this time it was not through Aloha's efforts. Hardly had they set foot on land before they were swarmed by excited reporters asking for details of their expedition for Colonel Rondon. How long would they stay? Where were they headed? Was it true they would search for Colonel Percy Fawcett? Someone, it seemed, had let slip that the Wanderwells were working with Colonel Rondon, and in Rio, Fawcett was a name that captured attention.

Colonel Cândido Mariano da Silva Rondon, a short man with a tall forehead and watchful, deep-set eyes, was a fierce advocate for indigenous rights and had just resigned as the head of Brazil's Indian Protection Bureau. Like Aloha and Walter, Rondon was an adventurer who had crossed vast territories against insurmountable odds. In 1908 Rondon led an expedition into the northern Mato Grosso region. After four months of travel in dugout canoes and slashing their way through untouched jungle, his party ran out of supplies. The work, however, was not completed so the expedition foraged from the forest and continued.[1] Despite illness, hunger, the depredations of animals, and the threat of hostile tribes, the expedition managed to complete its survey of the area, including the discovery of a major Amazon tributary that Rondon named the River of Doubt. When the expedition returned to Rio the following year, Rondon was hailed as a hero — no one had imagined he could still be alive.

Four years later Rondon's fame surged again when he was appointed to guide former US president Theodore Roosevelt on a scientific expedition into the Mato Grosso. In his account, *Through the Brazilian Wilderness*, Roosevelt wrote that Rondon "has been for a quarter of a century the foremost explorer of the Brazilian hinterland," and that shortly after meeting him, "It was evident that he knew his business thoroughly and it was equally evident that he would be a pleasant companion."[2]

The opportunity to follow in the footsteps of an American president and share the same guide was thrilling. The expedition, however, would be the most dangerous they had yet attempted. Roosevelt considered his voyage along the River of Doubt had been gruelling, remarking that it had shaved ten years off his life. In fact, Roosevelt never recovered. Within five years, the president was dead of complications arising from injuries and illnesses contracted on the trip.[3]

It was clear why Rondon had agreed to play host to a US president. What was less clear was why he was so willing to assist the Wanderwell Expedition, providing guides, maps, equipment, and even the use of two government planes.

Although best known as a Brazilian nationalist, Rondon was also an ardent defender of indigenous peoples. The son of a native Bororo mother, he forbade the men on his expeditions to use violence against the indigenous peoples, telling them, "Die if you must, but never kill."[4]

One explorer who had aroused Rondon's suspicion was the famous Percy Fawcett, sponsored by England's Royal Geographical Society, which itself had a reputation for using scientific exploration as a disguise for colonial designs. In response to Fawcett's request to lead a team into the Mato Grosso, Rondon

Walter Wanderwell and General Cândido Rondon on the terrace of the
Copacabana Hotel in Rio de Janeiro, at the outset of their
Mato Grosso adventure, Brazil, 1930.

said it was not necessary "for foreigners to conduct expeditions in Brazil, as
we have civilians and military men who are very capable of doing such work."[5]
And after Fawcett vanished, Rondon even protested the arrival of search
parties whom he feared would negatively impact the indigenous tribes. As
late as 1932, the British Foreign Office in Rio de Janeiro was warning:

> General Rondon has been publishing in the press the severest
> strictures on foreign explorers in Brazil, whose intentions he considers
> suspect, especially in connection with attempts to search for Colonel
> Fawcett. The Ambassador gravely doubts whether General Rondon
> will give any facilities to expeditions of this kind and fears that he
> may even cause special legislation to be passed in order to hinder
> them.[6]

And yet for the Wanderwell expedition Rondon offered every assistance
possible, short of accompanying them. For years, Rondon had worked to
publicize the plight of Brazilian native peoples and his own Indian Protection

Bureau, but with almost no success. As one historian wrote, "Rondon and his officers were reduced to publishing appeals in newspapers, for public opinion was their only source of support."[7] But the Wanderwell Expedition promised a means to create international sympathy for Brazil's indigenous people and an appreciation for their land and way of life. Rondon understood that the best tools were not political, but visual. Half an hour of film could do more to raise awareness than a dozen fiery speeches. In exchange for a plane, a crew, and a bit of fuel, the Wanderwell Expedition could not only make movies but also carry them to audiences around the globe.

During their initial meeting, Wanderwell and Rondon found much common ground: they were both explorers, both experienced publicists, and, at least for each other's benefit, both concerned with shaping public policy for the better. It's not hard to see that Rondon would have supported Walter's idea for an international police (Brazil had struggled to secure its borders for decades), and according to Aloha, the two were soon chatting with an easy familiarity. Photographs show Walter and Rondon, each in their respective uniforms, smiling warmly in a friendly embrace. It was a vital success, because without Rondon's support Aloha and Walter could not have pursued their adventures in the Amazon jungle.

The expedition stayed at the Copacabana Hotel and basked in the attention of Rio's adventuring elite, accepting daily invitations to white table-cloth functions from businessmen, important local families, and politicians. Photographs reveal Aloha in a beautiful beaded gown and Walter in a traditional tuxedo, the only images of them out of uniform. The Carl Zeiss Company donated equipment, Standard Oil obliged with fuel, the Brazilian government provided two planes, and smaller companies provided food, clothing, and walking shoes. For Walter, though, the most significant achievement was the rush of people wanting to start their own WAWEC units. With so many groups capturing so much media (and sending in fees), he hoped the Work Around the World Educational Club would soon be large enough to influence political opinion. As a hedge against competition, Walter instructed the office in Miami to proceed with securing copyright for the WAWEC manual. Papers were duly filed and the Library of Congress issued its certificate of copyright registration on April 13, 1931, Class AA Entry N° 65746.

❁

In late March 1931, Aloha, Walter, and a cinematographer known only as "C" completed a three-day train journey to the town of Corumbá, a small, European-style town with large government buildings and a thriving population. The town sat on a waterway at the tip of the Pantanal region, the world's largest wetlands. The Pantanal covered more than 42,400 square miles, an area almost as large as England. At the train station, Aloha, Walter, and C were met by town officials and the men appointed to be their mechanic and pilot. The pilot was a German Aloha refers to as "Tech," a former First World War flying ace. The mechanic was an exceptionally handsome young man nicknamed Practico who, according to Aloha, had a commission to rule over part of northern Brazil — an impossible task owing to its remoteness and the lack of any major settlements.[8]

The following morning, Aloha and company hauled their cameras down to the harbour, where "a gleaming silvery fliers' delight" awaited them.[9] The Junkers F.13 was a German-built floatplane that featured plush upholstery, reading lights, and swivel chairs. Affectionately called an "air limousine," the plane offered quick and luxurious transportation into regions that would otherwise take weeks to access. This particular vessel, with call letters P-BAJA, belonged to the German-Brazilian Condor Syndicate, the same airline that was now co-operating with the Graf Zeppelin to provide the world's fastest transatlantic mail and passenger service.

For the next two weeks Aloha and Tech made short exploratory flights over the region. They mapped villages, took aerial photographs and con-sidered the logistics of a multi-week expedition: "rations for 30 days, a large supply of maté, trade clothes and gifts, calico and old clothing. A .303 Enfield rifle, a Luger, dysentery pills, Atabrin for malaria (and) snake serum were included."[10] Rondon had made it clear that the disposition of the Mato Grosso tribes ranged from mildly hostile to murderously aggressive. Certain tribes he advised they avoid, while others, like the Bororo, were considered reasonably safe. Still, as Rondon himself made clear, the plane would undoubtedly "terrify the Indios" and if the natives decided to attack, there was nothing to do but let them. Injury or death was a distinct possibility.

❁

Aloha climbed into the pilot's seat, nodded to Tech seated beside her, then waved once more through the open window. After a tentative rumble, the engine gushed smoke, rose to a roar and began pulling the aircraft across the water's corrugated surface. The once distant shore of trees rushed forward as the heavy plane began to bounce and stutter until it peeled away from the lake's surface and climbed into the air.

The flight from Corumbá took them north along the Paraguay River across vast stretches of green, marbled with lakes, streams, and marshes that made the land look like an enormous soaked sponge. Throughout the journey they did not glimpse another settlement, or even a wisp of camp smoke. After several hours, Aloha began her descent. She would attempt to land on a mile-wide stretch of the Paraguay River. As the water drew close, however, Aloha froze, afraid that she would get the angle wrong or touch down too abruptly. When she asked the German pilot how he managed it, he had said, "I wait, and then I think about it a minute, and then I just set it down." Aloha harrumphed. "Well, that's alright for you buddy...flying all your life."[11] She swallowed her fear and the plane touched the water, sliding to a safe and frothy stop.

A staged film sequence depicts how the expedition was able to initiate contact with members of a Bororo village. Aloha is shown leaving several hand mirrors on a log before climbing a tree to watch. Moments later, a curious man, naked except for a necklace and a sheath over his penis, comes to collect one of the mirrors. He examines it briefly before racing back into the forest. In the next scene, Aloha is in the Bororo village, surrounded by a coterie of curious and equally naked tribe members, all smiling with the exception of a small, muscular man wearing a monkish haircut and a stony expression. Aloha would later write that she had "made a devastating blunder. To the Caciquè I should have presented the gifts."[12] The Caciquè, or chief, would ultimately decide their fate, so it was vital that he should be appeased.

Ruffled feathers were smoothed by the presentation of another gift. Aloha, seated on a mat, held up what looked like a bundle of rope to the unsmiling chief. Each holding one end, Aloha and the leader unfolded the

Aloha celebrates the delivery of her Junkers F.13 seaplane from
Colonel Rondon, Córdoba, Brazil, 1930.

bundle to reveal a large hammock. Aloha and company were allowed to stay
and, slowly, everyone — the crew and the natives — began to relax.

Before long, Aloha had worked up the courage to swim nude in the river
with local girls. The film and photographs of Aloha with three Bororo
women in the water are among the most memorable of the trip, revealing
her willingness to connect with the cultures she was among. While the
Bororo women walk nonchalantly into the river, a blindingly white Aloha
races into the water after them and is the first to duck under, her body
language that of someone skinny-dipping on a dare.

Aloha and Walter focused much of their footage on the Bororo: muscular
old women pounding a mortar of maize using logs taller than they were,
close-ups of Bororo faces with blunt-bangs haircuts, easy smiles, and fantastic
jewellery. Several men wore necklaces with a pendant made from the front
claws of a giant armadillo and shaped to represent a bird.

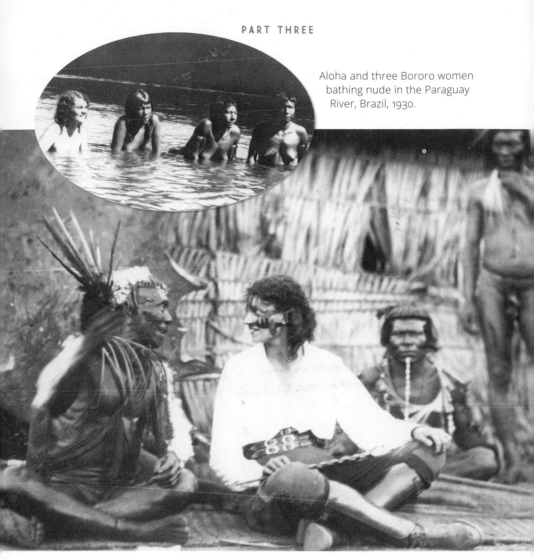

Aloha and three Bororo women bathing nude in the Paraguay River, Brazil, 1930.

In the Amazon jungle Aloha tries her hand at traditional Indian face painting, Mato Grosso, Brazil, 1931.

The villagers prepared a celebration that included transforming their guests into "extraordinary beings." While Aloha sat cross-legged on a mat, three village men fixed her hair and painted her face with black genipap dye and brilliant red annatto. The colour red and black were significant, with red representing goodness, power, and fertility, while black denoted spiritual power and life after death. When her make-up was in place, Aloha donned a small beak, completing her transformation to bird. Walter was likewise painted on his face, chest, and arms by a young Bororo woman — and judging by the expression on Walter's face, he was doing what he loved best in life, encountering people with drastically different world views and being made welcome among them.

✻

The expedition spent several weeks at Bobore before Aloha continued east and north to the Rio das Mortes, or River of Death, where she began her search for Colonel Fawcett. In a postcard to his brother Janec, Walter tells how Aloha spent nearly two months flying around the Pantanal, making films of the Indian peoples. "We have worked hard," he wrote "on producing a better film with our limited means so that the WAWEC project will have a healthy foundation." He told how an advance party had driven Unit N° II along the east coast to Buenos Aires, since there were no roads to the country's interior, and then stated, with seeming nonchalance, that he "didn't see Aloha for almost a month while I sat waiting in an Indian village and burned smoke signals for the 'Iron Bird,' as the Bororos have christened the airplane."[13] His card made no mention of Colonel Fawcett or of the plane crash Aloha would later describe. Aloha was later adamant that she really *did* make flyovers of the areas Fawcett had been.

Many theories suggest Fawcett's expedition was killed by some jungle tribe. Aloha, however, said she learned little from the natives, mostly because they couldn't see why anyone would care, and what information she *did* get pointed to natural rather than human disaster. According to a Bororo chief, whom she called Taboré, Fawcett and his crew had been drowned in a whirlpool — a major menace to transportation in the Mato Grosso.

Aloha also suggests that Fawcett's disappearance may have had something to do with his mental state at the time.

It seems the colonel's actions were most irregular prior to his starting out.... The only word that Fawcett had given to the outside world was that he was going into the Brazilian wilderness to make a more intensive study of the savages. Rumors also hinted to search for the gold of a lost race which had frequently been, over the centuries, the secret goal of explorations in South America. His departure did not indicate a long stay in the jungle. He had left practically his entire equipment at base camp, not even taking the ever essential matches, according to reports.[14]

Aloha's search for Fawcett was cut short by a fuel leak that necessitated an emergency landing near another Bororo village. She managed to land the plane on the river only to have it flung against shore by a hidden whirlpool. With the help of villagers, C travelled south by canoe for fuel and parts while Aloha and Practico waited with the plane. While they waited, they began an affair that would last until their rescue, and by correspondence thereafter.[15] In the film *Last of the Bororos*, Aloha described how the Bororo women would, after mating, rush into the river and "create a douching effect by quickly tightening the abdomen muscles and then relaxing, causing a vaginal action of intake and outflow — very simple and effective."[16]

✺

By the time Walter and Aloha were emerging from the jungles of Brazil, Margaret had once again left British Columbia (the kids remained in Miki's care) to lead WAWEC units through Cuba and the US. Justine and her crew had reached Asia, but there had been no word in some time and fears grew that WAWEC Nº III had disbanded. This proved true, although Tibesar continued across Asia to Europe by motorcycle, achieving her own driving records.[17] Other units in the US and Europe were sending successful reports to Miami. The challenge now was to recruit WAWEC members in South America.

✺

A photograph taken on July 15, 1931, shows Aloha in front of an advertising-clad Unit Nº II, surrounded by a curious crowd in front of the *Palacio de Correos*, the central post office of Buenos Aires. Aside from Walter, the only other crew member in the photograph is a blurred crouching figure, still recognizable as Olga. The expedition was growing again, and while Aloha and Olga played shows, Walter interviewed and selected eight new recruits.

The original plan was to drive the newly developed Pan-American Highway from Buenos Aires to the United States, but they soon discovered

Members of the expedition posed in front of one of their vehicles.
Aloha is third from the right, Brazil, 1930.

that the highway was nowhere near completion. Even near Buenos Aires, the road north was passable only in good weather and was often congested with meandering wagons and reluctant farm animals. It was, Walter decided, not the way to introduce his new recruits to the travelling life. He negotiated train transportation with a steel boxcar to house Unit N° II and the men of the expedition. The women would travel in a first-class berth.[18]

By late August a crew, transportation, and an itinerary were in place. Two days before the expedition was to leave, a couple arrived at the Wanderwell's hotel and asked for Aloha. "They were young, married, good-looking. The girl was British, tall, beautifully proportioned. She had been a model and a champion swimmer in London. The man had a rather odd accent that suggested Australian, but he said he was a naturalized American citizen."[19] The couple introduced themselves as William and Vera Guy. They were travelling through South America and, after seeing the Wanderwell show, felt inspired to join up. They could speak Spanish, had worked with newspapers, and were in top physical shape. Curly-haired William even knew how to fly a plane and was fast friends with some Americans who had run flights to Chile. Aloha liked the couple but the expedition was full—there was, she told them, simply no room for more.

The couple returned the next day. They "explained how anxious they were to get away. The husband said that he had seaman's papers and would soon be able to find work on a ship and so reach the United States. If only we would take his wife along their problem would be settled."[20] Walter relented. A uniform was hastily assembled and Vera Guy became the newest member of the Wanderwell Expedition. William promised to meet her in the United States.

※

Aloha was glad for the new company. After the adventure and pleasure of the Brazilian jungle, every day spent crawling through a South American hinterland was a wasted day that could be better spent back in Los Angeles, editing what she knew was blockbuster adventure footage.

As it was, she bounced through a ten-hour train ride from Buenos Aires to Córdoba, swapping travel stories with Vera, while Olga and the two other girls talked about Mexico City, where one of them had a rich uncle. Out in the boxcar, Walter and the other men shouted halting conversations, mostly about cars and South American road conditions. The only light inside the car came from open vents in the ceiling and, as the train climbed inland, temperatures fell. It was spring in Argentina and though nights no longer froze, it remained cold. By the time the train reached Córdoba, the grumbling had already begun. Apparently some of the men did not think that travelling like hobos in an unheated boxcar was much fun. So, at Córdoba, Walter acquired a second car: a black Ford Model T sedan that could carry the expanded gear and crew in some comfort, but also served as a backup in case one of the cars failed on the terrain ahead.

San Miguel de Tucumán was the largest city in northern Argentina, and the launching point for what was expected to be the most difficult portion of their trek through South America. Travelling along roads little better than wagon trails, their route would take them nearly 1,000 miles through remote river valleys, across arid plateaus, and over dozens of treacherous mountain passes to the high altitude city of La Paz. It was the most ambitious motoring attempt Aloha and Walter had made since Africa, and only they had an idea of how difficult and dangerous the journey might be.

The crew was just tightening the straps on the loaded cars when another unexpected visitor arrived at their hotel. A smiling William Guy, dressed in uniform, snapped a salute at Walter and announced that he was ready to join the expedition. Aloha was appalled. "We didn't want him, he was one too many." William quickly explained that recent political instability had made finding work difficult. Trade with the US was plummeting and what ships there were, weren't hiring. Annoyed but resigned, Walter allowed William to join. As Aloha would later say, "at that stage we felt we couldn't turn him back."[21]

William Guy was an expert at surviving by his wits. A native of Cardiff, Wales, he had spent most of his childhood in Manchester, England, living with an aunt and uncle. He was a rambunctious youth, with a short temper and a habit of getting into fights with neighbourhood toughs. He flunked school and was often in trouble with local authorities. When his guardians threatened to place him in reform school, William fled to Portsmouth. There he joined the crew of a ship bound for Rotterdam and points beyond. The year was 1924; he was just fourteen years old. Months later he was in China, and the year after that he had drifted to Egypt, where he survived as a prize-fighter. By 1928 he was in Nicaragua, where he was captured by guerrilla leader Augusto Sandino. After escaping his captors, he fled to South America and found work with an airline, making the acquaintance of American pilots who taught him to fly. In late 1929 he met and married Vera, and the two had rambled around Argentina until late 1931, when they met the Wanderwells. William had been searching for a means to get to the United States for some time and the expedition seemed purpose-made.

For all his resourcefulness, Aloha felt that William's greatest asset was his charm, and a gift for subterfuge. He was a slick talker with a disarming smile, quick to surmise the way to people's hearts. Within a week, he and Vera had been appointed assistant leaders, "he with the men and she with the girls."[22]

Walter, far left with arm raised in the Fascist salute that he adopted for his WAWEC organization. Aloha, kneeling front row, second from left. William Guy is to Aloha's right, La Paz, Bolivia, 1931.

The road north to La Paz began easily, over terrain that reminded Aloha of the Canadian prairie, lightly rolling and with wide grassy plains. As the expedition entered the scenic valley of Quebrada de Humahuaca, they travelled along what had been a caravan road during the Inca Empire, stretching from Buenos Aires to Peru. Aloha marvelled at the starkly contrasting colours on display: green fields, orange wildflowers, rust- and cappuccino-coloured mountains beneath a shocking blue sky. They passed villages of mud brick with not a car or railroad or electric light bulb in sight. The dry valley, complete with cactus and sagebrush, must have looked much as it did five hundred or even five thousand years earlier.

By the time they'd crawled up the Choqueyapu River canyon to the bowl containing the city of La Paz, several crew members were feeling the effects of altitude. At almost 12,000 feet, the city is high enough to induce cerebral edema, swelling in the brain. Though no one became seriously ill, tempers were short and even the cars struggled, losing 40 per cent of their power in the thin air. The exhausted cadets pleaded for a few days off to acclimatize and regain their strength. Even Olga complained the itinerary was too demanding. But Walter would not be swayed. Once they were across the Andes and into Peru's warmer climes, they could rest and recuperate. For now the work was what mattered: the better they documented their travels through film and literature, the better for them all.

To commemorate their visit to La Paz, the expedition visited a photography studio where they posed in two rows — eight in front, nine behind. In the resulting postcard, Aloha is crouching in the front row, between William and Vera. All except Walter are holding rifles, some with bayonets. Walter, grinning like a proud father and standing directly behind Guy, does not have a gun but is holding his arm aloft in his version of the Boy Scout salute. The postcard's caption reads in translation: "The cadets of the Wanderwell Expedition class 1931 in La Paz, Bolivia. More than 40 groups of volunteers for the International Police are traveling around the world."

No boxcars were available for the trip over the Andes to the city of Arequipa in Peru, so the cars were lashed to an open train bed. Female crew members purchased tickets for carriage travel, while the men travelled in the cars for the five-hour journey. By the time the train reached Arequipa, having crossed through high mountain passes and sub-zero temperatures, the men were rigid with cold and burning with anger.

Walter quickly announced a rest stop in Arequipa, but even after ten days' rest, the grumbling continued. Nor did it abate during the 475-mile drive along the Pan-American Highway to the coast at Lima. It was the toughest leadership challenge Captain Wanderwell had ever faced, and he struggled to balance discipline with morale. Aloha suggested another rest stop in Lima and Walter agreed.

It took a week to reach the Pacific, where they turned north to pass through a landscape filled with ancient burial sites, marine and dinosaur fossils, and, near Nazca, gigantic geoglyphs that were visible only from the air. The so-called Nazca Lines had been discovered by air travellers in 1927, and it's unlikely that the Wanderwell Expedition knew of their existence. By the time they rolled into Lima, the crew was sunburnt, blistered, parched, and ready for a holiday. But Walter changed his mind. The political situation in Lima was unstable and Walter feared their international police activities might cause trouble.

It was the last straw. The crew accused Walter of not keeping his word and refused to drive any further. The situation was serious enough that Walter agreed to a change in plan. Rather than attempt to drive through Ecuador and Colombia, they would take a ship directly to Panama. From there they could proceed to Costa Rica and leave troubled South America behind. Once again, the Wanderwell Expedition had failed to reach its goal.

Without seeing Lima, the crew sped to Callao. From there they boarded the *Zenon*, a 5,390-ton steamer belonging to the French line *Cie de Nav d'Orbigny*. Passage to Panama would cost $800 for the crew and cars. As usual, cabins were booked for the women, while the men slept in tents on deck. As the ship prepared to set sail, Walter called for a meeting. Aloha would later recount that "at the conference Captain Wanderwell asked to see Guy's American passport. Guy took a red booklet from his pocket, just flashed it, then put it away." It emerged that Guy was not, in fact, American. He was a British citizen who had never actually *been* to the United States. His passport belonged to an American who, Guy claimed, had died. Walter, already annoyed at having to travel by ship, was appalled. His "whole attitude changed. He sternly ordered Guy not to use the passport and not to pass himself off as an American citizen while a member of our expedition. Guy said nothing, but he was angry."[23]

As they approached Panama, Walter and Aloha had to decide how to conduct the rest of the expedition — the length of time allowed for it and the crew. The decision was made easier by the shock delivery of a petition from William Guy. Written in Spanish, the document declared, "Guy and certain other members refused to do any more work for the expedition. The majority of the members had signed the petition."[24]

Nonplussed, Walter reminded the crew that Panama was a military zone. It was essential they present a united front on arriving. Once they were safely landed in Panama, he said, any member who wished to leave would be free to do so.

On arriving in Panama, "all passports were returned to their owners and the Captain and I became relieved of all responsibilities.... We afterward learned that Guy's wife had gone to England, while he had shipped as a sailor upon Vincent Astor's yacht."[25] Walter made sure to keep Guy's mutinous letter close — it was proof that Guy had not fulfilled his duty as a WAWEC member and, therefore, was not entitled to the deposit he and Vera had paid on joining.

✻

A photograph taken in Costa Rica shows a clearly exhausted Wanderwell seated on the running board of Unit N° II. For once, there is no smile and no salute. Only one crew member, an unidentified male, had elected to continue through Central America. Even Olga had quit. By the time they'd passed through Costa Rica, Nicaragua, Honduras, El Salvador, and Guatemala — almost 1,000 driving miles from Panama — they were in a ruinous state. Another rest stop was called at Guatemala City in order to recuperate from what Aloha called "jungle jaundice," possibly yellow fever.

The Wanderwells re-entered the United States in early February 1932, one year and twenty-six days after their departure at Port Arthur, Texas.[26] In that time they had travelled over 30,000 miles — roughly 6,000 miles greater than the circumference of the earth.

MAKE THE WANDERLUST PAY

JOIN THE WORK AROUND THE WORLD EDUCATIONAL CLUB

Apply NOW

1. Write that you will live up to the rules, state sex, age, linguistic ability, profession, travel experience, include two passport photos. Also mention in detail if you own a vehicle and if you use stimulants (Address this to the nearest Wawec expedition Captain, care Poste Restante or to forwarding address 614 N. W. N. Riverdrive, Miami, Florida.)

2. When accepted, paint your vehicle olive drab, Wawec emblem and No. of your unit in black.

3. Get passport and visa.

4. Prepare custom deposit for vehicle.

5. Fill in membership card, fee 5 Dollars per annum.

6. Provide the following equipment: a strong valise 12cm. x 30 x 44. Olive drab waterproof trenchcoat with shoulderstraps having WAWEC and Unit No. above, embroidered in gold. Wool blanket. Wool olive drab tailored shirt with sports collar and two large patch pockets. Wool olive drab pair of shorts 70 cm. circumference on bottom, 28 cm. length in crutch. (For ladies, breeches of same material.) Aviation cap (R.A.F.) same material. A second suit as above in tropical khaki. Pair of olive drab, one colour wool golf socks and one pair of cotton. Pair of low heeled brown shoes. Wool pullover. Brown leather belt plain metal buckle 5 cm. wide. Set of Toilet articles. All buttons 2½ cm. diameter, plain.

Lodgings and breakfast are provided by group leaders. Salary, a percentage of work or sales on agreement. Daily six hours' campaign work, one hour vehicle maintenance. Sundays, two hours' open forum by Captain.

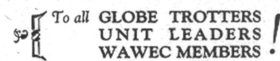

To all **GLOBE TROTTERS UNIT LEADERS WAWEC MEMBERS** !

Come to the

International Wawec Jamboree

December, 1931,

at MIAMI, the Magic Sunshine City of Florida.

Free camping accommodation—Open Forum.
Important organization plans for the future.

Notify **WAWEC**, Gen. Fowarding Secretary, 614 N.W.N. Riverdrive, Camp Wanderwell, MIAMI, of your arrival.

The expedition pamphlet announcing the International WAWEC Jamboree to be held at the Wanderwell compound in Miami in December 1931.

TWENTY-TWO

CLOSE QUARTERS
AND FRIGID SEAS

IN FEBRUARY 1932 the Winter Olympic Games took place at Lake Placid, New York. Crowds flocked to watch contestants from seventeen countries compete in speed skating, Nordic skiing, bobsleigh, ice hockey and, most popular of all, figure skating. Audiences gasped as Sonja Henie gave a flawless performance, sweeping her way to gold and into the record books. At only twenty years old, Henie had already won gold at the 1928 Olympics and five world championships. Newspapers gushed that "for perfection of figures, grace, showmanship, and mastery of the most difficult spins and jumps, there appeared to be no real competition for her."[1]

Henie's performance was the gloss on a very successful Olympics, but this was a rare patch of blue in an otherwise dark sky. Even during the games, front-page headlines blared alarm at the nation's destroyed economy. In the time that Aloha and Walter had been away, nearly five thousand banks had collapsed, the nation's productivity had fallen some 30 per cent, and industrial stocks had shed nearly 80 per cent of their value.[2] By 1932 half of all workers in Cleveland, Ohio, were jobless. And in Toledo, Ohio, four out of five were jobless.[3] Many blamed President Hoover for the nation's economic woes and public anger would soon sweep him from office, replacing him with Franklin D. Roosevelt, the man who would become the longest-serving president in US history.

✲

The economy in Mexico, though hardly robust, was faring better than America's. After checking that their savings still existed in the US, Walter and Aloha elected to stay in Mexico for a while. Years later, Aloha would still wonder that among so many bank closures, their account in Florida was somehow intact.[4]

Using Nogales, Mexico, as their forwarding address, Aloha began contacting various offices of the Shell Petroleum Corporation in Seattle, St. Louis, Denver, San Francisco, and Los Angeles. Long a major sponsor of the expedition, they had used Shell's distribution network to assist with the shipping of various pieces of equipment and collateral. This time Aloha asked that all available Wanderwell pamphlets (more than 35,000) be sent to Mr. F.M. Schlegel of the Shell Petroleum Company in Los Angeles. By late March, the Shell-sponsored pamphlets were concentrated in a Shell warehouse at 1298 Alhambra Avenue, and Aloha and Walter were ready to begin.

The original plan had been to work theatres all the way to Canada, collect the children, then return to Hollywood to edit the South America films. But given the "Hoover wagons" that lined California's streets, Walter was leery about their chances of earning much. There were more beggars here than they'd seen in India, and the highways were lined with stands selling anything: teacups, shoe shines, scrap wood, empty milk bottles, rescued nails. He and Aloha decided to head for Canada first, then work their way back. At least this was the scenario that Aloha painted in her memoirs. But there was another major issue hounding them: those 35,000-plus pamphlets were evidence of another failed venture.

The latest pamphlet had been one of the largest and most descriptive of any the expedition had produced, and why not — Aloha and Walter had spent years travelling the globe, and now there were many WAWEC units scattered across it. This act of WAWEC franchising was a masterful feat of marketing, and they had every right to be proud. On the back cover of the warehoused pamphlet, Walter had advertised the "first WAWEC Jamboree." It was a rallying cry to all WAWEC worldwide members to attend, and it was to be held at their "Camp Wanderwell" headquarters in Miami in December 1931. This would have been the first and largest collection of expedition crew members present anywhere and would be a confirmation of Walter's long-held dream.

But there was a problem: it was now early 1932, and Walter and Aloha hadn't attended. They couldn't have; they had been stuck in South America, dealing with their failure to complete the continental crossing and sorting out the ramifications of their crew's rebellion. For the founders of both the Wanderwell Expedition and WAWEC to simply not show up at their own convention would have raised holy hell among the hundreds of WAWEC members who had offered their trust (not to mention thousands of dollars in fees) in the cause. With this failure dogging them too, Aloha and Walter headed for Vancouver Island in British Columbia. It was the first time in the Wanderwell Expedition history that they did not stop in town after town to sell pamphlets and postcards or present their films. Their trip north to Canada looks very much like an extension of their lying low in Mexico.

On a sunny day in early June, the sound of crunching gravel sent six-year-old Valri Nell Wanderwell racing out through the front door of her grandmother's house on Vancouver Island. Barefoot, she ran to the edge of the yard and watched the familiar car with its wonderful letters emerge from the forest trail leading to the house. After two years away, Mom and Dad were back and their arrival was certain to bring hugs, kisses, and presents.

From the porch, Valri's five-year-old brother Nile, always more reserved than his vivacious sister, watched as the car doors opened and the grown-ups stepped out. Soon, the tall lady he knew was his mother had swept a giggling Valri up into her arms. Reaching into the car, his mother pulled out a white stuffed toy rabbit and gave it to Valri. Now Grandma and Tia-Miki were there too, hugging and shaking hands with the new visitors. Then the man dressed like a soldier strolled over and crouched down. He looked into Nile's eyes and smiled, holding out his hand. On it was a small toy car, a blue racer, and a silver coin with a flying bird on it. The boy took the gifts and mumbled, "Thank you, sir."[5]

Before long, the adults were sipping tea in the dining room. Aloha told tales of South America, recalling the Bororo tribe, their strange customs, their habit of living naked and swimming in piranha-infested rivers. She described the wonderful Junkers F.13 and the fuel leak that had sent them down. The footage, Aloha boasted, was unlike anything seen in theatres before. This film, when it was done, would cement her place in history. Miki sighed and said she was ready to get out and see something — like the sun. It had been a long dark winter in British Columbia.

"Well, why not come to Los Angeles?" Aloha suggested. The South America footage would take time to edit, so it would be lovely to have someone to help watch the kids. Perhaps Miki could even look into starting a career in Hollywood. It was decided.

❀

After two weeks, they said goodbye to Margaret and headed south. In Seattle they added three new members and, much to Aloha's disgust, purchased yet another car — a 1928 Cadillac. Among the new crew members was diminutive twenty-year-old Dorothy Dawn, a prettier version of Olga, who acted as backup driver and assisted with publicity. Another girl, sixteen-year-old Lynette Pollard, from nearby Tacoma, was unable to join the tour immediately but promised to travel to Los Angeles as soon as she was able to provide the $250 deposit required to join.

❀

When Walter told Aloha of his idea to purchase a schooner for a South Seas expedition, she was speechless. Since their arrival in the United States, Walter had droned on about the need to shore up their finances, to proceed with caution, to redouble their efforts. Now he had purchased another car and wanted to squander what remained of their savings on a boat? What about her *film*? Editing alone would cost a fortune.

Walter explained that having a boat would safeguard their lifestyle and provide a ready means of generating income. More than that, he wanted it to be the headquarters of a new organization he would legally register: the International Police, Inc. Aloha was unmoved. Walter described how by incorporating the international police he would be setting a legally verifiable precedent for the idea and also have a more stable means of creating and preserving value from their travels. It was, he assured her, the logical next step in the evolution of the Wanderwell Expedition. From now on, the sole focus of the expedition would be to further the international police idea and its originator. It was, in other words, the end of Aloha as the face of the expedition.

On July 5 an Associated Press article noted that Captain Walter Wanderwell and his wife had arrived in San Francisco after driving from Buenos Aires. On July 20, the *San Jose Evening News* announced that Walter Wanderwell had returned to their city after a sixteen-year absence but that he wouldn't stay long because he planned to "continue moving as long as he lives."[6]

According to a postcard Walter sent to his brother Janec, the expedition was travelling with a Cadillac, a Ford, and a house trailer en route to Los Angeles. He wrote, "business here is very tight. Bartering is very popular now and especially for our own needs. Actual cash is extremely limited."[7] Yet he was also hopeful that a schooner named *Carma* would soon be ready for a trip to the South Seas. The *Carma* was a sleek, fast, 110-foot, two-masted schooner. Originally christened the *Norma P. Coolen* in Mahone Bay, Nova Scotia, in 1913, her early days were spent trawling the Grand Banks of Newfoundland, where she gained a reputation as one of the fastest ships in the area. Over the years she was owned by a procession of dreamers and schemers, each failing in their plans for the boat, thanks to malfunction or misfortune. One day, during a routine fishing trip, the ship was caught at the edge of a sudden violent storm. The captain trimmed the sails and attempted to head home with the day's catch but was overtaken by the storm. A violent gust sent the main mast crashing to the deck where it killed the captain. Later, when Prohibition took effect, the *Norma P. Coolen* was sold to a French liquor syndicate that renamed her *Cherie* and began running booze between Canada, America, and the French islands of Saint-Pierre and Miquelon off the south coast of Newfoundland. Later, she became *Carma*. She was eventually seized by the US Coast Guard and sold at auction. The last owner had planned a trip to Vladivostok, but his plans were scuttled by Soviet red tape and the stock market crash.

Walter contacted the ship's current captain, Haakon H. Hammer, and inquired about purchasing the ship for a South Seas cruise. Hammer said that the ship needed extensive repairs but that a group of Scandinavians had rented the boat to take fishing parties down to Mexico. The group had paid one month in advance and had promised to make required engine repairs. If Walter could wait for a month or two, the ship might suit his purposes. Walter agreed.

✿

By August 11 the *Los Angeles Times* was reporting the triumphant arrival of the Wanderwell Expedition all the way from Buenos Aires, unaware they had already been to Canada and back again. Unsatisfied with their own "world's record for touring," the article explained how the expedition had come to Los Angeles to prepare for a "schooner trip to South Seas Isles and a journey through the eleven countries not already crossed by the intrepid organization."[8] The articles, clearly arranged by Walter, made no mention of a forthcoming film or of theatre engagements or of Aloha.

Aloha sniffed around Hollywood until she found suitable lodgings: two adjoining suites, located at the Arcady Apartments on the corner of South Rampart and Wilshire Boulevard. It was not an ideal location, but would do until they could find something closer to the film labs in Hollywood. For Aloha, the apartments were a place to sleep and to store the children while she worked. But rumours had begun to swirl. By some accounts, Aloha and Walter were no longer getting along and were in fact sleeping apart.[9] She later said the second suite was occupied by former expedition members, including Eric Owen.

Whatever the climate of her relationship with Walter, Aloha's infatuation with the world's entertainment capital was undiminished. It was the place where things *happened.*

Particularly in 1932, the Summer Olympics. More than 100,000 people had flocked to the opening ceremonies of the Games of the X Olympiad, held at the Olympic Stadium (now called the Los Angeles Memorial Coliseum). There was every reason to believe that the influx of visitors to the city could be a boon to the expedition's sales of their newly revised pamphlets, but the apartments Aloha had rented were only a few blocks from the Chapman Park Hotel, where female Olympic athletes were being housed. The crush of reporters, tourists, and official traffic made driving next to impossible and badly hindered pamphlet sales: without a place to showcase the cars, the Wanderwells were just grifters in funny costumes.

When the games ended, Aloha set about editing her film. Mindful of the criticisms levelled at *With Car and Camera Around the World*, she made certain that she was *not* in every scene and that the story was more than just a gander at the Mato Grosso. The search for Colonel Fawcett, the downing of the plane, the jungle's perils, and the "savage" Bororo tribe would supply enough drama to carry the story. But there was no doubting who the hero of the film would be, or of its greater purpose: this was Aloha's best chance to become a star.

✿

Aloha returned to her apartment one afternoon and heard shouting in the adjoining suite. Then a cry for help. She ran into the hallway and banged on the door. The noise stopped, and moments later, the latch fell and the door swung open. A dark-haired man stood at the threshold. Chairs and a table had been overturned. Two expedition members stood in a corner and near an open window she saw Walter, his hair ruffled and his clothing in disarray. Then "a man stepped from an adjoining room and I saw that it was Guy. Everyone was talking; someone said that Guy had demanded money that the Captain owed him. I heard the Captain say: 'You can't blackmail me; you can't choke money from me that I don't owe.'"[10]

Eyeing Aloha, Guy seemed to change his mind. He motioned to his friend and the four men brushed past Aloha and left. Appalled, Aloha insisted that Walter contact the police, or better still, the immigration authorities. But Walter refused. Straightening his tie, he said that Guy had demanded the mutinous declaration written in Panama, as well as the money he had paid to join the expedition. When Aloha worried that Guy might return, Walter shook his head. "Guy's a young fellow, he's hot-headed and later he'll realize his mistake. If he is in the country illegally he will be caught sooner or later."[11]

One of the men accompanying Guy that afternoon was the American aviator Edward Orville DeLarm.

✿

Towards the end of August, Walter learned that the US Patent Office had approved his claim to an "ornamental design for an automobile," awarding him a patent for a term of fourteen years.[12] The design showed a car with a rounded back, looking much like the sloped, aerodynamic cars that Cadillac

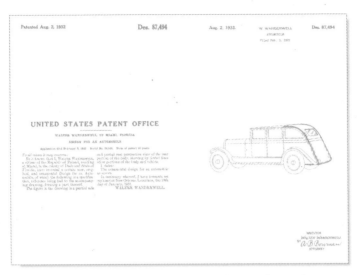

Walter Wanderwell's official papers for his aftermarket
Speed Slope for automobiles, dated August 2, 1932.

would begin producing in 1934 and would evolve into a hallmark of 1930s automotive design. At about the same time, Walter began his submissions to the Division of Corporations of the State of California — the first step towards establishing the International Police, Ltd., a company that would be legally permitted to issue and sell shares.

While continuing to push forward, Walter heard that the schooner he intended to purchase had been seized off San Clemente Island, and its captain, a man identified only as Kollberg, arrested for transporting several hundred cases of whiskey, purchased from a Canadian boat in international waters.[13] Walter scrambled to find a replacement ship but called off his search on September 18, when District Judge McCormick condemned the vessel and ordered it sold at auction to satisfy a fine of $2,200 — less than half the purchase price Walter had originally agreed to. The ship's owner, Mr. W.L. Doyle, protested saying that Kollberg was not the ship's owner, but the judge was unmoved and ordered the sale to proceed.

On the morning of October 5, a large crowd gathered at the county courthouse to attend the federal auction. Walter, Aloha, and the children pushed their way into a row of seats normally reserved for criminal trials. By the time United States Marshal Albert Sittel announced bidding on the former rum runner, Walter was wiping the palms of his hands on his thighs. This was by far the largest purchase he had ever attempted. The room fell silent as proceedings began. As promised, the bidding for the schooner opened at $2,200. Walter indicated that he would meet that price. The marshal then raised the price to $3,200. Walter waited nervously, but there were no takers. The *Carma* was declared sold, after just one bid, to Walter Wanderwell.

On October 7 the Harbor Shipping section of the *Los Angeles Times* announced that Captain Walter Wanderwell was seeking a crew of about twenty for a cruise to Tahiti "and away places." Within days, applications were pouring in from as far away as New England. Some people offered to pay extra while others cited long and formidable lists of skills and qualifications. Walter soon realized he could charge far more than the original $50 they had advertised. The price was raised to $200 (enough to cover the boat's entire purchase price) and planning for the expedition began in earnest.

Aloha suddenly had more to spend on the Bororo film, allowing for animated maps, proper film titles, and for the first time, a narrative soundtrack. It would be expensive but with a soundtrack, it would be possible to send the film into wide distribution, delivering her name to a multitude of new audiences while simultaneously freeing her from the stage.

Three days after the *Carma*'s auction, Judge Paul John McCormick learned that Wanderwell was not an American citizen and, therefore, not legally entitled to purchase at government auction. The sale order was rescinded and Walter's money returned. It didn't take long, however, for Walter to untangle these latest knots. With the assistance of attorney David H. Cannon, he told the court that the boat had been purchased on behalf of his daughter, Valri. Naturally, those attempting to prevent the ship's sale raised a howl of protest — who would buy a 110-foot schooner for a six-year-old girl? Nonetheless, on October 10, Judge McCormick ordered the sale to proceed. An article in the following day's *Los Angeles Times* pronounced "Valry [sic] Nell Wanderwell...the youngest master of any vessel plying the Pacific Ocean, according to Deputy United States Marshal Minnick."[14]

Coincidentally, on the same day the court released the *Carma*, Walter received a letter from the Commissioner of Corporations informing him that

LEFT: US Department of Justice letter releasing the *Carma*, purchased "illegally" only days earlier by Walter, into the hands of his daughter, Valri, the only American of the bunch, Los Angeles, California, October 10, 1932.

RIGHT: The Wanderwell Expedition's schooner *Carma* under full sail, Long Beach, California, November 1932. This picture was framed and sitting on Valri's coffee table when the authors visited her in Honolulu.

the IP project was now legally registered in the state of California as International Police, Ltd. In the space of a few hours, the Wanderwells had set a new course for themselves.

❁

Aloha's reservations about the ship vanished once it actually became theirs. On a sunny morning, the *Carma* was officially released to Valri, in the care of her parents, and the family climbed onto the boat. "We loved [the *Carma*] from the first day," Aloha said. "We thought it would give us the happiest days of our lives."[15]

The *Carma* was taken to the P&O docks at the Long Beach Marina for a month-long refurbishment. The troublesome diesel engine would be overhauled, rotten timbers replaced, and the ship furnished. Within days, the *Carma*'s railings had been repainted a gleaming white and the words "International Police R.E.," standing for the International Police Research Expedition, had been painted on the bow. A smiling Aloha posed for photographs with the children, looking out to sea from behind the wheel or grinning from high in the riggings.

While the boat was overhauled, Aloha and Miki rented an apartment in Hollywood closer to the film lab and paid visits to Hollywood studios and distribution companies. Walter began sorting and hiring new crew members.

❀

On October 27, the first meeting of the shareholders of International Police, Ltd. took place aboard the *Carma*.[16] Because neither Walter nor Aloha were American citizens, the organization's founding members were listed as *Carma* crew members Eric Owen (president), Cuthbert Wills (secretary), and Cuthbert's wife Elsa G. Wills (treasurer). Evidently, founding a company was not something six-year-old Valri was legally permitted to do. Cuthbert, called "Bert" by family and friends, was an English-born sailor, tall and lanky, with a pencil-thin moustache and a sceptical, mildly fastidious expression. He was a relative of Australian explorer William John Wills, who in 1860 led the first south-to-north crossing of Australia, from Melbourne to the Gulf of Carpentaria. A naturalized American, Wills had recently married Elsa, a girl from Guyana, and the Wanderwell Expedition was to mark the beginning of their adventuring life together.

Aloha's plans were finally coming together too. In mid-November she met a young film executive named M.J. Kandel, president of Ideal Pictures Corp., a film distribution company with offices across the country. Kandel was interested in the Bororo film and even more interested to know that further films were forthcoming. In 1933 Ideal Pictures was about to release a documentary called *A Jungle Gigolo*, written by A. Carrick and F. Izard, about the trials of a man living on the island of Sumatra with more wives than he can support.[17] Another drama called *Found Alive* told the story of a boy who had been hidden in the jungle during a messy divorce, only to

Aloha about to climb into the rigging aboard one of the expedition's many transoceanic ship excursions, undated.

grow up and discover the "lure of savage passions."[18] The Wanderwell films, with their exotic locations and thrilling sequences, would fit nicely into the company's plans.

❋

Of those who had applied to join the crew of the Wanderwell International Police Research Expedition, twenty were provisionally selected and fifteen might actually sail. Among the crew were the sisters Mary and Marian Smith of Rockmart, Georgia; Mary "Nellie" Parks, a twenty-six-year-old schoolteacher from Boston; and in a most bizarre piece of casting, an English nobleman, Lord Edward Eugene Montague, second son of the Duke of Manchester.[19] Several members came as a result of ads placed in the Seattle and Portland newspapers, including James E. Farris, who would act as ship's captain; his fiancée Ruth Loucks; and student sailor Jack M. Craig. The only familiar name was Eric Owen.

It was not long before federal officials were back causing trouble for the expedition. Following the US Marshal's condemnation of the *Carma* as "about as seaworthy as a cardboard box," naval authorities threatened to put a stop to the proposed expedition, citing the ship's unseaworthiness and insufficient life-saving equipment.[20] In fact, there *was* only one rowboat, hardly big enough for three people, never mind fifteen or twenty. Walter once again stepped in, revealing once more how careless he could be about the safety of his crew. He pointed out that he was *not* selling passage aboard the *Carma*, he was casting about for working *crew members* and, as such, they were all exempt from US transportation laws. Authorities were powerless to prevent the voyage from proceeding.

The charge that the ship was not seaworthy shook several crew members, including Aloha. She asked Walter to delay the trip and to purchase adequate life-saving equipment for the vessel. At the very least, Walter should chart a course that kept them close to land for as long as possible. Walter flatly refused. They would set sail for Hawaii, a crossing of more than 2,400 miles through open sea. There they would take film and earn money lecturing before continuing on to Polynesia, Tonga, Fiji, New Zealand, and Australia.

On November 29, Eric Owen and the Willses resigned their directorships with International Police, Ltd.

By Sunday, December 3, the Bororo film was nearing completion. A few scenes needed to be edited, some voice-overs added, and the titles completed; however, there was more than enough to show Ideal Pictures. Because it was Sunday, the film lab was closed, so Aloha travelled the 30 odd miles from Hollywood to spend the day on board the *Carma*, visiting the kids who were now living on board the vessel. Although the ship was hardly in pristine condition, it had come a long way since auction day. Broken furniture and empty boxes had been cleared out, all the rooms had been freshly painted, and new furniture installed where necessary. Each room was decorated in the style of a different country, reflecting the international flavour of the ship and her crew. A long table was installed in the galley and a piano and a gramophone were placed in the community room — shades of her stepfather's *Inlet Queen* — along with a comfortable sofa, a divan, and a small library. Foodstuffs, tools, drinking water, cameras, pamphlets, a small printing press, thirty rifles, and ample ammunition had all been securely stowed below.

Late in the afternoon, while most of the crew continued cleaning and tinkering, Walter called Aloha to their cabin. She later said that he told her that one of his pistols was missing — a .38 calibre revolver. The gun had been in a locked chest, but the chest had been opened. Together they combed the ship and asked crew members if they had seen the gun. No one had. A number of crew members were sent into town by Walter to canvas pawn shops. After more than an hour of looking, they gave up. The pistol had vanished.

✿

The following Tuesday, December 5, Aloha was back in Hollywood working on the film soundtrack. The *Carma* was still docked at Long Beach, ready, at long last, for her South Seas voyage. A fifteen-member crew had been selected, supplies and fuel had been gathered, and newspapers in Hawaii had been alerted to the expedition's arrival sometime within the month, depending on wind conditions. All that was left was to repair the ship's interior lighting, and for that an electrician had already been hired.

December's arrival meant cooler temperatures even in Southern California, and by evening, a fog had crept over the coast, haloing the single light on the dock near the ship and magnifying the watery sounds of the harbor. There was nothing left to do aboard the *Carma* so most of the crew decided to go to a movie. Several new films were in theatres, including the Marx Brothers' *Horse Feathers* and a Betty Boop short called *I'll Be Glad When You're Dead You Rascal You*, featuring a score by newcomer Louis Armstrong and his orchestra.

Four members stayed behind to watch over the ship and the kids. When Valri and Nile had been put to bed, Walter gathered with Ed Zeranski, Cuthbert Wills, Marian Smith, and Mary Parks in the ship's galley, where they played rummy and discussed plans for the morning. At some point a discussion arose regarding the sailing distance between two ports, and unable to agree, Walter headed for the ship's community room, presumably to retrieve a book or some maps. Shortly afterwards, a man appeared at the screened porthole outside the cabin. He asked the crew members where Captain Wanderwell was.

Wills stood up and walked to the galley door, where the fellow was now standing — a middle-aged man dressed in a long grey coat. Wills asked if he was the electrician.

Oddly, he replied, "No, but I know a lot about electricity."[21] Wills would later say the man spoke with a German accent. He asked again where the captain was. Wills led the stranger along the deck to the community room, where Walter was still looking for a map. The man thanked Wills and stepped inside. As Wills walked back to the galley he heard the captain greet the man in a tone that suggested surprise but familiarity.

Walter Wanderwell lays dead from a single bullet wound to his back, slumped against the divan of his stateroom on board the *Carma*, Long Beach, California, December 5, 1932.

In the galley, Wills re-cranked the phonograph, set the needle on "St. Louis Blues," and resumed his seat at the card game. According to his later testimony, he had just picked up his cards when there was a shout from somewhere outside. Mary craned her neck to look through a porthole; perhaps there was a party in the harbor. But then there was a muffled *pop* followed by a high shriek so loud it seemed to come from just outside the door. Wills and Zeranski threw down their cards and raced from the cabin. They hurried up the ship's ladder to look over the wharf. With only one light on the dock competing with the thick fog, they could see no one. Perplexed, they climbed down and combed the ship's deck, looking for anything unusual, but all was in order. The children were still fast asleep, and the moorings were tight. Then Wills noticed that the door to the common room was ajar. Zeranski reached down to light the kerosene lamp, but even as his matchstick crackled to life it was clear that something was terribly wrong. The captain was sitting on the floor, slumped against the divan. Two streaks of blood ran down the back of his jacket, issuing from the spot, about mid-back, where a bullet had smashed its hole and tore through his heart. Wills and Zeranski rushed into the cabin. Captain Walter Wanderwell was already dead.

Winnipeg Free Press

VOL. 38—NO. 133   WINNIPEG, WEDNESDAY, DECEMBER 7, 1932   Price 5c per Copy; Edition with Comic, 10c   22 PAGES

GLOBE-GIRDLING HUSBAND OF WINNIPEG WOMAN MYSTERIOUSLY SLAIN ON YACHT

BRITAIN AND FRANCE MEET TODAY ON NEW WAR DEBTS SITUATION

MacDonald, Chamberlain and Boncour to Confer on Latest Developments in Question

Problem Must Be Faced Directly if U.S. Does Not Alter Stand on to Payment

Tug Feared to Have Sunk With 18 Men Off Newfoundland

Belief Vessel Was Lost in Heavy Gale Strengthened by Reports of Finding of Second Body After Discovery of One in Ship's Lifeboat—Craft Had Been Engaged in Salvaging Operations.

BRITISH SPEED DRIVER RACES ANCIENT CAR

Speed budget at the wheel.

Shot Dead in Darkened Cabin of Ship Chartered For Trip to South Seas

Captain Walter Wanderwell, Colorful Leader of Strange Little Band of Adventurers, Victim of Bizarre Murder at Long Beach, Cal.—Expedition Composed of Nine Women and Seven Men, Including Reputed Scion of British Nobility.

MAN ROBBED OF ALL HIS CLOTHES HAS LAST LAUGH ON RELATIVE

NEWS OF THE DAY

U.S. ARMS PLAN NOT ACCEPTED BY BERLIN

Proposals Declared To Be Unacceptable to Germany In Present Form

First Day of Five-Power Conversations at Geneva End in Stalemate

Says Unauthorized Use of "U" Moneys Went on 20 Years

OPPOSE RECOGNITION OF MANCHUKUO STATE

Representatives of Three Nations Indicate Stand at League Session

Members Are Urged to Follow Advice of Lytton Commission on Controversy

CAPE-TO-LONDON HOP AMY JOHNSON'S PLAN

Famous British Aviatrix to Take-off Sunday After New Record

THREE HAVANA YOUTHS GRAVELY WOUNDED IN ATTEMPTED SLAYING

FREE STATE TREATY WITH CANADA PASSED

Dail Gives Approval to Trade Agreement; Rejected at Ottawa

MARILYN MILLER AND SIX STOWAWAYS NOT ADMITTED TO FRANCE

HUNDREDS SLAIN IN HONDURAS FIGHTING

Smashing Victories Are Claimed by Nationalist Troops

Mrs. Wanderwell Has Lived Adventurous Life Since She Last Left Winnipeg

LOOKING BACKWARD

Five Masked Men Stage Daring Mail Robbery in Heart of Chicago Loop

16 MORE SHOPPING DAYS

Prospective Mother Faces Death in Electric Chair

"Hunger Marchers" Start To Evacuate Washington After Peaceful Parade

TWENTY-THREE

THAT'S THE GUY!

A T FIRST ALOHA THOUGHT the pounding came from somewhere in the house. But as her mind swam clear of dreaming, she understood it was the door. She looked across the room at Miki, who was sitting up too. Aloha grabbed her robe, slipped it on, and rushed into the hallway. The landlady was already at the landing, fumbling to unlock the door. As it swung open, Aloha could see a man who said something she couldn't hear, but it was clear he was looking for her. The landlady turned to gape at Aloha. Across the street, lights popped on in the upper bedrooms.

✿

Aloha would recall only a pastiche of impressions: the catastrophe implied by detective Lieutenant Miller's manner, jamming into a car with as many as six plainclothes policemen, the wail of the siren as they crossed the intersection of Santa Monica and Western Avenue, the impression that paperboys were already on the streets yelling "Extra!" (when in fact no one in the press corps had yet heard of the murder), and especially the nauseating fear that left her unable to speak.

At the Long Beach police headquarters Aloha was taken to the office of the evening chief of police, where she was asked to take a seat. The chief closed the door. There was a pause as he considered how to proceed. Aloha asked for an explanation. Had the boat sunk? Was there a fire? Had someone been kidnapped? Finally, the officer said, "I am just a simple man and I can only put this to you in a simple way. Your husband, Captain Wanderwell, has been shot."[1] For a moment Aloha's mind did not register the officer's words. Walter was injured or missing or had *almost* been shot. But seeing the expression on the officer's face, she understood.

> When I gathered my wits, the second thought was for the children. He assured me they had been removed immediately from the yacht by the juvenile authorities and that I would see them there as soon as possible but first we would together and surrounded by both the Long Beach and Los Angeles officials return to the yacht.[2]

While she waited, the chief asked who she thought had killed her husband. But she had no idea. In tears, she explained that Walter had many friends and, naturally, a few enemies. He was headstrong and decisive and not everyone liked his manner. Members of his own crew, she revealed, had recently argued with him about the *Carma*'s seaworthiness. One member, Elsa Wills, had even threatened to organize a competing expedition to Mexico, on a boat that *would* sail. But these were professional disagreements, not blood feuds. She could think of no one on board the *Carma* who would have wanted to see Wanderwell dead.

The man sighed. He closed his notebook and asked Aloha to follow him. They travelled down a long hallway, past a throng of newspaper men, and turned into a small room. Inside was a table with a tray and what looked like strips of gauze. Aloha was asked to sit down. A man in a white coat and latex gloves told her to rest her hands over the metal tray. He explained that, simply as a formality, they needed to perform a paraffin test. Aloha did as asked but was not really listening as the investigator talked about nitrates and making a wax mold, the kinds of chemicals they would add, or the little blue flecks that might arise. What she *did* understand was that nitrates, if present, would suggest gunpowder.

After the test, they returned to the main office where Aloha was surprised to see the entire *Carma* crew now crowded into the precinct. At least two girls were in tears, while others looked at Aloha with a hand over their mouths. She was not permitted to speak to any of the crew but would be taken directly to the *Carma*.

Just as they were about to leave, Detective Miller appeared again. He sat down on the corner of a nearby desk and began telling her the story Cuthbert

Wills had told, about a man at the porthole. In an instant, Aloha believed that she knew who Wills was describing. The man's last name was Guy, she said. He was a British adventurer and former expedition member who had tried to rough up the captain as recently as two weeks ago. Then, with increasing certainty, she declared that Guy was "the only person living who might have done the shooting."[3]

As soon as word of this slipped out of the room, the waiting newspapermen bolted for the telephones.

❀

Aloha was taken to the *Carma* and her arrival caused a flurry of flashbulb explosions and a volley of shouted questions, but Aloha refused to speak to anyone except Detective Miller. He took her to the community room where Walter's body had been found, a small stain of blood still visible on the floor. He asked if she noticed anything unusual, to which she replied, "Everything." Looking down, however, something did catch her eye. She bent down and picked up Wanderwell's flutophone, his small tin whistle. "The police did not seem much impressed by my discovery, yet I knew things about the Captain's flutophone that they did not know. The Captain had loved to construct these little objects, he had made them all around the globe, he had presented them to rulers in India, Negro chiefs in Africa, little boys in New York. He could play a nice tune on his flutophone and he loved to teach other people to play them."[4] Most importantly, though, Aloha knew the captain had always kept the instrument clipped to his wallet. "The spot where I had picked up the flutophone was about ten feet from the cabin door." From this, Aloha deduced that Walter had reached for his wallet at some point shortly before his death — perhaps to pay someone off — but had been unable to replace the whistle. Aloha asked the police if they had located her husband's wallet, and if a letter, written in Spanish, had been found inside. She was told that his wallet had been found, but there was no letter. Walter had always carried Guy's mutinous petition with him, and she found it odd that the letter should be missing. "I thought this was interesting and important but the police did not seem to share my view."[5]

✻

By morning the story was in all the newspaper headlines, causing a sensation. This story had it all: love, travel, murder, whispers of sexual impropriety, jealousy, smuggling, espionage, a beautiful and mysterious widow, a scion of British nobility, and a disproportionate number of young, attractive girls. Less than twenty-four hours after the murder, newspaper articles and radio reports were already quoting Secret Service information revealing that Wanderwell's true name was Valerian Johannes Pieczynski, that he had been interned as a German spy during the war, and arrested in 1925 for impersonating an army officer.

The Associated Press ran stories that read like summaries printed on the backs of pulp novels:

> Mutiny, an attempted strangling and a fatal shot in the back, fired in the darkened cabin of an adventure yacht, were the clews [sic] detectives were following tonight in the hopes of finding the killer of Capt. Walter Wanderwell.
>
> Globe trotter, suspected spy, and untiring seeker of the bizarre in life, Wanderwell, when felled by an assassin last night…left a murder mystery as keen as any of the adventures he sought in life.[6]

The pitch of high drama often came at the expense of accuracy. Some articles claimed that Walter specialized in cruises for "landlubbers to remote places" or that he was married three times: first to a Canadian girl named Gilvis Hall, then to an American named Nell Miller, and finally to a French girl called Aloha Wanderwell.[7] Some articles presented statements as facts that are never repeated again. A United Press article made the sensational claim that "the pistol was lying on the floor at his feet. Fingerprints of the group aboard were taken to compare with those found on the gun." The article even quoted the chief investigator, misnamed Lieutenant Ralph C, Witler (it was Miller), as saying, "he hoped fingerprints on the gun would clear members of the party of suspicion."[8] The presence of a gun directly contradicts every other version of the story as reported by the press, the police, and Aloha herself.

The murder of a world-roving, oversexed, mystery man was an interesting story, but it wasn't long before papers latched on to the living spouse, Aloha.[9] The *Los Angeles Times* recalled Aloha's arrest and described her underage "escapades" of 1925. The competing *Los Angeles Record* branded her the "Granite Woman" and printed a sketch of a chisel-featured, empty-eyed woman beneath which they invited readers to "catch the cold glint of bravery in the face of this 'granite woman'…[who] wants the world to know that she comes of solid stuff." Although supposedly an appreciation of a young widow's ability to keep her wits in a trying situation, the article implied a kind of monstrous frigidity that came from being the wife of a man "schooled in German sturdiness."[10]

By December 8 newspapers had widened their focus to include interviews with, of all people, Nell, who was now Mrs. Nell Farrell. In one paper Walter's former wife said, "Walter's murder was a terrible shock. I haven't the slightest idea who could have killed him, but undoubtedly he had enemies."[11] Not to be outdone, two days later the *San Mateo Times* reprised the theme on page one, announcing "Former Wanderwell Wife in S.M. Says Girl is Killer." Here Nell insisted that, "A woman, a woman of one of his adventures murdered Captain Wanderwell. He had it coming, and someone was bound to get him sooner or later." Describing him as "the eternal lover," Nell sighed that Walter might have become a great man had it not been for women.

> My life with him was one of constant problems, difficulties, getting him out of scrapes, leaving town in the middle of the night so I wouldn't have to testify against him. There were innumerable seduction and betrayal charges, and he was just slick enough, as a rule, to talk himself out of each.[12]

She even claimed to know William Guy, declaring that he was "innocent of the crime. I am positive of that. I knew Guy and I know there was no motive for him to kill Captain Wanderwell. A woman is the one to look for."[13] Nell had retired from the road a few years earlier, but her assertion, true or not, made for good copy.

⚙

A man named Harry Greenwood, employee of a local gambling ship, had been at the Long Beach docks on the night of the murder and reported seeing a man who fit the description of the Man in Grey. When shown a selection of photographs, he immediately pointed to the picture of Guy that Aloha had supplied. Greenwood described him as "an extremely nervous man who rushed from the vicinity of the *Carma* to a point a block away from the craft." The man had asked how to get to the city centre, but after being shown where he could catch a street trolley, opted to run the distance. This report, combined with descriptions of Guy's threatening visits to Wanderwell, made him the prime murder suspect.

What investigators could not understand, however, was why the *Carma*'s crew seemed so reluctant to share details about what they knew. Every answer seemed hedged, every description couched in the vaguest of terms. Exasperated, another detective, Lieutenant Murphy, announced that "certain persons, for reasons best known to themselves, have been withholding information from the police." He warned, "Unless this attitude is changed, I will demand a grand jury investigation to determine if a conspiracy exists to cover up evidence."[14]

⚙

On the night of December 8, Los Angeles detective Lieutenant Joe Filkas paid a visit to a house at 2054 Blake Street, in a district known as the LA River Bottoms. With him were two men, one of them Carleton Williams, the lead crime reporter for the *Los Angeles Times*. The house they wanted to search was dark and, judging by its ramshackle appearance, unoccupied. The men walked quickly up the steps and then Filkas kicked in the front door and shined his light on the interior. There, lying on a sofa eating tuna from a can, was William Guy. Far from looking startled, however, he simply put his hands in the air and with the faintest trace of a grin said, "I know what you want — I've been expecting you fellows. But I didn't kill Wanderwell. I just moved here a day or two ago because I knew I would be suspected. I was thinking of giving myself up — I think I would have done it tomorrow but you fellows beat me to it."[15] When asked why he had gone into hiding,

Guy freely admitted that he was in the country illegally and had even voted in the last election.

After his arrest, Guy was taken, not to the police station, but to the headquarters of the *Los Angeles Times*, where he was questioned by Carleton Williams and other *Times* staffers until the early hours of the morning. Newspapers would soon trumpet Guy's own version of events, protesting his innocence, admitting his hatred for Wanderwell, and incredibly, claiming that no less than six people could prove he was nowhere near Long Beach on the night of the murder. According to Guy, he had gone to bed at 8:30 p.m. the night of the murder at the home of his good friend, the aviator Edward Orville DeLarm. Though Guy didn't know it yet, Eddie had been the third man in the police vehicle.

When reporters had finished with him, Guy was brought to the Long Beach Police Department, booked, and then stuffed into a car and driven to the port of Long Beach. Wills, Zeranski, and others still living on board the *Carma* were asked to state whether they thought the man they had in custody was the Man in Grey. Guy smiled his glossy smile and looked at Wills through the porthole. "You know, I'm not a first class murderer," he said. All present felt "pretty sure" Guy was the assailant. "I wouldn't want to put a noose around any man's neck," said Cuthbert Wills, "but I think he is the man."[16] The crew was temporarily uncertain because, they said, the man who had appeared at the porthole was moustachioed and spoke with an accent that suggested a trace of German. Detectives, however, noted that a razor and shaving cream had been found at the rented house, and Guy himself admitted he had recently worn a moustache and that he was fluent in German.[17]

Within hours newspaper headlines announced the capture of the Man in Grey. The crew's positive identification appeared alongside Guy's own explanation of his whereabouts and details of why he had so disliked Walter Wanderwell. In his version of events, there had been no mutiny, but Walter and Aloha had simply abandoned the expedition in Colón, Panama. When Guy heard that Walter and Aloha were in Los Angeles, he paid them a visit and asked for his $200 fee to be returned since he had not, as promised, been delivered to the United States. Walter refused, smashing a window with his fist and calling for police assistance.

Most of the Los Angeles–based dailies had crafted disparaging nicknames for Aloha, calling her "the Granite Widow" or "the Rhinestone Widow," based on a necklace she had worn in the early days of the investigation. Ironically, it may have been a necklace of diamonds she had had made in Italy from stones she collected in Africa. And because crew members had been forbidden to speak to reporters, the press latched on to anyone remotely connected with the murder. One paper, desperate to heighten the drama, carried a front-page photo of the ship's *cat*, Rasputin. A discouraged Long Beach policeman was quoted as saying, "If only this cat could talk." The newspaper agreed, but noted that "Rasputin, with a cold, stony stare as icy as that of Aloha Wanderwell, the 'Granite Widow,' can't put into words what he saw happen Monday night."[18]

On December 8, 1932, the front page of the *Los Angeles Record* carried the headline "Murder Yacht Widow Breaks" and reported that Aloha "today broke under the strain of her husband's murder and was reported in complete collapse." Shortly after Guy's arrest, police had asked Aloha to come to the station and confront the accused. Much to the press's disappointment, Aloha reported that she was too ill for such a meeting. Earlier, a reporter had asked Miki how her sister could be so stoic. She replied that Aloha was working hard because everyone was depending on her. "If she did not act this way, the whole crew would go to pieces. There'll probably be a big reaction later."[19]

Despite the collapse of her personal life, Aloha had work to do. Voice-overs for the Bororo film had not yet been completed and an orchestra had already been booked — if she didn't finish the recording, she would forfeit everything. So Aloha went to the Metropolitan Studios and narrated what turned out to be her last adventure with Walter Wanderwell. It was the worst performance she ever gave. Her voice, normally so lively and clear, was flat and muttering. She stumbled over her words but didn't bother to correct them.

Aloha's despondency did not go unnoticed. Douglas Fairbanks got in touch and reassured her that the best cure for a broken heart was to get working. He offered double billing with his latest picture *Mr. Robinson Crusoe* at the United Artists Theatre at Broadway and Ninth. Desperate for money, Aloha agreed. Walter had died without a will and their family funds were frozen until the estate could be settled. Within days, ads appeared for Fairbanks's movie with an equally sized "special added sensation." The specific wording of the ad, however, could not have been greatly encouraging: "The 'Rhinestone' Woman of the Hour!...Aloha Wanderwell In Person!... With Her Amazing Film 'The River of Death' Recording her last adventures with Capt. Wanderwell."[20]

It was Hollywood voyeurism at its most shrill, but with Fairbanks's help, Aloha was able to negotiate a generous fee. Engagements would begin on December 15 and run for a week. The ink was hardly dry on that contract before Aloha signed another with the Universal Service newswire to tell her life story. It was an opportunity to manage her image, while also raising interest in what the Wanderwell Expeditions had achieved through stories in short segments that would appear from December 12 to 15.

Wanderwell Witness

Edward De Larm (above), Yaqui Indian aviator, was held in Long Beach, Cal., as a material witness in the slaying of Capt. Walter Wanderwell, adventurer. He is a friend of William James Guy, arrested as a suspect in the slaying. (Associated Press Photo)

Circulated press photo of pilot and murder trial witness Edward "Eddie" DeLarm, Long Beach, California, January 1933.

☼

Investigators continued their inquiry, looking for enough evidence to charge William Guy with murder. Subpoenas were issued for Eddie DeLarm and his wife, Isobel. Both claimed Guy was at their house at 325 Madison Way, Glendale, on the night of the murder — 30 miles from Long Beach. During separate questioning, however, Eddie and Isobel disagreed on when they had last seen Guy. Eddie stated that he "went to bed about 8 o'clock Monday evening, as near as I can remember. I think that Guy went to bed soon after. My wife remained up about an hour later. I don't know whether Guy left the house or not." Isobel wasn't sure how late she'd seen Guy but asserted that "to the best of her knowledge" he was in bed when she retired at 9:00 p.m.[21]

Eddie denied that the Wanderwell case had been discussed with Guy the next morning. He said Guy had asked to borrow his (Eddie's) Studebaker so he could look for a job. He "said he would return it to the Grand Central Airport, where I had my airplane in a hangar. I let him take the automobile and when I got to the airport about 10 o'clock the car was there and that was the last I saw of him."[22] According to Isobel, however, on the morning after the shooting, Guy and Eddie had driven away together at around 8:00 am.

Eddie told investigators he'd met Guy in Buenos Aires in December 1930 while "conducting some airplane flights."[23] He admitted that he had accompanied Guy on a visit to Wanderwell in August and that the incident had turned violent — directly refuting Guy's claim. The most damaging reports, however, came from DeLarm's mechanic, Ralph Dunlap, who had visited the DeLarm residence on the evening of the murder. He told police that Guy had been there and that he had even announced he was going to Long Beach, though he (Guy) refused to say why he was going.[24]

❀

An inquest was held at 9:30 a.m. on December 9 at the Patterson & McQuilken Funeral Parlor. While crowds surrounded the premises, Aloha and members of the crew joined Long Beach police, William Guy, and state prosecutors to give testimony before a coroner's jury. *Carma* crew member Marian Smith reiterated that she had seen the Man in Grey at the porthole, but now also added that she had seen him standing at the galley's open doorway. "When the stranger came aboard the boat I saw him the first time as he halted momentarily at the doorway. ...I had a good look at him at that time. A moment later I had another look at him when his face appeared at the porthole to the dining room. I am positive the man I saw is the man here."[25] After making her announcement, Miss Smith fainted.

Next were Cuthbert Wills, Ed Zeranski, and Mary Parks, all of whom agreed that Guy was the man who had visited the *Carma* Monday night. To everyone's surprise, however, Deputy district attorney Clarence Hunt refused to allow a charge of murder to be brought against Guy. The reason, according to one reporter, was that, "Not once was the name of the suspect brought into the testimony."[26] The coroner's jury, however, did agree that Wanderwell had died from "gunshot wounds inflicted by an unknown person on the ship *Carma*," and that, "from the evidence produced we find the killing to have been with homicidal intent and we recommend further investigation."[27] In fact, evidence of powder burns on Walter's jacket showed that he'd been shot from a distance of about six inches.

❀

On the morning of Monday, December 12, Aloha was getting ready for the trip to Long Beach Harbor, where Walter's funeral was scheduled to begin at 9:00 a.m. Before she could leave, however, the police were, once again, knocking on her door.

Deputy District Attorney Clarence Hunt questioned Aloha for more than two hours, forcing her to recount every aspect of the trip to South America, of Guy's desertion and threats. What, exactly, was Guy's motive for killing

335

Walter? Why not just rob him or beat him senseless? When Aloha was finally permitted to leave, she stepped into the corridor and collapsed. According to the Associated Press, "Authorities said they had questioned Mrs. Wanderwell only about Guy's past and his connection with the Wanderwells." The article also noted, however, that "what was brought out during the questioning of the attractive blond widow and what caused her to falter and swoon into the arms of her sister was not made known by officers."

The failure to bring a murder complaint against William Guy had become an embarrassment to the Long Beach police force. Aloha was brought to the station to extract as much information as possible to bolster their case. When they were done, warrants were issued for the arrest of both Eddie DeLarm and his mechanic Ralph Dunlap — as material witnesses for now, but with the possibility that they could be charged as accomplices to murder.

With Miki's assistance and her head held high, Aloha left police headquarters, telling reporters only that she had a husband to bury.

✿

The body of the slain Walter Wanderwell, traveller of the world's long trails, went to an ocean grave under a brooding storm.

Cold rain fell, thick fog lay over the harbor, and a chill wind furrowed the waters as the little schooner, on which the adventurer had been shot in the back just a week ago, put out in an angry sea.[28]

So the newspapers described the *Carma*'s sad trip into open waters. Befitting the proceedings, it was even snowing slightly. A crowd of men in long coats and fedoras had gathered at the dockside, waiting in the gusting rain for the widow to arrive. Walter's body, laid out in a sea grass coffin and draped with the American flag, had been carried from the hearse and lowered to the deck of the *Carma*. Among those waiting, only Eric Owen wore a Wanderwell uniform.

When Aloha arrived, in uniform and with a black veil of mourning across her face, the procession began. In most photographs she looks frozen. One shot captures an expression verging on grief, her hand stretching to touch the sea grass coffin.

The *Carma* motored several miles west towards Santa Catalina Island over choppy seas. Captain Farris, a tall handsome man with a booming

The seagrass casket containing the body of Walter Wanderwell is lowered onto the deck of his beloved Nova Scotia schooner, *Carma*, in preparation for his burial at sea, Long Beach, California, December 12, 1932.

voice, read out a short speech on Aloha's behalf. He recalled Walter's many achievements, the values he fought for, and the country he loved. Aloha stood next to the flag-draped coffin that rested on a plank pointing over the railing. Eric W. Owen stood beside her, bugle in hand, while just over her shoulder was Art Goebel. As the *Carma* heaved on the unsteady seas and the rain mixed with snow, the eulogy ended with a short quote from Walter's favorite countryman, Joseph Conrad:

May the deep sea where he sleeps now rock him gently,
wash him tenderly, to the end of time.

Captain Farris closed his book, a seaman's whistle sounded, and Eric Owen raised his bugle to play a final "Taps." Attendants lifted the plank and Walter's coffin slid into the water. A wash of bubbles frothed and dispersed as the casket receded into the sea. After a life on the road, a million vagabond miles, and who knows what else, Walter Wanderwell was gone.

The front of United Artists Theatre in Hollywood the week after Walter's murder, Hollywood, California, December 1932. Aloha shared top billing with Douglas Fairbanks. Expedition Unit Nº IX was part of the theatre lobby exhibits.

TWENTY-FOUR

WHAT'S PAST IS PROLOGUE

L OS ANGELES DISTRICT ATTORNEY Buron Fitts abruptly took control of the case. He announced that all witnesses and principals would be questioned again — and the DeLarm household, including mechanic Ralph Dunlap, would face a grand jury inquiry. He also announced that important new evidence had surfaced, allowing a murder complaint to be made against William Guy. Most intriguing for the press, however, was Fitts's comment that he did not believe Walter's murder had been a "one man job." Headlines were soon announcing, "Suspect Gang Killed Skipper."[1]

Aloha began her appearances at the United Artists Theatre on the evening of December 15. The box office had been decorated with garlands and a large poster announced "The Rhinestone Woman of the Hour." Another sign told theatregoers that the guns and backpacks of the late Captain Wanderwell would be on display, and indeed his rifles and knapsacks were piled outside the theatre for the curious to examine.

The *Los Angeles Times* described the *The River of Death* as a search for the lost explorer Percy Fawcett and said that, as a travelogue, it was "fair and convincing enough" but decried the "incendiary finish" where Mrs. Wanderwell said she was working in the interests of an international police force to promote world peace.[2] Theatregoers were even less charitable.

Whereas previous Wanderwell films had drawn audiences with travel and adventure stories, these ticket-buyers just wanted to ogle the Rhinestone Widow. They were not interested in the search for a moustachioed English explorer or in watching a documentary on bark-eating Amazonian tribes who moved naked through the forests. They wanted Aloha to talk about the murder. Aloha introduced her films in person but refused to take questions. During one presentation hecklers began urging her to "Take it off!!"[3] Aloha did not oblige.

Those interested in hearing Aloha's thoughts about her late husband would have done better to read the stories she had agreed to write exclusively for Hearst's United Service newspaper syndicate.

> I was with Captain Wanderwell for ten years. During eight of them I was his wife. I could never have found a more congenial mate, or a truer one.
>
> I won't be lonely, as I continue to journey the earth, for I shall always feel that Cap is with me, taking the brunt and carrying the burden, encouraging, guiding, leading the way.
>
> And I shall always regard him as I thought of him ten years ago while a sixteen-year-old school girl in the south of France — the gayest, most gallant, most romantic adventurer in all the world.[4]

❁

On December 19 a tired-looking Aloha, dressed in a trench coat and rain hat, was escorted through a crush of onlookers at the Long Beach Superior Court. It took a while to get through because there was no actual courthouse. Instead, court facilities were located in the Jergins Trust Building, a multi-use building that also housed, among other things, the enormous Loew's State Theater. The offices of the Superior Court within it were tiny and the crowds who came to watch the trial made the narrow hallways almost impassable.

When court finally came to session, participants learned that William Guy would be defended by Eugene McGann, a veteran attorney known for representing clients who operated at the margins of the law.[5] McGann was reportedly retained by a friend of Eddie DeLarm named Edward J. Moffett.

McGann, in turn, enlisted Moffett as part of Guy's defence team — a sly legal manoeuvre that prevented Moffett from being called to testify. The press referred to him simply as "The Mysterious Mr. Moffett." The defence team was rounded out by "second chair," George W. Rochester. No one representing Guy was court-appointed, yet no one questioned that a penniless Welshman was able to afford such an august defence.

Judge Charles F. Cook commenced proceedings by asking the prosecution to produce their evidence against Guy. Several members of the Wanderwell crew were asked to take the stand, including Marian Smith, who repeated that she was "sure Guy was the man she saw at the porthole on the night of December 5. Cuthbert Wills did likewise. When asked if he could reproduce the sound of the scream he'd heard, Wills paused before emitting a high, piercing scream that electrified the courtroom and echoed down the building's corridors. Attempting to defuse the drama, McGann hurriedly asked if the sound might not have come from a seagull, or perhaps a siren. Wills looked at the attorney for a moment before replying, "It struck me as more of a man's scream than anything else."[6]

When Aloha took the stand, she described Guy's threatening visit to Walter the previous August, although this time she claimed it was DeLarm who had done most of the talking, including a warning that if the captain didn't pay up, they would "make him pay eventually."[7] She also repeated the tale of Guy's mutinous actions in Panama, flatly refuting that he was "owed wages" of any kind. When she was excused from the stand, Aloha, a cigarette dangling from her lip, amazed onlookers by crossing the courtroom and entering into a whispered conversation with the accused.[8] At the end of their brief conversation, however, and to the surprise of all present, the two shook hands briefly before Aloha hurried away.

Incredulous reporters clamoured to know what had been said, but both Guy and Aloha refused to say. Later McGann said Aloha had questioned Guy about the missing letter of mutiny that Guy and several other crew members had signed. Apparently, she asked if he knew what had become of the letter, and Guy had supposedly replied, "No, but I hope Mrs. Wanderwell, that you don't think that I shot the captain."[9]

Newspapers reported that Guy appeared pleased as he was being led back to his cell, commenting to reporters, "Well, that doesn't look as if she thought

I killed her husband."[10] At the end of that morning's proceedings, however, the court felt that there was sufficient evidence to warrant a trial. William James "Curly" Guy was ordered held for trial without bail on a charge of murder in the first degree. Buron Fitts would seek the death penalty.

❀

According to the Long Beach coroner, Walter was wearing two pairs of pants at the time of his death. The inner pair was found to conceal a second wallet containing as much as $800. This was a vast sum to be carrying around. In 1932 the average annual American income was just $1,650, so to carry half an annual salary in his billfold was odd to say the least.[11] Since Walter had died without a will and the murder investigation was ongoing, all monies were held as evidence. Aloha needed to gain administration of Walter's property. She filed her claim on December 23, asking that she, Valri, and Nile be made legal heirs to his estate. According to a notice in the *New York Times*, the estate was valued at just $1,500, of which $1,000 was cash and another $500 in property.[12] No mention was made of the property in Miami.

On Christmas Day newspapers reported that the Wanderwell crew had called off the South Seas trip.[13] Members who were not directly involved in the investigation turned in their WAWEC and IP insignia and left town. Gradually, while Aloha was forced to wait in Los Angeles, WAWEC units around the world began disbanding and the International Police, Inc. was mothballed.

❀

On December 30, Guy was formally arraigned and a trial was set for Thursday, February 2, 1933. When asked how he would plead, Guy threw back his shoulders and said, "Not guilty." In the intervening weeks, however, more stories trickled out. A "lunchroom employee" and "friend" of Guy named Sylvia Anderson said she saw Guy driving around Glendale at 6:45 p.m. on December 5. This was contrary to Guy's claims that he did not leave the DeLarm residence all night.[14] Then it was revealed that DeLarm's car had been repossessed the day *after* Walter's murder and had been thoroughly cleaned inside and out. There were odd stories, too, like the letter discovered in the trash bin of the DeLarm home. It had been written in code, torn up, and covered in tooth marks. Detectives used a substitution code method to discover that the note was to "Curley [*sic*]" from someone named June Churchill and expressed her affection for Guy, wishing he was there so they could walk together beneath the moon. Police announced they were actively searching for June Churchill.[15]

Aloha was bound to Los Angles for the duration of the trial. While she waited for a decision on the estate settlement, she and five other crew members declared themselves destitute and applied for financial aid from the district attorney's office. They were granted nine dollars each for their appearance at the preliminary hearing and advanced a small sum for the forthcoming trial. Then, on January 24, Aloha was granted guardianship of Valri — allowing her to assume control of the *Carma*, which still legally belonged to her daughter.[16] Within days, the *Carma* was chartered as a "showboat" for a year-long cruise to Central and South America, with a first stop in Mexico. The charterers were listed as John T. Branson, who would make the trip to gather animals for the California zoological gardens, and Thomas J. Hughes, who would oversee the transport and operation of carnival amusements, including a Ferris wheel, merry-go-rounds, high-dive performers and several trained animals.[17]

❃

By the time the trial began, the Wanderwell murder case was a worldwide sensation. Curious throngs queued outside the court several hours before the trial — so many that drink and hot dog vendors soon lined the street. Inside the courtroom, jury selection proceeded with surprising speed, although according to one reporter, the session had been "confused by the violent attempts of an eager throng to gain admittance to the courtroom." Three hundred observers were packed into the tiny room, while several hundred more who were denied entry reacted by pulling down restraining ropes, tearing the hinges off and splintering doors, and shoving guards aside.[18]

It had been expected that Los Angeles County Superior Court judge Walter Desmond would preside, but instead the case was passed to a newly appointed judge — and former reporter for the Hearst chain of newspapers

— Robert Walker Kenny. An ambitious man, Kenny would become California's attorney general and be credited with outlawing the Ku Klux Klan in the state.

With the jury selected, prosecutor Clarence Hunt made his opening remarks, announcing that Aloha would appear the following day as the state's first witness. Not to be outdone, defence attorney Eugene McGann asked Judge Kenny to permit a field trip. As one reporter wrote, "By the aid of an almanac McGann showed the court that by singular coincidence meteorological conditions, including the position of the moon and the tide, will be practically identical tomorrow night with what they were on the night of the murder."[19]

The field trip was approved and, oddly, Judge Kenny waived the use of a police vehicle and took Guy as a passenger in his own car. Although not much happened during the tour of the *Carma*, the scene at the boat was described with typical flair by Carleton E. Williams, the *Los Angeles Times* reporter who had led Detective Filkas to Guy's hideout. "The scene aboard the ship," he wrote, "was made more unusual by the gathering of scores of pelicans, regular denizens of Fish Harbor. The somber visaged and long-beaked birds perched on every available pier and vantage point and solemnly observed all that went on."[20]

The next morning, it was Aloha's turn to take the stand. She outlined Guy's actions in South America: how he had forced his way into the expedition, his refusal to work, and the mutinous petition he had written. She said Walter had always kept the note in his wallet and wondered why it should now be missing.

One reporter noted that throughout her testimony Aloha ignored Guy, refusing even to glance at him, but that the "curly-haired, faintly smiling defendant...kept her under a steady gaze."[21] Late in the afternoon, to the disappointment of the court, the prosecution called Aloha down from the stand, saying that she would return the next day.

The following day, McGann unwrapped a new surprise, a confession signed by a woman named Olga Labrulitz. The letter, found in a local dance-hall washroom, said, "I killed Wanderwell. He was my sweetheart for eight months. I did not know he was going to the South Seas. He told me he would kill me. I told him, 'No, you'll go first.' I shot him." Prosecutors Hunt and Brayton accepted the note with scepticism but promised to make a full inquiry. When court was adjourned, journalists rushed to file their stories, with one reporter making special note that "Aloha wore her blouse open at the throat."[22]

❄

On Monday morning Judge Kenny issued a bench warrant for Aloha's arrest — she hadn't shown up. When she eventually arrived fifteen minutes late, Kenny angrily remanded her in custody until the end of her testimony. But even this dramatic event was eclipsed by Eugene McGann's introduction of Eddie DeLarm as principal witness for the defence. While the courtroom murmured, McGann began questioning Aloha. He asked her to repeat what had happened in South America, how the mutiny letter had been delivered, and whose idea it had been to disband in Panama.[23] Aloha told him Walter had "suggested that for the benefit of the whole that we stay together until we got to Panama, where other arrangements could be made."

"Wasn't that Guy's suggestion?" asked McGann.

"No, it was not."

"Were you present when the paper was turned over to your husband?"

"I was not."[24]

McGann then turned to the question of money. Aloha explained that Guy had demanded $160 be paid to him. McGann asked if Guy had received any payments in money or equipment. "None to my knowledge," she answered. With that reply, McGann quickly focused on the night of the murder. Having established that Guy was supposedly after money, he asked Aloha whether her husband had been robbed on the night of the murder. With great reluctance, she admitted that he had not. McGann leaned forward and placed a wallet in front of Aloha. "Whose wallet is this?" he asked. But as she attempted to acknowledge whose wallet it had been, she lost her words and began sobbing so forcefully that Judge Kenny ordered a short recess.[25]

The evening's newspapers offered critiques of Aloha's tears and fainting "performance." But Aloha insisted her tears were real. "The truth was I couldn't talk about those events; at the time I was dazed and confused...when

I was called to the witness stand the happenings of the immediate past seemed blurred and chaotic to me... I couldn't discuss certain things in relation to the crime; they were too near and terrible."[26]

The following day Aloha concluded her testimony and the prosecution's focus shifted to other crew members. Cameraman Ed Zeranski and Marian Smith from Georgia were both asked, "Do you see anyone in the courtroom who resembles the man at the porthole?" Both crossed the courtroom and placed a hand on Guy's shoulder.

In response, McGann summoned state witness Joseph Burzinski, who had been present when DeLarm and Guy had threatened Walter in August. According to Burzinski, when Guy first walked into Wanderwell's apartment, Walter had offered to shake hands, but Guy declined, remarking, "That's unnecessary."[27] Then, contradicting his earlier statements, Burzinski denied that Guy had threatened Walter with physical violence but noted that Walter had seemed exceedingly frightened by Guy's appearance.

Next on the stand was ship engineer Cuthbert Wills. Dressed in a suit that had been borrowed from family members in Canada, Wills spoke in sharp, clear sentences and described, once again, the events of December 5. When it came time to identify the Man in Grey in the courtroom, Wills, like the others, walked across the courtroom. "Guy looked cooly [sic] at Wills and a trace of a smile flitted across his face as the engineer, color rising in his cheeks, touched his coat."[28] Among those on board the *Carma* the night of the murder, only Mary Parks refused to identify Guy as the Man in Grey, saying that she was not absolutely certain. McGann began a withering cross-examination of Wills, challenging every detail of the story and eventually forcing Wills to admit that he had initially refused to pick Guy out of a police lineup. Wills, who grew progressively more annoyed, explained that he had wanted to be sure the accent was the same. He needed to *speak* with him first.

As the session drew to a close, Eugene McGann announced that he would call a surprise witness. Al "The Boatman" Mauzy, caretaker of a hulk that lay alongside the *Carma*, would testify that several days after Cuthbert Wills and Marian Smith had viewed the police lineup, they had said that it was, in fact, too dark on the boat to be 100 per cent sure it was the same man.

McGann then announced he would also call two Glendale automobile dealers who saw Guy in their town at the hour of the murder.[29] There is no surviving account of prosecutors Hunt and Brayton complaining that Guy was supposedly in bed at that hour. Nor did they call Harry Greenwood, who claimed to have spoken with Guy at Long Beach's harbour just minutes after the murder.

※

By February 9, anyone watching the trial must have felt there was strong evidence to convict Guy. All but one on board the *Carma* said Guy was the Man in Grey. Prosecutor Hunt had intricately outlined Guy's dislike of Wanderwell and detailed his past threats towards him, including the August visit to his apartment. Prosecution had also shown that the testimonies of Guy's own witnesses did not agree. Surely the evidence was strong: there was a motive, several witnesses whose testimony agreed, and the accused's own admitted hatred for the victim.

Prosecutor Hunt announced that the state had one last witness. Called to the stand was E.T. Liller, an embalmer, who explained that Wanderwell was found to have been wearing two pairs of pants at the time of his death. The argument went that since a wallet containing $800 was found on the *inside* pair of pants, this might explain why Wanderwell had not been robbed. The killer, quite simply, would not have known about the inner pants. And with that the prosecution rested.

When Eugene McGann stood up, he approached the bench smiling and asked that the case be dismissed. The prosecution, who had to show the burden of proof that Guy was guilty, he said, had completely failed to prove its case, or even a "chain of circumstances" linking Guy to the murder.[30] Judge Kenny denied the motion but adjourned proceedings so that the jury could be taken to visit the house of Eddie DeLarm and the LA River Bottoms house that Guy had used as his hideout. Just before the gavel fell, however, McGann announced that the defence would be calling two surprise witnesses the following day: Ed Zeranski and Aloha Wanderwell.

✿

When the trial reconvened at 9:00 a.m. the following morning, McGann grumbled that he was unable to call his first witness to the stand because Mrs. Wanderwell "was unable to reach court immediately."[31] Instead, he called three newspaper reporters to the stand.

First to testify was *Los Angeles Record* reporter Agness Underwood, who had branded Aloha the "Granite Widow." Underwood claimed that three days after the murder she overheard Cuthbert Wills remark that he "could not be sure" that Guy was in fact the Man in Grey. Reporters Vincent Mahoney and Marian Rhea gave similar statements.

With his "shadow of doubt" planted, McGann called a stream of witnesses, including Eddie DeLarm, Mrs. DeLarm, their two daughters, Betty and Juanita, and neighbours Mr. and Mrs. Harry Wilson, all of whom testified that Guy could not have been anywhere near Long Beach at the time of the murder. Then there was mechanic Ralph Dunlap — the man who had said Guy told him he was heading for Long Beach. On this day, however, he said that as he approached the DeLarm house at 8:45 p.m. he saw Guy through a window, walking towards his bedroom.[32] The prosecution, evidently unaware of Dunlap's earlier statements to police, said nothing.

By the time Aloha took the stand, McGann was in blazing form.

[I] was drilled as if by a dentist's tool. The attorney, in an endeavor to confuse me or entrap me, picked on the most minute of events such as my having given permission to a secretary while in Bolivia to sign business letters which the expedition had sent regarding some trivia... It seemed to me they were hammering away at me rather than at the man who was suspect and, in fact, one day I told the judge I thought the whole hearing was a farce. It was common knowledge much gossiped about at the time, that Long Beach had never convicted a person for murder and as this suspect was a Britisher and he would eventually be deported, they would be able to wash their hands of the whole thing having done their duty.[33]

An unidentified newspaper photo of Aloha in court
waiting to be called to testify, February 1933.

When it was announced that Guy would speak in his own defence on February 14, Valentine's Day, the crowds doubled. The press's focus now shifted from kooky Captain Wanderwell and his band of misfits to the plight of the dashing Welsh adventurer who wore a permanent smile and claimed that all he wanted to do was get back to his darling wife, Vera. As Carleton Williams observed, the courtroom was packed "largely with women."

It was afternoon before Guy finally took the stand. In a low voice he identified himself as William James Guy and said that he had been born in Cardiff, Wales. He repeated his claim that on the night Walter Wanderwell was murdered, he was at the home of his friend Edward DeLarm, about 30 miles from Long Beach. He had, he said, arrived at the DeLarm home at 6:30 p.m. and did not leave until morning. McGann had no further questions, and the prosecution, unbelievably, did not see fit to cross-examine. Guy, much to the courtroom's disappointment, left the stand.

A page from the court reporter's transcript in the murder trial of William James
"Curly" Guy. Note the annotation for February 15, 1933:
"Trial returned verdict Not Guilty."

McGann's final remarks took nearly three hours, at one point shouting
at jurors, "Picture to yourselves this young man, Mr. Guy, dangling from the
end of a rope, and ask yourselves if this evidence warrants such a verdict."[34]
Brayton closed for the prosecution, calling Guy a killer and taking special
aim at the ridiculous revisions and contradictions of the DeLarm family
testimony, calling it a "mass of untruths." Then, at precisely 5:00 p.m. on
February 16, the case was turned over to the jury for deliberation. As Judge
Kenny gave his final instructions to the jury, Los Angeles district attorney
Buron Fitts left the courtroom. When someone asked him what was
happening inside, Fitts responded: "Judge Kenny is closing for the defence."[35]

It took the jury 5½ hours and four ballots to reach their decision. The
lead juror, a small, middle-aged man, read out the verdict: "We the jury find
the defendant...William James Guy...Not guilty." The courtroom erupted.
Female spectators mobbed Guy, kissing and hugging him, grabbing at his
clothes. According to the foreman, jurors were simply not convinced that
lighting conditions aboard the *Carma* had been sufficient for witnesses to
positively identify the mysterious Man in Grey.

When asked how he felt about his trial and acquittal, Guy shrugged and said, "After facing starvation as a prisoner in Russia, a firing squad commanded by Sandino, fever in the South American jungle and torture at the hands of Chinese brigands, a murder trial didn't look so dangerous...I knew I wasn't guilty, but if that jury had thought so, I guess I could have stood the rope around my neck."[36] One newspaper, reflecting on the story of Walter, called it a strange tale, "so strange, indeed, that if written as a novel most publishers would probably say it was not a story but a nightmare."[37]

For Aloha, the episode certainly *was* a nightmare. But still the question remained: who killed Walter Wanderwell? It was a question the press would trot out on the anniversary of his murder well into the 1950s. Aloha, however, never spoke publicly of the murder again, although privately she maintained her position that Guy had been Walter's killer. "The first thing he did upon gaining his temporary freedom," she wrote, "was to apply to authorities for the bullet that had killed the Captain."[38]

This iconic studio photo of Aloha Wanderwell posing with the newly acquired Russian cuff would be used by German skin care company Nivea in several advertising campaigns featuring her.

TWENTY-FIVE

ALIAS ALOHA WANDERWELL

IT HAD BEEN TEN YEARS since Idris Hall first met the dashing Walter Wanderwell, and she had happily traded her homebound life for the promise of fame and adventure at his side. But now her reel was empty again and the people who flashed across the screen were ghosts. In some ways, the decade had brought no changes at all: she was still free to drink and smoke (which she did), and she still had only the vaguest idea about what to do with her life. Her plans for the future had died with Walter.

With Guy's acquittal, the Wanderwell name fell from the headlines. Theatre engagements dried up, Wanderwell units worldwide disbanded, and most of the automobiles that had once heralded the arrival of the "Great Expedition" were being sold for scrap. The crew of the *Carma* likewise dispersed. With the boat leased, there was no seafaring means for an expedition to travel. WAWEC and the International Police had ceased generating income, and what little cash Aloha had (mostly what had been on Walter's person at the time of his murder) wouldn't last long.

She had two cars, a trunkful of films, some camera equipment, and a bit of land in Miami. And two children. Aloha once again relinquished guardianship of Valri and Nile, placing each into separate foster homes. Aloha claimed it was to keep the children safe, but she had always been willing to leave them in other people's care. Valri would later talk of being placed in an orphanage for a year and records show that she was placed under the guardianship of a couple named Keown, who would later lease the *Carma*.

Before Aloha could make plans for the future, a magnitude 6.4 earthquake shook Long Beach on March 10, killing 120 people and causing widespread damage. The scale of carnage did not match the Miami hurricane of 1926, but the city was brought to a standstill. Emergency crews arrived to distribute food and water in the town's main park, while those left homeless were placed in hotels and churches and billeted in private homes. The few remaining theatre engagements Aloha had scheduled were cancelled and there was no prospect of new work. In spite of this catastrophic event, Aloha could count herself lucky; the home in which she was staying on Westbourne Avenue was undamaged and the *Carma* had not sunk.

❋

By early April 1933 Aloha was in Los Angeles, signing a Declaration of Intention to become a United States citizen.[1] As with so many of Aloha's official documents, the declaration contains numerous bizarre inaccuracies, including claims that she had emigrated from Havana, Cuba, that she was twenty-five years old, that her "lawful entry for permanent residence" was at New York, New York, and that her son's name was "Walter Wawec Nile." Regardless, Aloha was permitted to stay in the country.

The *Carma* that had been leased to the circus operator arrived in Mexico only to be prevented from landing at Mazatlán by customs officials who insisted the ship pay a large deposit on the carnival equipment. The ship's captain, Branson, was unable to pay the duties. The crew remained stranded for several weeks until, faced with starvation and a lack of drinking water, the government allowed members to land and accepted the carnival equipment as security for import duties, lighterage, and taxes. The next day, Captain Branson and the *Carma* disappeared from port, leaving the crew — including Miki and Eric Owen — to forage for food and accept the charity of the locals.[2]

With only her cars to rely on and her money dwindling fast, Aloha decided that the only path open to her was the one with well-worn grooves. "I steeled myself to examine sheafs [sic] of letters from persons anxious to help me start a new expedition. I picked out three people and we started."[3] One particularly interesting letter came from Captain D. de Waray of Colombia's Legión Extranjera, or foreign legion. Unaware that Captain Wanderwell was no longer alive, Captain de Waray offered the organization's services as "International Police Secret Service agents or Intelligence Officers." The group comprised more than two hundred military-trained mercenaries, including British, French, German, Austrian, and American officers. Although the letter did not say exactly what kind of work they proposed to do, de Waray closed his offer "trusting that we may be able to work together for mutual benefit."[4] Two hundred well-armed mercenaries offering their services to an organization whose main goal was to disarm the world was nothing short of jaw-dropping. Aloha filed the letter away as a curious keepsake.

❀

While Aloha sought a new beginning, Curly Guy fought with US immigration authorities and tried to cash in on his new-found fame. After posting a $3,000 bail bond (arranged by DeLarm), he was offered a role in a movie but the deal collapsed when authorities reminded the producers that Guy was not eligible for employment as he was not an American citizen. He also tried boxing, at which "he looked very capable — or at least he didn't fall down every time he let one fly."[5] At his deportation hearing Guy claimed that he was, in fact, an American citizen, despite a birth certificate saying he been born in Wales. But Guy said his *father* had been born in San Francisco, thus qualifying him for citizenship. Conveniently, all San Francisco birth records from that era had been destroyed in the earthquake of 1906. To further bolster his case, Guy called on the testimony of Eddie DeLarm — but this time Eddie refused. Outraged, Guy threatened DeLarm, warning that he would "bump him off."[6] DeLarm begged the sheriff to appoint a bodyguard until Guy could be questioned. But just two days later the men had settled their differences, and Guy arrived in court to give testimony on behalf of DeLarm who was seeking damages from a former business partner. Incredibly, DeLarm was also in court facing a charge of possessing 16 gallons of illegal liquors — and not for the first time, it seems.

DeLarm's name had "figured in several sensational airplane liquor traffic affairs."[7] None of this had come to light during the Wanderwell trial.

Eventually, Guy *was* deported. Immigration officials allowed him to choose any destination he wanted, provided it was not contiguous to the United States. Either Guy misunderstood the terms, or he deliberately chose to play for more time. He picked Mexico. Bizarrely, the authorities agreed. However, while immigration agents were escorting Guy to the border, he gave them the slip during a routine bathroom break at a service station. He simply disappeared.[8]

Over the years, Guy would re-enter the United States many times, always under an assumed name, and frequently "doing business" with Eddie. In late 1936 police in Los Angeles were summoned to a disused warehouse by an anonymous caller claiming there were loud noises coming from inside. With weapons drawn, two officers found DeLarm and Guy hiding behind a false wall. They were both detained, and later Guy was once more deported.

In the summer of 1940, he and Eddie climbed an ornate stairway to the second floor of the Hotel Roosevelt in downtown Los Angeles and knocked on a door painted with the words "Canadian Aviation Bureau." Soon both were flying new Hudson bombers to a small makeshift airstrip in North Dakota on the Manitoba border. On the Canadian side a wheat field had been ploughed under to form an identical landing strip. When the planes landed in North Dakota they taxied to the end of the runway and turned off their engines. A team of horses was hitched to the nose gear and the planes were dragged across the border into Manitoba, where they were refuelled and flown to Scotland.[9] In 1940 the United States was officially neutral and had not yet joined the European war effort. While an international agreement stipulated that warplanes could not be *flown* beyond American air space, nothing was said about horses dragging them through a field.[10]

As part of the so-called "Ferry Command," Guy and DeLarm flew dozens of aircraft across the Atlantic. DeLarm flew until September 11, 1941, re-signing shortly after crash landing in a field near Sainte-Cécile-de-Masham, 25 miles north of Ottawa. Guy, however, continued his airborne activities, and shady past notwithstanding, he was enlisted to fly a top secret mission, ferrying Canadian Prime Minister William Lyon Mackenzie King and Major

General Georges Vanier (future governor general of Canada) to England for war meetings with Winston Churchill.[11]

Guy's swashbuckling, adventurous life came to an end on another routine ferry flight to Scotland. On October 16, 1941, Guy radioed that his plane had been hit by enemy fire. According to one report, his last words were, "Ditching, tanks all empty, cheerio."[12] Eddie DeLarm, on the other hand, lived a long and healthy life, surviving many more adventures (and occupying many more column inches of newsprint) before dying of cancer at his home in Tucson, Arizona, on December 19, 1975.

※

Guy and DeLarm were, at the very least, opportunists who may have had more than a passing association with one or more American government agencies. At most, they were swindlers, hoodlums, and racketeers, but they were hardly alone. Almost everyone connected with the Wanderwell trial seems to have oozed corruption. District attorney Buron Fitts, who had forced Guy's prosecution (only to later declare that he never thought he was really guilty), was indicted for bribery and perjury in 1934 after accepting payments from a real-estate promoter, purportedly in exchange for dropping a statutory rape charge.[13] Fitts was also implicated in a sex ring the press dubbed "Love Mart" that offered virgin, underage girls to wealthy clients — mostly movie moguls. It was rumoured that Fitts was being paid a "retainer" by Louis B. Mayer of MGM, among others, so that many a Tinseltown star's "indiscretion" never saw the light of day. Money followed influence and, in Fitts' case, vice versa. The deaths of popular film director William Desmond Taylor, actress Thelma Todd, and director Paul Bern (Jean Harlow's husband) are just three of the many mysteries that occurred during Fitts's tenure that were never adequately nor officially explained.

On March 29, 1973, two men paid a half-hour visit to the now retired Fitts at his home. As they left, Fitts followed them to his driveway, got into his car and killed himself with a single shot to the head. Rather than assist the dying Fitts, the two men drove away. Some reports claimed the gun Fitts used was the same weapon used in the unsolved murder of William Desmond Taylor.[14]

Even the man who had originally fetched Aloha from her home in

Hollywood, Detective Lieutenant Ralph C. Miller, did not escape unscathed. Within months of Walter's murder, Miller was given a desk job and then fired from the force. The reasons for his dismissal were never made public, but according to news reports, an internal police investigation had linked Miller to a prostitution and smuggling ring involving several law enforcement officers.[15]

＊

Aloha had been back on the road for only two months when word came that the *Carma* had been sold to a Mexican coffee magnate and renamed the *Neutal*. During a test run of the ship in early October, she struck a reef near Mazatlán and sank in shallow water. After a notorious run of twenty years, during which the vessel had been a rum runner, bankrupted several owners, and had seen the death of at least two people, the schooner was no more. Aloha immediately called her lawyer in Los Angeles and instructed him to reapply for guardianship of Valri. As one reporter observed, "The petition, if granted, would give the mother charge of the daughter's estate of $1,100, representing money received from the sale of the schooner."[16]

According to Valri, it took several weeks to locate her, since her temporary guardians had sent her to yet another foster home where her name was changed. With guardianship granted, and newly flush, Aloha continued her lecture tour across the United States, travelling in Unit N° IV, the supercar Walter had purchased just before the National Air Races of 1930. Valri was placed into yet another foster home.

A short time later, while tanking up at a gas station outside Laramie, Wyoming, Aloha met a strikingly handsome youth named, of all things, Walter. He was fascinated by the car and its pilot, while she in turn was more than a little beguiled by his well-proportioned frame, thick wavy hair, strong jaw, and perfect smile. She invited him to attend her show that evening in town. The next day Aloha received a handwritten note:

Laramie, Wyo
Oct. 26, 1933

Dear Miss Wanderwell,

Since having met and talked with you, I have decided that life is too short to live in the same place all one's life.

If I remember correctly, you said that you were planning on getting someone to travel with you. I would like to apply for that position, or do you think that I could fulfill the requirements? Saturday will probably be my last day on this job, so before making other plans, I would like to hear from you.

Hell, all one's life is a trial, so you cannot blame me for trying. Can you?

Sincerely yours,
Walter Baker

By December 1933 Aloha, Walter Baker, and a crew of three young women had made their way to New Orleans, where they planned to lecture and sell pamphlets over the Christmas holidays. In an interview published on December 18, Aloha said that in a life like hers, a sense of humour was indispensable.

You can get along without a tropical hat or a pair of shoes... but you just can't do without a sense of humor. When you're drenched to the skin through four days of rainstorms, when you're cold and hungry and weak from exhaustion, you've got to look at your experiences from the humorous side — else you won't last... [A person must look for] all the good he or she can get out of every 24 hours.[17]

It was vintage Aloha, and as if taking her own advice, a newspaper notice appeared several days later.

Romance fluttered behind theater wings in New Orleans Thursday when it became known that Aloha Wanderwell, prominent figure in one of America's thrilling unsolved murder mysteries, had eloped to Gretna and had married Walter Baker, a member of the troupe.[18]

The marriage was intended to remain secret, but the Wanderwell car had been spotted outside the residence of Judge G. Trauth. Curious reporters began snooping and eventually found the wedding licence, which stated that Idris Hall, twenty-five years old, widow of Walter Wanderwell, had married Walter Baker, twenty-one, of Wyoming (Aloha was in fact twenty-seven, and Walter was barely eighteen). Just one year and twenty-one days after the murder aboard the *Carma*, Aloha was married again. When asked about Walter's murder, she refused to elaborate.

The murder is still as it always has been to me — an unsolved mystery.
"I had thought I would never marry again. But now, with the new world trip before us, everything seems so bright, and Walter and I are so happy."[19]

The marriage was sudden. Not even Miki and Margaret knew of it. When Miki (who had made her way home from Mexico thanks to some of Aloha's Mexican friends) read the news in a local newspaper, she sent a hilarious letter to her sister, telling her, "You should really have sent our maternal parent a wire like you did last time. She's sort of old fashioned in a way and likes those little proprieties kept up."[20] At the letter's close, Miki advised her sister to "be smart and get this one well insured, lambkin." Walter N° II was good insurance for Aloha in any event: with an American husband, she was free to stay in the United States permanently.

As for Miki, despite numerous trips via planes, trains, and ships (after her Wanderwell experiences she refused to travel by car), she would call Canada home for the rest of her life. Following a short stint in Victoria, where she worked as an artist's model, she returned to Vancouver Island's eastern coast and to land she received courtesy of her father's veterans' land grant.

Her property line ended at an easement leased by the Esquimalt & Nanaimo Railway (E&N) — land that was originally planned for the coastal railroad. Since it was waterfront and very desirable, people were allowed to squat on the land, so long as they maintained it. From the mid-1940s until

Miki Hall sits on the deck of her summer encampment on the east coast of Vancouver Island, in Merville, British Columbia, 1958. She called this place "Happy Shack." Windsong would be built just to the north of this spot in 1962.

the early 1960s Miki spent her springs and summers here — practically on the rocky beach itself — living first in a canvas tent erected on a wooden platform and then in a shed she called "Happy Shack." The rest of the year she travelled or spent time with Margaret at her new home in Jamaica, where she moved in the mid-1930s. During the Second World War Miki joined the Royal Canadian Air Force, deciphering intercepted Japanese codes. Sometime during the war, she attracted the romantic attentions of a superior officer and the affair lasted throughout the war. Not long after the war, the officer admitted he was already married and would be returning to his wife, somewhere out east. Miki remained unmarried for the rest of her life.

By 1961 the E&N had been completed further inland and had no more development plans for its coastal lease. The British Columbia government and the E&N decided to sell off the land and end squatting rights. Squatters like Miki, however, had the right to keep their land (and purchase more) if

ABOVE: The name and year of completion of Miki's beloved Windsong home, hand-carved into the end of the hearth, April 2008.

RIGHT: Miki's Windsong cabin on Vancouver Island. The hearth piece with the Hall family motto carved into it was once the mantelpiece in Margaret's home on the Hall property in Qualicum Beach, Vancouver Island, British Columbia, 1962.

they could afford to build a permanent structure on the property. Thanks to her inheritance, Miki did have the money and she purchased several lots, eventually owning 78 acres, some with Aloha. Here she built a home that survives to this day. She christened it "Windsong" when it was completed in October 1962. Nestled against the seashore and backed by a high wall of thick forest, Windsong was a paradise where Miki could watch the ocean tides and befriend the local deer, with whom she shared her home-brewed beer.

Miki remained at Windsong until the last two years of her life, when illness forced her to move to town. She passed away in her Comox condominium on May 23, 1995, and her ashes were spread at sea, opposite her beloved Windsong. The new owners of Windsong added a two-bedroom structure, maintaining the look and feel of Miki's original design, and they still call it Margaret's Place — after the Wanderwell era, Miki had begun using her full name, Margaret.

Mother Margaret eventually left Jamaica (donating the property to the local Salvation Army, much to the family's consternation) and returned for a time to Canada, where she sold off the remaining Qualicum Beach holdings. She came to an arrangement with an entrepreneurial educator named Ivan Knight, who was building the Qualicum Beach Boys School on the family's former property: in exchange for selling the land, her grandson Nile would receive free education (plus room and board) at the school. Sadly, once the properties were sold, the patriarch of the family, Herbert Hall, was largely forgotten — so much so that local records contain no explanation of why a main street running through Qualicum Beach (and terminating at the former school property) is called Hall Road. Margaret Hall lived to be eighty-three, dying at Newport Beach, California, on November 20, 1961.

❁

True to her word, Aloha continued travelling, lecturing, and film-making — working under the name Aloha Wanderwell and usually described as *Miss Wanderwell.* Her South America movie *Aloha Wanderwell and the River of Death* played in only a few theatres and earned very little money, but she persevered. She and Walter Baker toured throughout the United States during 1934 and, by the end of the year, had purchased an aircraft for a proposed flight around the world in 1935. In one of a series of articles she wrote for the Hearst newspaper chain, Aloha announced that she was in New York planning a "Wanderwell World Peace Flight." It was a dramatic reassertion of her former husband's ideas. "There is always tomorrow, with new adventures beyond the horizon, new friendships to make and perhaps new mysteries to encounter... Captain Wanderwell is gone but his way of life and his guiding hand stay with me."[21]

But the flight never happened. By October she, Walter Baker, and Eric Owen were in China, giving lectures, catching crocodiles, posing for news photos, and attending hotel-sponsored soirées. In January 1936 they reached Indochina by car. One particularly memorable image depicts an arrestingly attractive Aloha in Siam (now Thailand), standing in front of her Ford Phaeton and cradling a clouded leopard kitten. Of all the photos ever taken

Aloha holds a young clouded leopard in Siam (now Thailand), 1934.

of Aloha, this one may best sum up her professional persona: beautiful, fearless, and potentially dangerous.

In Sydney, Australia, Aloha struck lucrative advertising deals with Texaco, Ford, and Nivea and made dozens of appearances in theatres around the city and throughout the continent. In November 1936 Aloha and her new Walter reached Wellington, New Zealand, before proceeding to Auckland and, one month later, the Philippines. Somewhere along the way, Aloha had begun filing radio reports to be aired in the United States and in Britain via the BBC.

A story filed in February 1937 came from Calcutta, India, and Lahore, Pakistan. Two months later she was in Ceylon and two months after that back in Port Said and Egypt, where she revisited the pyramids at Giza. The travelling continued through Europe, England, and Scotland until December 1937, when after more than two years of travel, Aloha and Walter settled in Cincinnati. When not working on radio programs for the radio station WLW,[22] Aloha spent much of 1938 writing books, one "In the Lap of the Gods,"[23] featuring text by Aloha and photographs by Walter Baker, and another entitled *Call to Adventure!* Her radio stories eventually attracted the attention of NBC, with whom she created a radio series called "Adventures in Paradise" dramatizing (and fictionalizing) several of Aloha's exploits.[24]

Aloha should have been famous, and yet, somehow, it eluded her. In the wake of Walter's death, she relied on her ability to persevere. She stuck to what she knew and pursued it with relentless determination. But while she was a quick study and had an almost superhuman ability to endure, she did not possess the genius for self-promotion and reinvention that her late husband had demonstrated. With the notable exception of her work in radio, Aloha did not reinvent herself or her expeditions. Even her approach to filmmaking remained much as it had been in the 1920s — self-focused travelogues that offered some remarkable scenery *but no sound*.[25] As late as the 1950s, when Aloha produced *My Hawaii*, she still had not embraced sound recording, believing, perhaps, that live presentations could do without. Instead, Her approach guaranteed that only a limited number of people would ever hear her remarkable stories. Theatrical distribution dried up, and while a handful of her travelogue contemporaries made the transition to television, Aloha never did. It was a fatal choice, condemning her to irrelevance and even casting her as a pathetic figure, unable to adapt.

❈

Aloha's book *Call to Adventure!* was published on November 22, 1939, by Robert M. McBride Publishers of New York, who decided to aim the title at young adult women. Much of Aloha's text had been rewritten by a ghostwriter who, in the style of the day, heightened the drama while subduing the trials and tribulations. Aloha was appalled and would never again trust someone else to tell her story. The book received tepid reviews and soon went out of print. Aloha agreed to purchase the remainders from her publisher. Fatefully, Aloha was not home when the delivery of the books was made, so the boxes were left at the edge of her property. A short while later, city garbage trucks arrived and carted away the apparently discarded packages. The books were incinerated.[26]

As the Second World War crept across Europe, Aloha's ability to travel was curtailed. Her radio show ended, and except for the occasional engagement speaking at ladies' groups, she made almost no public appearances. Realizing that the occupation of a wandering filmmaker was ill-suited to

LEFT: Aloha with Nile and Valri in front of their Lazy-U Motel, Laramie, Wyoming, 1943. Valri was by this time attending the University of Wyoming just across the road.

BELOW: After Aloha married Walter Baker, they "retired" to Laramie, Wyoming, where they built Lazy-U, one of the first post–Second World War motor hotels in the West, 1946.

times of war, she and Walter moved to his boyhood home of Laramie, Wyoming, where they built the region's first motor hotel, calling it the Lazy-U Motel. One of the motel's more famous guests arrived in the 1950s. As well as teaching literature at Cornell University, Vladimir Nabokov was also an avid butterfly collector. The southeast corner of Wyoming is home to many different varieties of butterflies, and it attracted Nabokov and his wife Vera to the area — they lodged at the Lazy-U. When he wasn't chasing butterflies, he continued his work on a book about a precocious, twelve-year-old girl named Lolita.

In 1941 Walter Baker legally adopted Valri and Nile, and they came to live at the Lazy-U in Laramie. Since 1934 Valri and Nile had been living with Margaret in Qualicum Beach, and then Victoria. For the first time in her life Aloha came to know her children and was surprised to discover that she enjoyed their company. Nile, now taller than both Aloha and Walter, demonstrated a keen creative streak, a stupendously sharp intellect, and an equally sharp temper. Valri, far more easygoing than her brother, had blossomed into beauty. A film taken in the early 1940s, when Valri was about sixteen, shows her swimming lengths in a large pool at a nearby friend's ranch. This film needed no sound. While onlookers watch Valri swim, Aloha sits beneath a giant sun hat with an expression that looks very much like pride — and she was, after so much separation, fiercely proud of her children.

Valri attended the University of Wyoming in Laramie until 1945, when she transferred to the University of New Mexico in Albuquerque. Two years later she met and married her first husband, Louis Ruffin Jr. Valri would marry once more before meeting her third husband while modelling in Mexico. A Kodak executive named Melvin Lundahl, he would become the father of her three children: Margaret (also known as Miki), Leinani, and Jonathan. Valri was even more beautiful than her mother and, in her younger days, was a stage dancer, TV game show assistant, Mexican soap opera actress, and successful model appearing in countless magazines, including *Vogue*, and most famously as Pan Am Airlines Hawaii Clipper girl. Her blond hair and radiant smile continue to shine from vintage posters around the world.

Nile attended school in Wyoming and, during the war, was a member of the US Navy Seabees (or CBs, Construction Battalions) in the South

Pacific. After the war, Nile settled in San Francisco, where he changed his name (to Jeffrey Baker[27]) and became an artist and art dealer, eventually specializing in studies of classical paintings. Nile never married but had one son, Richard.

✺

By the 1950s Aloha had retired from the lecture circuit altogether. After *Explorers of the Purple Sage*, a film showcasing the cowboy life on Wyoming's rugged expanses, Aloha would make only one more film, this one called *My Hawaii*. It was perhaps the best-crafted film she would ever produce. One particularly affecting scene shows Aloha standing with a bouquet of flowers at the rim of the Kīlauea volcano. With a sorrowful expression, she looks down at the flowers before allowing them to slip from her hands into the crater.

When the kids had gone, Aloha and Walter moved back to California, settling in Newport Beach where Walter became a developer specializing in adobe houses, including the one he built for Aloha. It was a grand two-level house on a quiet corner and had a large bay window in the upper-level living room facing west. Aloha often sat in a large cozy chair with her cat Sinbad, looking out at the boats in the harbour, the magnificent sunsets, and occasionally Santa Catalina Island would peek through the haze.

They earned a good income and spent most of their free time socializing with friends or attending horse races. Walter Baker was said to be exceptionally lucky and routinely attended races carrying rolls of cash exceeding $1,000. In later years, when the grandkids came to visit he would hand them each $100 and tell them to bet on whichever horse they wanted. Valri's daughter, Miki, would recall winning $500 at the age of twelve, all of which he insisted she keep.[28]

✺

As the years drifted by, Aloha began to feel that the best days of her life had been spent adventuring with Walter Wanderwell. She worried that their stories, photographs, films, and mementoes would soon be lost forever. For years she queried the Ford Motor Company, asking what had become of her beloved Unit Nº II, the car that had taken her so far around the world.

Finally, in 1979, a letter came from the curator of the Henry Ford Museum. He wrote:

> After a considerable amount of research by our registrar, we learned that this car was included in a group of old vehicles that Henry Ford decided in 1942 were of marginal historical importance. These vehicles were transferred to the Highland Park plant and eventually scrapped (for their metal content as part of the war effort). In subsequent years, many of us associated with the Museum have had occasion to express disappointment and dismay that such a decision was made, but it is a fact that we must accept obviously. We hope this information is of some help to you.[29]

After so many miles and so many years, the car that had carried their dreams of peace was melted down in the service of war. It was Aloha's last link to the cars in which she had circled the globe. By 1970 not a single Wanderwell car was known to exist.[30]

For the next twenty years, Aloha continued to organize and annotate her collected materials, promoting them to film and historical archives, with limited success.[31] Increasingly lonely, she wrote letters to contacts around the world, asking for translations of articles or follow-ups on what had happened to people she'd met along the way. At one point, overwhelmed and frustrated, she disposed of 200,000 feet of film. Then in 1989 a television producer from New York asked if she would agree to appear on camera to talk about her meeting with the famous American flyers who had been the first to circle the globe by air. Aloha said that not only would she be happy to appear, she could provide footage of their meeting in Calcutta. Producers were dumbfounded. Months later, at the age of eighty-three, Aloha made her first and only television appearance on the PBS series *American Experience* in an episode called "The Great Air Race of 1924." Her appearance stirred some interest among documentary filmmakers, yet no projects came together. Some of her films were, however, placed with the Academy Film Archive and the Library of Congress.

By the early 1990s Aloha's energy was beginning to wane, and following the death of her beloved sister Miki in May 1993, she seemed, finally,

Aloha and Walter Baker in the house that Walter built for them
on Lido Isle in Newport Beach. Their cat, twelve-year-old
Sinbad, sits at their feet, California, 1952.

to have given up. Two years later, after more than sixty years of marriage, Walter Baker died too. Just then, however, word came from the National Automotive History Collection in Detroit that they were willing to accept her Wanderwell memorabilia (including almost five hundred photos and negatives) and would issue a tax receipt for $7,500 in return.[32] Aloha rallied, writing an introduction to accompany the collection that was not so much a review of her intrepid career as it was a remembrance and tribute to Walter Wanderwell.

With clear affection and nostalgia, Aloha described the captain as "a man of originally Polish roots" but ultimately a citizen "of the universe."

> Gradually, the reader will discover the far, far deeper obsession and involvement of this truly extraordinary, charismatic man — imbued with his overwhelming esprit de corps, motivated by towering respect for the care and protection of body and soul, ever reflected in song,

written word, film (the extension of spirit) and human contacts, who dedicated his life's mind, effort, energy to the protection and expansion of universal intercommunication via technology...and by spirituality....

One small but inciteful [sic] portion of the legacy of a very young man, very well named "Captain Walter Wanderwell."[33]

Six months later, on June 3, 1996, just a few months shy of her ninetieth birthday, Aloha died of heart failure at Newport Beach. According to her wishes, she was not buried in the cemetery next to Walter Baker. Instead, she was cremated and her ashes scattered near Walter Wanderwell's final resting place in the waters near Santa Catalina Island.

Aloha Wanderwell's ability to rewrite her own history, exploit government bureaucracy, and confound her critics didn't end with her passing. In what was perhaps a final grace note, her official California death certificate lists her date of birth once again as 1908 instead of 1906. And the Social Security number neatly typed into the corresponding document box belongs not to her, but to an African-American man named Carl Frazier, also deceased.

A beautiful painting of Aloha that formed the cover of an invitation card to the memorial service and celebration of life when she passed away, July 1996.

EPILOGUE

CURTAIN CALL

O N THE EVENING OF DECEMBER 2, 1980, a small crowd gathered in
the Jean Delacour Auditorium of the Natural History Museum of Los
Angeles County to see a free presentation about an old-time explorer named
Aloha Baker. In the minutes before 7:00 p.m., children were clowning
impatiently in their seats while parents glanced at the black-and-white photos
in the program.

As the lights dimmed, a woman in her seventies strode across the stage,
dressed in khaki pants, a white shirt, and a tailored military style vest. In a
clear voice that carried the hint of an English accent, the woman asked if
there were any travellers in the audience. A few hands shot up and the lady
asked them where they had travelled and how they gotten there — mostly
cars on highways, trains, or planes. She had travelled this way too, she said,
but before there were highways or airlines. She began painting a picture of
a world before television, ballpoint pens, self-winding watches, bubble gum,
or canned beer. It was a time when electricity was not yet universal, when
cars and airplanes were novel. And when the lady's movie started, Ms. Baker
began narrating, with humour and vivid descriptions, a world like nothing
anyone had seen before.

There were scenes of tiny cars scaling great mountains and crossing vast
deserts. One car was parked on the back of the Sphinx, another drove along
the Great Wall of China. There were images of war and pristine jungles, of
exotic women and African tribes, and again and again, shots of a young and
beautiful adventurer. The rapt audience listened to Ms. Baker describe how,
during a search for missing explorers in the Amazon jungle, she had crashed

a plane and befriended a tribe of Bororo Indians. The tales were so spectacular that, had it not been for the film footage, they would have been difficult to believe.

For more than an hour her audience sat spellbound. As the film ended and the lights came up, Ms. Baker said that although the technology has changed, the world itself is pretty much the same. People are people, with the same needs and dreams as they ever had. She challenged her listeners to approach their world with curiosity and wonder. Travel, she said, is the best education and the best way to promote peace. Despite our differences, whether primitive or civilized, we need to find a way to share our planet in peace. "Go with your hat in your hand and wherever you are they will treat you as a guest."[1] After thanking her audience she placed her hands together, bowed slightly, and left the stage. The applause was long and heartfelt.

ACKNOWLEDGEMENTS

Since this project began in 1998, the aim has been to tell the story of a remarkably adventurous young woman who accomplished amazing feats of skill and daring and set many world records, yet has somehow been lost to history. Our research sent us in all directions, chasing the bits and pieces of Aloha's life that had blown about the great wide world. And though we didn't need to drive around the world, we have been assisted and encouraged by people on every continent.

The subject of this biography, in both her Idris and Aloha personas, assisted us in ways she would not have dreamed possible while circling the globe in a "flivver" ninety years ago. It's to her that we offer our deepest thank you, not only for understanding the wisdom of keeping journals and notes and scrapbooks about her life and experiences, but also for actually living that astonishing life. She continues to be an inspiration.

Our heartfelt thanks go out to the following:

Aloha's two children, Valri and Nile, for so generously sharing your memories and memorabilia with two authors whose single-minded purpose was to return your mother's legacy to its rightful place in history. She was a "first" in more ways than one.

Valri's two daughters, Margaret and Leinani, and to Nile's son, Richard, for sharing your stories of life with your mother and grandmother, your gracious hospitality, your family photos, artifacts, and for entrusting us with the telling. We hope this book introduces Aloha to a whole new generation.

Pat Reynolds and Ruth Stewart, librarians at the Long Beach Public Library, for your historical interest and excitement about the project, and especially for that surprise manila envelope containing Long Beach newspaper clippings.

Barbara Thompson, Laura Kotsis, and Paige Plant at the Detroit Public Library's National Automotive History Collection, for unfettered access to the Aloha Baker Collection.

Jake Homiak, Daisy Njoku, and Pam Wintle of the Smithsonian Institution's Human Studies Film Archives, and Amy. J. Staples of the Smithsonian's National Museum of African Art, for access to tape recorded interviews with Aloha, copies of films, especially *Last of the Bororos*, her narration scripts, and assessments of the historical importance of those films.

Richard Peuser and the staff of the National Archives and Records Administration in College Park, Maryland, for assistance in sorting through the mass of early twentieth century Department of Justice, military, and intelligence records on Walter Wanderwell and help in understanding their impact.

Daien Ide of the North Vancouver Museum and Archives, for helping us locate the Hall family's original residence and some of Herbert's business interests.

John Waggener of the American Heritage Center, University of Wyoming in Laramie, for allowing us to be the first to open the Walter Baker Papers that detail so much of Aloha's life post-1933.

Claude Zachary of the University of Southern California's Doheny Memorial Library Archives, for access to Walter Wanderwell's international police papers.

DeSoto Brown of the Bernice Pauahi Bishop Museum in Honolulu, for access to Aloha's film *My Hawaii*.

Deborah Griffiths, executive director of the Courtenay and District Museum on Vancouver Island, for continued encouragement and for help putting the Comox Valley's early twentieth–century history, and the Hall family's place in it, in perspective.

Deborah Chapman, curator of the Salmon Arm Museum, for helping to locate and assess the local residency records of Margaret and Robert Welch, and the marriage records of Margaret and Herbert.

The staff of the Historical Society of Long Beach for supplying much-needed background information on the city during the 1930s and especially for locating two "hidden" glass negative plates showing the burial of Walter Wanderwell.

Rose Katsuki, Police Services Specialist, Homicide Cold Cases, Long Beach Police Department, for digging into cold cases and unsolved murders to help locate pertinent files and information on Walter Wanderwell and others.

The late Joe Bell, columnist and staff writer for the *Los Angeles Times* and the *Daily Pilot*, for sharing reminiscences of his friendship with Aloha during the 1980s and writing so eloquently of her accomplishments.

David Coppen, Kodak archivist, for his fond memories of Aloha and his insight into working with her during the preparation of her mementoes and archives.

Miriam Ramos and the staff of the Los Angeles Superior Court Archives, for help finding the microfilmed court records and transcripts of the William Guy trial and intervening with Kodak when the microfilm disintegrated due to age.

Ranju Alex and the staff of the Oberoi Grand Hotel in Calcutta, for help in understanding the relevance of Aloha's visit there. We hope to visit one day soon!

Toby Parker, archivist, Haileybury and Imperial Service College, for information on Herbert Hall.

Deidre Simmons, author and former archivist, and Christine Godfrey, archivist, for St. Margaret's (and St. George's) School for girls on Vancouver Island.

Patrick Dunae, PhD and honorary research associate (History) at Vancouver Island University, for clarifying aspects of the Vancouver Island education system at the turn of the last century.

Don Tarasoff, past president of the Society of Saanich Peninsula Museums, for an exhaustive analysis of handguns and ammunition in use in Southern California circa 1920s and 1930s.

Dan Hinman-Smith, humanities instructor at North Island College, for clarifying issues of US immigration policy between the two world wars.

Eileen Whitfield, author of *Pickford: The Woman Who Made Hollywood*, for the many wonderful, inspiring conversations and emails about Mary Pickford and Douglas Fairbanks and for sharing your unique knowledge of Hollywood during the 1920s and 30s.

Ced Pearce, for pointing us in the right direction when trying to understand travel through Africa during the 1920s and for sharing your own materials on Aloha and Walter's legacy.

The late R.H. Johnston, Vancouver Island native, South Africa resident, for details of the Wanderwell Expedition in Africa and a personalized copy of his amazing book *Early Motoring In South Africa*. Don't give up the wheel, Bob!

To the staff of our publisher, Goose Lane Editions, whose enthusiasm and guidance was second to none — thank you... more than you know.

To our talented and perceptive editor, Susan Renouf, who, in a twist of fate worthy of Aloha herself, was the first to say "yes" and the last to say "done."

And of course, Google.

On a personal level, to our friends and supporters:

To Richard Mackie PhD, historian and author, and Susan Safyan, editor and author, for guidance, contacts, limitless encouragement, and for insight on early drafts of the manuscript (and more than a few dinners), but mostly friendship ... we think you know how we feel.

To Mary and Tom Reed, and Craig and Edie Roland, for your friendship, hospitality, and your fiery enthusiasm about Aloha's story, and especially for keeping Windsong — Margaret's Place — the spiritual escape it always was.

To Devra Robin and Jamie Baker, for your support, encouragement, and on one occasion, your sleeping quarters. We're so glad you live in California!

And finally, to our own families and friends for supporting our work, weathering our absence, buying us a beer every now and then, and telling us they knew there was a good story at the end of the road.

A NOTE ON SOURCES

Discovering the "real" Aloha has been no easy task.

Even with our dogged determination and collective "nose" for uncovering the tiniest of details, securing secondary and tertiary sources of information about Aloha and the entire Wanderwell Expedition was difficult.

Our discovery of a locked, dust-covered tin box in her daughter Valri's apartment that no one had set eyes upon in decades was literally an Indiana Jones moment for us. It contained two of Aloha's handwritten diaries along with her original expedition passport, annotated maps, and dozens of candid family photos dating back to her birth. The contents were in a very real sense our Rosetta Stone. The maps of Africa with notes and routes drawn in red grease pencil showed us exactly where the expedition drove and what alternate directions might have been followed due to lack of real roads and forced detours. Her passport gave us dates and places — international border entry and exit visas — to cross reference against Aloha's own writings and published reports. The wealth of photos are among the few extant pictures of life before Walter Wanderwell, when Aloha was still Idris, and "adventure" was defined as a short walk to the beach at the bottom of the Hall property on Vancouver Island. Its discovery allowed us to confirm or challenge many of the assertions Aloha made throughout her peripatetic life.

Walter had forbade members of the expedition from keeping notes about their journey (diaries, specifically), and newspapers following their expedition and performances only reported what they saw or what they believed their audiences wanted to read. Aloha's surreptitiously written first-person entries in these logbooks provide the rarest of glimpses into the day-to-day mechanics of every aspect of the Wanderwell tour. We see what life on the road between two world wars was like through the experiences of a teenager who grows up before our very eyes. But are there embellishments? Does she gloss over certain events? Does she make up anything? Aloha, in later life, did edit some of the material, going so far as to literally cut and paste, physically removing one paragraph with scissors, while pasting in a newly written one with glue. What's missing? And why?

The judicial sources and court records from the time regarding the events, trials, and tribulations of the Wanderwells — marriage, divorce, probate, tax, smuggling and Mann Act allegations, arrest, incarceration, murder, trial, and even Walter's own death — are almost entirely non-existent. The microfilm reel we helped locate in the underground repository of the Los Angeles Superior Court records office on Hill Street (which disintegrated upon being loaded into a mechanical viewer) hadn't been seen since 1962. Its backup in a humidity-controlled vault in Chatsworth had never been unspooled at all. We were told the original paper source material of William Guy's murder trial from which those microfilms were made would likely have been incinerated fifty years after the event, which was standard operating municipal and state practice. A fifty-year destruction mandate meant the originals would have been destroyed in the early 1980s. The trial ended in acquittal, and as such all evidentiary materials — from both the prosecution and the defence — were returned to their original owners. Also, because it was an acquittal the records had been sealed, with the result that the identification number on the microfilm reel, CR50818, meant it was a "Confidential Reel." The only reason we were allowed access to the evidence contained on that reel in the first place was because we could prove that all people involved had long since passed away. The law states that privacy expires with the person.

Marriage and divorce records for Walter and Nell in Florida could not be attained; likewise, real estate, tax, and probate records regarding Walter's estate and property holdings in Miami cannot be found. If his land was sold off prior to the Second World War (it probably was), those records, if they still exist, are likely mouldering away in a box in the forgotten corner of some old warehouse. We were told as much by a Dade County court clerk. Historical records that far back are simply not a priority, and never were. For the most part even old reference card files don't exist, which means computerized backups that would have been based on those card files were never made.

In many cases, governmental budget cutbacks are to blame for the dearth of materials and the lack of access. Beginning twenty-five years ago, government austerity programs hit the civil service hard; staff numbers at municipal and state levels were reduced and entire departments were folded into other portfolios. In many instances we encountered overworked clerks who kindly passed our requests for records on to volunteers or interns who failed to locate the files.

These research obstacles will be familiar to any non-fiction writer. Attempts to confirm, challenge, or deny assertions made by the key characters of a biography becomes difficult if all you have is that person's word for it. This is especially true of Aloha and Walter, since they were engaged in peculiarly public endeavours and used "spin" to explain, apologize, and promote.

It is possible that as this book gains wider attention, new material, new "evidence" will come to light, and we welcome that. Attics, basements, warehouses, vaults, and safety deposit boxes have a mysterious way of revealing themselves.

This is the story of Aloha Wanderwell's amazing life, warts and all, based on the best available sources. It is the tale of an extraordinary woman who welcomed risk, adventure, and accomplishment into her life. The four corners of Aloha's world had wheels, and the ends of the Earth were merely a challenge to her perseverance and indomitable spirit. No roads? No worries. Maybe Peter Pan had it right: "All the world is made of faith, and trust, and pixie dust."

Aloha certainly thought so.

NOTES

LEGEND

TDP ("The Driving Passion"): An unpublished collection of reminiscences that Aloha wrote towards the end of her life, drawn from various journals, newspaper clippings, and memories. Aloha planned to publish "The Driving Passion" but was unable to find a suitable publisher during her lifetime.

CTA (*Call to Adventure!*): A ghostwritten account of Aloha's adventures until 1927, aimed at teenagers. Published in 1939 by Robert M. McBride & Company, New York, under her married name Aloha Baker.

Logbooks: Logbooks from 1923 (including December 1922) and 1924 still survive and are held in the private collection of Aloha's daughter, Valri Baker-Lundahl. These are handwritten accounts of expedition events, recorded en route. Aloha references other journals in her later writings, but their whereabouts remain unknown.

NARA: National Archives and Records Administration, College Park, Maryland.

NAHC: The National Automotive History Collection, Aloha Baker Collection, Skillman Branch Library, Detroit, Michigan.

PROLOGUE

1. Aloha quoted and misquoted many of her favourite writers throughout her personal reminiscences. The authors have chosen to leave any malapropisms in her own words.

CHAPTER ONE

1. In Canada's 1911 Census Idris's grandfather (the respondent) had no idea of her birthdate. His guesstimate was off by six months and in the wrong year.
2. Information about Herbert's time at Haileybury was provided by Toby Parker, archivist, Haileybury and Imperial Service College, November 14, 2007.
3. Canadian Immigration and Population figures from Statistics Canada, Table 075-0001 — Historical statistics, estimated population and immigrant arrivals, annual (persons), CANSIM (database), using E-STAT (distributor), accessed September 5, 2011, http://estat.statcan.gc.ca/cgi-win/cnsmcgi. exe?Lang=E&EST-Fi=EStat/English/CII_1-eng.htm.
4. "Seeding Time," *High River Times*, April 10, 2012.
5. At least one book has claimed that the High River Agricultural School was a fake enterprise, aimed at extracting fees from problematic English boys "of the Little Lord Fauntleroy variety, sloshing around the place in the first flush of bucolic enthusiasm." Grant MacEwan and James Martin, *Eye Opener Bob: The Story Of Bob Edwards* (Victoria: Brindle and Glass Publishers, 2004), 197.
6. Birth certificate for Idris Welsh, Manitoba Vital Statistics, http://vitalstats.gov.mb.ca.
7. The correct spelling of Robert's last name was probably Welch. Official and private documents vary. The authors use Welch from this point forward.
8. Undated typewritten letter from James Hedley to siblings Sadie and Neville Hedley, in Goleta Family Archives, accessed by authors August 2007, 4.

9. Herbert and Margaret were both members of the Church of England. Marriage between two such parishioners in a private home, and by a Baptist minister no less, strongly suggests the wedding was a hurried affair. If Margaret and Robert had not been married, and Idris born out of wedlock, then this scenario makes some sense. In an almost surreal twist, one of the witnesses listed on the marriage licence is named Robert Welch; local census records from the time period show several residents named R. and Robert, Welch and/or Welsh.

10. TDP, 3.

11. As described by Valri Baker-Lundahl to the authors, May 2006.

12. James A. Gibbs, *Shipwrecks off Juan de Fuca* (Portland, OR: Binford & Mort, 1968), 78.

13. See Imperial War Museum: Posters of Conflict — The Visual Culture of Public Information and Counter Information, Current Accession: IWM PST 4903, http://www.vads.ac.uk/large.php?uid=26762. This and several other propaganda posters appeared in Canada and England.

14. By the war's end 628,736 Canadians had signed up — almost 8 per cent of the country's 1914 population.

15. CEF (Canadian Expeditionary Force) Attestation Paper No. 75359. Dated, signed, and witnessed in Vancouver, British Columbia, Dominion of Canada, May 11, 1915.

16. Idris would later write about the loss of her mother's first love, though she did not say whether the love in question was Robert Welch.

17. It is also possible that Idris was denied "hardship" travel and accommodation by the military, because she was not a "blood" Hall, and therefore, according to military regulations, not direct family.

18. Detail of the leg injury from a conversation between Nile Baker and the authors, April 2007.

19. TDP, 4.

20. Ibid.

21. From the last will and testament of Herbert Cecil Victor Hall, dated November 5, 1914. Private collection of Valri Baker-Lundahl.

CHAPTER TWO

1. "The War Was Over — but Spanish Flu Would Kill Millions More," *The Telegraph,* November 11, 2009, accessed June 7, 2012, http://www.telegraph.co.uk/news/health/6542203/The-war-was-over-but-Spanish-Flu-would-kill-millions-more.html.

2. TDP, 6.

3. Ibid., 5

4. A.F. Pollard, *A Short History of the Great War* (Lenox, MA: Hard Press, 2006), 287.

5. TDP, 7

6. David Silbey, *The British Working Class and Enthusiasm for War, 1914-1916,* ill. ed. (London: Routledge, 2005).

7. Martin Gilbert, *The First World War* (New York: Holt Paperbacks, 2004).

8. Spencer Tucker, Laura Matysek Wood, Justin D. Murphy, *The European Powers in the First World War: An Encyclopedia,* ill. ed. (Oxfordshire: Taylor & Francis, 1999), 178–80.

9. TDP, 6.

10. "Everyone liked Miki..." is evident from Idris's various writings, but also through authors' interviews with family and friends who knew her. Miki is consistently described as Idris's opposite: gentle, compassionate and extremely private. In later life, even her closest friends had no idea of the wild adventures she'd once had with her mother and sister. More than once we've had to produce photographic proof to convince disbelieving friends.

11. TDP, 7.
12. Ibid., 7, 11.
13. Ibid., 9.
14. Ibid., 10.
15. Ibid., 23.
16. Roland Herbert Bainton, *Christianity*, (Boston: Houghton Mifflin Harcourt, 2000), 129.
17. TDP, 13.
18. Ibid., 12.
19. Ibid., 15.
20. Ibid.
21. Ibid., 18.
22. Ibid., 21.
23. Ibid.
24. Ibid., 23.
25. As described by Valri Baker-Lundahl to the authors, May 2006.
26. TDP, 24.
27. Ibid., 28.
28. This title is Idris's. The school was more commonly called the *Raspini Pensionnat de Jeunes Filles de Nice.*
29. 1922 Logbook, n.d.
30. Unfortunately, no record of Eliza's last name survives.
31. TDP, 30.
32. Ibid., 30, 31.
33. Ibid., 40.
34. Idris doesn't record the name of the film company, but it was likely the Gaumont Film Company that was located in the nearby town of Grasse. Today, that company is the oldest running film company in the world. Richard Abel, *The Ciné Goes to Town: French Cinema, 1896-1914* (Oakland: University of California Press, 1994), 10. A few months later, Idris would gain a small role in a film called *Esclave* (*Slave*), directed by Rose Pansini and filmed at Cap d'Antibes. The French Government chose to preserve the film in the 1970s.
35. "Golden Years of Aviation: Civil Aircraft Register", France, accessed June 5, 2009, http://www.airhistory.org.uk/gy/reg_F-23.html.
36. Idris was not consistent regarding the aviator's first name and the authors have been unable to verify his identity. There was, however, an Auguste Maïcon who matches Idris's description. Auguste Maïcon was a well-known aviator in Nice with a habit of flying under bridges in the South of France. He was also involved in the local film industry.
37. TDP, 34.
38. Ibid., 36.
39. Ibid., 41.
40. Ibid., 42.
41. The authors made numerous attempts to discover if archives of *Le Petit Niçois* exist. After numerous queries, representatives of the paper responded that they were not inclined to answer questions.
42. TDP, 43. Apparently, Idris's explanation to the Raspini school that her mother "needed her" was enough to secure her freedom. Given the time of year, it's possible that classes had been recessed for the Christmas holiday.
43. Ibid., 44. Descriptions are also drawn from photographs from the day, NAHC, and family collection.
44. TDP, 44.
45. In later life Burton Holmes and the Halls became good friends, exchanging Christmas cards and birthday wishes.
46. 1922 Logbook, n.d.
47. No firm date had been set for the next World's Fair, but it was assumed to be in Chicago in 1926.
48. TDP, 44–46.

CHAPTER THREE

1. TDP, 48–49.
2. Ibid.
3. TDP, 55.
4. Brochures and postcards were also sold before and after each show, but the intermission was invariably the most

profitable. A captive audience was good for business.

5. TDP, 53.
6. Ibid.
7. Ibid., 54.
8. Ibid., 55.
9. 1922 Logbook, n.d.
10. TDP, 42.
11. Ibid. The paper may also have been *Le Petit Niçois*. That paper, although still in existence, did not respond to our numerous inquiries.
12. From the private journals of Margaret Hall, 1942. Private collection of Margaret Lundahl-Hammel.
13. TDP, 51.
14. Ibid.
15. Ibid.
16. Ibid., 52.
17. Ibid., 53. Even in her own ghostwritten autobiography *Call to Adventure!* she refers to herself as American. Also, it is entirely likely that Walter had much to do with the change of Idris's name. His knack for creative public relations had gotten him this far, and "Aloha" was more mellifluous than "Idris." The first expedition pamphlet for sale in the South of France shows a young photogenic Idris billed as, "Aloha Hall, Mécanicienne [mechanic]." To reflect this change in her life, from this point forward the narrative will refer to Idris as Aloha.
18. 1923 Logbook, Saturday December 30, 1922.
19. TDP, 60–61.
20. Ibid.
21. Ibid., 92.
22. Ibid.
23. 1923 Logbook, Wednesday, January 3. Walter Wanderwell was not the first to propose an international police, but his plan to task such a force with supervising the manufacture and trade of armaments was unique.
24. 1922 Logbook, n.d.
25. *New York Times*, January 8, 1923.
26. "Wanderwell Has Mania," *New York Times*, January 14, 1923. There may be more to the story than Aloha's later writings would admit. The pages in her handwritten journal from the day were cut out and replaced with text written much later (in ballpoint ink rather than fountain pen). Whatever the exact details, there was something about the incident that she did not want anyone to know and didn't want history to record.
27. 1923 Logbook, Sunday, January 7.
28. When the expedition returned to Nice from Menton, they moved from the Normandie to the Royal.
29. TDP, n.p.
30. Ibid.

CHAPTER FOUR

1. A reference to Missouri's reputation as the "show me" state, the inference being that people from Missouri won't (or can't) take people at their word. They need to be shown.
2. TDP, n.p.
3. Although admonished by her mother after the Geneva incident not to use her real name from that point forward for fear of sullying the good Hall name, it's interesting that she does use her real name on this most official of all documents. She only used the initial A for Aloha, clearly identifying herself as Idris Hall with the additional alias (and noted as such in the passport) of Wanderwell.
4. Taken from a loose notepad sheet slipped between the pages of the 1923 logbook. Aloha apparently made notes of her days' activities and converted them to prose in her journals when she had time.
5. 1923 Logbook, Monday, January 22.
6. TDP, 113.
7. 1923 Logbook, Monday, January 22.
8. Ibid., Tuesday, January 23.

9. Ibid.

10. The hotel was later renamed Palais Wilson after the American president who championed the idea of a League of Nations.

11. 1923 Logbook, Tuesday, January 26.

12. 1922 Logbook, n.d.

13. 1923 Logbook, Sunday, January 28.

14. Old newspaper clipping inserted into 1923 Logbook, n.d.

15. TDP, 105.

16. 1923 Logbook, Saturday, February 1.

17. TDP, 101.

18. 1922 Logbook, n.d.

19. TDP, 114.

20. About fifty seconds running time at 16 frames per second.

21. TDP, 114.

22. Ibid., 123.

23. Ibid.

24. 1923 Logbook, circa Wednesday February 21.

25. TDP, 124.

26. Ibid., 117–18.

27. Interestingly, Cap was more interested in the coverage of the event provided by Arthur Weigall's wires to the *Daily Mail*. Lord Carnarvon had struck an agreement with the *London Times* newspaper, offering them an exclusive in exchange for his ability to control the stories that would be published. Consequently, only the *Times* reporter, H.V. Morton, was actually allowed on site. Cap knew enough about the media to realize that alternative coverage was more likely to produce the unvarnished truth.

28. TDP, 125.

29. 1923 Logbook, Monday, February 26.

30. Ibid.

31. Ibid.

32. 1922 Logbook, n.d.

33. 1923 Logbook, Tuesday, March 13.

34. Although the Expedition was not directly sponsored by Ford, local Ford agents frequently offered a quid pro quo — vehicle support in exchange for promotion. One of the reasons Walter had chosen a Ford for his expedition was that farm machinery was also manufactured by Ford, and even in war-torn Europe, tractors using Ford mechanicals were ubiquitous. Showroom dealerships as we know them today were rare outside the United States.

CHAPTER FIVE

1. Even today, the bullfighting season begins on or after Easter.

2. 1923 Logbook, March 25.

3. Three loose pages were inserted into Aloha's 1923 Logbook around March 25, material written about the "journalists." The first of the pages contains the date Saturday, March 17, but seems to have been added much later.

4. The proper spelling is "duro," and it was the equivalent of five pesetas at the time.

5. 1923 Logbook, March 25.

6. 1923 Logbook, March 29.

7. Ibid.

8. TDP, n.p.

9. 1923 Logbook, April 3.

10. Ibid.

11. Ibid.

12. Ibid., May 24.

13. TDP, n.p.

14. 1923 Logbook, n.d.

15. Ibid., n.d.

16. "Opportunity Knocked, He Was Home," *Boca Raton News*, June 19, 1975.

17. TDP, 182–83.

CHAPTER SIX

1. TDP, 186.

2. The acronym WAWEC would go through several derivations and translations throughout the expedition, depending on Walter's objectives.

3. TDP, 186.

4. Interestingly, in 1923 German car company Audi produced an experimental

aluminum bodied car (the Type K), but it wasn't until 1989 that the Acura NSX became the first all-aluminum body production car. Today, aluminum is the preferred material of leading-edge car manufacturers, such as Tesla.

5. TDP, 187.

6. In her unpublished reminiscences, Aloha often changes the names of crew members. Her notes actually call Sommers "Winters." The correct names are borne out by surviving visas and border crossing papers.

7. Peter Benson, *Battling Siki: A Tale of Ring Fixes, Race, and Murder in the 1920s* (Fayetteville, AR: University of Arkansas Press, 2006), 129.

8. Aloha's spelling is never reliable. Amanda's last name may have been Hertig, Hörtig, or some other variation. She did not stay with the expedition long enough to surface on any of their literature.

9. TDP, 188.

10. Ibid., n.p.

11. Ibid., 187.

12. Ibid., n.p.

13. Ibid., 196. Chief White Elk was actually an Italian con man named Edgardo Laplante who earned his living by wowing Europeans with tales of Indian glory and raising money for starving children on reserves. He was eventually jailed in Italy for fraud. Aloha certainly knew of his shifty ways, writing in her journal about him, "The New York promoter had booked an assortment of Quebec Indian 'savages' threatening to fire one and all if any man dared utter a single word of English."

14. It's hard not to wonder if the duo ran into Hemingway, who was just about to leave for Spain.

15. Les Apaches was the name ascribed to criminal youth of the Parisian underworld in the late nineteenth and early twentieth centuries. The name also denoted a circle of French musicians, writers, and artists who lived mainly in the Montparnasse district of Paris.

16. TDP, n.p.

17. 1923 Logbook, n.d.

18. TDP, 201.

19. Another changed name, in her notes Aloha calls van der Ray, "Elvi van Zelingen." Even "van der Ray" is likely a transcription error of "van der Raay" or "van der Ree."

20. TDP, n.d.

21. From original documents at the NAHC.

22. TDP, 214.

23. Ibid., 215.

24. Ibid., 217. Order of quotes reversed.

25. 1923 Logbook, n.d.

26. TDP, 221.

27. See Mel Gordon, *Voluptuous Panic: The Erotic World of Weimar Berlin* (Port Townsend, WA: Feral House, 2006).

28. Hyperinflation reached its peak soon after.

29. TDP, 222.

30. Eric D. Weitz, *Weimar Germany: Promise and Tragedy* (Princeton, NJ: Princeton University Press, 2007), 102-3.

31. TDP, 226.

32. 1923 Logbook, n.d.

33. Ibid.

34. TDP, 232.

35. Ibid., 231.

36. Ibid., 235.

37. 1923 Logbook, n.d.

38. TDP, n.d.

39. 1923 Logbook, n.d.

40. TDP, 239.

41. Ibid., 240.

CHAPTER SEVEN

1. Neither Walter nor Aloha ever lived in Detroit. However, Walter's promotional savvy in securing a Ford Model T as the signature vehicle for the expedition, and using the Ford name in all publicity even though they weren't officially

sponsored, gave the Detroit media a local angle.

2. TDP, 243.
3. Ibid., 242.
4. Ibid., 245.
5. While the Wanderwell Expedition had
its own unique style, it was neither a
new nor an exclusive globetrotting enterprise. They were constantly rubbing
shoulders with others engaged in similar "ventures."
6. 1924 Logbook. Date unclear.
7. Maritime Timetable Images, accessed
on June 28, 2016. http://www.time-
tableimages.com/maritime/images/
mm.htm.
8. TDP, n.p.
9. 1924 Logbook, April 1.
10. Ibid.
11. Letter from the Eastern Automobiles
Supplies and Transport Company to
Walter Wanderwell dated March 3,
1924. NAHC.
12. TDP, 253.
13. 1924 Logbook, April 1.
14. Ibid., April 2.
15. In 1817 British diplomat and explorer
Henry Salt and Italian explorer Giovan-
ni Caviglia investigated cave catacombs
at Giza for a distance of several hundred yards before arriving at a spacious
chamber. Egyptian authorities to this
day remain unconvinced that any such
man-made catacombs exist, though
they concede that natural catacomb-
like formations may. In 2009 British
science writer Andrew Collins published a book called Beneath the Pyramids, which announced the discovery
of just such a system of catacombs at
the Giza complex. The publication
prompted an angry denouncement by
Egyptian authorities.
16. 1924 Logbook, n.d.
17. Ibid., April 3.
18. Ibid., April 2.
19. Martin Isler, *Sticks, Stones, and Shad-*

ows: Building the Egyptian Pyramids
(Norman, OK: University of Oklahoma Press, 2001), 92. See also Leon
Gray, *The New Cultural Atlas of Egypt*
(Tarrytown, NY: Marshall Cavendish,
2010), 125.
20. Steve was the crew's name for Stefanowi
Jarocki.
21. 1924 Logbook, April 17. Recounting
events of earlier days.
22. TDP, n.p.
23. The currently accepted spelling is Port
Taufiq.
24. 1924 Logbook, May 3. Recounting
events of earlier days.
25. A piastre, or piaster, is 1/100 of an Egyptian pound.
26. 1924 Logbook, May 3, 1924. Recounting
events of earlier days.
27. Ibid.
28. Ibid.
29. Ibid.
30. As Aloha defines it here, "making love"
was merely flirting, caressing, and perhaps whispering "sweet nothings" as a
form of seduction prior to the physical
act. Apparently, Aloha wanted none of
it.
31. TDP, n.p.
32. 1924 Logbook, n.d.

CHAPTER EIGHT
1. TDP, 274.
2. 1924 Logbook. Recording events of May
5, 1924.
3. This was another temporary Laissez-
Passer and not actually a full passport.
4. 1924 Logbook. Recording events of May
5 through 9, 1924.
5. Ibid.
6. Ibid.
7. Ibid., n.d.
8. Ibid. Recording events of May 11, 1924.
9. Ibid.
10. John H. Downing et al., *The SAGE
Handbook of Media Studies* (London:
Sage Publications, 2004), 520.

11. The actual problem was the front axle — it was bent and it impeded steering.

12. A horse-drawn cab, not unlike what we would call a tuk-tuk today.

13. 1924 Logbook. Recording events of May 26, 1924.

14. Although neither Aloha nor Walter held American passports, Walter was considered an American resident and the expedition flew the American flag.

15. Though Aloha's journals and other writings make no note of it, she succeeded in getting a new proper passport for herself at the British Embassy in Bombay. It is dated May 28, 1924, and carries the official Empire of India registry number 18392. It also reveals that she stood at five ten in stocking feet and was born in 1906. However, the six in the date has been traced over with a different pen, turning the six into an eight. Whether the issuing officer did this at the embassy based on her "correction," or whether Aloha performed the edit herself is unknown.

16. Letter from Havero Trading Co. (Bombay Branch) Berlin Aniline Department to Agfa Rollfilm Corporation of New York (Hollywood, California), May 27, 1924. NAHC.

17. Letter from the Asiatic Petroleum Company (India) to Captain Wanderwell, May 30, 1924. NAHC.

18. TDP, 283; and 1924 Logbook, May 26.

19. TDP, 283; and 1924 Logbook, n.d. but recording events of June 4, 1924.

20. Rudyard Kipling, *Kim* (Salt Lake City, UT: Project Gutenberg, 2009), http://www.gutenberg.org/files/2226/2226-h/2226-h.htm#chap03.

21. South Asian–style inns, not unlike the small motor hotels of today.

22. 1924 Logbook, n.d.

23. *CTA*, 78.

24. Conrad Anker, *The Call of Everest: The History, Science, and Future of the World's Tallest Peak* (Washington, DC: National Geographic, 2013), 29.

25. Today the Kadwa is partially dammed, making it a much more formidable crossing. In 1924 the depth was less than 3 feet.

26. CTA, 101.

27. TDP, 289.

28. "A Dak Bungalow Book," *New York Times*, August 17, 1873.

29. Rudyard Kipling, *My Own True Ghost Story*, (Newburyport, MA: Weiser Books, 2012), 3

30. 1924 Logbook, n.d.

31. 1924 Logbook, circa June 5. Entry dated as "4th day."

32. TDP, 294.

33. Ibid., 295.

34. Ibid., 297.

35. 1924 Logbook, n.d.

36. "Varanasi," *Encyclopædia Britannica Online (Official)*, accessed April 2010. https://www.britannica.com/search?query=varanasi.

37. Mark Twain, *Following the Equator: A Journey Around the World*, vol. 1 (Mineola, NY: Dover, 1989), 480.

38. Ibid. Twain was referring to the durian fruit, famous for its rank smell. Of eating durian, American chef Anthony Bourdain said, "Your breath will smell as if you'd been French-kissing your dead grandmother." Quoted in Layla Eplett, "Forbidden Fruit: What's Up With Durian?!" *Food Matters* (blog), *Scientific American,* July 23, 2014, http://blogs.scientificamerican.com/food-matters/forbidden-fruit-what-8217-s-up-with-durian/.

39. The deadly disease was not unique to India. In 1924 Los Angeles was battling its own epidemic of bubonic plague.

40. 1924 Logbook, n.d.

41. James Hastings, *Encyclopedia of Religion and Ethics, Part 2* (Whitefish, MT: Kessinger, 2003), 197.

42. TDP, 302.

43. Ibid., 310.
44. 1924 Logbook, n.d.
45. TDP, 311.
46. 1924 Logbook, n.d.
47. "Telegrams in Brief," *Times* (London), June 24, 1924.
48. TDP, 313.
49. The change in attire suggests that Aloha and the pilots got together after the media event. Aloha's journal suggests the same.
50. NAHC, Accession No. 33, Box 2.
51. "The Great Air Race of 1924," season 2, episode 1 of PBS's *The American Experience*, October 3, 1989. Directed by David Grubin. See also Spencer Lane, *First World Flight: The Odyssey of Billy Mitchell*, (US Press, 2001), 285.

CHAPTER NINE
1. TDP, 320.
2. Based on sponsorship letters contained in the NAHC.
3. 1924 Logbook, n.d.
4. TDP, n.p.
5. *CTA*, 123.
6. TDP, n.p.
7. Hannah Beech, "Shanghai Swings!," *Time* magazine, Monday, September 20, 2004, http://www.time.com/time/asia/covers/501040927/story.html.
8. Aldous Huxley, *Jesting Pilate: The Diary of a Journey* (London: Chatto & Windus, 1926).
9. 1924 Logbook, n.d. and unattached. The page was possibly torn from the journal and reinserted later.
10. TDP, 337.
11. Ibid., n.p.
12. Ibid., 339.
13. Ibid.
14. 1924 Logbook, n.d.
15. TDP, 343.
16. Jurov had left the expedition shortly before their arrival in Peiping.
17. "Peking," The China Marines, 2014, accessed May 13, 2010, http://chinamarine.org/Peking.aspx.
18. *CTA*, 132.
19. Ibid., 137.
20. TDP, n.p.
21. *CTA*, 138.
22. NAHC, Cards Box 3 and Box 7.
23. TDP, 352.
24. TDP, 355. Italics Aloha's.
25. NAHC, Box 3.
26. Gavan McCormack, *Chang Tso-lin in Northeast China, 1911-1928: China, Japan, and the Manchurian Idea*, ill. ed. (Redwood City, CA: Stanford University Press, 1977), 130.
27. 1924 Logbook, n.d.
28. *CTA*, 145-46.
29. Arthur Waldron, *From War to Nationalism: China's Turning Point, 1924-1925* (Cambridge: Cambridge University Press, 1995), 64.
30. TDP, 365.
31. Ibid.
32. Waldron, *From War to Nationalism*, 146.
33. TDP, 367. Caps on *He* and *Her* as well as quotation marks on *"to make arrangements"* are Aloha's.
34. 1924 Logbook, n.d.
35. *CTA*, 148.
36. Where they would have secured "Soviet courtesy flags" outside the Soviet Union is anyone's guess.
37. TDP, n.p.
38. *CTA*, 151.
39. Even more improbably, today Vladivostok has two Versailles Hotels.
40. TDP, 378.
41. 1924 Logbook, n.d.
42. TDP, n.p.
43. 1924 Logbook, n.d.
44. TDP, 390.
45. Ibid., 394.
46. Ibid., n.p.
47. Ibid., 398.
48. Ibid., 400.
49. Ibid., n.p.

50. Ibid.
51. Although the story seems almost impossibly convenient (the Prince Regent happened to be passing through?), footage of the event survives — and seems to have happened exactly as Aloha described.
52. TDP, n.p.
53. Ibid.
54. Ibid.

CHAPTER TEN
1. US Application for Certificate of Arrival contained at the NAHC.
2. TDP, 417.
3. TDP, 423.
4. *CTA*, 178.
5. Ibid.
6. TDP, n.p.
7. "Traveler Faces Charges," *Los Angeles Times*, January 8, 1925, sec. A.

CHAPTER ELEVEN
1. Fred D. Ragan, "Obscenity or Politics? Tom Watson, Anti-Catholicism, and the Department of Justice," *The Georgia Historical Quarterly* 70, no. 1 (Spring 1986): 17–46.
2. "Pennsy Police Show that 'Hiker' Is Four-Flusher," *Fort Wayne Journal-Gazette*, April 12, 1916.
3. NARA, File 9-16-12-73.
4. David M. Kennedy, *Over Here: The First World War and American Society* (New York: Oxford University Press, 2004), 24.
5. NARA, File 9-16-12-73.
6. Ibid. All subsequent quoted interview excerpts in this chapter are from the same source.
7. The ship's name was actually *Cambuskenneth*, a three-mast, square-rigged ship. Wanderwell never corrected Alexander's mistakes and certainly did not mention that the *Cambuskenneth* was sunk by German submarines in June 1915, but only after six German crew members were removed by row boat. Alexander may or may not have been aware of this.
8. Enden was A. van den Enden (given name unknown). He was an associate of Walter's and was arrested under similar circumstances the day after Wanderwell. Enden was from the Netherlands and made it clear to Hooper during separate questioning that he was sick and tired of being lumped in with other "foreigners" as a possible national security risk merely because of his Dutch accent. Hooper asked A. van den Enden if he was willing to "eavesdrop" on Wanderwell and relay everything Wanderwell spoke about to Hooper. He readily agreed and was placed in the same cell as Walter.
9. Chad Millman, *The Detonators* (New York: Little, Brown, 2006), 31.
10. Ibid., 32.
11. See "Hindu–German Conspiracy," Wikipedia, last modified June 23, 2016, https://en.wikipedia.org/wiki/Hindu–German_Conspiracy.
12. "N.Y. Firemen Work in Rain of Bullets," *New York Times*, July 31, 1916.
13. Letter from US Attorney Hooper Alexander to US Attorney General, dated April 12, 1917, received at the Department of Justice, office of Warren Bielaski, April 14, 1917, NARA.
14. "Wanderwell Reaches New York City in 'Special' Hanson Six Car," *Atlanta Constitution*, October 5, 1919, sec. A.

CHAPTER TWELVE
1. TDP, n.p.
2. "Wanderwell Held On White Slave Charge," *Trenton Evening Times*, January 15, 1925.
3. Leonard Pitt and Dale Pitt, *Los Angeles A to Z: An Encyclopedia of the City and County* (Oakland, CA: University of California Press, 1997), 299.

4. "Traveler and Woman in Custody," *Los Angeles Times*, March 5, 1925.
5. TDP, n.p.
6. Ibid., 444.
7. Ibid.
8. "Wanderwells Fined for Wearing Belts," *Los Angeles Times*, March 10, 1925, sec. A.
9. TDP, 446.
10. Ibid., 448.
11. Ibid.
12. Aloha writes that it was Joan Crawford who taught her to dance the Charleston.
13. Canadian-American co-founder of Warner Bros. Studios.
14. TDP, n.p.
15. Ibid.
16. Ibid.
17. Ibid., 455.
18. Ibid., 459.
19. Ibid., n.p.
20. From Ralph Colvin to J. Edgar Hoover, April 23, 1925. From declassified FBI field reports released to the authors on September 18, 2008, under FOIA.
21. TDP, 462.
22. Ibid., 315.

CHAPTER THIRTEEN

1. Correspondence from Special Agent L.C. Wheeler, Department of Justice, Bureau of Investigation, Los Angeles, to the Department of Justice in Washington, DC, bureau file 31-925-19, case file 43-7-4. Petitioned for release by authors in 2007. Released to authors on June 25, 2008.
2. TDP, 465.
3. Ibid., 467.
4. Jeffrey Vance, *Douglas Fairbanks* (Redwood City, CA: University of California Press, 2008), 297.
5. Ibid., 470.
6. "Too Much Producer," *Los Angeles Times*, April 29, 1925, sec. A.
7. TDP, 475.

8. Unfortunately, no photographs survive from this portion of the tour and Aloha's journals from the trip have likewise been lost.
9. TDP, 478.
10. "Barrow-Pushers Reach Vancouver," *Vancouver Daily Province*, June 18, 1927.
11. TDP, 486.
12. Ibid., 496.
13. Ibid.
14. Ibid., n.p.
15. Ibid., 501.
16. Ibid., n.p.

CHAPTER FOURTEEN

1. Solon E. Rose, "Traffic Violations and the Court — Detroit's Violation Bureau," *The Annals of the American Academy of Political and Social Science* 116 (1924): 185–90, http://www.jstor.org/stable/1015986.
2. TDP, 505.
3. Ibid.
4. Ibid., 509.
5. Ibid., 511.
6. NAHC.
7. TDP, 511.
8. Ibid.
9. Ibid., 512–13.
10. Ibid., 513.
11. Ibid., 514.
12. Ibid., 515.
13. Ibid., 516.
14. Leigh Summers, *Bound to Please: A History of the Victorian Corset* (Oxford: Berg, 2001), 38.
15. Various online advertisements of Ferris Bros. Co, New York, 1922.
16. TDP, 519.
17. Personal interview of Aloha's daughter, Valri Baker-Lundahl, by the authors, May 2009.
18. TDP, 523.

CHAPTER FIFTEEN

1. Fernando Ortiz, *Cuban Counterpoint, Tobacco and Sugar* (Durham, NC: Duke University Press, 1995), 63.
2. Rosalie Schwartz, *Pleasure Island: Tourism and Temptation in Cuba* (Lincoln, NE: University of Nebraska Press, 1999), 80.
3. Advertisement in *Miami Daily News*, n.d.
4. TDP, 525.
5. Reference Library, Vessel Record, Library and Archives Canada, Canadian Heritage, vol. #348, reel #C-2444, 7.
6. TDP, 527.
7. Ibid., 528.
8. John P. Parker, *Sails of the Maritimes* (Aylesbury, Buckinghamshire: Hazell, Watson and Viney, 1960), 119.
9. Letter from Felix S.S. Johnson, American Consul, to The Honorable Secretary of State, Washington, June 8, 1926, NARA.
10. Letter form Lorin A. Laterop, American Consul, to The Honorable Secretary of State, Washington, May 13, 1924, NARA.
11. See "In Landing Liquor," *Globe and Mail*, April 30, 1926.
12. TDP, 534.
13. Certificate of Discharge, issued at Quebec City by the Marine and Fisheries Dept. of Canada, June 18, 1926, signed by the Deputy Shipping, NAHC.
14. TDP, 539.
15. Wanderwell pamphlet "Aloha Wanderwell — The World's Most Widely Travelled Girl," n.p., n.d.
16. Ibid.
17. "Peace Missionaries Advocate International Police System," *Christian Science Monitor*, August 14, 1926, sec. A.
18. "Husband Reports Woman World Tourist Missing," *The Hartfort Courant*, September 3, 1926.
19. TDP, 541.
20. Ibid., 542.
21. Ibid., 543.
22. Ibid.
23. Ibid.
24. Ibid., 545.
25. Ibid., 546.
26. Craig Woodward, "1920s Hurricanes," Coastal Breeze News, accessed November 2010, http://coastalbreezenews.com/2010/06/17/the-%E2%80%9Cgreatest-storms-on-earth%E2%80%9D-%E2%80%93-part-iii-hurricanes-of-the-twenties/.
27. TDP, 546.
28. See "1926 Miami Hurricane," *Wikipedia*, last modified May 2, 2016, https://n.wikipedia.org/wiki/1926_Miami_hurricane.
29. TDP, 547.
30. Ibid., 548.

CHAPTER SIXTEEN

1. TDP, n.d.
2. *CTA*, 189.
3. TDP, n.p.
4. Ibid.
5. Ibid., 190.
6. Ibid., 551.
7. Ibid., 552.
8. "Medicine: at Sea," *Time* magazine, November 29, 1926, http://content.time.com/time/magazine/article/0,9171,729724,00.html.
9. TDP, 554.
10. Ibid., 560.
11. Ibid., 564.
12. Ibid., 565.
13. Ibid., 566.
14. *CTA*, 202.
15. TDP, n.p.
16. Ibid.
17. Ibid., 572.
18. Ibid., 573.
19. Ibid., 574.
20. Ibid., 575.
21. Ibid., 576.

CHAPTER SEVENTEEN

1. Moitsadi Moeti, "The Origins of Forced Labor in the Witwatersrand," *Phylon* 47, no. 4 (1986): 276–84.
2. TDP, n.p.
3. Ibid., 582.
4. Ibid., 583.
5. Ibid.
6. Ibid., 584.
7. Ibid., 585.
8. Ibid., 587.
9. Ibid., 589.
10. Ibid., 591.
11. Ibid., 593.
12. Joseph Conrad, *Under Western Eyes* (Salt Lake City, UT: Project Gutenberg, 2006), http://www.gutenberg.org/files/2480/2480-h/2480-h.htm.
13. TDP, 595; and *CTA*, 232.
14. *CTA*, 233.
15. TDP, 596.
16. Ibid., 597.
17. Ibid.; and *CTA*, 234.
18. *CTA*, 234.
19. TDP, 600.
20. Ibid., 602.
21. Ibid., 604.
22. Ibid., 613.
23. Ibid., 617.
24. Ibid., 624.
25. Ibid., 634.

CHAPTER EIGHTEEN

1. TDP, 644.
2. "Dole Air Race," *Wikipedia*, accessed February 14, 2011, http://en.wikipedia.org/wiki/Dole_Air_Race; and Burl Burlingame, "Breese-Wilde Monoplane 'Aloha,'" 2003, accessed February 14, 2011, http://hsgalleries.com/breesewildebb_1.htm.
3. TDP, 646.
4. Ibid.
5. Ibid., 647.
6. Ibid., 659.
7. Ibid., 660.
8. Ibid., 661.

9. As described on the official website of the Norfolk Hotel at "Hotel History," accessed February 21, 2011, http://www.fairmont.com/EN_FA/Property/NRF/AboutUs/HotelHistory.htm.
10. TDP, 663.
11. Ibid., 662.
12. Ibid., 664.
13. Beryl Markham, *West with the Night* (Boston, MA: Houghton Mifflin, 1942), 5.
14. TDP, 670.
15. *CTA*, 270.
16. TDP, 674.
17. Ibid., 678.
18. Ibid., 679.
19. Ibid.

CHAPTER NINETEEN

1. See "This Day in History, 1927: Ford reveals its Model A to an eager public," *Hemmings Daily*, accessed December 12, 2013, http://blog.hemmings.com/index.php/2013/12/02/this-day-in-history-1927-ford-reveals-its-model-a-to-an-eager-public.
2. *Die Tagebücher von Joseph Goebbels* (The Diaries of Joseph Goebbels), Part I, Records 1923-1941, vol. 1/3, June 1928-November 1929, ed. Anne Munding (Munich: K.G. Saur, 2004), entry for October 21, 1928.
3. Charles Douglas Stuart and A.J. Park, *The Variety Stage: A History of the Music Halls from the Earliest Period to the Present Time* (London: T. Fisher Unwin, 1895), 191.
4. *By Car Round the World, Times* (London), September 17, 1929, 12.
5. David Grann, *The Lost City of Z: A Tale of Deadly Obsession in the Amazon* (New York: Vintage Books, 2010), 275.

CHAPTER TWENTY

1. "In His 82 Years He's Done It All—Lots Of Times," *Tucson Daily Citizen*, October 6, 1971.

2. "Near End of World Tour," *Atlanta Constitution*, November 10, 1929.

3. "Travelers to Earn Million," *Oakland Tribune*, November 12, 1929, sec. D.

4. "Globe-Circling Car to be Gift to Ford," *New York Times*, November 30, 1929, accessed June 2011, http://query.nytimes.com/gst/abstract.html?res=9403EFDD173BE23ABC4850DFB7678382639EDE.

5. Review of *With Car and Camera Around the World* by Aloha Wanderwell, "Miss Wanderwell's Exploits with Camera Shown at Fifth Avenue," *New York Times*, December 19, 1929.

6. "Una Teniente De La 'WAWEC' Llega En Avion Como Avanzada De La Expedicion Que Viene A Cuba" (One Lieutenant with WAWEC Arrived by Plane in Advance of the Expedition that Will Come to Cuba), *El Pais-Excelsior*, February 17, 1930.

7. US Census Bureau, "Fifteenth Census of the United States: 1930, Population Schedule," Miami, Florida, Precinct 36, sheet 2A. https://archive.org/details/1930_census?and[]=subject%3A%22Florida%22

8. Don Berliner, "A Concise History of Air Racing," last updated March 6, 2013, http://www.airrace.com/ConciseHist.htm.

9. Letter from Briggs Manufacturing Company to Captain Wanderwell, Detroit, Michigan, July 3, 1930, NAHC.

10. "Captain Wanderwell's South American Tour 1930-32," *Veteran and Vintage Magazine*, 1975, 189.

11. "Chile Insists Army Is Loyal to Regime," *New York Times*, September 24, 1930.

12. Elinor Smith, *Aviatrix* (New York and London: Harcourt Brace Jovanovich, 1981), 186.

13. Ibid., 272–73.

14. Handwritten letter from Aloha to Miki, Aloha Family Archives, Goleta, California, n.d.

15. "Tells Thrilling Tale of Escape from Chile," *New York Times*, November 16, 1930, accessed June 2011, http://query.nytimes.com/gst/abstract.html?res=9A04EEDD1F3AEE32A25755C1A9679D946194D6CF.

16. Advertisements, *Times-Picayune*, December 1, 1930; and Advertisements, *Times-Picayune*, December 7, 1930.

17. "Globe Trotters Sail from Here to Pernambuco," *Galveston Evening News*, January 25, 1931.

CHAPTER TWENTY-ONE

1. "Roosevelt–Rondon Scientific Expedition," *Wikipedia*, last modified May 11, 2016, https://en.wikipedia.org/wiki/Roosevelt–Rondon_Scientific_Expedition.

2. Theodore Roosevelt, *Through the Brazilian Wilderness* (Charles Scribner's Sons, 1914), 8 and 51.

3. Candice Millard, *River of Doubt: Theodore Roosevelt's Darkest Journey* (New York: Broadway Books, 2010), 642, Kindle edition.

4. Rondon quoted in Grann, *The Lost City of Z*, 381, ePub edition.

5. Ibid., 347.

6. Peter Fleming, *Brazilian Adventure* (Evanston, IL: Marlboro / Northwestern, 1999), 49.

7. Todd A. Diacon, *The Human Tradition in Modern Brazil*, ed. Peter M. Beattie (Wilmington, DE: Scholarly Resources, 2004), 115–16.

8. Interview with Aloha W. Baker conducted at her home by Dr. Jake Homiak, Human Studies Film Archives, Smithsonian Institution, February 12–14, 1993. Sound recording.

9. Transcript for *Last of the Bororos*, (B&W film, 1,200 feet, 32 minutes, 1930) by Aloha W. Baker, Smithsonian Institution, Human Studies Film Archives, 6.

10. Ibid.

11. Interview with Aloha W. Baker conducted at her home by Dr. Jake Homiak, Human Studies Film Archives, Smithsonian Institution, February 12-14, 1993. Sound recording.

12. Notation on a photograph contained in the NAHC.

13. Postcard written to Janec Pieczynski from Walter Wanderwell, date stamped August 11, 1931. Courtesy of Valri Baker-Lundahl.

14. Transcript for *Last of the Bororos*, (B&W film, 1,200 feet, 32 minutes, 1930) by Aloha W. Baker, Smithsonian Institution, Human Studies Film Archives, 3.

15. "Heart Affair Revealed By Letters," *Long Beach Press-Telegram* (Home Edition), January 5, 1933, B1.

16. From the soundtrack of *Last of the Bororos*, courtesy Smithsonian Institution, Human Studies Film Archives.

17. "Justine Tibesar Rides Motorcycle from Vietnam to Belgium!" (1931). Used with permission, http://www.berndtesch.de/English/Continents/Asia/Asia.html.

18. Transcript for *Last of the Bororos*, (B&W film, 1,200 feet, 32 minutes, 1930) by Aloha W. Baker, Smithsonian Institution, Human Studies Film Archives, n.p.

19. Aloha Wanderwell (under exclusive contract to Hearst Newspapers), "Around the World Before and After the Famous Wanderwell Yacht Tragedy," *Atlanta Constitution*, March 3, 1935, sec. SM.

20. Ibid.

21. Ibid.

22. Ibid.

23. Ibid.

24. Ibid.

25. Ibid.

26. US Immigration Border Card #724 issued at Nogales, Arizona, February 2, 1932. NARA.

CHAPTER TWENTY-TWO

1. "Sonja Henie Defends Title," *Dubuque (IA) Telegraph-Herald*, February 11, 1932.

2. The American banking situation in 1932 is well described in Murray Newton Rothbard, *America's Great Depression*, 5th ed. (Auburn, AL: The Ludwig von Mises Institute, 2008), 304.

3. Stephen Feinstein, *The 1930s: From the Great Depression to the Wizard of Oz*, rev. ed. (Berkeley Heights, NJ: Enslow Publishers, 2006).

4. TDP, 11.

5. Ibid. n.d.

6. "World Traveler Here Again After 16 Years," *San Jose Evening News*, July 20, 1932, 3.

7. Postcard from Walter Wanderwell to Janec Pieczynski, July 15, 1932, courtesy Valri Baker-Lundahl.

8. "Tour Champions Visit City," *Los Angeles Times*, August 11, 1932, sec. A.

9. From a conversation between Nile Baker and the authors, April 2007.

10. A. Wanderwell, "Around the World," (see chap. 21, n. 18).

11. Ibid.

12. Walter Wanderwell, "Design For An Automobile," US Patent Des. 87,494 (Serial Number 38,536), filed February 3, 1931, and issued August 2, 1932.

13. "Rum Ship's Sale to Pay Fine Slated," *Los Angeles Times*, September 18, 1932, sec. C.

14. "Little Girl Now Sea's Youngest Shipmaster," *Los Angeles Times*, November 1, 1932, sec. A.

15. A. Wanderwell, "Around the World," (see chap. 21, n. 18).

16. Share Certificates, International Police, Ltd., (Capt. Wanderwell), University of Southern California, Doheny Memorial Library, Department of Special Collections, Collection No. 112.

17. Allyn Carrick and Forrest Izard, *A Jungle Gigolo*, 1933, black-and-white docu-

mentary, accessed on June 2011, http://www.imdb.com/title/tt1270659/.

18. Charles Hutchison, *Found Alive*, April 11, 1933, black-and-white film, 65 min., accessed June 2011, http://www.imdb.com/title/tt0024035/. The "Lure of Savage Passions" is taken from the film's original promotional poster.

19. "Lord Montagu, [sic] Eleven Others Signed for Tour," *Berkeley Daily Gazette*, (Evening Edition), December 7, 1932.

20. "Rum Ship's Sale to Pay Fine Slated," *Los Angeles Times*, September 18, 1932, sec. C.

21. "Murder Is Done in Bizarre Tub," *The Spokesman Review* (WA), December 7, 1932.

CHAPTER TWENTY-THREE

1. TDP, 12; see also A. Wanderwell, "Around the World," (see chap. 23, n. 1).

2. Wanderwell Baker, précis to TDP, 12.

3. "Sea Adventurer Slain," *Milwaukee Sentinel*, December 7, 1932.

4. A. Wanderwell, "Around the World," (see chap. 23, n. 1).

5. Ibid.

6. "Mrs. Wanderwell Gives Killing Clew," *Washington Post*, December 7, 1932.

7. "Man Arrested as Spy During War Killed in Mystery," *Berkeley Daily Gazette*, December 7, 1932; see also "Globe Trotter's Old Associate Under Arrest," *Daily Courier* (Connellsville, PA), December 8, 1932.

8. "Globe Trotter Slain in Cabin of Schooner," *Sheboygan (WI) Press*, December 6, 1932.

9. "Former Wife Tells of Love Affairs of Murder Victim," *Reading (PA) Eagle*, December 10, 1932.

10. Agness Underwood, "Granite Woman In Yacht Murder," *Los Angeles Record*, December 7, 1932.

11. "Wanderwell's Ex-Wife Tells Divorce Reason," *Los Angeles Times*, December 9, 1932, sec. A.

12. "Former Wanderwell Wife in S.M. Says Girl is Killer," *San Mateo Times*, December 10, 1932.

13. Ibid.

14. "Sea Slaying Suspect's Alibi Hit," *Rochester Evening Journal*, December 9, 1932.

15. "Yacht Murder Suspect in Custody of Police to Face Grave Charge," *Evening Independent* (St. Petersburg, FL), December 8, 1932. Florida newspapers took special interest in the Wanderwell case because of its connection to their state. Headquarters of WAWEC and the International Police remained in Miami. See also "Mystery Baffles," *Lewiston Morning Tribune* (Lewiston, ID), December 9, 1932.

16. "Woman Aids Alibi He Was Not Aboard Death Ship," *Seattle Times*, December 8, 1932.

17. "Nab Man in Gray in Murder Case," *Spokesman Review* (Spokane, WA), December 9, 1932.

18. Ibid.

19. "Widow Is Brave," *Los Angeles Record*, December 7, 1932.

20. Advertisement, *Los Angeles Times*, December 15, 1932, sec. A.

21. "Murder Suspect's Friends Subpoened [sic] to Inquest," *Los Angeles Times*, December 9, 1932, sec. A.

22. Ibid.

23. "First Indian Aviator," *Cheyenne & Arapaho Tribal Tribune* 7, no. 8 (February 1, 2012): 8.

24. Ibid.

25. "Curley Guy Definitely Pointed Out," *Saskatoon Star-Phoenix*, December 10, 1932.

26. "Fail to Swear Out Charge in Yacht Murder," *Pittsburgh Post-Gazette*, December 10, 1932.

27. "Curley Guy Definitely Pointed Out,"

Saskatoon Star-Phoenix, December 10, 1932.

28. "Wanderwell Buried at Sea," *Poughkeepsie (NY) Eagle News*, December 13, 1932.

CHAPTER TWENTY-FOUR

1. "Suspect Gang Killed Skipper," *Spokane Daily Chronicle*, December 13, 1932.

2. "Doug Goes Back to Nature," *Los Angeles Times*, December 17, 1932.

3. Theodore Orchards, "Once Aboard the Lugger," *The Graveside Companion*, ed. J. Francis McComas, (New York: Ivan Obolensky, 1962), 117.

4. Aloha Wanderwell, "Mrs. Wanderwell to Carry on Mate's Work," *Rochester Evening Journal*, December 16, 1932.

5. In later life, McGann would represent a case in which a company that marketed a "health oil" attempted to convince the court that advertising with testimonials about a product's efficacy in treating certain health conditions did not mean the company was claiming its product *had any effect* on such conditions.

6. "Held For Trial," *Lewiston Morning Tribune* (Idaho), December 20, 1932.

7. "Pair Identify Accused Man," *Los Angeles Times*, December 20, 1932.

8. Courtroom Scene Adds New Puzzle," *Los Angeles Times*, December 20, 1932, sec. A.

9. "Held For Trial," *Lewiston Morning Tribune* (Idaho), December 20, 1932.

10. "Wanderwell's Widow Shakes Hand of Suspect in Murder Case," *The Telegraph Herald and Times-Journal*, (Dubuque, IA), December 20, 1932.

11. For further context, see "The Year 1932 News, Prices and Popular Culture," The People History, 2004, accessed July 26, 2011, http://www.thepeople history.com/1932.html; and "1932 Ford," *Wikipedia*, last modified June 22, 2016, http://en.wikipedia.org/wiki/Ford_Model_B_%281932%29.

12. "Wanderwell Left $1,500 Estate," *New York Times*, December 24, 1932. Digital reproduction purchased April 6, 2008.

13. "Wanderwell Cruise Off," *Cleveland Plain Dealer*, December 25, 1932.

14. "Girl Throws Doubt on Alibi Given by Young Adventurer," *Dallas Morning News*, December 21, 1932.

15. "Torn Code Love Note Fogs Wanderwell Quiz," *Los Angeles Times*, January 13, 1933.

16. "Wanderwell's Daughter Made Mother's Ward," *Los Angeles Times*, January 24, 1933, sec. A; "Mrs. Wanderwell and Three Girls Given Aid," *Oakland Tribune*, January 24, 1933, sec. D.

17. "*Carma* to be Showboat on South Seas Cruise," *Los Angeles Times*, February 1, 1933, sec. A; "Guys' Murder Trial toOpen," *Poughkeepsie (NY) Eagle News*, February 2, 1933.

18. "Doors Splintered as Crowd Rushes to Murder Trial," *Dallas Morning News*, February 3, 1933.

19. "Wanderwell Trial Shifts to Vessel," *Seattle Daily Times*, February 4, 1933.

20. "Jurors Visit Death Craft," *Los Angeles Times*, February 4, 1933.

21. "Sea Rover Slain for Paper, Charge," *Baltimore Sun*, February 4, 1933.

22. "Wanderwell's Widow Heard," *Los Angeles Times*, February 4, 1933.

23. Quotes from the trial are based on newspaper accounts, not court transcripts. The authors conducted extensive searches of the archives within the Los Angeles Police Department, the Long Beach Police Department, and the Los Angeles County court records, but found nothing. A microfilm reel of the actual trial transcripts (N°. CR50818) was eventually located at the LA Superior Court Archives. However, as the technician placed the microfilm on the take-up reel, the film disintegrated. We were later informed that the destroyed reel was only a copy and

that a master reel was housed at their backup archive in Chatsworth, California. After six months, the master file was retrieved but also began to disintegrate upon inspection. At the authors' request, the reels were sent to Kodak's head offices in Rochester, New York, where the microfilm had originated, but they were also unable to extract any content from the film. Original paper files may still exist in an archive somewhere, but despite years of effort, none have materialized.

24. "Mrs. Wanderwell Tardy as Trial of Guy Is Resumed," *Reno Evening Gazette*, February 6, 1933.
25. Ibid.; and "Aloha Breaks on Stand," *Nevada State Journal*, February 7, 1933.
26. A. Wanderwell, "Around the World," (see chap. 23, n. 1).
27. "Guy Identified as a Visitor to Murder Yacht," *Dallas Morning News*, February 7, 1933.
28. Ibid.
29. "Guy's Counsel Offers New Witnesses to Refute Wanderwell Killing Tale," *Charleston Daily Mail*, February 8, 1933.
30. "Prosecution Rests in Wanderwell Case," *Berkeley Daily Gazette*, February 9, 1933.
31. "Defence Attacks Identification of Guy as Slayer," *Seattle Daily Times*, February 10, 1933.
32. "Two More Add their Support to Guy's Alibi," *Dallas Morning News*, February 12, 1933.
33. Wanderwell Baker, précis to TDP, 16.
34. "Long Beach Jury Find Guy Not Guilty of Slaying Capt. Wanderwell on Yacht *Carma*," *Los Angeles Times*, February 17, 1933, sec. A.
35. Robert Kenny, "My First Forty Years in California Politics, 1922-1962," interview transcript, interviewer Doyce Blackman Nunis (Los Angeles: Oral History Program, UCLA, 1964), 91.
36. "Freed in Murder Trial, Guy Faces Fed-

eral Charges," *Dallas Morning News*, February 18, 1933.
37. "A Queer Thing in Life," *Reno Evening Gazette*, February 18, 1933.
38. Wanderwell Baker, précis to TDP, 16.

CHAPTER TWENTY-FIVE

1. "Wanderwell Widow is Left on Shore," *Oakland Tribune*, March 21, 1933.
2. "Yacht Carma Abandons Crew," *Oakland Tribune*, May 8, 1933.
3. A. Wanderwell, "Around the World," (see chap. 23, n. 1).
4. Letter from Captain W. de Waray, Commandant in Chief, Legión Extranjera, to Captain J. [sic] Wanderwell, March 9, 1933, Barranquilla. Courtesy Valri Baker-Lundahl.
5. "Guy and Martin Fail to Show Up," *Los Angeles Times*, March 22, 1933, sec. A.
6. "DeLarm, Alibi Witness, Given Bodyguard as He Charges Guy Threatened His Life," *Los Angeles Times*, August 15, 1933, sec. A.
7. "DeLarm's Plea Fixed for Today," *Los Angeles Times*, July 17, 1933, sec. A.
8. "'Curly' Guy Trace Lost by Agents," *Los Angeles Times*, September 2, 1933, sec. A.
9. Carl A. Christie, *Ocean Bridge: The History of the RAF Ferry Command* (Toronto: University of Toronto Press, 1995).
10. This was a wonderful piece of military sleight of hand. The planes would arrive in southern Manitoba fresh off the assembly line in Burbank, California. After refuelling, they were flown to Montreal, refuelled again, and this time rebranded with the livery of Britain's RAF. After a third stop for fuel in Labrador's Goose Bay, they were flown to Scotland, outfitted with armaments, and prepared for bombing runs into Germany.
11. "From Murder Trial To Post of Honor — Curley Guy Pilot of Plane Bearing

British Notables," *Long Beach Press-Telegram* (Home Edition), August 21, 1941, cover (with photo of Guy and Aloha Wanderwell).

12. Stuart Palmer, "Once Aboard the Lugger," in *Murder Plus: True Crime Stories from the Masters of Detective Fiction*, compiled by Marc Gerald (New York: Pharos, 1992), 211. First published in *Detective: The Magazine of True Crime Stories*, 1951.

13. "While we were splashing in the surf, who bobbed up in an adjoining wave but Buron Fitts. It was all very cordial. I don't think Fitts believed Guy was guilty either." Kenny, "My First Forty Years," 91–92.

14. "D.A. Fitts Was Good Match for Scandalous '30s," *Los Angeles Times*, September 19, 1999, accessed June 2011. http://articles.latimes.com/1999/sep/19/local/me-12084/2.

15. "Officers Continue Quizzing," *Long Beach Sun*, February 10, 1933.

16. "Slain Captain's Widow Asks Control of Child," *Washington Post*, October 20, 1933.

17. "Sense of Humor Great Essential States Traveler," *Times-Picayune* (New Orleans), December 18, 1933.

18. "Widow of Slain Adventurer Wed," *Times-Picayune* (New Orleans), December 29, 1933.

19. Ibid.

20. Letter courtesy of Valri Baker-Lundahl. Some punctuation has been added for clarity.

21. A. Wanderwell, "Around the World," (see chap. 23, n. 1).

22. During this period WLW Cincinnati had the most powerful radio transmitter in North America — one of the most powerful in the world, in fact. On a clear evening its 500,000-watt signal could be heard as far west as California, as far south as Mexico, and, it was rumoured, as far east as parts of Europe and Africa. It was so powerful, that Canadian radio stations in Ontario and Quebec had to lobby America's broadcast regulator to force the station to reduce their signal — it was overlapping their frequencies and drowning them out!

23. As far as we know, this book was never published.

24. Happily, an audio copy of this program still exists at the Library of Congress in Washington.

25. As far as these authors know, *Aloha Wanderwell and the River of Death* (later recast as *Flight to the Stoneage* and *The Last of the Bororos*) was the first and only sound film Aloha ever produced.

26. What few existing used copies remain — mostly delisted library editions — can still be found on Internet auction sites such as eBay, some fetching more than $1,000 per copy!

27. "He Seeks Luck of the Irish," *Long Beach Press-Telegram*, women section, June 19, 1968, sec. B.

28. Personal interview with Margaret Lundahl-Hamell conducted by the authors, Goleta, CA, February 2009.

29. Letter from Greenfield Village & Henry Ford Museum to Ms. Aloha W. Baker, October 29, 1979, NAHC.

30. Members of Aloha's extended family are still searching.

31. In 1978 she managed to place her film *The Last of the Bororos* with the Smithsonian Institution's Human Studies Film Archives.

32. Of course, its real value is inestimable.

33. Aloha Wanderwell, "Introduction" to the Aloha W. Baker Collection, NAHC.

EPILOGUE

1. "All Humanity 'Savage,' Finds Famous Woman Wanderer," *Washington Post*, July 2, 1934.

BIBLIOGRAPHY

NEWSPAPERS AND PERIODICALS

Ada Evening News (OK)
Adelaide Advertiser (Australia)
Albuquerque Journal (NM)
Amsterdam Evening Recorder (NY)
Anaconda Standard (MO)
Appleton Post-Crescent (WI)
Atlanta Constitution (GA)
Auburn Citizen-Advertiser (NY)
Augusta Chronicle (GA)
Australian Ford News
Baltimore American (MD)
Baltimore Sun (MD)
Barrier Miner (Australia)
Beaver Daily Times (NY)
Bellingham Herald (WA)
Berkeley Daily Gazette (CA)
Berkshire Evening Eagle (MA)
Biddeford Weekly Journal (ME)
Binghamton Press (NY)
Bismarck Tribune (ND)
Border Cities Star (ON)
Brisbane Courier (Australia)
Brooklyn Daily Eagle (NY)
Burlington Daily Times (NC)
Burlington Hawk-Eye (IA)
Cairns Post (Australia)
Calgary Daily Herald (AB)
Cape Girardeau Southeast Missourian
Catalina Islander (CA)
Cedar Rapids Republican (IA)
Centralia Daily Chronicle (WA)
Ceylon Daily News (Sri Lanka)
Charleston Daily Mail (SC)
Charleston Gazette (WV)
Charlotte Sunday Observer (NC)
Chicago Tribune (IL)
China Mail (Hong Kong)
Christian Science Monitor (Boston, MA)
Chronicle-Telegram (OH)
Cleveland Plain Dealer (OH)
Coshocton Tribune (OH)

Council Bluffs Nonpareil (IA)
Daily Courier (PA)
Daily Democrat-Times (MS)
Daily Herald (MS)
Daily Illini (University of Illinois)
Daily Independent (PA)
Daily Intelligencer (PA)
Daily Journal-World (KS)
Daily Kennebed Journal (ME)
Daily Messenger (NY)
Daily News (PA)
Daily Northwestern (IL)
Daily Republican (MS)
Daily Washingtonian (Washington, DC)
Dallas Morning News (TX)
Danville Bee (VA)
Decatur Review (GA)
Deming Headlight (NM)
Deseret News (UT)
Detroit News (MI)
Detroit Times (MI)
Dothan Eagle (AL)
Dunkirk Evening Observer (NY)
Edwardsville Intelligencer (IL)
El Cronista del Valle (TX)
El Orden (Mexico)
El Pais-Excelsior (Cuba)
Ellensburg Daily Record (WA)
Evening Independent (FL)
Evening Independent (OH)
Evening News (CA)
Evening Tribune (MN)
Evening Tribune (RI)
Every Week Magazine (US National
  Supplement)
Eugene Register-Guard (OR)
Fitchburg Sentinel (MA)
Flesherton Advance (ON)
Florence Morning News (SC)
Florence Times (AL)
Fort Wayne Journal-Gazette (IN)

Frederick Post (MD)
Free Lance Star (VA)
Fresno Bee (CA)
Galveston Daily News (TX)
Gettysburg Star and Sentinel (PA)
Gettysburg Times (PA)
Gleaner (Jamaica)
Globe and Mail (ON)
Gloversville Morning Herald (NY)
Greensburg Daily Tribune (PA)
Grosse Pointe News (MI)
Hartford Courant (CT)
Helena Daily Independent (MT)
Herald – Melbourne (Australia)
Herald Press (MI)
Hobart Mercury (Tasmania)
Holland Evening Sentinel (MI)
Honolulu Advertiser (HI)
Honolulu Star-Bulletin (HI)
Illustrated Weekly of India
Independent Record (MT)
Independent Star-News (CA)
Indiana Evening Gazette (PA)
Indiana Progress (PA)
Indianapolis Star (IN)
Iowa City Press-Citizen
Ironwood Daily Globe (MI)
Jackson City Patriot (MI)
Japan Times and Mail
Joplin News Herald (MS)
Kalamazoo Gazette (MI)
Key West Citizen (FL)
Kingsport Times (TN)
La Crosse Tribune and Leader Press (WI)
La Opinion (Spanish Los Angeles paper)
La Prensa — Spanish (TX)
Lewiston Daily Sun (ME)
Lewiston Evening Journal (ME)
Lewiston Morning Tribune (ID)
Lethbridge Herald (AB)
Lexington Herald (KY)
Lima Sunday News (OH)
Lincoln Daily Star (NE)
Literary Digest (NY)
Long Beach Independent (CA)
Long Beach Press-Telegram (CA)
Long Beach Sun (CA)

Los Angeles Record (CA)
Los Angeles Times (CA)
Ludington Daily News (MI)
Macon Daily Telegraph (GA)
Manitoba Free Press
Mansfield News-Journal (OH)
Marcellus Observer (NY)
Meriden Record (CT)
Miami Daily Metropolis (FL)
Miami Daily News (FL)
Miami Herald (FL)
Milwaukee Journal (WI)
Milwaukee Sentinel (WI)
Modesto Bee (CA)
Modesto Evening News (CA)
Modesto News-Herald (CA)
Montreal Gazette (QC)
Morning Observer (PA)
Morning Olympian (WA)
Morning Oregonian (OR)
Mombasa Times (Kenya)
Nambour Chronicle (Australia)
Nashua Telegraph (NH)
Nevada State Journal
New Castle News (PA)
New Orleans States-Item (LA)
New York (Evening) Post
New York Times
New Zealand Evening Post
New Zealand Radio Record
Niagara Falls Gazette (NY)
Oakland Tribune (CA)
Ogden Standard-Examiner (UT)
Olympia Daily Recorder (WA)
Oshkosh Northwestern (WI)
Ottawa Citizen (ON)
Oxford Mirror (IA)
Oxnard Press-Courier (CA)
Palm Beach Post (FL)
Paris Match (France)
Pittsburgh Post-Gazette (PA)
Pittsburgh Press (PA)
Port Arthur News (TX)
Poughkeepsie Eagle-News (NY)
Prescott Evening Courier (AZ)
Reading Eagle (PA)
Regina Leader-Post (SK)

Regina Morning Leader (SK)
Reno Evening Gazette (NV)
Rochester Journal (NY)
Rockhampton Morning Bulletin
  (Australia)
Roundup Record (MO)
Rutland Daily Herald (VT)
St. Louis Post-Dispatch (MI)
St. Petersburg Times (FL)
Salt Lake Telegram (UT)
San Antonio Express (TX)
San Antonio Light (TX)
San Francisco Chronicle (CA)
San Jose Evening News (CA)
San Mateo Times (CA)
Santa Barbara Morning Press (CA)
Saskatoon Star-Phoenix (SK)
Seattle Times (WA)
Sheboygan Press (WI)
Singapore Straits Times
Spartanburg Herald (SC)
Spokane Daily Chronicle (WA)
Spokesman Review (WA)
Star (OH)
Star of India
State Beacon (NJ)
Sydney Morning Herald (Australia)

Syracuse Herald (NY)
Sunday Oregonian (OR)
Sunday Sun and Guardian (Australia)
Telegraph-Herald / Times-Journal (IA)
Time magazine (NY)
Times-Leader (PA)
Times-Picayune (LA)
Times of Ceylon (Sri Lanka)
Times Recorder (OH)
Toledo Blade (OH)
Toledo News-Bee (OH)
Tonawanda Evening News (NY)
Trenton Evening Times (NJ)
Tucson Daily Citizen (AZ)
Tuscaloosa News (AL)
Uniontown News Standard (PA)
Vancouver Morning Star (BC)
Vancouver Province (BC)
Vancouver Sun (BC)
Variety magazine (CA)
Vaudeville News and New York Star
Vista Press (CA)
Washington Post (DC)
Winnipeg Free Press (MB)
Wisconsin Rapids Daily Tribune (WI)
Youngstown Vindicator (OH)
Yuma Daily Sun (AZ)

KEY SOURCES

Agness M. Underwood Collection, California State University Northridge Oviatt Library.
  http://library.csun.edu/SCA/Peek-in-the-Stacks/Underwood.
Allen, Stookie. (Editorial Cartoon). *Women of Daring: True Story in Pictures.* New York:
  Argosy Weekly. December 24, 1938.
Aloha W. Baker Holdings, Bernice Pauahi Bishop Museum, Honolulu, Hawaii.
Ancestry.com (and co.uk & .ca).
Archives of the Anglican Diocese of British Columbia, Victoria, BC.
Austin, John. *Hollywood's Unsolved Mysteries: The Unsolved Murder of Walter Wanderwell.*
  New York: Ace Publishing Corporation, 1970.
Baker, Aloha. *Call To Adventure!* New York: Robert M. McBride, 1939.
———. "The Driving Passion." Unpublished memoir.
Baker-Lundahl, Valri. Personal records and photographic materials, private collection.
  Goleta, California.
Burnett, Claudine. *Prohibition Madness: Life and Death in and around Long Beach,
  California, 1920-1933.* Bloomington, IN: AuthorHouse, 2013.
Cairns, Kathleen A. *The Enigma Woman: The Death Sentence of Nellie May Madison.*
  Nebraska: University of Nebraska Press, 2007.

California Department of Health Services, Office of Health Information and Research, Vital Statistics, California Death Index. http://searches.rootsweb.ancestry.com.

Collins, Frederick L. *Homicide Squad: Adventures of a Headquarters Old Timer.* New York: G.P. Putnam's Sons, 1944.

Cook, Beverly Blair. "Moral Authority and Gender Difference: Georgia Bullock and the Los Angeles Women's Court." *Judicature* 77, no. 3. (1993): 144–55.

Dammann, George H. *Illustrated History of Ford: 1903-1970.* Illinois: Crestline Publishing, 1970.

Doe, Ernest. *Centennial History of Salmon Arm.* Salmon Arm: self-published, 1971.

Finney, Guy W. *Angel City in Turmoil: A Story of the Minute Men of Los Angeles in Their War on Civic Corruption, Graft and Privilege.* Los Angeles: Amer Press, 1945.

Grann, David. *The Lost City of Z: A Tale of Deadly Obsession in the Amazon.* New York: Doubleday, 2005.

Johnston, R.H. *Early Motoring in South Africa.* South Africa: C. Struik Publishers, 1975.

Lovell, Mary S. *The Sound of Wings: The Life of Amelia Earhart.* New York: St. Martin's Press, 1989.

Lundahl-Hammel, Margaret. Personal records and photographic materials, private collection. Goleta, California.

Marsh, James H., ed. *The Canadian Encyclopedia,* 2000 ed. Toronto: McClelland & Stewart, 1999.

McComas, J. Francis, ed. *The Graveside Companion: An Anthology of Infamous California Murders.* New York: Ivan Obolensky, Inc., 1962.

Military Heritage, Library and Archives Canada. http://www.bac-lac.gc.ca/eng/discover/military-heritage/Pages/military-heritage.aspx.

Millard, Candice. *The River of Doubt: Theodore Roosevelt's Darkest Journey.* New York: Broadway Books, 2011.

Newton, Michael. "Wanderwell, Walter, Murder Victim." *The Encyclopedia of Unsolved Crimes,* 2nd ed. 1932. Reprint. New York: Infobase Publishing, 2009.

Oakes, Jill, and Rick Riewe. *Voices from the Dorms: Qualicum Beach School, Qualicum College School for Boys, 1935-1970.* Winnipeg, MB: Aboriginal Issues Press, 2010.

Qualicum Beach history (general), British Columbia Archives Collection, Royal British Columbia Museum.

Rayner, Richard. *A Bright and Guilty Place: Murder, Corruption, and L.A.'s Scandalous Coming of Age.* New York: Anchor, 2010.

Sherman, Carl. *Last Cruise of Spymaster Wanderwell's International Joy Ship.* New York: For Men Only (September 1961): 34–52.

Treatt, Stella Court. *Cape to Cairo: The Record of a Historic Motor Journey.* Boston: Little, Brown, 1927.

Underwood, Agness. *Newspaperwoman.* New York: Harper & Brothers, 1949.

Walker, Joseph B., and Juanita Walker. *The Light on Her Face.* Hollywood: The ASC Press, 1984.

Walter Nicholas Baker Papers, 1915-1945. American Heritage Center, University of Wyoming, Laramie. Account #10417.

Wilson, Robert E. "The Wanderwell Case." *Foreign Service Journal* (April 1967): 46–47.

Whitfield, Eileen. *Pickford: The Woman Who Made Hollywood.* 2nd ed. Lexington: University Press of Kentucky, 1997.

INDEX

ABOUT THE AUTHORS

CHRISTIAN FINK-JENSEN's writing has appeared in numerous magazines and newspapers, including the *Toronto Star, Philadelphia Inquirer, New York Quarterly, Rampike, Vancouver Sun,* and *Ottawa Citizen.*

RANDOLPH EUSTACE-WALDEN has worked as a writer, editor, researcher, television producer, and director. He has twice been nominated for Emmy and Gemini awards and has won several Leo awards.